THE WORLD AND THE PERSON

The World and the Person
And Other Writings

ROMANO GUARDINI
Translated by Stella Lange
Introduction by Robert Royal

REGNERY GATEWAY
Washington, D.C.

Cataloging-in-Publication data on file with the Library of Congress

ISBN: 978-1-68451-449-6
eISBN: 978-1-68451-464-9
Library of Congress Control Number: 2022950140

Published in the United States by
Regnery Gateway, an Imprint of
Regnery Publishing
A Division of Salem Media Group
Washington, D.C.
www.Regnery.com

Manufactured in the United States of America

10 9 8 7 6 5 4 3 2 1

Books are available in quantity for promotional or premium use.
For information on discounts and terms, please visit our website:
www.Regnery.com.

Contents

The Wisdom of the Psalms

The Gentleman from Verona

by Robert Royal

Romano Guardini was born in 1885 in Verona in Northern Italy, but his family moved to the German city of Mainz, where his father served as the Italian consul while he was still very young. Except for regular trips back to his birthplace, he lived in Germany during his formative years and wrote in German. For many thinkers, this history might be a mere biographical detail. In Guardini's case, however, it has considerable significance. He was a beloved figure in his day among his students and had an enormous influence on the Catholic Church and European culture in the twentieth century and beyond. He inspired later thinkers as diverse as Hans Urs von Balthasar (who wrote an interesting book about him), Josef Pieper, Luigi Giussani, Joseph Ratzinger (Pope Benedict XVI), and Jorge Mario Bergoglio (Pope Francis). His influence probably owes something to the dual heritage that shows in all his work, which combines the academic rigor of the heyday of German intellectual life with the gentler human qualities of Italian culture.

The present collection is a highly valuable retrieval of texts that supplement Guardini's greatest and best-known books, such as *The End of the Modern World*, *The Spirit of the Liturgy*, and *The Lord*, which have remained in print and have influenced generations. He makes a point of calling the works in this collection "reflections," not systematic treatments. But in truth they "reflect" the author's deep and internally consistent theological, philosophical, and—unusual among religious writers—literary culture. His books on Dante and Rilke, along with his frequent references to Augustine, Pascal, Dostoyevsky, Heidegger, and even Nietzsche, present an eclectic but deep and coherent vision of the Church and the world. Varying approaches to fundamental questions, of course, have their advantages and disadvantages. But as these texts make abundantly clear, Guardini had the kind of mind—the living virtue, as he puts it in his book on the virtues, included here—that can move flexibly but faithfully through whatever questions it encounters. This is why these books are less like academic treatises and more like living dialogues with a wise and experienced and learned friend.

In recent years, there have been efforts to enlist Guardini into present-day conservative or liberal camps. It is misguided, however, to try to place him on some crude ideological spectrum, because he was a subtle and supple thinker, not a simplistic partisan. Guardini warned about the dangers of a soulless world of science and technology, for example, but welcomed advances in knowledge if they could be seen within a deep theological context. His vocal opposition to the Nazis led to his "retirement" from university teaching at only fifty-three, but he also had grave doubts about the highly secularized political foundations of the democratic nations. He was one of the early advocates of liturgical reform and greater lay participation in liturgy, but he died just three years after the close of Vatican II and before the bitter liturgy wars and other post-conciliar controversies began. It is quite enough to appreciate his radical rootedness in the biblical realism that has always marked the Catholic Church, and to recognize the many insights and questions that he brings to bear on almost all modern and postmodern developments, without trying to turn him into a protagonist in current controversies.

In this brief introduction, it is impossible to do justice to all this intellectual wealth, but it may be helpful to highlight some of the main lines of Guardini's work.

Several of the characteristics of Guardini the writer and thinker appear most clearly in his late book *The Virtues: On Forms of Moral Life* (1963). After a few years of studying science and then economics, Guardini felt called to the priesthood and turned to theology in the early decades of the twentieth century. Thomism—with its obvious roots in Aristotle—was undergoing a rich revival led by Réginald Garrigou-Lagrange, Jacques Maritain, Étienne Gilson, and many others. Guardini, however, chose to study the thought of Saint Bonaventure, who drew more from the Platonic-Augustinian side of Catholicism. While he was also part of the scholastic flowering of the thirteenth century, Bonaventure was a Franciscan, and his works lend themselves more easily to modern currents of personalism and communitarianism. The Thomists are known as rigorous philosophers and theologians, but the Franciscan tradition, at least in the hands of Guardini, has its own intellectual precision and power.

It is no surprise, then, that Guardini opens his study of the virtues by quoting not a Christian figure but Plato, who observes the union of the Good, the True, and the Beautiful in the divine. While he differs with Plato on whether the state should be "the protector of the moral order"—the experience of Germany in the first half of the twentieth century had shown the dangers of such a view—he wants to reinforce the notion that men must acknowledge the existence of truth and the absolute moral principles that flow from it. As he puts it in his highly influential *The End of the Modern World*, "As long as men are unable to control themselves from within...they will inevitably be 'organized' by forces from without." At the same time, he warns that moral principles and the virtues that embody them should not, in the deepest understanding, be regarded as "external limitations to rebellious man. Here we shall regard the good as that whose

realization makes man truly human." Virtues are not (as they are sometimes taken to be) an imposition on human freedom but something "living
and beautiful" that perfects human nature from within. By their very nature, the virtues inform and promote a full and fruitful life. It is a paradox
of human life that in forming ourselves to virtue through self-discipline
we attain real freedom. Without self-discipline, we remain slaves of igno-
rance, impulse, emotion, and external forces, never becoming true masters
of ourselves. Each of us will proceed upon that path in a uniquely personal
way, but all those paths lead to the same destination: the Good that is God.

Guardini not only describes this flexibility of living virtue, he embod-
ies it in his work. In *The Virtues*, he examines two of the four Cardinal
Virtues—Justice and Courage—but he devotes most of the work to more
workaday virtues that are often overlooked, among them truthfulness,
patience, loyalty, reverence, courtesy, and gratitude. As all good virtue
theorists do, he shows how all the virtues are interrelated. Kindness or
loyalty toward others is always shaped by truthfulness and justice, and
vice versa.

And he goes further. In the concluding section, "Justice before God,"
he not only examines this traditional subject but shows how it reflects back
on all the previously examined virtues. Because from a Christian perspective, the general ethical principles and virtuous habits, useful as they are
in certain circumstances, achieve their full purpose only in their engage-
ment with the whole of reality. Human failures are daily evident in both
the public and private spheres, and it is therefore crucial that man realize
that Christ alone is able, ultimately, to remedy those failures: "everything
depends on man's understanding himself from this viewpoint." Individual
persons and God's universal kingdom are linked not merely by an ethical
system but by the mystery of grace. As Guardini puts it in his little book
on the theological virtues, "we must do what the Christian always has to
do, change the order of things, give up the old starting-point and seek a
new one, put away our old measures and learn to use the new."

The Word of God: On Faith, Hope, and Charity, as the title indicates, deals with those three Theological Virtues. Written decades before the volume on the other virtues, it is an exploration of the deep realities that lie behind our everyday decisions and struggles. Guardini begins the discussion of Faith, for instance, with some startling reflections on the opening of John's Gospel, "In the beginning was the Word." Most readers rightly see this as an affirmation that Christ—the Word (*logos*)—was present in the Trinity and was indeed God. And it is clear that John is deliberately echoing the opening of Genesis, which recounts the Creation of the world. "But if we consider it carefully," Guardini notes, going deeper still, "the beginning of which the Prologue of St. John's Gospel speaks lies even beyond this. He does not mean the beginning of the world, but beginning itself."

What can this possibly mean? He explains:

> He is not Lord because there is something over which He rules, but in Himself and of His very essence, the one absolutely free, powerful, self-possessed and self-sufficient. So this Beginning is prime reality and being, the eternal, fulfilled forever through itself and in itself....
>
> In the beginning we find not that to which the present age reduces everything, mere nature with all the reserve, determinism, stuffiness, even stupidity, which is implied in this concept, but the bright, free, responsive word of the living God. From this everything proceeds.

And this realization lays upon us modern men, "the heirs of a dying age of reason," a task that "consists largely in rediscovering what the eye is, namely, not merely the beginning but the half of all understanding; in learning once again what true and complete seeing is, namely the grasping of the original reality." Faith has all the older characteristics of radical trust in God, but it also demands from us, half-blinded by materialism and scientism, that we try to see more clearly the Truth behind other truths.

Guardini follows this first deep insight with explorations of its consequences. About Hope, for instance, he reminds us that hoping in anything other than eternity—the only reality that does not pass away—however understandable from a human perspective, leaves us stunted: "No one becomes completely human who does not in some way reach this experience, that everything passes away and that nothing which is itself perishable can save us from this transitoriness." And when he deals with the "Canticle of Love" (that is, the theological virtue of Charity), he repeats the old Christian belief, "Love does not pass away," but warns those who think this mere sentimentality or religious fervor:

> Love is actually portrayed as Christian sobriety, but a sobriety which has nothing to do with barrenness of heart or narrowness of mind. If it gives significance to the *charismata* it must come from the heart of God, from the operation of the Holy Spirit. It must be moderation in fullness, the "sober intoxication of the Spirit," as the old hymn says, an attitude which in its serene self-control, its faithfulness and strength is incomparably greater, deeper and richer than all that is unusual.

The most wide-ranging treatment of that human depth in the pages included here is to be found in *The World and the Person*, which is a response to a two-fold crisis Guardini discerned as having emerged in Western culture over the past few centuries. On the one hand, we have enjoyed rapid and astonishing advances in scientific and technological knowledge of the world and our very own bodies—along with serious developments in the understanding of human psychology. On the other hand, we have tried to preserve the "humanistically philosophical" understanding of ourselves. Despite the differences and even contradictions between these two views of the nature of man, "both claimed to know what man is.... This conviction that they knew man, and the resulting security and the consequent narrowness in dealing with human affairs, has been shattered. The feeling, which was never openly admitted but crept surreptitiously through the 19th century, that the conditions of humanity might be different than the official opinion maintained, has now forced its way into the open." Various other answers began to appear, of course, but ultimately they have failed. And the modern, to say nothing of the postmodern, condition is that we no longer know what we are—or the nature of the world of which we are a part.

Guardini therefore sets out on a path of exploration of what it means to be human and, more importantly, Christian. His method is akin to what became known in the twentieth century as phenomenology. He considers a series of dimensions of human experience, particularly the question of "inwardness," which many, following Kierkegaard, have taken to be a crucial mark of Christianity, and height or depth. But there are evil as well as good forms of inwardness and depth, says Guardini, because we are free in our intentions. And besides, in the modern world inwardness and depth are often regarded as a kind of psychological therapy. Christianity operates in a different dimension because only Christ Himself can provide the very space for ultimate inwardness and depth. We cannot by these, or any other of the usual means, save ourselves:

> What Jesus means is not an unfolding of the naturally religious predisposition, such as takes place in the course of the history of religion or such as the mystical and ascetic systems of various religions strive for. But He came to reveal the God who is sovereign in relation to the world and unknown to it; He came to tell us what our condition is before this God and to announce what He is willing to do for us.... Here we have primarily and fundamentally not a matter of human experience but of a divine

action according to a sovereign decree. And to become a Christian means to take this action as a foundation and criterion of one's own existence through faith in the word of Christ, unconcerned about one's own experience, and whether one is "deepened" or not, whether one becomes harmonious or discordant, perfected or fragmentary.

True Christian inwardness, an "absolute gift of God," often leads to psychological healing, too, of course, but that is not its primary focus: "If then God comes in Christ to the believer, God's inwardness comes to him, for God is Himself His inwardness." In one of the many paradoxes of the Christian life, this frees the self from itself and leads us to that higher and truer human existence for which we were created.

So if that is man, the "person," what of "the world"?

"It is part of the problem of the world that it is possible not to see it, although it bears our existence, and that a certain effort is required in order to have sight of it." We have noticed earlier in the discussion of Faith that one of the modern tasks is to recover eyes that can better see both the parts and whole—and their true relations. And that means not simply a catalog of objective elements, however exhaustive. There is a human element, a drama, involved, a drama of *persons*, because without interaction with others we do not become persons even in the limited sense in which we ordinarily use the word.

Even so, mere interaction with others remains at the same level as our own personhood. And in Christian terms, there is a still larger context:

The person, then, is dependent on the condition that other persons should exist. Not this or that person, though they might be the most important or outstanding at any time, but just persons as such. It is different in the case of the absolute personality, God. Without Him I cannot exist....

Things come into existence by the command of God; the
person by His call. And this means that God summons it to
be His "Thou"—more exactly that He destines Himself to be
man's "Thou.". . .

This is the intrinsic "I-Thou" relation which cannot be
abolished. The world is also drawn into it.

Historically, of course, there have been different attempts to understand that fuller, interpersonal meaning of "world." The modern West was
nearly unique in that, for a time, it tried through empiricism, pragmatism,
scientism, and skepticism to live without a sense of the "beyond" and gave
rise to tragic movements such as Communism, Nazism, Fascism, and
secularism. But many felt something else was missing. Guardini sees in
great German poets like Hölderlin and Rilke imaginative attempts to create a sense of that "beyond," but they reacted against the pure objectivity
of much of modern culture by turning to an exaggerated and misdirected
"inwardness" and individualism. As Guardini's phenomenological examination of the nature of personhood and the world reveals, the only remedy
for this distortion is, again, Christ. He alone sets right the balance between
faith and reason and reorders all personal existence so that, as Saint Paul
says, Christ lives in us and we in Him, the person and the whole world, if
we recover the eyes to see, participating in the Divine Trinity.

It was only natural that Guardini would examine not only the intellectual response to the crisis of Western civilization but also the role that the
Catholic Church needed to play in the modern world. In the opening chapter of *The Church of the Lord*, written shortly after the close of the Second
Vatican Council, he lays out some of the gains that he felt had emerged:

- a reciprocal openness to the world, meaning that the
  Church could find truth and wisdom in the secular, even
  in other religions, while at the same time not isolating

Herself from "the world" (in the bad sense Scripture
sometimes uses) and seeing that world as God's Creation;

- a reform of the liturgy (a longtime concern of Guardini's)
that brought the laity into the heart of the Mass and
other rituals.

   With the passage of time, it became evident that these reforms had
also introduced troubles into Catholicism, and it would be interesting to
know how Guardini would tally up the balance sheet were he alive today.
We know that he would not take any of the usual approaches to such
questions because his understanding of the mystery that is the Church
(and of every other subject he touched) was deeper than what we are familiar with: "The Church cannot be resolved into merely natural concepts.
Her actions cannot be prescribed for her merely in view of natural demands. On the contrary, she lives by her mission and she must fulfill
this—even though it may be at the price of giving scandal."
   The unique nature of the Church is, properly speaking, a mystery. A
"mystery" is a reality that the human intellect cannot explain but can only
acknowledge, unlike a "problem," which we have the ability to solve. So
the full truth about the mystical body that is the Church cannot be captured by the usual sociological or institutional categories. Guardini reminds readers, for instance, that

the Church worked out and maintained for more than seventeen centuries a divine Revelation transcending all imagination; the doctrine of the triune God, as well as the message
of God's love, which, when understood in its fullest sense,
breaks asunder all natural intelligibility. According to all the
laws of nature such a structure should have disintegrated after
a short time. But the Church did not disintegrate, and so
something took place in it which, from the point of view of

all history and knowledge of life, is impossible. This fact indicates that the Church is based upon and supported by
something that is more than human.

Guardini asks the equally paradoxical question: "What do you think
of a social structure which proclaims to men doctrines that trouble them,
and make demands on them which do not accord with their immediate
wishes and needs, and yet is recognized and even loved by innumerable
persons?" The emphasis here is on the "social structure." The Apostles,
says Guardini, were not chosen for their brilliance or even their virtues
but for their sheer witness of Christ as Son of the living God and of the
Eucharist—a witness first given not in writing but by their very lives:

> [Christ's] own doctrine He entrusted not to a book but to men
> with whom He had lived and whom He had trained....
> "[T]he twelve" were not merely a group of men which might
> just as well have been larger or smaller, but they were—together
> with those who gathered around them—a figure, a whole, an
> organism, which stood in objective validity and authority.
> They were—the church!

And the Church was a structure that turned authority into service
and power into love: "that mysterious reality which has been moving
through history for two thousand years, loved as nothing earthly has been
loved but also hated and persecuted with a bitterness never experienced
by anything else."

Guardini's commentaries on Scripture, though written prior to the
admission of the historical-critical method in Catholic circles, also witness
to his supple imagination, as in his book *The Wisdom of the Psalms*, also
included here. Good student of literature that he was, he pays careful attention to imagery. So in his commentary on Psalm 1, for example, he

identifies three images—the "way," the tree, the wheat and the chaff—but places them, as he places nearly everything he touches, into a rich and living context that most of us, just reading the bare words, might miss. A "way" means there's a destination, and it is good for us to remember the possibility of going the wrong way as well as the right way; in a Palestine on the edge of the desert, a tree is fed by hidden streams of water that enable it to rise up tall and remain fixed in one place; and the ancient method of winnowing the wheat from the chaff is a vivid example of what is heavy with fruitfulness and the insubstantial husk that the wind and the winnowing fan carry away. Or as the New Testament echoes that image, the light chaff is fit only to be burned up and disappear forever. Although his commentary does not employ "historical-critical methodology," it is valuable because he tries to read the texts of the Psalms as poems, poems of revelation to be sure, but like all poems, words intended by the author (in the case of the Bible, both the human and divine authors) as a message addressed to a human reader, not an academic scholar. It is in that context and at that level that some of his deepest insights emerge.

For instance, he points out that the voice that speaks in the Psalms is not directed solely to the individual reader, as we might be tempted to think from our own circumstances. In Psalms 113 and 95, a discerning eye will see that the Hebrews are called out of slavery in Egypt by that voice and set on the way to the Promised Land. And similarly, especially in Psalm 95, we discern that the God of Abraham, Isaac, and Jacob has been at work specially in the history of Israel but also in the whole of Creation and human history. Moreover, that God manifests himself at specific times and places—a scandal to mere philosophies that think of the divine only as an abstraction outside our world but an integral part of how the biblical God relates to His Creation, including human beings.

As a consequence, "We are living in a vast historical whole, a series of events stretching from the beginning of the human race to the present day and going on to an end of which the Lord says no one knows when it shall be reached, 'not the day nor the hour.' We are living in the midst of these events." So even though the situation of a modern reader of the Psalms is different from that of the ancient Hebrews, who may have heard them read aloud in the synagogue, we all—whatever our station—are part of this same sacred order and sacred history and must strive to live accordingly.

The language of the Psalms is often poetic and inspiring. In Guardini's description of them, his own lyrical gifts come to the fore, as when he writes, "The eye of the believer sees God's greatness in the vast expanse of space; he sees His mantle in the brightness of the firmament. And how luminous is He himself, light of all light, if the beams of the sun and the stars are His covering!" An exhilarating prospect, if also frightening, even before we come to the rigors of sin and death. And yet Guardini believed that the ultimate truth is one our modern and postmodern world urgently needs to hear. As he put it in commenting on "The Canticle of Love":

> Man does not know God. Between him and the living Lord lies the dullness of his earthly nature. His earthliness separates him from the mysterious and remote divinity. His sin makes him blind to the one who is all-holy. Hence his experience of God remains inadequate, uncertain and ambiguous. But when the Spirit visits a man, then he comes face to face with God in immediate experience, and knows who He is.

And we know who we are as well.

THE VIRTUES
On Forms of Moral Life

Preface

In Plato's *Republic* there is a passage in which Socrates demonstrates how the supreme truth is united in "the Good" with the divine itself. In reply, his young interlocutor, Glaucon, cries out in amazement, "You speak of an inconceivably transcendent beauty!" (509 B)

In regard to the manner in which the great master of philosophic thought makes the state the protector of the moral order one may well differ with him. We have learned by bitter experience what happens when government officials take into their hands what belongs to personal freedom. There is one thing, however, that Plato's philosophy has made clear once for all; that is, after the confusion and chaos introduced into thought by the Sophists, he showed that absolute values exist, that these can be known, and that therefore there is such a thing as truth. He likewise showed that these values are summed up in the majesty of that which we call "the Good," and that this good can be realized in the life of man according to the potentialities of each individual. Plato showed that the good is identical with the divine; but that its realization leads man to true humanity, as virtue comes into being, and this virtue signifies perfection of life, freedom and beauty. All this is everlastingly valid, even for us today.

These are the matters of which we intend to speak in this work. The ensuing reflections—they are purposely called by this name to distinguish them from scholarly treatises—have grown out of the spoken word, and the reception given these talks has shown that our age, in spite of all its scepticism, longs for an interpretation of everyday life based upon the eternal.

This interpretation shall be carried out in a very unsystematic way. The first chapter deals with the determining points of view. Our interpretation does not pretend to be exhaustive. Rather, it lays hold upon ordinary reality as it came to our attention and seeks therein the starting-points of moral self-realization. At all points it appeals to the personal experience of the reader and strives from there to progress to a unity of ethical consciousness.

Moral teaching has become too negative; these reflections seek to do justice to the living majesty, nobility and beauty of the good. We tend too much to view the ethical norm as external to rebellious man; here we shall regard the good as that whose realization makes man truly human. The young Glaucon was seized by a reverent transport at the words of his master. This book would attain its purpose if the reader felt that the knowledge of the good is a cause of joy.

In 1930 a collection of "Letters on Self-Culture," which had been composed during the preceding years, was made and published in book form. These letters were addressed to young people and in many ways presupposed the atmosphere of the Youth Movement. The present reflections are addressed to the more mature and presuppose a knowledge of the bitter years which we have experienced since that time. A historical abyss separates these two attempts at a doctrine of life and yet they belong together, as in the same man youth and maturity belong together.

As regards the "epilogue," the reader would do well if, after taking note of it, he reconsidered the preceding reflections in the light of this knowledge.

On the Nature of Virtue

I n these reflections we shall deal with something that concerns us all, each in his own way, namely virtue. The word probably affects us strangely, perhaps even unfavorably; it is likely to sound old-fashioned and "preachy."

Forty years ago the philosopher Max Scheler wrote an essay entitled "Toward the Rehabilitation of Virtue."* This title is a bit strange, but understandable, if we consider that at that time ethics, which under the rule of Kant had petrified and become merely a doctrine of duties, was loosening up and people were beginning once again to think of the good as something living, which concerns the whole man. In that situation Scheler pointed out the changes that the word and the concept "virtue" had undergone in the course of history until they took on the wretchedly deficient character which still clings to them.

For the Greek, virtue, *areté*, was the nature of the noble-minded, culturally developed man; for the Roman, *virtus* signified the firmness and solidity which the noble man maintained in public and private life; the Middle Ages understood by virtue (*tugent*), the conduct of the chivalrous

---

* Max Scheler, "On the Reversal of Values," collected works (Bern, 1955), III, 13ff.

man. But gradually this virtue became well-behaved and useful, until it received the curious tone which causes aversion in the normal man.

If our language had another word we would use it. But it has only this one; therefore we want to begin by agreeing that virtue denotes something living and beautiful.

Then, what does it mean? It means that the motives, the powers, the actions and the being of man are gathered at any given time into a characteristic whole by a definitive moral value, an ethical dominant, so to speak.

Let us choose as an example a very modest virtue, such as orderliness. This means that a person knows where a thing belongs and what is the proper time for an action, also what measure is valid in any instance and what is the relation of the various matters of life to each other. It indicates a sense of rule and recurrence and a feeling for what is necessary so that a condition or an arrangement may endure. When orderliness becomes a virtue then the person who practices it does not wish to realize it only in a single decision; for instance, if he ought to work and instead would like to do something else, yet he pulls himself together and does what the occasion requires. Orderliness becomes an attitude of his whole life, a disposition which prevails everywhere and determines not only his personal actions but even his surroundings, so that his whole environment acquires a quality of clarity and reliability.

But the virtue of orderliness, in order to be a living thing, must also touch the other virtues. So that a life may be ordered in the proper way, this orderliness must not become a yoke which burdens and constrains; rather it must contribute to growth. Hence it includes a consciousness of what hinders life and what facilitates it. So a personality is rightly ordered if it possesses energy and can overcome itself, but also if it is capable of breaking a rule when this is necessary to avoid being cramped, etc.

A true virtue signifies an ability to penetrate with a glance the whole existence of man. Within it, as we have said, one ethical value becomes dominant and gathers together the living fulness of the personality.

Now there are two ways in which the virtue of orderliness is realized. It may be innate; then it comes forth easily and self-evidently from the nature of the person in question. Everyone probably knows such a person, whose desk is always clear and at whose touch things seem to find their place of their own accord. The task of such a person consists in cultivating his native quality and developing it so that it becomes a matter of course which makes existence clear and fair. But he must also guard against a degeneration, for an excess of orderliness can make one hard and narrow. It can produce the pedant, around whom life dries out.

But there are also persons of a different disposition, for whom orderliness is not a quality of nature. They are inclined to follow the impulse of the moment, and in consequence their actions lack consistency. They leave off what they have begun because it is boring; they let objects lie as they fell because they are in a hurry to get away. Indeed, order as such annoys them. They consider a neat room uncomfortable; to look ahead over the day and apportion it seems to them pedantic; to account for receipts and expenses and to balance them seems irksome constraint. The fact that there is a rule irritates them and stirs the desire to break it, because for them freedom means the possibility of always doing just what their feelings urge them to do. Persons of this type can attain orderliness only through their understanding of the fact that it is an indispensable element of life, the life of the person and of the community. They must discipline themselves, begin again after each failure and do battle for orderliness. In this way the character of the virtue in them is something conscious and toilsome, eventually reaching a certain degree of naturalness, but always endangered.

Both of these forms of virtue are good and both are necessary. It is as great a mistake to think that only that virtue is genuine which springs naturally from one's disposition as it is to say that only that is ethical which is acquired with pain and toil. Both are virtue, morally formed humanity, only realized in different ways.

We might also point out that proper order takes on a different character according to the sphere with which it deals. Lifeless objects in a warehouse are ordered differently than, let us say, living beasts in a stable, or persons in an industry; soldiers in service are ordered differently than children in school.

So a great many things might be said on the subject. In connection with the feeling for human worth and social position the sense of order results in a proper behavior in social life; together with a sensitivity to situations, a feeling for what is proper, tact, etc.

Virtue is also a matter of our attitude toward the world. How does a person in whom the feeling for order has become effective view the world? He observes that everything in it is "ordered according to measure, number and weight," as Scripture says. He knows that nothing happens by chance and that everything has a meaning and connection. He rejoices at the sight of this order. He may think, for instance, of the cosmology of the Pythagoreans who equated the laws of the cosmos with those of musical harmony and said that what guided the course of events was the sound of Apollo's lyre. He who has this disposition sees also the order in history, sees that profound laws prevail there, that everything has its cause and nothing is without effect. The Greeks expressed this by the concept of *themis*, according to which all human activity is regulated by divine law and justice. Consequently, this virtue signifies a relation to the whole of existence and enables us to discover aspects of it which never become clear to the one who lives in disorder.

Of course this orderly view may also become rigid so that it sees order merely as natural order and even this as only a mechanical necessity. Then the original form and living productiveness disappear; likewise, all that may be called spiritual fullness, freedom and creativity, and existence congeals in dull and soundless inevitability.

But a person sensitive to order can also suffer in consequence. Indeed every genuine virtue entails a predisposition to spiritual joy and also to spiritual suffering. The disorderly person remains indifferent to the confusion of human affairs, insofar as they do not affect him personally, or he may even consider them his native element and enjoy them. But he who knows the meaning of order senses the danger, even the sinister quality, of disorder. This may be expressed in the ancient concept of chaos, the destruction of existence. Form has become formlessness in the monster, the dragon, the werewolf, the midgardserpent. Here we see the nature of the true hero (Gilgamesh, Heracles, Siegfried) who does not go forth to seek adventure or glory, but knows that it is his task to overcome chaos. They conquer that which makes the world monstrous, and unlivable; they create freedom and suitable conditions for life. For him who desires order, every disorder in the interior life of man, in human relations, in his life work and in the state is alarming, and can even be a torment.

Virtue may also become morbid. We have already touched on that point. Order may become a shackle by which man suffers harm. I knew a very talented man who said, "When I have once made up my mind to do something I would not be able to alter my decision even if I wished to do so." In this case order has become compulsion. Or we may think of the scrupulousness of conscience which torments a man with the feeling that he must do something and do it again and again, endlessly, compelled by an urge that never leaves him. Then there is the teacher who forces everything into rigid rules in order to remain master of his pupils, because he is unable to create an elastic order which serves the purposes of life. And there is also the pathological condition in which a person feels "Now is the time, now 'it' must be done, or something terrible will happen," but he does not know what it is that must be done. Here we have a compulsion to order which has lost its content.

In every virtue there is the possibility of constraint. Therefore man must become master, even of his virtue, in order to attain to the freedom of the image of God.

Virtue extends through the whole of existence, as a harmony which gathers it into unity. And it also ascends to God, or rather it descends from Him.

Plato already knew this, when he invented for God the name of *Agathon*, the "good." It is from the eternal goodness of God that moral enlightenment comes into the soul of the receptive man. It imparts to different characters their respective dispositions for good. This understanding reaches its perfection in the Christian faith. We may recall the mysterious vision in the Apocalypse where the embodiment of order, the Holy City, comes down from God to man. (Apoc. 21:10ff). Due to the limitations of space, we shall mention only a few fundamental points.

First of all, there is a truth, a reality upon which every order of existence depends. It is the fact that God alone is "God" and that man is his creature and image—that God is really God, not an anonymous principle of the universe, not a mere idea, not the mystery of existence, but He who is himself the real and living one, Lord and Creator—and man is His creature and is obliged to obey the supreme Lord.

This is the basic order of all earthly conditions and of all earthly activity. Against it, the first man rebelled when he let himself be persuaded that he might "be as God," and this rebellion continues to the present day, on the part of great and small, genius and gabbler. But if this order is disturbed, then no matter how much power is gained, how much welfare secured, or how much culture developed, all things remain in chaos.

Another way in which the virtue of order is established by God is the irrevocable law that all wrong demands expiation. Man likes to attribute his own forgetfulness to history and thinks that, when he has done wrong, things continue undisturbed: the intended effects remain, the wrong is past, is annihilated. A concept of the state has grown up, according to which the state is permitted any wrong for the purposes of power, prosperity and progress. If these ends are attained, the wrong is blotted out.

As a matter of fact, the wrong is still there, in the matter and the continuity of history, in the lives of those who have committed it and in those who have suffered it, in the influence it has had upon others, and in the impression upon the opinions, the language, and the attitudes which characterize the age. And it shall be expiated some day; it must be expiated—inescapably. God vouches for that.

The third point is the revelation of the judgment. History is not a natural process which is self-justified; rather, it must render an account but not to public opinion, or to science and scholarship. It is likewise incorrect to say that the course of history is itself the judgment, for much remains hidden, much forgotten and the responsibility for many things is placed where it does not belong. No, judgment is reserved for God. Everything will come before His truth and will be revealed. Everything will come under His justice and receive His final verdict.

We see that what we have called the virtue of order, which at first appeared so commonplace, reaches ever deeper, becomes more and more inclusive and finally ascends to God himself—and descends from Him to men. This concatenation is what the word "virtue" means.

In the following, we shall work out a series of such structures of man's relation to the good. We shall do this without any system, but rather use image upon image as these present themselves in the manifold varieties of human experience. This will help us to understand man better, to see more clearly how he lives, how life becomes his task, how he performs it meaningfully or gambles it away.

This will also help us in the practical conduct of our own life. For there is a relation of choice between our various predispositions to the different virtues. These are not a general pattern to be imposed on men but are themselves living humanity, insofar as it hears the appeal of the good and fulfills itself therein. And the good is a living treasure, radiating from God, at its source infinitely rich and yet simple, but breaking up and unfolding at its contact with human existence.

Every virtue is a diffraction of this infinitely rich simplicity upon a potentiality of man. But that means that different individuals according to their potentiality are more or less related or alien to the different virtues. So a socially inclined person who readily establishes relations with others will find the virtue of understanding quite easy and natural, whereas it is naturally strange to the active resolute person fixed upon his goal. A person of creative temperament has an originality which enables him to grasp a given situation vividly, while the person who is of more logical temper holds to fixed rules.

To see all this is important for our understanding of the moral life of different individuals. It is also important for our own daily life, because in our moral development it is well to begin with that which is familiar to us and then to advance to the conquest of that which is more alien.

Truthfulness

A virtue which has suffered great damage in our day is truthfulness, which taken in its widest interpretation includes also the love of truth, and the will that truth should be recognized and accepted.

First, truthfulness means that the speaker should say what is so, as he sees and understands it, and that he should express what is in his mind. Under certain circumstances this may be difficult, and may even cause annoyance, harm and danger. But our conscience reminds us that truth is an obligation, that it is something absolute and sublime. It is not something of which we may say: "You may tell it if it is convenient for you or serves some purpose," but "When you speak you must tell the truth, not abbreviate it or change it. You must tell it absolutely, simply—unless the situation urges you to be silent or you can evade a question in a decent and proper way."

But apart from this, our whole existence depends upon truth. We shall say more about this later. The relations of people to each other, social institutions, government—all that we call civilization and man's work in its countless forms—depend on a respect for truth.

Truthfulness means, then, that man has the instinctive feeling that the truth must be told, absolutely. Of course, we must emphasize this point again, this obligation is based on the assumption that the questioner has the right to be informed. If he does not, then it becomes the task of experience and prudence to find the proper way of avoiding an answer.

We must also note that in regard to truthfulness in daily life it makes a difference if one possesses interior certainty in regard to the various situations, and also if one is a master of the language and quick to define and distinguish. This is a matter of ethical culture with which education should deal. Many a lie arises from shyness and embarrassment, and also from insufficient mastery of the language.

Special problems arise from circumstances such as we have known in the past and still meet today, when a totalitarian tyranny places all under compulsion and permits no personal convictions. Then man is perpetually on the defensive. Those who exercise violence have no right to demand the truth, and they know that they cannot expect it. Violence causes speech to lose its meaning. It becomes a means of self-protection for the one who is violated, unless the situation is such that it demands a testimony by which the speaker risks property and life. To determine this is the affair of conscience and he who lives in secure freedom may well consider whether he has a right to pass judgment in such a case.

At any rate, truthfulness means that one tells the truth, not only once but again and again, so that it becomes a habit. It brings to the whole man, his being and his action, something clear and firm.

And one should not only speak the truth but do it, for one can lie also through actions, attitudes and gestures, if these seem to express something which is not so.

But truthfulness is something more. We have already spoken of the fact that virtue is never isolated. Surely we have already observed that nature does not know the absolutely "pure" tone, that there are always overtones and undertones forming a chord. A pure color also does not occur, only a mixture of colors. Similarly, "bare" truthfulness cannot exist. It would be hard and unjust. What exists is living truthfulness, which other elements of the good penetrate and affect.

There are persons who are truthful by nature. They are too orderly to be able to lie, too much in harmony with themselves—sometimes we may even say, too proud to lie. This is a splendid thing in itself. But such a person is often in danger of saying things at the wrong time, of offending or hurting others. A truth that is spoken at the wrong moment or in a wrong way may so confuse a person that he has difficulty in getting his bearings again. That would not be a living truthfulness but a one-sided one, damaging and destructive. Of course, there are moments when one must not look to the right or left but state the plain truth. But, as a rule, it holds good that we are in the context of existence, and here consideration for the other person is as important as truth-telling. Therefore truth-telling, in order to attain its full human value, must be accompanied by tact and kindness.

Truth is not spoken into a vacuum but to another person; therefore the speaker must try to understand what its effect will be. St. Paul makes a statement whose full meaning is untranslatable: he says that those whom he is addressing, the Christians of Ephesus, should *aletheuein en agape*. Here the noun, *aletheia* is turned into a verb: "to speak, to do, to be truth"—but "in love." (Eph. 4:15) In order that truth may come to life, love must accompany it.

On the other hand, there are persons in whom this feeling for others is very strongly developed. They perceive immediately how they feel, understand their nature and situation, are aware of their needs, apprehensions and troubles, and consequently are in danger of giving in to the influence of these conditions. Then they not only show consideration, but adapt themselves; they weaken the truth or overemphasize it, indicate a parity of opinion or meaning where it really does not exist. Indeed, the influence can predispose their own way of thinking, so that not only external independence of speech and action is lost, but even the interior independence of judgment.

Here too the living quality of truth is endangered, for it includes the liberty of spirit to see what is true, the determination of responsibility which upholds its judgment even in the face of sympathy and helpfulness, and the strength of personality which understands that its own dignity stands or falls with its loyalty to truth.

So we have two elements which must accompany the desire for truth if the complete virtue is to develop: consideration for the person addressed and courage when truth-telling becomes difficult.

Other things are also necessary. For instance, one needs experience of life and an understanding of its ways. He who sees life too simply thinks that he is telling the truth when he may actually be doing violence to it. He may say of another: "He is a coward!" Actually, the other man does not have the forthrightness of one who is sure of himself; he is timid and uncertain and does not dare to act. The judgment seems correct, but the one who pronounces it lacks knowledge of life, or he would have understood the signs of inhibition in the other person.

Again, one may judge that another is bold, whereas he is really shy and is trying to overcome his interior inhibitions.

We might add many other examples. They would lead us to see that living truth claims and requires the whole man. A friend of mine once remarked in conversation: "Truthfulness is the most subtle of all virtues. But there are persons who handle it like a club."

All relations of men with each other, the whole life of the community, depend on faithfulness to truth.

Man is a mysterious being. If someone stands before me, I see his exterior appearance, hear his voice, grasp his hand; but what is going on within him is hidden from me. The more real and vital it is, the more deeply it is buried. So there arises the disturbing fact that the association of persons with each other—and that means the greater part of life—is a relation which moves from one mystery to another. What forms the bridge? The facial expression and gestures, the bearing and actions, but, above all, the word. Through the word man communicates with man. The more reliable the word, the more secure and fruitful the communication.

Moreover, human relationships are of varying depth and significance. The gradation passes from mere getting along with one another and man's simple needs to the life of the soul, to the workings of the mind, the question of responsibility, and the relation of person to person. The way leads ever deeper, into the special, individual, profoundly personal, into the range of freedom where our calculations fail. So the truth of the word becomes ever more important. This is applicable to every kind of relationship, above all to those upon which life in the proper sense depends: friendship, collaboration, love, marriage, the family. Associations that are to endure, to grow and become fruitful must become ever more pure in the truthfulness of each toward the other; if not, they will disintegrate. Every falsehood destroys the community.

But the mystery goes deeper. It does not consist merely in the fact that every communication passes from the hidden depths of one person to those of another, but everyone also communicates with himself. Here man, so to speak, separates into two beings and confronts himself. I consider myself, test and judge myself, decide about myself. Then this duality again unites into the single self and thereafter bears within itself the results of this encounter. This is constantly happening in the process of the interior life. It is the way in which it is accomplished.

But what if I am not truthful in dealing with myself? What if I deceive myself, pretend? And do we not do this constantly? Is not the man who is always "in the right" most perilously "in the wrong"? Does not the man in whose opinion others are always at fault constantly disregard his own fault? Is not the one who always gets his way living in a tragic delusion, unaware how foolish, how conceited, how narrow, how brutal he is and what harm he is doing? If I wish to associate properly with myself and so with others, I must not disregard my own reality, must not deceive myself, but must be true in dealing with myself. But how difficult that is, and how deplorable our state if we honestly examine ourselves!

Truth gives man firmness and stability. He has need of these, for life is not only a friend but also an enemy. Everywhere interests oppose each other. Constantly we meet touchiness, envy, jealousy, and hatred. The very differences of disposition and point of view cause complications. Even the simple fact that there is "the other," for whom I am in turn "the other" is a root of conflict.

How shall I manage? By defending myself, of course. Life is in many respects a battle, and in this battle falsehood and deceit might sometimes seem useful. But what on the whole give us firmness and strength are truth, honesty, and reliability. These qualities bring about an enduring result: respect and confidence.

This is also true in regard to that great power which penetrates the whole of man's life and which is called "the state." It is not an accident that whenever the state, whose basic principles should be liberty and justice, becomes a tyranny, lying and falsehood grow proportionately. Even more, truth is deprived of its value; it ceases to be the norm and is replaced by success. Why? Because it is through truth that the spirit of man is constantly confirmed in its natural rights, and the person is reassured of his dignity and freedom. When a person says, "It is so," and this statement has weight in public because truth is honored, then he is protected against the force which is inherent in every government. But if the government succeeds in depriving truth of its value, then the individual is helpless.

The most hideous manifestation of tyranny is this, when a man's conscience and consciousness of truth is broken, so that he is no longer able to say, "This is so... this is not so." Those who bring this about—in political and judicial affairs, or elsewhere—should realize clearly what they are doing: they are depriving man of his humanity. This realization would crush and destroy them.

Truth is also the means by which man becomes stable and attains character. This is determined by the fact that a man's nature has taken on that firmness which is expressed by the statements: "What is, is. What is right, must be done. What has been entrusted to me I uphold." In the measure in which this comes about, man gains stability and self-reliance.

But is this not self-evident? Does not everyone possess stability by the mere fact that he is himself—as every animal is itself, the swallow, a swallow and the fox, a fox?

Here we must not be careless in our thinking, for much depends upon exactness in these matters. Why does an animal make so strong an impression of stability, of being at one with itself? This is so because it is "nature," a living being without a personal soul. The "spiritual" element within it—order, meaningful being, and behavior—is the spirit of the Creator, not its own. But man possesses a spiritual soul, a free and rational personality. Through this he is worlds above the animal, but for this very reason he lacks the animal's natural stability and unity. He is endangered by his own spirit which constantly tries to overstep its own nature and to become self-determined, and thereby also to question and deceive itself. If we add to this all that faith tells us about the disorder caused by original sin and all that followed, then we see that man is a being endangered by his very origin and that he must constantly resist the evil possibilities within himself. From this point of view man "*is*" not simply himself, his true self, but he is on the way toward it and seeking it. And when he acts rightly, he "*becomes*" himself.

How important it is, then, to ask what is the way in which a true selfhood comes into being, in the profoundest depths of existence, beyond all tensions and disturbances. The answer—above all answers that could be given—is this: it comes from the will to truth. In every true thought and word and deed the interior center, the true self, is confirmed, imperceptibly but really. How dangerous it is when man is deceived about his own nature, in speech, in literature and in pictures. Often we say to ourselves in terror: that which science, literature, politics, newspapers, and films call man is not really man at all. It is an illusion or an assertion for some ulterior motive, or a weapon, or simply thoughtlessness.

Our considerations have advanced far. We said in our first reflection that every virtue involves the whole man. This has been confirmed again. Indeed the virtue extends far beyond man, to God.

Let us just think deeply about this: if I say, two and two are four, then I know that it is wholly four, and only four and always four. I know that this is correct and there will never be a moment when it is not correct, unless certain but definite conditions of higher mathematics are involved. What brings about this certainty that cannot be anything but what it is? What is the reason why, beyond these simple relations of sense objects, every true knowledge at the moment of its flashing upon us brings with it the certainty that it is so? Of course I can err if I have not observed carefully enough or thought clearly enough. That can happen and it happens every day. But when I really know, then I say: It is so. What brings about this strange certainty of the mind depending on nothing tangible? It can only be something that comes from God. Something that does not come from man himself here enters into human action and experience. It is a power, not of compulsive force, but of the reason appealing to us and bearing witness of itself: a power of the mind which brings about that firmness in man which we call "conviction." Plato built his whole philosophy upon this basic experience. He called this power a "light"; the highest, indeed, the real light, that comes from the true sun. This sun is God, whom, as we have mentioned before, Plato calls the *agathon*, the "good." St. Augustine, relying upon St. John, introduced this idea into Christian thought where it became eternally fruitful.

In the last analysis, what is truth really? It is the way in which God is God and knows himself, is knowing and in his knowledge bears himself. Truth is the indestructible, untouchable solidity with which God, by knowing, is based upon himself. From him truth moves into the world and gives it solidity. Truth penetrates all being and gives it its nature; its light shines into the human mind and gives it that brightness which we call knowledge.

This is a valid conclusion: He who holds to the truth holds to God. He who lies rebels against God and betrays the rational basis of existence.

In this world, the truth is weak. A trifle suffices to hide it. The most stupid persons can attack it. But some day the time will come when things will change. God will bring it about that truth will be as powerful as it is true; and this will be the judgment.

"Judgment" means that the possibility of lying ceases because omnipotent truth penetrates every mind, illumines every word and rules in every place. Then falsehood will be revealed as what it is. However expedient, clever or elegant it may have been, it will be exposed as an illusion, as a nonentity.

We should let these thoughts occupy our minds, our understanding, and our hearts. Then we shall perhaps sense what truth is, its steadfastness, its calm radiance, its nobility. Then we will enter into union with it, through all that is most intimate and loyal within us. We will accept responsibility for the truth and expend our efforts in its behalf.

All this will suffer opposition and trials, because we are human. But our lives must testify to the fact that truth is the basis of everything—of the relation of man to man, of man to himself, of the individual to the community—and, above all, of man to God—no, of God to us.

Acceptance

If someone should ask, "I should like to make progress in moral life; where shall I begin?", then we would probably answer, "Wherever you will." You can begin with a fault of which you have become conscious in your profession or occupation. Or else, you can begin with the needs of the community, the family or friends, wherever you have ascertained a failing. Or else you may be aware that some passion has power over you and you may strive to overcome it. Basically, all that matters is that you should be honest and sincere and make a determined effort. Then one thing will lead to another. For the life of man is a whole. If he grasps it anywhere with determination then his conscience awakes and strengthens his moral power in other respects as well, just as a fault anywhere in his life makes its influence felt everywhere.

But if the questioner urges us further, "What is the presupposition for all moral effort if it is to be effective, to change what is amiss, to strengthen what is feeble, and to balance what is uneven?" then, I believe, we would have to answer, "It is the acceptance of what is, the acceptance of reality, your own and that of the people around you and of the time in which you live."

Perhaps this sounds somewhat theoretical, yet it is not only correct but deserves the special attention of everyone who is making an honest effort; for it is by no means self-evident that we accept what is, accept it interiorly as well, with a ready heart. Someone might object again and say, "But this is affectation. What is, is, whether we 'accept' it or not, quite apart from the fact that such a disposition is very convenient and must lead to passivity." So we must make it clear at once that we are not dealing with a weak submissiveness but with seeing the truth and taking one's stand upon it, resolved, of course, to work for it and, if necessary, to fight for it.

Here true humanity begins. An animal is essentially in harmony with itself. More accurately, for the animal the question does not exist. It is naturally adapted to its environment just as it is and is absorbed in it. That is why it gives us the impression of "naturalness." It is exactly as it must be according to its nature and the surrounding conditions.

Man's situation is different. He is not absorbed in his own being and environment. He can depart from himself and think about himself. He can judge himself and can raise his desires above what he is to that which he would like to be or should be. Indeed, he can lift himself in fancy to the impossible. So there arises a tension between his actual being and his desires, which may become a principle of growth insofar as he keeps before him in his striving an image of himself, which he seeks to overtake with that which he really is. But the tension may also cause a harmful split, a flight from one's own reality, a phantasy existence which disregards the given possibilities and also the threatening dangers.

This is what we meant when we said that all effective moral striving must begin with a man's sincere acceptance of existence as it is.

Let us try to understand what this acceptance means by seeking to understand more clearly what it is that we accept.

There is first of all myself. For I am not man in general, but this particular person. I have a certain character and no other, a certain temperament among all the various ones that exist, certain strong and weak points, definite possibilities and limitations. All this I should accept and build upon as the fundamental basis of my life.

This is, we repeat, by no means self-evident. For there is—and this throws a glaring light on the finiteness of our existence—a disgust with our own being, a protest against one's self. We must remember again that man is not, like an animal, enclosed in himself, but can rise above himself. He can think about how he would like to be. And many a person lives more in a dream world than in the consciousness of his reality. We know, too, the curious activities by which a person tries to slip out of what he is, dressing up, masking, plays. Does not all this indicate the vain, but ever renewed attempt to be someone different than we really are? So there appears the command, strict and not easy to fulfill, really to wish to be who we are—convinced that behind this there is no dull necessity of nature, nor a malicious chance, but the allotment by eternal wisdom.

This means that I must accept not only the strong points that I have but also the weaknesses; not only the possibilities but also the limitations. For we strange human beings are so constituted that what supports us also burdens us, what brings security also endangers us. Every mode of being has a positive side and also a negative, and we cannot select.

We have attained great wisdom if we have learned that we cannot pick and select among the foundations of existence but must accept the whole. This does not mean that we should approve of everything, and leave everything unchanged. Certainly not. I can and should work on myself and my life and mold and improve it. First, however, I must admit the existing facts; otherwise everything becomes false.

The person endowed with a keen reason, a practical view, and a firm hand often lacks the creativity of imagination, the beauty of the dream which belongs to the artistic temperament. In return the latter is burdened with the dark moments of emptiness and discouragement, and the difficulty of adjusting to the real world and its calculations. The person of strong feelings who tastes the joys of existence must also endure its pains and sorrows. No one can expect to keep the one and reject the other, but if he wishes to live true to reality he must accept his own nature. The person who is cool-headed and can easily shake off unpleasant things does not know the heights and depths of existence.

Again, this does not mean that we should call good what is not so. The bad is bad, evil is evil and what is ugly should be called ugly. But all efforts to develop the one and overcome the other depend on the assumption that we have first recognized and admitted what is. How many people build up phantasies about themselves and seek to circumvent by lies what really is. They are indignant if we call their attention to a fault and surprised if something goes wrong. The beginning of all effort is the recognition of what is, even if that happens to be one's faults. Only when I honestly take upon myself the burden of my faults do I really become serious and only then can the work of overcoming them begin.

We must also accept the situation and circumstances of our life as they have been allotted to us. Of course, we can change and improve many things and shape them more according to our wishes, especially if these wishes are definite and the hand that seeks to carry them out is firm. But, basically, the tendencies that have grown out of our earliest years remain and determine what follows. Psychologists say that the fundamental characteristics of a child are fixed by the end of the third or fourth year. These accompany him through his later life, as also do those influences which the persons around him, the social group, the city and the country have exercised.

Another step is the acceptance of our destiny. Destiny is not accident. It possesses a logical consistency which is determined externally by the connection of events but also internally by the nature and character of the person involved.

The life of the average man will not know the triumphs or the catastrophes experienced by the genius. The man whose talents lie in economics and organization will not be seized by the perplexity and despair that often overwhelm the man of artistic nature, and the latter will not experience the victories and defeats of the man who has the ability to acquire and use power. So the nature of a person forms, as it were, a sieve which permits certain experiences to pass through and retains others.

Even those things which may happen to one—perhaps the lightning which strikes a house during a thunderstorm—will be something different if the owner of the house is madly carried away by his misfortune or has self-control and is able to stand firm. So we may say in a certain sense that the individual possesses in his disposition a preliminary sketch of his destiny. Not a fixed necessity—this is contradicted by the fact of freedom which again and again, in small things and in great, has its part in building a life—but a direction, a basic character, often a probability of definite events. Again the important thing is that one accept one's destiny and then work more resolutely in guiding and shaping it. The life of modern man is governed by an idea which is the counterpart of the fear that grips his nerves; that is, the idea of obtaining security against increasing dangers. Of course we can do many things in this respect. To mention only one thing, we can calculate how great the life expectancy is in a certain occupation, and how great the percentage of accidents in another; but, we cannot insure ourselves against life itself. Rather, we must accept it with all that it brings, both great and small, of possibilities of fortune and misfortune. To accept one's destiny really means to accept oneself and to be true to oneself. This idea took the form of the *amor fati* in pagan scepticism, the "love" of one's own fate, born of defiance. Its Christian form is the assent given to the way that is outlined for us by our own nature, because of our confidence that everything rests upon Divine Providence.

The logical consistency of the thought leads us further, to the point where we do not merely resist pain and misfortune, or, if they cannot be avoided, endure them courageously, but where we accept their bitterness. In order to be able to do that, we must have been taught in the school of Christ, for our nature inclines otherwise. It protests against pain, and, to begin with, we cannot object to that, especially since there is a yielding to pain that grows out of weakness; there is even a morbid desire for it. But mere rejection destroys the meaning of pain for our life. If it is rightly understood and borne, it deepens life, cleanses it, and brings man into harmony with himself, because he comes into harmony with the divine will, which is behind all events.

And finally there is this: Acceptance of self means that I consent simply to be.

This statement sounds odd, as long as all is going well. Then we live on in our own being and action and think no further. But when other times come—times of misfortune, of failure, of disgust—then there is a cleavage between myself and me. I did not confront the possibility of my own existence and decide that I wished to be, but I was cast into being. I came forth from the lives of my parents, of my ancestors, out of the conditions of the age. The event of my birth said to me, "Now you are. So live your life." At certain moments we are intimately aware what a grace it is to be, to be permitted to breathe, to feel, to work. But it may happen otherwise, so that our own existence appears to us not in the nature of a gift but of a burden. When our strength fails, the world turns gray and duties weigh upon us; in times of protracted illness or sorrow, in moments of discouragement or of melancholy the protest may arise, "I was not asked. I did not want to be. Why must I?" Then we feel that it is unreasonable to demand that we should be, and that it is an act of the deepest profundity of being to accept our existence. For it can be declined, in a dull and weary fashion, when a person continues to live, merely shrugging his shoulders in resignation, but also in a desperate action, for the number of those who cast away their life is frighteningly large and seems to be growing. They are those for whom the gift of existence becomes a burden and who are unwilling to carry it, or perhaps are unable, because no faith and no love teaches them to understand the difficult riddle.

In all this we make no progress with merely human motives. We really should have said this at the beginning of our reflections. For when we considered that we cannot construct our own existence but receive it, the next question should have been, "From whom?" And the answer would have been, "From our parents, from the historical situation, from our ancestors. But ultimately and through all the intermediaries—from God." So we cannot attain to a true acceptance if we do not clearly understand from where we receive our existence: from the blind course of nature, the senselessness of chance, the malice of a demon—or from the pure wisdom and love of God. And we must again and again remind ourselves that the basic revelation of Christ was how God is disposed toward us.

True acceptance is possible only if we have proof upon which we can rely. This we have in the living God. The more closely what we should accept touches our life, the more clearly the acceptance involves a conquest of ourself, an interior abandonment of self, as the spiritual masters of the Middle Ages expressed it, a surrender of oneself to that which is, the more we need to understand the nature of the omnipotent intention which is directed toward each one of us.

There is a question which is really foolish, but must be asked, since it helps us in our relations with the transcendent God: Does He really know what He demands of us, He who has no destiny because there is no power that could impose it upon Him? Must not His dispensations, if we may say so, always come "from above," in Olympic fashion, from the calm aloofness of the unapproachable?

Here revelation tells us of a mystery which is as comforting as it is incomprehensible. In Christ, God laid aside this unapproachability. Through the Incarnation He stepped into the space which forms a single chain of destiny for him who lives in it. God stepped into history. When the eternal Son became man He did so in reality, without protection or exception, vulnerable by word and act; woven, like us, into the stifling web of effects that proceed from the confused hearts of men. Yet there is a difference; for the greater his soul, the deeper his feelings, the more intense his life, the more one is affected by these things. To have a destiny means to suffer; the more capable of suffering one is, the greater is the element of destiny in his life. What vistas of thought does this open to us! What a climax does the concept attain! The Son of God steps into history to atone for our sin and to lead us to new possibilities. He does this prepared for all that would happen to Him, without reservation, without evasion, without resorting to resistance or craft. Men, who have really no power over Him to whom "is given all power in heaven and on earth," inflict a bitter destiny upon Him. But this is the form of his Father's will for Him. This will is His own will; to accomplish it is the "food" of His life. (John 4:32) So the weight of destiny is transformed into freedom. The highest freedom and the heaviest duty become one. We may recall His mysterious word on the way to Emmaus: "Ought not Christ to have suffered and so to enter into his glory"? (Luke 24:26)

But God is not "the absolute Being" of mere philosophy, but He who is such that His most intimate nature, His love, is expressed in this way. And His sovereignty is that supreme freedom which is able and willing to accomplish it.

Only from this point of view can existence be comprehended and mastered. Not through some philosophy of personality and its relation to the world, but through faith in what God has done and in union with Him. The image for this is the Cross, as He said, "If anyone will come after me let him deny himself and take up his cross and follow me." (Matt. 16:24). Each "his own," that which is "sent" him. Then the Master accomplishes in him the mystery of holy freedom.

Patience

O ur first reflection endeavored to remove from the concept of virtue the narrow, moralistic tone that it has acquired in the course of time, and to view it as something living, great and beautiful. So it might seem strange if the title of the following reflection claims that this description also identifies patience. Is not patience something dull and insignificant, a miserable means by which a narrow life seeks to justify its own poverty?

Therefore we shall begin our consideration on the heights with the Lord of all virtue. For the great example of patience is God because He is the omnipotent and loving one.

Have we ever tried to understand how mysterious it is that God created the world at all? The unbeliever knows nothing of this mystery, for he sees the world as "nature"; that is, as something which simply exists. But even the believer is usually not conscious of it because he thinks of the creating power of God in a natural way, as the first cause in the series of causes which operate in nature. He has faith, but this faith has not yet determined his way of thinking and feeling. This is still similar to the ordinary way of the age. But as soon as faith penetrates the core of the personality, the nature of the finite becomes mysterious and the question arises, "Why did God create it?"

If we were able to answer that question, really to answer it, then we would know much. But on earth this is impossible, for it would presuppose that we could think from God's point of view and such knowledge will be given to us only in eternity. Here on earth the question remains unanswered: why He, who is all things, can do all things, is Lord of all riches; why He created the world. The world which is indeed great, immeasurable for our mind, but always and absolutely finite. God does not need the world. Of what use is it to Him? What does He do with it? Perhaps these considerations give us some inkling of the roots of divine patience.

For God not only created the world, but He upholds and sustains it. He does not become weary of it. There is a myth which may open our eyes—for myths can do that. There is much truth in them, of course in ambiguous form, so that he who hears them is always in danger either of under-rating it or of being misled by it. An Indian myth tells of Shiva, who fashions all things, that in an exuberance of delight he creates the world but then grows weary of it, treads it into fragments and produces another. This suffers the same fate and creating and destruction continue indefinitely. How impressive is the image of this divinity of impatience. It shows us how different is the relation of the true God to the world.

He creates it—the reason is an unfathomable mystery. In spite of its profusion of powers and forms, it is finite, measured and limited throughout. So it does not "suffice" for God himself, and can never satisfy His eternal demands. Yet He does not become weary of it. This is the first manifestation of patience; that is, that God does not cast away the world, but keeps it in existence, respects it, and that He, if we may use the expression, is faithful to it, forever.

In this world there is a being possessing consciousness, inwardness, heart and mind. This being is man. To him God has entrusted His world, so that it may not merely exist but be experienced. Man should continue

God's work with understanding, feeling and loving. He should administer the first world and shape it in truth and justice. In this way, the second world shall come into being, the real world that God intends.

But how does man treat the work of God? Anyone who has gained some experience and has looked more carefully into history and who does not let himself be blinded by the superstition of progress must be terrified to notice how much disorder there is in the world—how much error and folly, greed, violence and falsehood, how much crime. All this exists in spite of science, technology and welfare—or rather together with it—mixed with it, inextricably confused. Even in religion, in men's ideas of the divine, their relations with it, and their defense of it. Modern man is inclined simply to accept everything that happens. He arranges one thing next to the other, derives one from the other, declares everything to be necessary, and calls the whole "history." But he who has learned to distinguish, to call the true true and the false false, the right right and the wrong wrong, cannot do this and must be frightened to see how man deals with the world.

And yet God does not cast away the badly spoiled creation and form a new one. What a terrible threat we glimpse in the account of the flood. If we look into it more deeply, we discern the hint of a possibility of universal destruction in the words: "The Lord God repented that He had created man upon the earth." (Gen. 6:6) But in God—if we may say this—the "Yes" is stronger than the "No," and he carries the world on, "endures" it through time and eternity.

This attitude of God toward the world is the first patience, absolute patience, possible only because He is the omnipotent one, because He, who knows no weakness, is the true Lord whom no one threatens, the eternal one for whom there is neither fear nor haste. We may recall Jesus' parable of the sower and the seed. The master of the field had sown good wheat but in the midst of it the weeds sprang up. His servants came and asked, "Shall we tear it out?" But he answered, "No, otherwise you will tear out the wheat with the weeds. Let both grow. Later the harvest will come and they will be separated from each other." (Matt. 13:24ff.)

This is the patience of the one who could use force but spares, because he is truly Lord, noble and gracious. But man is the image of God; he should imitate him in this respect also. The world is placed in his hand, the world of things, of persons and of his own life. He should make of it what God expects, even now, after the weeds have spread their rank growth through everything. Patience is the prerequisite for the growth of the wheat.

Can an animal be impatient? Obviously not, it can be neither impatient nor patient. It is fitted into the interrelation of nature's laws; it lives as it must live and dies when its time has come. Impatience becomes possible only for a being which is capable of rising above the immediately existing and of desiring what has not yet come to be. It is possible only for man. Only he is faced with the decision whether he is able to allow time for growth and development.

And this must be done again and again, for in this existence in time and finiteness we constantly find the tension between what man is and what he would like to be; between that which has been realized and that which remains to be accomplished. And it is patience which endures the tension.

It is patience, above all, with that which is given and apportioned to us, our destiny. The environment in which we live is allotted to us; we are born into it. The events of history continue without our being able to change them essentially, and everyone feels their effects. Personally we experience, day by day, what happens to come along. We can resist or change many things according to our wishes; but basically we must accept what comes and is given to us. To understand this and to act accordingly is patience. Anyone who is unwilling to do this is in constant conflict with his own existence.

Let us recall that character who rebels against all laws, Goethe's Faust. After he has renounced hope and faith, he cries out, "And cursed above all be patience!" He is the ever-immature who never sees reality or accepts it as it is. Always he flies above it in his fancy. Always he is in a state of protest against his destiny, whereas the maturity of man begins with his acceptance of what is, of reality. Only this gives him the power to change and to re-shape it.

We must also have patience with the people who are associated with us. Whether it be our parents, husband or wife or child, a friend or a fellow-worker or whoever it may be. Mature, responsible life begins with our accepting people as they are.

It can be very difficult to be bound to a person whom one gradually comes to know intimately, of whom one knows how he speaks, how he thinks, what his attitude toward everything is. One would like to put him away and take another. Faithfulness here is pre-eminently patience with what he is, how he is and acts, and what he does. If this patience is not exercised everything goes to pieces and the possibilities that lay in the relationship are lost.

But we must also have patience with ourselves. We know to some extent, in the form of a more or less definite wish, how we should like to be. We should like to be rid of one characteristic, to possess another, and we are annoyed at being just what we are. It is difficult to be obliged to remain the person we are, humiliating always to find in ourselves the same faults, weaknesses and deficiencies.

Disgust with oneself—the greatest spirits have most often felt this. Here patience must again take over and help us to accept ourselves and persevere. Not to approve of that in ourselves which is not good; not to be self-satisfied—that would be the way of the Philistine. Dissatisfaction with our own imperfection and insufficiency must remain; otherwise, we would lose that power of self-criticism which is the prerequisite for all moral development. But it should not cause us to escape into illusions about ourselves. Every sound criticism must begin with what is given and work on from that point, knowing that it will be slow work, extremely slow. And this very slowness guarantees that the change is taking place not in our fancy, but in reality.

Wherein does the moral life consist?

Perhaps we have realized that we lack self-control. We must keep a firmer hold on ourselves, become more quiet in speaking, more prudent in action. We recognize and admit this, but it is at first only in our mind, as a thought, or a plan. It must be worked out in real life, and that is difficult. We may dream ourselves into a virtue, and how much wishful thinking consists of imaginary virtues! But the dreams vanish and everything is as it was—no, it is worse, phantasy consumes moral energy, apart from the lack of truthfulness that is inherent in it. How often, under the impression of a lofty moment or a new resolution, we think, "Now I've made the grade!" But on the next occasion we notice that our own reality, which seemed to have taken on the form of that which we know to be right, slips back into the old way, and everything is as it was.

A real moral growth would take place if our acts of restraint and self-moderation became more conscious, if our awareness of what our violence might bring about increased, and if we did not let ourselves be carried away so easily by the impulse of our feelings but remained more free, and attained a mastery over our emotions and our inner selves. This would not be phantasy but real processes of the interior life, changes in the relation of various acts to each other, the molding of their character. But that sort of thing takes place slowly, very slowly.

Therefore patience, which always begins again, is a prerequisite if something is really to be done. In the *Imitation of Christ* we find the phrase: *semper incipe!*—one of those clear and concise expressions of which the Latin language is master. At first sight, it is a paradox for a beginning is a beginning and then we go on. But that is true only in mechanical matters. In actual life beginning is an element that must operate constantly. Nothing goes on if it does not at the same time begin.

So he who wishes to advance must always begin again. He must constantly immerse himself in the inner source of life and arise therefrom in new freedom, in "initiative"—the power of beginning—in order to make real what he has purposed: prudence, temperance, self-control, or whatever it may be that is to be accomplished.

Patience with oneself—of course not carelessness or weakness, but the sense of reality—this is the foundation of all progress.

Goethe's Faust, who was formerly the idol of the bourgeoisie, is impatient through and through; he is a dreamer who never grows up. He sells himself to magic, a way of expressing that he does not know how definitely the acceptance of reality, endurance and perseverance amid the things that are, form the basis of all growth and accomplishment. Instead, he makes speeches, everything around him goes to pieces, and at the end there is a "redemption" which no one believes who understands what that word means.

When we were thinking about the concept of virtue we noticed that there is no virtue which, if we will permit the old expression, is chemically pure. As in nature we do not find the pure tone, the pure color, but only refractions and chords, so there is no attitude which is pure patience, but many other elements must be mingled with it.

So, for example, patience is impossible without insight, without knowing the ways of life. Patience is wisdom, understanding what it means that I have this and not something else, that I am of this nature and not another, that the person with whom I am associated is as he is and not like another. I would like it to be different, and by persevering effort I may be able to change many things, but basically things are as they are and I must accept that. Wisdom is insight into the way in which realization comes about; how an idea is lifted from the imagination and worked into the substance of existence. Wisdom is knowing how slow this process is and how greatly endangered; how easily we may deceive ourselves and slip from our own hand.

Patience demands strength—great strength. The supreme patience rests upon omnipotence. Because God is the omnipotent He can be patient with the world. Only the strong man can exercise living patience, can take upon himself again and again the things that are; only he can always begin anew. Patience without strength is mere passivity, dull acceptance, growing accustomed to being a mere thing.

Love, too, belongs to true patience—love of life. For living things grow slowly, take their time, and have many ways and turns. Life demands confidence, and only love can trust. He who does not love life has no patience with it. This leads to short-circuits and to violence; and then there are wounds and destruction.

Many other things could be said on this subject.

Living patience is the whole man, standing in tension between what he would like to have and what he has, between what he ought to accomplish and what he is able at any given time to do, between that which he wishes to be and that which he really is. Working out this tension, again and again gathering things together in relation to the possibilities of the moment—that is patience. So we might say that patience is man in the process of becoming, with a true understanding of himself. And it is only in the hand of patience that those who are entrusted to us can thrive and grow. A father or mother who does not have patience, in this sense, will only harm the children. A teacher who does not have patience with those entrusted to him will frighten them and deprive them of sincerity. When life has been placed in our hands, the work can prosper only if we carry it on with this deep and quiet power. It resembles the manner in which life itself grows. When we were children we perhaps had a little garden, or just a flower pot on the window-sill, and we planted seed. Was it not difficult to adapt ourselves to the way in which growth in the earth took place? Did we not dig up the ground to see if the seed was growing—and then the germ perished? Did we not feel that growth was too slow, until the insignificant sprout appeared? And when the buds formed did we not squeeze them to make them open? Instead, they turned brown and withered. The power under whose protection life can unfold is patience.

Again and again we shall turn to the patience of the powerful one under whose protection we should grow, the living God. Woe to us if He were like Shiva, the impatient and foolish one; if He did not have the wisdom and long-suffering which, in quiet attention, holds the world, which He does not need but which He loves, permitting it to ripen.

Again and again we shall turn to Him: "Lord, have patience with me, and give me patience so that the possibilities granted to me may, in the short span of my life-time, those brief years, grow and bear fruit!"

Justice

Now we shall speak of justice. The word has a lofty but also a tragic sound. It has enkindled noble passion and inspired the practice of the finest generosity. But it also reminds us of great wrongs—of wide-spread destruction and suffering. The whole history of mankind could be recounted under the heading: "The battle for justice."

In the Sermon on the Mount, in the Beatitudes, the words of Jesus express the greatness and also the whole tragic quality of the matter concerned. He says, "Blessed are they that hunger and thirst after justice, for they shall have their fill." (Matt. 5:6) The one who says this is no idealist remote from the world, but He of whom the Gospel says that "he knew what was in man." (John 2:25) Here He figuratively connects justice with that urge which determines the presence or absence of physical life—with hunger and thirst. In the heart of man—of the right-minded man, whom Jesus calls blessed—the desire for justice is as elementary as hunger and thirst are in his physical life. How terrible is the lack when this desire is not fulfilled. But some day, this is Christ's promise, it shall be satisfied.

By the word "justice" Jesus means something which receives its full meaning only from Revelation: justification before God, the grace of pardon and sanctification.* But to bring home to us what that means he connects the idea of salvation by God's grace with that of justice as the basic value of all moral existence and that of hunger and thirst for bodily satisfaction. So he suggests something elementary which concerns the whole man.

This basic and elementary thing shall now be the subject of our meditation.

We can speak of justice only in relation to man; it does not exist in the animal world. Where we seem to discern something of the sort—perhaps in noble horses or highly bred dogs—it is a reflection of the human being in the animal which lives with him. Of its own nature, the animal knows nothing of justice, for it lacks what is central to justice, the person. But what is a person? It is the manner in which man is man. A lifeless thing in nature exists as a thing, something without feeling, whose form, qualities and energy are determined by the laws of nature. A living creature exists as an individual, a being that lives, grows from an inner center, maintains itself, unfolds, propagates and dies. It too is determined by interior and exterior necessity. Man, however, exists as a person; that means, he is not merely there, but he is conscious of himself. He knows about himself; he is master of himself; he carries out his own work with judgment and in freedom. He stands not merely in a physical or biological relation to other persons, but converses with them and lives in a community which is established on a basis of intelligence. The fact that man is a person gives to his existence the frightening seriousness and significance which we express by the words "conscience" and "responsibility." Man not only exists, but his existence is committed to him and he is accountable for the use he makes of it. He is not merely active, he *acts*, and he is responsible for his actions. This gives man dignity and honor. For this he desires freedom and a right order. He must desire them, inevitably,

---

* On this, see the epilogue to the meditations at the end of the book.

for the sake of spiritual self-preservation, for himself and for others, for mankind as such. This is, primarily, the desire for justice.

Justice then is that order in which man can exist as a person, in which he can form his judgment about himself and the world, can have a conviction which none can touch, and can be master of his decision and act according to his judgment. Justice is that order of existence in which man can participate in the world and carry on his work, and can form with other persons relations of friendship, of association, of love and fruitfulness according to the demands of his conscience. And, we must emphasize this again, this is true not only of one or another, not only of the powerful or fortunate or talented person, but of every man because he is human.

The order which would guarantee this would be justice. But is there such a thing? Is not history really the tragedy of justice? Is it not a concatenation of the deeds by which selfishness, violence and falsehood have constantly endangered and destroyed this order? In any case, such an order would be justice and the man who desires it and strives for its realization we call a just man.

Justice would go deeper if it determined destiny, and if the man who is good would in consequence be happy, or if the man of good disposition were successful, and the pure of heart were always beautiful, and the good man had a rich and full life; if, on the other hand, an evil disposition rendered its possessor ugly, injustice brought misfortune, and every sin brought vengeance upon the one who committed it, only upon him, and never upon an innocent person.

This would be justice not merely in action but in destiny. But does it exist? Is it not the subject of fairy tales? Is this not the reason why we—even as adults and with our experience of life—never grow weary of these tales, whereas reality is so completely different? In this deeper sense the just man would be the one who desired this state of affairs and did what he could to bring it about, but he would also be Don Quixote, the dreamer, who pursues the impossible and makes himself ridiculous.

Perhaps the matter goes deeper still and here we seem to find something that we must call the justice of being. This is so improbable that one must almost fear to speak of it. We surmise what it means if we listen to the complaints of human hearts, complaints about its non-existence: Why was I not born strong and healthy instead of sickly? Why do I have these qualities and not others? Why do I not have the possibilities for which I envy my friend? And so on.

In the speech of all men there appear questions which no wisdom can answer—those questions in which we find the word "why" and the word "I." Why am I so? Why am I not so? Justice of being would exist if every man from the very first could agree to be as he is and who he is. But here we touch the basic mystery of ultimate being. The answer to these questions can be given only by God himself; an answer which does not merely solve the problem but removes it in a living encounter.

But let us stay within the confines of everyday reality. How would it be if man strove for justice?

In regard to the existing order he would do what he could to see that the laws of the land gave everyone his rights, that burdens were apportioned according to true capacity, that needs would be properly met, etc. These are great things, but let us disregard them for a moment. It often seems as if great things exist for the purpose of diverting people from those things that touch them seriously. Where does the justice of the existing order really become a serious matter? Here the answer would be less imposing but far more concrete. It would concern matters that touch our own life.

For example: if you spend ten dollars for yourself and later are supposed to do it for another, does the amount carry the same weight for you in both cases? Or do you say, or think, or feel, in the first case, "only" ten dollars, and in the second, "all of ten dollars"? Why the difference? It would be justice if you considered the amount as equivalent in both cases, for that means that another's need touched you as closely as your own. And even if there were a difference in the immediate feeling, yet your intention and action would be the same in both cases.

What is the situation in your home, in your family? Do you consider the different persons there of equal worth? Does an unkind word about one distress you as much as such a word spoken about another? Or do you like one person and become indignant about an injustice done to him but think the matter not so serious if the injustice is done to another? Ought not at least your practical conduct in both cases be the same?

Here, and not in the apportionment of taxes, does real justice begin: it begins at home, in our dealings with our friends, in the office, wherever we are associated with people. It consists in saying and giving and doing, in so far as possible, that which the other has a right to expect.

And the justice of destiny, in which the life of man were to be arranged as his disposition merits, how would this justice, in so far as we can speak of such a thing, appear in everyday life? What could one do who "hungers and thirsts" for it? He could not change much in the actual situation, for higher powers are in operation there; but he could, for example, make an effort to judge another not according to external appearances, but according to his intentions. But how do we act in everyday matters? Do we give to those who live around us that first beginning of the justice of destiny which consists in trying to understand what they mean? At home among our family or in business, when dealing with our associates, in short, among persons who are close to us, do we consider how somebody meant the word which offended us, why he was so irritated in a particular case, or what may have been the reason why his work was so unsatisfactory?

Only in that way would we be dealing seriously with everyday reality; that is, not by attempting to establish a general culture of justice in which the interior and the exterior would correspond, but by giving to those persons with whom we are dealing a little of such justice.

The deepest stratum of justice is touched, as we saw, by the question concerning the differences of existence. Why are persons different in disposition? Why is one healthy and another an invalid? Why does one come from a harmonious family and another from a broken one? And so on through all the inequalities which press upon us everywhere. We cannot grasp their roots. Let us rather consider what would be possible in daily life.

There is, for example, the elementary question of whether we actually grant to the other the right to be as he is. If we consider the matter, we shall soon see that we usually do not do this at all but, by aversion, ungraciousness or bias, reproach him for his own nature. But his existence gives him the right to be as he is; so we should grant it to him, and not only in theory but also in our disposition and in our thoughts, in our daily attitude and actions. This we should do especially in our immediate environment, in our family, among our friends, our associates and colleagues. It would be justice to seek to understand the other person from his own point of view and to act accordingly. Instead we emphasize the injustice of existence by sharpening and poisoning the differences through our judgment and actions.

But if things are so in the small circle which we can influence, how can they be otherwise in world affairs? Everyone should say to himself: the history of nations moves in the same way as the affairs in my home. The state mirrors the way in which I order my small sphere of action. All criticism should begin with ourselves, and with the intention of improving things. Then we would soon see how much goes wrong because we do not permit the other person to be who he is and do not give him the room which he requires.

But will things never be properly ordered? If we put aside wishful thinking we must reply: evidently not in the course of history. Of what avail are all the attempts to bring about justice on earth if we look not at ideologies and party politics but at reality, the whole reality?

Let us consider the present situation. Let us presume that those who live and fight today are really concerned about the establishment of justice; that is, a proper order of society, sufficient food for all, suitable working conditions for everyone, the possibility of education without special privileges, and so on. Then much would have been accomplished. But how much all this is intermingled with striving for power and self-will! How much injustice enters into it, how much falsehood, how much even of crime! Millions of persons are crushed in order that the supposedly correct form of economic conditions, of the social order, of government—even of justice—may be established. And let us assume that in all this a forward step is taken. Does this take away and nullify all the terrible things which brought it about? Or is the evil still there, in the context of life, poisoning what has been attained?

A person is worthy of his humanity in so far as he strives to bring about justice in the place where he is; but as a whole, as that which it should be, as a condition of existence and an attitude of mankind, justice can never be attained. And here the idea of "progress" which has at present become a dogma, and the notion of the evolution of man beyond himself to ever greater heights must not confuse us. Personal experience as well as history tells another story. There is a basic disorder working in man which makes itself felt anew in every one who is born.

Only by God will true and complete justice be established, and only through His judgment. We should try to let the revelation that this judgment will be passed upon all mankind affect us deeply. The first thing that everyone who thinks of the judgment should say to himself is, "Judgment will be passed upon me!" But there will also be a judgment upon all the human institutions and powers about which we are so likely to feel that they are sovereign and subject to no examination: the state, civilization, history.

The judgment must be taken into account in all being and action. It is God's verdict upon every finite reality. Without it everything is half balanced in space. Only God determines it. He it is who sees through all, fearing nothing, bound by nothing, just in eternal truth. If a man does not believe in Him, his hunger and thirst shall never be satisfied.

Reverence

I f one wishes to think about a phenomenon of human existence it is well to notice the word by which language designates it, for language expresses more than the mind of the individual. We wish to do this in dealing with the virtue upon which we now intend to meditate; that is, reverence.*

It is a strange word, this combination of "fear" and "honor." Fear which honors; honor which is pervaded by fear. What kind of fear could that be? Certainly not the kind of fear that comes upon us in the face of something that is harmful or causes pain. That kind of fear causes us to defend ourselves or to seek safety. The fear of which we shall speak does not fight or flee, but it forbids obtrusiveness, keeps one at a distance, does not permit the breath of one's own being to touch the revered object. Perhaps it would be better to speak of this fear as "awe."

This word leads us to an understanding of the phenomenon. The feeling of reverence has a religious origin. It is the perception of the holy and unapproachable which, in the experience of early man, surrounded all that

---

* Translator's note: The German word for reverence, *ehrfurcht*, combines the two words, *honor* and *fear*. The English word, from the Latin *vereor* also implies the idea of fear and respect.

was lofty, powerful and splendid. It included several things: a surmise of greatness and holiness and a desire to participate in it combined with the apprehension of being unworthy of it and of arousing a mysterious anger.

In the measure in which cultural evolution progressed, and a rational understanding and technical mastery of the world increased, the religious element receded. The concept of significance and value became predominant and awakened a respectful attitude in which there was still an echo of the old awe, that feeling of reverence of which we are speaking and by which a man of proper discernment still pays tribute to greatness.

In reverence man refrains from doing what he usually likes to do, which is to take possession and use something for his own purposes. Instead he steps back, and keeps his distance. This creates a spiritual space in which that which deserves reverence can stand erect, detached and free, in all its splendor. The more lofty an object, the more the feeling of value which it awakens is bound up with this keeping one's distance.

And yet the experience of value makes us wish to participate in it. So we must determine more exactly for modern man why reverence steps back instead of pushing forward, why it removes its hands instead of grasping. What demands reverence is, above all, the qualities of the person, his dignity, freedom and nobility. But also worthy of respect are the qualities of any work of man which reveal nobility or delicacy. And finally the phenomena of nature which express the sublime or mysterious.

Perhaps we can say that all true culture begins with the fact that man steps back. That he does not obtrude himself, seize hold of things, but leaves a space, so that there may be a place in which the person in his dignity, the work in its beauty, and nature in its symbolic power may be clearly discerned.

Reverence can also assume, so to speak, an every-day form. Every genuine virtue extends over many levels and stages because it is an attitude of a living person. Hence reverence can and should appear in everyday life, and then we call it respect.

Respect is the most elementary thing that must be perceptible if people are to associate with each other as human beings. We need not consider particular values, talents, accomplishments, moral nobility, or the like, but simply the fact that the other is a human being with freedom and responsibility.

So respect would mean that one takes another's conviction seriously. I may fight against it, for if I am of the opinion that what he says is wrong then I have a right and, under certain circumstances, a duty to defend the truth as I see it. But I must do this with respect, conscious of the fact that I am dealing not with an abstract sentence in some book but with a person, who on the basis of his conscience has decided upon this opinion. If I see that he is mistaken I may contend with him, but I may not violate his opinion nor wish to trick him by cunning.

Respect desires privacy for the other person, in the sphere of his own being and in connection with those among whom he lives and to whom he is related, his family, his friends. This is something which is increasingly forgotten in our day. Everywhere we see the urge toward publicity; a mania to see just that which is reserved; a greed for sensation which finds an odious pleasure in unveiling, stripping, causing shame and confusion—and with this the technique which renders it possible, the money behind newspapers, magazines, films and television. What an atmosphere of disrespect for everything personal all this fosters!

How crude it is, for instance, to photograph a child that is praying, or a woman who is weeping because an accident has caused the death of her husband! The desire to strip what had previously been surrounded by reverence has actually glorified itself; it claims to be courage and frankness and speaks of "taboos" that must be destroyed. No one thinks of the destruction of security and sensitivity that is actually involved, or perhaps this is also desired and enjoyed.

On the other hand, how great is the desire to be publicized. For if the average reader of the illustrated paper had not the expressed or secret wish to see his own picture, then the force of public opinion would grow strong enough to abolish the whole show. Moreover we must not forget how much this dwindling of respect, which shows itself in the destruction of privacy, prepares man for dictatorship. If a man no longer has a sphere reserved for himself he is at the disposal of totalitarian usurpation.

We might point out many other things. Respect is the guarantee that the relations of one person to another preserve their dignity. If a friendship disintegrates then the persons concerned may well ask themselves if there has not been a lack of respect. If a marriage goes bad and those who are bound by it no longer feel secure in each other, we are justified in assuming that they have treated each other like a piece of furniture or worse, for furniture costs money.

Here we also find the root of what we call courtesy. This does not signify something external. True courtesy is the expression of respect for the human person. It makes it possible that the many who constantly encounter each other in the limited space of life can do so without offending each other; in fact, even do so in such a way that the encounter is humanly valuable. We shall need to think about this point more carefully.

Respect is necessary wherever things human are concerned, either persons or works. But reverence awakes before what is great, the great personality and the great creation.

What is "greatness"? It is not something quantitative; not what we mean when we say: "The number one hundred is greater than the number ten." Rather, it is a manner of thinking and of meeting the world. It means the strictness of man's demands upon himself and the willingness to stand for what is important, a breadth of vision and boldness of decision, a depth of involvement, originality and creative power.

It is not an easy thing to confront greatness. It can discourage, even paralyze, for the greatness of another makes me feel my own littleness. Goethe said that there is only one defence against great superiority and that is love. I wonder if this is true. It may not always be possible to love. Perhaps it may be more correct to say that the defence against great superiority consists in truth and reverence which say: "He is great, I am not. But it is good that greatness should be, even if it is not in me but in another." Then there is an open space and envy disappears.

The greatness of another, if one does not accept it honestly, awakens an anger which seeks to belittle it, a resentment. One begins to find fault, looks for imperfections in order to be able to say that what is praised is really not so worth while, maintains that it is just a matter of luck, and so on. If this succeeds, then everything becomes paltry and we have debased the envied person. But if one freely affirms and accepts the great man because greatness is beautiful, even if it is found in another, then a wonderful thing happens; at that moment the one who reveres stands beside the one revered, for he has understood and recognized his greatness.

A similar reverence is demanded by a great work and a great deed. It is so important to encounter them, even if they cause our own accomplishments to shrink. I once asked a friend what culture really is. He answered: Culture is the ability to judge. For in order to judge we must have standards, which have become a vital part of our feelings, standards for great and small, genuine and false, noble and base.

To meet a great achievement wherever it may be, in scholarly research, poetical creation, the fine arts, or political action, and not to armor ourselves with the offended resentment of the man who wishes to achieve and is unable, but instead to open our mind and to recognize that it is good that someone had this ability—that is what gives us standards and enables us to judge.

We have seen that reverence is awakened in a well-ordered mind by a great person and a noble work, and that we can measure the degree of culture of a man by his ability to feel these and respond freely and joyously to them. But it is strange, and an honor to man, that this feeling can also be aroused by what is small or defenceless, incapable of making its own way.

The low and vulgar man feels the impulse to exploit the defencelessness of the child, or the inexperienced or weak person; the decent man
feels impelled to respect the defenceless. But why? It would seem a sensible
thing to say that it is a matter of course for every right-feeling man to wish
to help a child or a feeble person. Helpfulness, yes—but why reverence?

Perhaps it is because the decent man, when confronted by helplessness, is touched by the proximity of destiny and stops.

Then the matter takes on a religious meaning. We recall how Jesus
speaks of children and the "woe" that he pronounces upon those who
harm the mind of a child, a statement by the way, that is generally forgotten today. (Matt. 18:6ff.) How many are there who seriously concern themselves about such harm? How many are even conscious of the destructive
impressions that those who are not yet morally capable of defending themselves can receive from magazines, radio, film and television? Jesus says:
beware "for their angels always behold the face of my father who is in
heaven." Behind the defencelessness of the child stands the watchfulness
of the angel who beholds the holiness of God. And what holds true of the
child holds true of all who are defenceless.

These are profound matters which we should take to heart.

The right-minded man feels reverence before a great personality, or
a great work, but also before the defenceless person, the inexperienced,
the weak, the suffering and afflicted. It is a sign of increasing barbarism if
misfortune is manhandled and turned into a sensation in illustrated pa-
pers and magazines. The decent man feels sorrow for human suffering
and respects the privacy of those involved. Beware that they may not take
vengeance upon you in the coarsening of your feelings, and also that similar misfortunes may not befall you as well.

Ultimately, however, all reverence culminates in reverence for the
holy.

We feel it when we enter a church. Churches are built in such lofty
and impressive style that, even as we enter, the space affects us. If this does

not happen, then it is not, in essence, a church that we see but merely an assembly-hall. For this reason we step softly in a church and speak in a low tone. How the barbarism of our time is revealed when travellers in a church behave as if they were in a museum or a stadium. But there is something even worse: the holy provokes the rebellious spirit in man, drives him to mockery, to blasphemy, and to violence. Half the world is full of this. Such feelings and dispositions have made atheism a political power. And let no one say that he is a stranger to them; actually, they lurk in everyone in consequence of the primeval rebellion. So it is well if we keep alive the feeling of reverence toward the holy.

The basic act of this reverence is the adoration of God. It expresses the true nature of man most perfectly, especially if the body also performs the act in bowing. It must give us pause to note that this attitude is so very inconspicuous in religious life. Usually we find only petition or thanks, less frequently praise; adoration scarcely ever appears. And yet it is so essential. "I adore God" means I am aware that He is and that I stand before Him; that He is the one who essentially is, the creator, and that I am His creature; that He is holy and I am not, and that I adapt myself with heart and mind to the holy one who confronts me. Adoration is truth in act.

And now we shall go a step farther. We have constantly tried to carry the virtue which we are considering even into God himself, because "the good" is ultimately the One who is good. He alone is good, as Jesus said to the young man (Mark 10:28) and all that is good in man is an element of the divine image. How does this apply? Does God himself show reverence?

We certainly do not wish to talk nonsense, but I believe that we must answer this question in the affirmative. The reverence is revealed in the fact that God created man as a free being. We often encounter a kind of humility which, in order to honor God, debases man. This is not Christian. It is fundamentally the converse of the idolizing of man, and converse attitudes tend to interchange.

God wishes man to be His image, that is, possessing knowledge and responsibility. This expresses a divine will to reverence, for God might have created man so that he would be bound to the good. This would imply nothing base, perhaps even, if we think of the horrible flood of evil and crime which inundates the world, something great and blissful. He might have permitted His truth, even from the beginning, to send its beams so powerfully into the mind of man, might have set up the nobility of the good so basically in man's conscience that it would have been quite impossible for man to err or to sin. Then the world would have been a work of art, beautiful and harmonious, but the wonderful fact of a free creature would have been lacking, and also God's attitude toward this freedom, which we can only express by saying, God reverences man. This brings about the holy world of the kingdom of God, which grows, by His grace, out of the freedom of man.

This also throws a new light upon another basic truth of Revelation, the event which concludes the whole of history and fixes man's destiny for all eternity: the judgment. When one speaks of this it is usually as of something dreadful. In reality the judgment is a testimony of honor for man, for it places him in a position of responsibility. Only a free and responsible being can be judged.

Here a mystery prevails which no one can fathom. God's will is the basis of all being and action, and yet man is free. He is truly free, so much so that he can even say no to God's will. But this freedom does not exist beside the will of God, even less is it an opposing power rising up against Him, but it is God himself through whom it exists and operates—His reverence.

The reverence of God for freedom and at the same time the decisiveness with which He wills the good and only the good—perhaps nothing has been reflected upon as much as this mystery, but no one as yet has penetrated it.

Is it possible to reach even greater depths?

God is the absolutely existent one, self-based and self-sufficient. How can anything finite exist "beside" Him or "before" Him, especially finite freedom? Must He not, as the only existent one rise up in the triumph of His absoluteness? You may reply: "That would be the icy triumph of eternal loneliness!" But Revelation tells us that He, the Triune God, possesses within Himself unending community, incomprehensible fruitfulness; that He is Father and Son and Holy Spirit, speaker and spoken and in infinite love comprehending and comprehended. It is a mystery, certainly, impenetrable for our minds, but revealing to us that He does not need the finite in any way, not in order to attain consciousness or to gain love, as the pride of pantheism maintained. And yet He wills that the finite should exist and should be free. Does this not reveal a mystery of divine reverence? That the absolute power of the divine act of being does not crush the finite being; the glowing majesty of the divine "I"—no, "We"—(Cf. John 14:23) does not consume the finite, but, on the contrary, wills it, creates it by a never-ending call and preserves it in its reality.

Truly "in Him we live and move and are," as St. Paul said on the Areopagus in Athens. (Acts 17:28) His creative reverence is the "space" in which we exist. In our day, when that terrible mixture of arrogance and folly which is called atheism is flooding the world, it is good to think of that truth.

Loyalty

I f in the following pages we are to deal with loyalty, then it is essential to the subject that we call to mind the connotations of the word at the present time. Generally, we avoid using the word loyalty. Like many another word expressing moral values it no longer sounds quite genuine to us. It seems too great, too lofty, and, in the face of the confused reality of our life, too simple.

Many factors have contributed to this thinking: poetical bombast, official rhetoric, and the dishonesty of politicians and newspapermen. Likewise, equally important is the fact that during years of terror an absolute and unconditional adherence, a readiness for every sacrifice was demanded of us, something which no earthly cause has the right to demand, while at the same time the very persons who demanded this betrayed us in most hideous fashion.

Nevertheless, it remains true that our life rests upon loyalty. So it is well to consider carefully what this worn-out word means.

First of all, we must understand clearly that the word is applied to two different ways of behavior. The one is a psychological disposition. In a person of this type psychic processes are slow but go very deep. Feelings are strong. They do not flare up quickly and then die out, but they continue and bring about an enduring state of mind. Decisions are formed slowly, but they remain as an interior direction and can be relied upon to determine action. When a person of this type bestows his affections upon another or determines to support him, then the bond is solid and survives every kind of vicissitude. These are fine qualities, although they also have their dark side, the danger of rigidity, of narrowness and of injustice. But, as we have said, they are a matter of natural disposition which we cannot bestow upon ourselves and cannot ethically demand of another.

Other natures are different, but they also are obliged to practice loyalty. In their case it is not supported by a particular psychic structure but must depend upon a basis which can be presupposed in everyone. That is the human person with his insight into true and false, right and wrong, honor and dishonesty, the freedom of decision and the firmness with which this decision is maintained for the sake of the other person and his confidence and for the sake of the choice that has been made. Or, if the decision threatens to waver, it is renewed and reaffirmed again and again.

What is the meaning of this virtue? We may describe it as a force which conquers time, that is, change and transition—but not with the hardness of a stone, in rigid motionlessness, but living, growing and creative. Let us try to imagine it.

Two persons have met, have fallen in love and decide to marry. This relationship is at first supported by the desire of the one vitality for the other, feelings of congeniality, common experiences, harmony in relation to nature and men, similar preferences and inclinations, and so forth.

These feelings at first seem to guarantee a life-long bond. But they can easily cease. Differences, such as we always find between different persons, appear. And now is the time for true loyalty: each of the two must be aware that the other trusts him, depends upon him, that they have formed a bond which determines their life, that this must be supported by what is best in them, the core of their humanity, the person and its dependability. And now self-conquest begins: to stand by the other and keep him, but not in order to possess and dominate, but to preserve the life that rests upon the bond and to bring it to full fruition and unfolding; to know that one is responsible for the other; not to prescribe to him what he should be, but to give him freedom to be what he truly is, to help him to become what his nature meant him to be; to accept him again and again and stand at his side.

We must consider too that when two persons come together each one comes with a definite character. But "to live" means to grow and consequently to change. Some characteristics show themselves in childhood, others in adolescence, others in later years. So it can happen that on some occasion the one person says to the other in consternation, "I just don't know you anymore! You were not like this when I began to love you." It may be that he feels himself abandoned, even deceived, as if the other had disguised himself, whereas it was actually only a living development that revealed his new qualities. Again this is the time for loyalty, so that the change may be surmounted and the relation may endure. And this must be done not in rigidity and constraint, but in such a way that the one receives the other again and again and accommodates himself to him. All this can be difficult, under certain circumstances, very difficult. The disappointed feelings may rebel. But to the extent to which this loyalty is practiced, it grows deeper and brings about what truly constitutes a marriage.

Let us continue our reflection: loyalty means remaining true to a responsibility in spite of loss or danger.

For example, one has assumed certain obligations. He has thought over the matter carefully, recognized it as proper, and the other person depends upon his decision. But now the circumstances change and losses threaten. Loyalty means that he keeps his word and assumes the losses, as he would expect the other person to do if the situation were reversed. Or a person is seized by an idea, recognizes the necessity of an action and commits himself to it. As might be expected, difficulties arise. Loyalty means that he stands firm and fights on. Or it may be a case of dangers resulting from one's profession. A physician feels that his work is wearing out his strength, perhaps threatening his life. A civil servant has a difficult post, perhaps especially difficult because others take it easy. Loyalty says, "Hold on!"

And what is this really which we call "conviction"? First of all, it is insight. One has seen that something is so, and then the thing is certain. It does not require any further support, for example, that it coincides with the opinions of the age, or brings advantages or anything of the sort. But wherever persons are concerned, mere logical reasons are not sufficient, the decision must be based upon a personal obligation. The strength with which this cleaves to what has been accepted and affirmed, even in times and situations in which the "reasons" seem pale and uncertain, this is loyalty.

Loyalty overcomes change, injury, and danger but not by a power of persistence inherent in one's disposition. That may exist, and happy is the one who possesses it. But loyalty is more than that; it is the firmness which results when a man has assumed a responsibility and abides by it. This quality overcomes the variability, the injuries and the dangers of life by the power of conscience.

A person of this sort can be trusted. We feel that in him there is a point which is beyond fear and weakness, and which gives him ever renewed strength to persevere in his resolve.

But we must not forget another loyalty; that is, loyalty to God.

What happens when a man in a mature decision resolves to believe? At first he is influenced by all that he has learned from his parents, from the atmosphere of his home, from his teachers, from the life of the Church and other sources. He himself may have had religious experiences. In a moment of heartfelt prayer he may have sensed something that was holy and loving and that supported him. Or he may have experienced on certain occasions what Providence means. The answers of the Christian religion to the problems of existence have convinced him. He noticed that if he followed its counsels he became better, more resolute, more possessed of interior resources, and the like. Thereupon he made his decision and gave God his faith. This first faith is fine, generous, and filled with the consciousness of profound meaning. But in time these feelings may change or even disappear.

Perhaps the feeling of God's nearness vanishes and the believer seems to be standing in a religious vacuum. Or he experiences how much of human weakness inheres in the religious world. Or events take place which he cannot harmonize with the concept of Providence. Or the views of the contemporary world move away from faith and make it seem antiquated. Then faith loses the support of feeling, of its environment, and of the circumstances and events of life, and the doctrines of revelation which at first seemed so wonderfully clear, grow pale. Then the question may arise in his mind whether he has not been mistaken, whether he has not been the victim of some idealistic illusion. At such moments one may feel very foolish in holding on to faith. But this is the time for loyalty, which says, "I will remain firm. When I first believed, it was not a mere inclination of feeling or the attraction of a beautiful idea that became effective, it was an act of the core of the personality, in all seriousness. The word faith implies a promise—a promise of loyalty—God relies upon this promise; therefore I cling to Him."

In this way faith acquires a new meaning; it is the act by which man endures through the period of God's silence and absence. When He lets us feel His nearness, when His word comes to life, then it is not difficult to be sure of His reality; then it is joy. But when He conceals Himself, when we feel nothing and the sacred word is silent, then it becomes difficult. But this is the time for true faith.

Loyalty is something that outlasts the flow of time. It has within it something of eternity. And since we are speaking of eternity: what of God himself. Does the word loyalty have any meaning in His case? This question leads us to profound matters; let us take them to heart very carefully.

When God created the world He gave it true greatness. The scientific researches of the last decades have brought this to our attention in overpowering fashion. Greatness in magnitude and, if we may say so, greatness in the minute. Our thought is staggered by what has been revealed. The world is greater than we can conceive. But compared with God it is small, for He is absolute. We cannot use the word "is" of God and of the world in the same sense. We cannot say that God and the world "are." He is absolutely, glorious in Himself and self-sufficing. The world is through Him, before Him, in reference to Him. But when He created it He did not do so in sport but in divine seriousness. He staked His honor upon it. He gave it—I think we may rightly say this—His loyalty, when He said it was "good." We read this six times in the first account of the creation, and at the end a seventh time: "God saw all that He had created and behold, it was very good" (Gen. 1:31). In this way He bound Himself to the world.

We have already spoken of the Indian myth in which the god Shiva produced the world in an exuberance of creative joy and then grew weary of it and shattered it and made a new one and after this another one and so on. This would be the image of a God who was not loyal to his work. His demands would always be frustrated by the finiteness of the world. After a while he would find it unsatisfactory and he would discard it. It would be terrible to be in the hands of such a god. But the God who has revealed Himself to us is not like that. He holds fast to His work; He keeps the world in being. It exists each moment as a result of His loyalty.

This was, if we may say so, the "test" of God's loyalty to the world which lies in the very finiteness of all that is created, a quality that can never be abolished. But there was another test, which should never have taken place. It came not from the nature of things but from history, from man's freedom, from a misuse of this freedom, from revolt, and it constantly springs forth again from man's rebellion. Now the loyalty of God becomes a basic principle of Revelation.

Sacred Scripture tells us how God, in order to bring about redemption, called a nation and entered into a covenant with it, which rested wholly upon His eternal loyalty. Out of this covenant, which again and again stood the "test" of man's unfaithfulness, grew the history of the Old Testament. Finally God's loyalty accomplished the inconceivable, taking upon Himself the responsibility for man's guilt, stepping into history by the Incarnation and so accepting a destiny.

The life of Jesus is one entire expression of loyalty. This is shown by the way in which He persevered in remaining in narrow, hostile Palestine, because He knew that He had been sent as a party to the covenant of Sinai, although the wide pagan world would readily receive Him. He persevered even to death—and what a death!

It is from God that loyalty comes into the world. We can be loyal only because He is so, and because He has willed us, who are made in His image, to be loyal also.

Disinterestedness

Perhaps this title surprises the reader, for who is likely, at present, to consider disinterestedness a virtue, that is, an example of moral value?

There is a proverb which comes from ancient China and which states that the fewer interests a man has, the more powerful he is; that the greatest power is complete disinterestedness. But that idea is foreign to us. The image of man which has become the standard since the middle of the past century is quite different. It presents the active man who moves with decision in dealing with the world and accomplishes his purposes. This man has many interests and considers himself perfect when everything that he does is subordinated to the goals that he sets up for himself.

That such a man accomplishes much would not be denied even by the teachers of that ancient philosophy. But they would probably say that most of it is superficial and bypasses that which is really important.

How, then, does the man live who is ruled by his interests?

In his associations with others such a man does not turn toward another person with simplicity and sincerity, but he always has ulterior motives. He wishes to make an impression, to be envied, to gain an advantage, to get ahead. He praises in order to be praised. He renders a service in order to be able to exact one in return. Therefore he does not really see the other as a person; instead, he sees wealth or social position and then there is always rivalry.

With such a man we are not at ease. We must be cautious. We perceive his intentions and draw back. The free association in which true human relations are realized does not develop. Of course our life with its many needs also has its rights. Many human relations are built upon dependence and aims. Consequently, it is not only right but absolutely necessary that we should seek to obtain what we need and should be conscious of doing this. But there are many other relations which rest upon a candid and sincere meeting of persons. If interests and ulterior motives determine our attitude in such cases then everything becomes false and insincere.

Wherever the essential relations of "I" and "thou" are to be realized, interests must give way. We must see the other as he is, deal simply with him and live with him. We must adapt ourselves to the situation and its demands whether it be a conversation, collaboration, joyfulness, or the endurance of misfortune, danger or sorrow.

Only in this way are true human values made possible; such as a real friendship, true love, sincere comradeship in working, and honest assistance in time of need. But if interests become dominant here, then everything atrophies.

A man who keeps interests in their proper place acquires power over others but it is a peculiar kind of power. Here we approach the ancient aphorism of which we spoke in the beginning. The more we seek to gain our own ends, the more the other person closes up and is put on the defensive. But the more clearly he perceives that we do not wish to drive him but simply to be with him and live with him, that we do not want to gain something from him but merely to serve the matter at hand, the more quickly he discards his defenses and opens himself to the influence of the personality.

The power of personality becomes stronger in proportion to the absence of interests. It is something quite different from that energy by which a man subordinates another to his will, and which is really a very external thing in spite of its "dynamic" quality. The power of personality stems from the genuineness of life, the truth of thought, the pure will to work, and the sincerity of one's disposition.

Something similar holds true of a man's relation to his work. When a man who is dominated by his interests works, then his work lacks precisely that which gives it value; that is, a sincere service to the thing itself. For him the first and chief consideration is how he can get ahead and further his career. He knows very little of the freedom of work and the joy of creation.

If he is a student, he works only with an eye to his vocation, and very frequently not even to that which really deserves the name of vocation, which is a man's feeling that he is "called" to a certain task within the context of human society. Rather, he works with an eye to that which offers most opportunities for financial gain and for prestige. He really works only for the examination, learns what is required, and what the professor in each case demands. We must not exaggerate; these things too have their rights. But if they are the sole motives then the essential thing is lost. That kind of student never has the experience of living in the *milieu* of knowledge, of feeling its freedom and its greatness. He is never touched by wisdom and understanding; his interests isolate him. What we have said of students also holds true of other forms of preparation for later life.

Naturally, we repeat, these other things have their rights. A man must know what he wants, otherwise his actions disintegrate. He must have a goal and must orient his life to that goal. But the goal should lie mainly in the object to which he devotes himself. He will pay attention to remuneration and advancement, since his work gives him the means of which he and his family have need, gives him wealth and the esteem of others. But the real and essential consideration must always be what the work itself demands, that it be done well and in its entirety.

The man who has this attitude will not let his actions be determined by considerations extrinsic to the task. In this sense he is disinterested. He serves, in the fine sense of the word. He does the work which is important and timely; he is devoted to it and does it as it should be done. He lives in it and with it, without self-interest or side-glances. This is an attitude that seems to be disappearing in most places. Persons who do their duty in sincere devotion, because the work is valuable and fine, seem to be becoming rare. Actions are increasingly based upon utilitarian motives and considerations of success apart from the real matter in hand. And yet disinterestedness is the only disposition which produces the genuine work, the pure act, because it frees man for creativity. It alone gives rise to what is great and liberating, and only the man who works in this way gains interior riches.

What we have said also opens the way to the final essence of humanity—selflessness. One of the most profound paradoxes of life is the fact that a man becomes more fully himself the less he thinks of himself. To be more precise, within us there lives a false self and a true self. The false self is the constantly emphasized "I" and "me" and "mine," which refers everything to its own honor and prosperity, wishing to enjoy and achieve and dominate. This self hides the true self, the truth of the person. To the extent that the false self disappears the true self is freed. To the extent that a man departs from himself in selflessness he grows into the essential self. This true self does not regard itself, but it is there. It experiences itself, but in the consciousness of an interior freedom, sincerity and integrity. The way in which a man puts away the false self and grows into the real self is that which the masters of the interior life call detachment. The saint is the person in whom the false self has been wholly conquered and the true self set free. Then the person is simply there without stressing himself. He is powerful without exertion. He no longer has desires or fears. He radiates. About him things assume their truth and order.

Shall we say, with reference to essentials, that that man has opened himself for God, has become, if we may use the term, penetrable for God.

He is the "door" through which God's power can stream into the world and can create truth and order and peace. There is an event which reveals this marvel. When St. Francis had lived through the long loneliness on mount La Verna and had received the stigmata of Christ's passion in his hands and feet and side and returned to his people, they came and kissed the wounds in his hands. Francis, so basically humble, would have, in former times, rejected with horror these marks of reverence. Now he permitted them, for he no longer felt that he, "the son of Bernardone of Assisi" was their object, but Christ's love in him. His exterior self had been quenched, but the real Francis shone—he who no longer stood in his own light but was wholly transparent for God.

Every genuine virtue, as we have seen before, not only pervades the whole of human existence but it reaches beyond it to God. More correctly, it comes down from God to man, for its true and original "place" is the divine life. How does this apply in the case of disinterestedness? Does not God have interests, He, through whose will everything exists and whose wisdom orders all things?

We must be careful not to confuse meanings. To "have interests," in the sense in which we have used the term, means something other than being active. Every activity has a goal, an end to be attained; otherwise, there would be chaos. In this sense, God looks toward the goal He has set, and directs His activity toward it. But it is a different thing when the person acting is not simply looking toward the other person or the work to be accomplished, but regards himself, wishes to be recognized, and to secure an advantage. How could God intend anything of the sort? He is the Lord, Lord of the world, Lord of the divine life and existence. What could He need? He has—no, He is—everything!

When He creates the world, He does not do so as a man would make something, in order to boast of it or to serve his own needs, but He creates through pure, divine joy in the act. We may use that term here, in its highest sense. He creates things so that they may exist, that they may be truthful, genuine and beautiful. We cannot conceive of the freedom and joyfulness of God's creative activity.

But what of the government of the world, that which we call "Providence"? Doesn't God have purposes? Doesn't He guide man, every man, and all the events of his life, to the end that He has proposed? Isn't the life of one man arranged in a certain way because the life of another is connected with it in this manner? Are not the lives of all men oriented toward each other, and is not the whole of existence arranged by divine wisdom according to God's plan? Again, we must distinguish the meanings of words. What is willed by supreme wisdom is not "interests" which accompany and are extrinsic to the essential thing, but the very meaning of that which is willed, its truth, and the fulfillment of its nature.

This divine will is the power which binds one thing to another, refers one event to another, brings one person into relation with another, and every man into relation with the whole. This does not constitute "interests" but "wisdom," the sovereign wisdom of the perfect Master who creates human existence as a woven fabric in which every thread supports all the others and is itself supported by all the others. At present, we do not yet see the pattern. We see only the reverse of the tapestry and are able to follow certain lines for a short distance, but then they disappear. But some day the tapestry will be turned, at the end of time, at the final judgment; then the figures will stand out brightly. Then the question never fully answered—or answered not at all—in the course of time—"Why"; Why this sorrow; why this privation? Why can one do this and not another?— all the questions of life's trials will receive their answer from the wisdom of God, which brings it about that things are not a mere mass of objects and events, are not a confusion of occurrences, but that all these together constitute a "world."

Asceticism

There was a time when people spoke not only scornfully but with annoyance about anything that can be called asceticism, as if it were not merely something wrong, but something unnatural and insulting. They thought that "asceticism" arose from the fear and hatred of life, even from perverted feeling; that it revealed the hatred of Christianity for the world, the corrupted sentiments of the priest who depreciated living nature in order to justify his own existence, and so on.

That was the time of liberal bourgeois prosperity. Things seem to have changed somewhat since then. Anyone who wishes can see what was involved in the "service of life." Nevertheless the word asceticism still awakens resentment, so it is worth while to ask what it really means.

Much of the resistance against asceticism stemmed from the desire for license in following one's urges and instincts. But this also involved a false concept of life, or, more exactly, of the manner in which life grows and bears fruit.

How does life function in nature? Men like to compare man with nature when they wish to make room for something which is contrary to the spirit of Christ. How does "life" go on in nature? How does a healthy animal grow and develop? By following its urges. Then everything turns out well, for instinct keeps it from going wrong. If an animal is satisfied, it stops eating. If it is rested it gets up. When the urge toward procreation is active, the animal follows it. When the time has passed, the urge is silent. The manner, the type, so to speak, according to which the life of nature is carried on is simply that of working out its fulfillment. The interior drive expresses itself in external action.

But what is the case with man? In him there is a force at work which we do not find in the animal. This is so plainly real and operative that one must be blind in order not to see it. It is the spirit. This brings all that we call "nature" into a new situation.

In the realm of the spirit the urge has a different meaning than it has in mere nature. It plays and works differently; so it is foolish to seek to understand the life of man by comparing it with the life of the animal. At present men often carry the folly to greater lengths and try to understand man by comparing him with a machine. But let us not go into that. In any case it is foolish to set up the life of an animal as the measure of the life of man.

What is the function of the spirit in regard to human urges? In the drive toward food, procreation, activity, rest, comfort? First of all, something surprising: it intensifies the urge. No animal follows the drive toward food as much as a man who makes the pleasure its own end and thereby harms himself. In no animal does the sexual urge reach the boundless extent which it has in a man who permits it to destroy his honor and his life. No animal has the urge to kill that man has. His wars have no real counterpart in the animal kingdom.

All that we can call an urge operates differently in a man than in an animal. The spirit gives a unique freedom to the life-impulses. They become stronger and deeper, with far greater possibilities of demand and response. But at the same time they lose the protection of the organic order which binds and secures them in the animal. They become unregulated and their meaning is endangered. The concept of "living to the limit" is a blind one. The animal lives to the limit; it must. But man must not. The spirit gives a new meaning to the urge. It works into the urge and gives it depth, character and beauty. It brings it into relation with the world of values, and also with that which bears these values, the person, and so lifts it to the sphere of freedom. In the animal the drives constitute "nature"; the spirit makes of them what we call "culture," taking this word as an expression of responsibility and self-conquest.

In the case of the animal, the drive builds the environment that is suited to its kind, but thereby also accommodates it to conditions and limitations. In the case of man, it leads to a free encounter with the breadth and wealth of the world, but thereby it is also endangered. All that we call excessive, overwrought, and unnatural becomes possible—and enticing.

The spirit elevates man above the urge, not thereby destroying it or becoming, as a foolish statement expresses it, the "adversary of life." Only a corrupt spirit, traitor to its own nature, does that. By the spirit man acquires the possibility of ordering and forming the urge, and so leading it to greater heights, to its own perfection, even as an urge. Of course it is thereby exposed to the danger of deformation and of going counter to nature.

May we emphasize once more that all this points to the fact that a drive or urge in man means something different from an urge in the animal and that it makes no sense if a man seeks the pattern for his life in the animal or in mere nature. Asceticism means that a man resolves to live as a man.

This brings about a necessity which does not exist for the animal; that is, the need to keep his urges in an order which is freely willed and of overcoming his tendency toward excess or toward a wrong direction.

This is not to imply that the urges are in themselves evil. They belong to the nature of man, and operate in all forms and areas of his life. They compose his store of energy. To weaken them would be to weaken life. But life is good. A deep current in the history of religion and ethics proceeds from the thought that the urges as such, sexual activity, the body, and even matter itself, are evil—indeed the very principle of evil—while the spirit as such is good. This is dualism, in which, certainly, noble motives are at work; but, as a whole, it becomes a dangerous error, and very often ends in a surrender to the urge. The motive for true asceticism does not lie in such a struggle to overcome the urges, but in the necessity of bringing them into proper order. The order is determined by various considerations: the question of health, regard for other persons, and our duties to our vocation and our work. Every day makes new demands and obliges us to keep ourselves in order. And this is asceticism. The word, derived from the Greek *áskesis*, means practice and exercise, exercise in the proper directing of one's life.

We must also consider the fact that there is a hierarchy of values. For instance, there are everyday values, those that pertain to our physical life; above these there are the values of our vocation and our work; still higher are those of personal relations and intellectual activity; and finally those which are attained by our immediate relation to God. We realize these values by means of the powers of our being; but these are limited and we must understand clearly to which tasks we want to turn them. We must choose, and then carry out our choice. This requires exertion and sacrifices—and that too is asceticism.

Apart from all this, everyone who knows the tendency of human nature toward self-indulgence also knows how necessary it is to impose upon ourselves voluntary exercises in self-control, such as are not demanded by our immediate purposes. They are necessary so that the will may more easily fulfill the demands of duty when these present themselves. They are necessary also as a way to freedom which consists in being master of oneself, of one's impulses and circumstances.

The physical urges which proceed from the somato-psychic organization of man present themselves so plainly to our consciousness that the mental and spiritual urges can easily be overlooked. But these, as a matter of fact, are more decisive from the point of view of our total community life. The building up of what we call the personality, its preservation in the world, its activity and creativity, is based upon mental and spiritual urges. There is the urge toward recognition and esteem, toward power in all its forms. There is the urge toward social and community life, toward freedom and culture; the urge toward knowledge and artistic creation, etc. All these urges have, as we said, their significance as impulses basic to self-preservation and self-development. But they are also inclined to become excessive, to bring our life out of harmony with the lives of others and so to become disturbing or destructive.

Therefore a constant discipline is necessary, a discipline whose principles are determined by ethics and practical philosophy; this discipline is asceticism.

But let us put aside generalities and look at a concrete situation, for example, a friendship. Two persons have learned to know and like each other. They have discovered a community of tastes and viewpoints. They find each other congenial and trust each other. They think that their friendship is secure and make no further efforts to preserve it. But, as we can expect, there are also differences between them and gradually these make themselves felt. Misunderstandings arise, annoyances, tensions. But neither of the two seeks the causes where they really are, namely in his own self-confidence and carelessness, and after a short time the two get on each other's nerves. The quiet confidence disappears, and gradually the whole relationship disintegrates.

If a friendship is to endure, it must be guarded. There must be something that will preserve it. Each of the two must give the other room to be what he *is*. Each must become conscious of his own failings and regard those of the other with the eyes of friendship. To will this and to carry it out in the face of the hypersensitiveness, sloth and narrowness of our own nature—that again is asceticism.

Why do so many marriages grow dull and empty? Because each of the two partners has the basic idea that the purpose of marriage is "happiness," which means that each can find fulfillment in simply living his own life to the fullest extent.

Actually a true marriage is a union of two lives; it is helpfulness and loyalty. Marriage means that "each shall bear the other's burden," as St. Paul says. (Gal. 6:2) So a spiritual responsibility must keep watch over it. Again and again each must accept the other as the person he is, must renounce what cannot be, must put away the mendacious notions fostered by the films, which destroy the reality of marriage. He must know that after the finding of each other in the first stage of love the task just begins. A genuine marriage can endure only through self-discipline and self-conquest. Then it becomes real, capable of producing life and of sending life into the world.

Someone founds an institution, undertakes a work, or does whatever his vocation entails. Let us suppose the most propitious case, that this is his true vocation and he is doing that for which he has talent or ability and so likes doing it. At first he enjoys the task and puts forth every effort.

Perhaps it would be necessary even then to tell him to keep within the measure of the possible and not to over-do. For after a time the tension relaxes, the more quickly as the original effort was more intense; but the tasks continue. What will happen if they are based only on the "full life," the joy in working and in accomplishing results? Then indifference will result and later aversion, and finally everything will collapse.

No work can flourish if it is not sustained by a responsibility which induces a man to perform his task faithfully and unselfishly.

Human life has many strata. There are superficial things, some that go deeper, and some that are quite essential—and each stratum has its requirements, values and fulfillments. Plainly, we cannot have everything at the same time; we must choose, must surrender one thing in order that the other can come to pass.

Let us consider everyday life once more. The man who constantly watches movies loses his taste for great drama; he no longer understands it. So he must ask himself what he really wants and must choose. He must put away the superficial charms of the movies in order to be capable of experiencing what is more valuable, perhaps to become so once more; or he must stay with the movies and persuade himself that these are the art of the times, that he needs the relaxation, and cannot force himself, after the toil of the day, to the mental exertion that real drama demands, and so on. The person who reads a great deal of trash loses the taste for good reading. So he must make up his mind as to what is more important for him. One who is constantly among people, talking and discussing, loses the ability to live with himself, and so loses all that which only reveals itself in solitude. Again it is a question of "either—or." And much self-control is required to triumph over the restlessness which drives one out.

If a man wishes to obtain from life the precious gifts that it can bestow then he must know that it is only by renouncing a lesser good that he can have the greater.

The people who preach the gospel of the "good life" say that we must not curtail this life; we must bring out all its possibilities and enjoy them. If we ask them what the true content of this life, its meaning and its standard, may be, they answer: "Life itself, the strong, sensitive rich life." But is that true? Is life its own meaning and measure? Not only ordinary people speak in this way. There have been whole philosophies that have taught the same thing. But is it not very revealing that today we have the opposite of this, namely a philosophy of disappointment and of nausea? The meaning of life does not consist in enjoying one's own sensations and powers, but in bringing about the fulfillment of the task assigned to us. Man lives truly and fully if he knows his responsibility; if he carries out the task that awaits him; and if he meets the needs of the persons entrusted to him. But to recognize and to choose the right thing and reject what is wrong—this constant effort to transcend one's own wishes and meet one's obligations—that is asceticism.

Let us finally consider that which determines the meaning of our existence, the relation to the One who created us, under whose glance we live and before whom we must appear after our few years upon earth—then we shall easily see that no relation to Him can be established without discipline and self-conquest.

Man is not driven forcibly to God. If he does not discipline himself, betake himself to prayer in the morning and in the evening, make the observance of the Lord's day an important occasion, have a book at hand which will show him again and again something of the "breadth and length and height and depth" of the things of God (Eph. 3:18), then his life continually passes over the quiet admonitions that come from within. When he should be with God he is bored, for everything seems empty. Lectures, newspapers and radio teach him that religious values and relations do not exist any longer for modern man, and he feels not only justified but progressive. To be at home with God, so that one associates with Him gladly and feels the joy of His presence, this again, like every other serious matter, requires "practice." It must be willed and carried out with much self-conquest, again and again. Then God gives us as a grace the sense of His holy presence.

So we shall have to learn that asceticism is an element of every life that is rightly lived. We shall do well if we practice setting limits to our urges, for the sake of proper measure. We shall learn to leave that which is less important but very attractive in order to attend to that which is more important. We shall take ourselves in hand in order to be spiritually free.

For example, we trust the reader will not mistake accuracy for pedantry, before going into the city we might resolve not to let ourselves be caught by advertisements and by people, but to keep our mind occupied with a fine thought or recollected in quiet freedom. Or we might turn off the radio so that the room will be still. Perhaps we might remain at home one evening instead of going out, or say *no* sometimes when eating or drinking or smoking—or many things of that sort. As soon as we turn our attention to the matter we shall find many occasions for a liberating "practice"; learning to endure pain instead of resorting immediately to medication, accepting inwardly the renunciation that may be salutary for us; greeting an uncongenial person with quiet friendliness.

These and other such actions are not great things. We are not speaking of strict fasting or night vigils and difficult penances, but of practice in right living; of the truth that our life is different from that of the animal. It is human life, in which the internal drives are lifted by the spirit into a glorious but dangerous freedom. This spirit gives them their motive force, but it must also supply the regulating power, by means of which life is not destroyed but brought to its fullness.

Courage

This meditation shall deal with courage—or bravery. The two words have related meanings, but there are slight differences. "Bravery" refers to men's behavior in a concrete situation; "courage" to the general attitude, the manner in which one meets life. The terms shall be used as seems most suitable in each case.

First of all we shall consider the distinction which we have found useful on several other occasions; that is, the distinction between a natural disposition and a moral attitude.

There is a kind of courage that is a natural quality. It may be that the person in question has no great sensitivity, and matters that would trouble another do not even enter his consciousness. His imagination is not very active, and he does not envision possible perils. So he passes through dangerous situations interiorly untouched or handles them easily. This is an excellent predisposition for practical living, but the one so predisposed must guard against becoming careless or brutal.

It can also happen that courage comes from a sound and healthy constitution, a strong *joie de vivre* which regards difficulties and dangers as a challenge; a confidence in life, secure in the feeling that things will turn out for the best. This is fine, and may be what we would call "a good stock." Of course this too has its dangers, and the person so disposed must take care that he remains thoughtful—and thankful.

Finally there is a predisposition to courage which belongs to the realm of the noble and unusual. For one so disposed bravery and honor are the same thing. He is aware of the challenge of life and feels bound by self-respect to meet it. He may not be very strong physically, and is perhaps very sensitive to suffering and so particularly subject to distress both exterior and interior. Nevertheless he stands firm, goes on quietly and meets events without fear. This is a natural nobility which may also foredoom such a person to a tragic destiny.

All this is a matter of natural disposition. One has it or does not have it and it may result in either good or evil. If a person so endowed comes under the influence of good teachers and recognizes his own possibilities, then a useful, good, and even noble life may result. But here we are speaking of something which—except in very unfavorable circumstances—is possible for everyone and hence may be a moral obligation, something which can be demanded of us, and for which we should train ourselves.

What would be the aspects of such a virtue? How would it develop and reveal itself? Let us begin with the main point which determines everything else, and which is the most difficult to realize. I mean the courage to accept one's own existence. We have spoken of this in our earlier reflections. Our existence is a tissue of good and bad, joyful and sorrowful, of things that assist and support us and also of those that hinder and burden us. Courage means the ability not only to select what pleases us or makes life easy, but also to accept the whole as it is, in the confidence that it reveals the providence of God.

Every man bears within himself that mysterious something which we call his essential character. It means that qualities are not just jumbled together, but form a whole, something integrated and decisive which supports us but also makes demands. Each element aids the others but also brings with it a danger and burden for the others. This essential character man brings with him into life. It determines what he is and what he can accomplish, favorable and unfavorable—"himself." Courage means that he accepts this basic form of his existence in its entirety, not choosing or rejecting anything.

For example, one cannot be a person of strong sensibilities and choose to feel joy but not pain, for the one implies the other. To be sensitive is a glorious thing. It bestows great things upon us, the beauties of the world, the depths of personal relations, the tensions of struggle, the joy of accomplishment. But this same sensitivity brings evil with it, the pain of loss, the sorrows of human conflict, the fruitlessness of labor. We cannot have the one without the other. So courage means, first of all, accepting oneself as one is, with the sensitivity of feeling and the painful experiences that it brings, as well as the precious gifts that it bestows. This does not mean that we must approve of everything; certainly not. But first we must accept, and then try to see what we can change, increase, moderate, improve.

The integrated whole of which we have spoken means something else. It is like a picture which stands before us and which we can survey, but it is also like a melody which goes on in time, a configuration which is experienced as it transpires. The basic principle is the same, for what happens to a person is not just a matter of choice but corresponds to what he is. Character and destiny are intimately related.

The person who is not technically and economically minded will not experience what the person so minded will experience when he establishes a business, knows the triumph of success and the pain of failure. These things are granted to the one and denied to the other. But in return the other person may have a natural appreciation of art and discover in it realities which the other never attains. A third person may be a scholar, perhaps a historian. He lives in all ages, understands the greatness of their achievements, feels the grief of their passing away—all of which remains unknown to the other two.

To the differences of temperament and character we must add those of sex, of health, of social conditions, and so forth, all of which help to determine that in a certain life some things take place and others do not.

So the existence of every man contains a pattern, a configuration of being and of events, and he must accept it as it is, and not desire to have the good without the bad. But he must first accept and affirm the whole, and then, certainly, do what he can to give it the form that he considers right and proper.

But in order to solve the problem, which is so vitally the problem of mankind, we must delve more deeply.

We may attempt to express the nature of man in various ways. In connection with the subject which we are discussing we can do so by saying that man has a relation to the world as a whole. The animal is enclosed in its environment, and even though this environment may be enlarged in the process of evolution of the individual and the species it remains essentially a partial thing. Only man is related to the whole world, is himself a microcosm.

Of course he too is individually limited and hemmed in by all the qualifications of nationality and country, talents, sex, culture, social position, vocation or employment and so forth; that is, by the very character of which we have spoken. But this contains a basic relation to the world as a whole, that which has been called the "microcosmic" element in man. This blending of individuality and universality composes the peculiarity of man: he is limited and at the same time related to the universe.

This tension in the character of man is bound up with another: the tension between necessity and freedom. Man lives under the universal laws, but bears within himself an abyss from which he can always draw a new beginning.

So, if he wishes to be true to reality, he must accept his limitations and his determination by the form of his character, but, because of his freedom in relation to the world, he has the ability of advancing toward the whole in his special way.

All this comes from God. He has given me to myself. I must accept my existence from His hand, must live it and carry it out. That is the basic courage and how necessary it is today when there is so much talk of nothingness, destruction, oppressive fear, disgust and dark things of all kinds. In large part this is merely talk, and those who speak and write in this way, do not take it seriously themselves. But it is true that our time is really hard pressed, from without and from within. It is a time of transition, in which a great deal is crumbling away, often without our being able to see what new structure shall take its place. Therefore it is doubly necessary that we confidently accept our existence from God and live it courageously.

This interior form of the individual being and life involves a practice of courage which a person of strong and cheerful temperament may not be consciously aware of, but which some may feel as a difficult task: the confidence requisite for living with a view to the future, for acting, building, assuming responsibilities and forming ties. For, in spite of our precautions, the future is in each case the unknown. But living means advancing into this unknown region, which may lie before us like a chaos into which we must venture.

Here everyone must make the venture in the confidence that the future is not a chaos or a totally strange thing. Rather, his own character, the ordering power within him, will make a way so that it is really his own future into which he moves.

This also forms the natural basis for the message of Christ about the Providence which guards every man; the message that the future, though all unknown, is not strange, not hostile, but is arranged for him by God; that existence, though it extends far beyond our ken, is not a chaos, but ordered by God for him.

To believe this and live accordingly may be difficult for a person who is of a hesitant or timid disposition. But here the courage to live coincides with trust in the divine guidance.

There is another point that we must consider, something particularly pressing in times when historical epochs end and new ones begin. This is man's relation to the future as a whole, to the course of history. The life of the individual does not flow along in the course of history like water in the bed of a stream; rather it forms a part of it. Sometimes the individual is so bound up with the past that the future is quite strange to him. Then he lives without confidence in the future and takes refuge in the past. What has been is so completely satisfactory to him and its form so fair, that all that is new repels him.

Here too courage is necessary, courage which dares to face the future in the confidence that God's plan will work out. This courage accepts what is to come, sees in it the individual's own task, and cooperates. This may be very difficult and can be accomplished only by means of true obedience to the will of Him who guides history.

Bravery means standing one's ground in danger. What is the root of all that we call danger? It is the evil which affects all hearts and makes it possible for hostile elements to touch us. It is the hypersensitivity of our nature which can be offended in so many ways. It is mutability, which causes our life to move toward death. These are facts that cannot be changed. And bravery means facing these conditions of our existence and standing firm before them, indeed, standing firm before life as it comes, first of all because one overcomes danger more easily if one goes to meet it than if one is intimidated by it; also, because one surmounts pain more easily if one bears it freely than if one becomes wrapped up in it. Moreover, difficulties are a part of our life. They are sent to us. If we meet them bravely, they prove to be a gain. Every situation contains a possibility for growth, for becoming a better man—the man we were meant to be. We waste this opportunity if we seek to evade the difficulty.

The courage that accepts life and meets it bravely in each instance implies a conviction that within us there is something that cannot be destroyed, but rather which derives nourishment from everything, becomes stronger, richer, deeper through every experience rightly faced and carried out, because this something comes from the creative power of God.

Actually, this something is the power of God itself. If in a favorable hour I penetrate quietly and recollectedly into the inmost depths of my being, ever more deeply until I, as it were, reach the interior boundary of nothingness—there I find God's power which maintains me in existence. This preserving power is indestructible, even though I pass through danger and through death. The reason for all present-day talk of anxiety and dissolution and nothingness, for all the grotesque figures of art and poetry, for the overwhelming force of political power, is that the consciousness of interior support, the confidence in the hand of God in the depths, at the edge of nothingness, is no longer alive in men.

There is another kind of courage of which we must speak; that is, the courage to take a risk if it is God's will. To everyone there comes in some way the call of God, and it decides his life. This call may take various forms. It may be a question of the occupation a man is to choose. How much depends on whether he chooses the lifework of which his deepest self says: "This is where you belong, to this you are 'called,'" or whether he chooses something that promises more money, easier success, greater human respect!

It may also be a question of a person, a friend, a love. Again what matters is whether man permits himself to be drawn into something which is alluring, flatters his self-esteem, yet of which his deepest self warns him that it may deprive him of what is highest; or, whether he chooses that which may be harder, more demanding, but which builds life and teaches responsibility.

There are also lesser decisions. Basically, every admonition of conscience is a call of God. For the good is not simply the useful or that which conduces to a fuller life or the progress of a culture, but it is the holiness of God which urges man to admit it into his life, and which is embodied in the ethical demands of each situation. Each situation is a call, for it addresses us and says, "Do this—do not do that!" Again and again we are faced with the decision, to dare to tell the truth or to lie, to be just or to seek our own advantage, to be pure or to permit ourselves to be defiled, to be noble or to slip into the mean and low. On each occasion God calls us.

Here courage means placing our hand in His and following Him, in small things and in great. The way may lead us very far. We know of persons who follow it so far that they escape our comprehension; these are the saints. We hear them speak, we read their writings, but essentially they have gone beyond us, with God. This is the highest challenge.

If there is a regret which is most bitter at life's end, then it is this: I heard the call but did not follow it.

In our reflections we have always applied the virtue which we were considering to God and attempted to know Him better in the light of that virtue. Can we also speak of courage in connection with God? We can, if we remove from it all that is merely human, and which, if applied to God, would detract from His holy sovereignty.

When was God, in this highest sense, courageous? He was courageous when He created man. When He—using the word with all the reservations that we must apply to every statement which brings God in relation to time—"decided" to create beings who possess freedom, and to put His world into their hands. But this meant—speaking once more with the proper reservations—that He put His honor in their hands. For God created the world in wisdom and in love. He called it "good" and "very good" (cf. the first chapter of Genesis), and it is so forever. These creatures, mankind, could be faithful but they could also revolt against Him. And yet he dared to expose His work to the danger of their freedom.

And when the danger became a reality and man refused to obey Him, God took a second "risk," so inconceivably great that it requires the whole power of confident faith not to be scandalized by it. He Himself took on the responsibility for man's guilt. He became man, and accepted a destiny in our confused history.

Have we ever thought about the truly divine courage of Christ? Have we understood the bravery that fired the heart of Jesus, when He, who came from the presence—St. John says "from the bosom"—of the Father, stepped into this earthly world? Into all the falsehood, the murderous cruelty, the pitiful narrowness of our existence? And He did this, not protected by the pride of the philosopher or secured by the tactics of the politician, not willing to repay guile with guile and blow with blow, but in the vulnerability of perfect purity.

Let us consider how we act amid the dangers of this world; how energetically we protect ourselves by all manner of means. Jesus never protected himself, but He accepted everything that the violence and unscrupulousness of men inflicted upon Him. We do not take the world as it is, but choose from it what pleases us. He accepted what the course of events brought upon Him, for this was the will of the Father. We know how to conform, to evade, and to seek advantages. His nature was such, and He spoke and acted in such a manner that what was most evil in men was challenged; that, as we read in Luke's Gospel, "the thoughts," the hidden disposition, "in the hearts of many were revealed." (Luke 2:35) He truly lived in the conditions of the world and endured them. The hour of Gethsemane lets us surmise what that meant. If we try to fathom all this we may well shudder before what we can call the courage of God in Christ.

And He dared to live this life not in order to accomplish something of earthly grandeur, glorious heroism, or a noble work of art, but as a "redemption," for our sake. He lived so that we might gain the courage to be "Christians" in the world in which He was "Christ."

To the extent to which we put away illusions and see how much so-called Christian morality and Christian culture is actually the product of a particular historical situation, to the extent to which we experience how the world does all the things which St. John in the prologue of his Gospel tells us of its behavior toward the incarnate Son of God, only to that extent shall we realize that the attempt to be Christians in this world and to order our existence in accord with Christ appears to be a most desperate undertaking. Then it becomes clear what, in the final analysis, is meant by "courage," that is, the attitude which says, "But nevertheless," and takes up the battle in spite of all that makes it appear senseless and vain. We must never forget that He has fought the fight before us and thereby made it possible for us to conquer.

Kindness

I n this chapter we shall speak of a virtue which is easily neglected because it is reserved, inconspicuous and quiet; that is the virtue of kindness. How often we speak of love. It challenges us, for it is noble and radiant. But we should speak of it less often, that would be better for it, and instead should speak of that which our callous age needs so sorely—kindness.

This word often misleads us to regard what it designates in a derogatory fashion, to misunderstand "kindness" as mere good nature, which is certainly nothing very valuable. Good nature is passivity, which lets things take their course, or indolence, which avoids conflict, or even stupidity, which believes anything. But kindness is something deep and strong, and for that reason it is not easy to define.

Let us attempt it in this way: a kind person is one who is well disposed toward life. But can one be ill disposed toward life? Yes, indeed, especially if we are dealing not so much with overt actions as with the disposition behind them, which may perhaps escape our notice.

It may be that a person desires to dominate over others. He says that he desires their best interests, but actually what he wishes is to dominate. Such a person is not well disposed toward life, for life is smothered in the grasp of tyranny. Many a domestic tragedy results from the fact that one person wishes to dominate over the others. It may be the husband or the wife, a son or a daughter. True kindness allows to life a proper space and freedom of movement; it even gives and provides these, for only in this way can life grow and develop.

Or it may be that a person is resentful toward life. He thinks that he has suffered an injustice; his expectations have been disappointed; his claims have been disregarded. This may perhaps really be the case, and he should try to make the best of the possibilities that remain. But he cannot overcome the feeling of resentment, and he takes revenge. "They are all like that," he says, because one was like that; "there is no justice," because he thinks he has not been given justice. Kindness pardons, for it is magnanimous and releases the offender; it trusts and always allows life to begin anew.

Much unkindness results from envy. Many a poor person sees another man enjoying his wealth. In some way or another everyone feels that others have what he lacks. If he cannot accept this fact, becomes bitter, and envies the other his possessions, then his mind is poisoned and he becomes an enemy of life. Kindness can look beyond itself; it does not begrudge to others what it lacks. In fact, it can even rejoice with the others. We might mention many similar things.

Kindness means that one is well disposed toward life. Whenever he encounters a living being, the kind man's first reaction is not to mistrust and criticize but to respect, to value, and to promote development. Life is sorely in need of this attitude—our human life—which is so vulnerable.

But in kindness there is strength, strength in proportion to its purity, and perfect kindness is inexhaustible. Life is full of suffering; if a person is well disposed toward life then the suffering touches him and makes itself felt. But that is wearing. Suffering demands our understanding; and that requires exertion. It demands help. But only he who truly understands the suffering in any particular case can really help, only he who can find the necessary words and can see what must be done in order to alleviate the suffering. Woe unto that kindness if it is merely well disposed but is weak. It can happen that it is destroyed by its own sympathy, or in order to protect itself becomes violent.

True kindness requires patience. Suffering returns again and again and demands understanding. The failings of others touch us repeatedly and become the more unendurable because we know them by heart. Kindness must constantly make the effort and turn to the others.

One other thing is required by kindness, something of which we rarely speak—a sense of humor. It helps us to endure things more easily. Indeed we could hardly get along without it. The person who sees man only seriously, only morally or pedagogically, cannot endure him for any great length of time. We must have an eye for the oddity of existence. Everything human has something comic about it. The more pompously a man acts, the greater is the comic element. A sense of humor means that we take man seriously and strive to help him, but suddenly see how odd he is, and laugh, even though it be only inwardly. A friendly laugh at the oddity of all human affairs—that is humor. It helps us to be kind, for after a good laugh it is easier to be serious again.

One thing more must be said about kindness; it is quiet. True kindness does not talk much, does not seek attention, does not fuss with organizations and statistics, does not photograph and analyze. The deeper it goes the more silent it grows. It is the daily bread by which life is nourished. When this disappears there may be science and politics and welfare, but in the end all remains cold.

And now we shall seek for kindness in the place from which all virtue comes; we shall seek for it in God.

God is essentially good. In the Psalms, the prayerbook of the Old Testament, we find beautiful statements about God's goodness. And they are authentic, for the men of the Old Testament were not soft-hearted; they could not be so, in view of the hard life they were compelled to live.

Israel was a small nation and lived in a poor land; indeed, half of it was a stony desert. The Israelites were always in danger, for around them lurked powerful cultures, wealthy and filled with the pride and luxury of paganism, hostile to the pure faith of divine revelation. When an Israelite spoke of the goodness and kindness of God it was the result of a genuine experience. So we read, for example, in the 144th Psalm: "The Lord is gracious and merciful, patient and plenteous in mercy. The Lord is sweet to all, and his tender mercies are over all his works."

If we could see God's goodness, this abyss of kindness, we would be joyful all our life long. That a world exists at all is a continuous expression of God's goodness. The world would not exist if He did not wish it. He does not need it for Himself—how could the infinite God need the world which disappears before Him? If He creates it and preserves it, then it is because of His goodness and kindness.

But now someone will ask: "Does the world look as if God were well disposed toward it? Does human existence appear to be a work of divine goodness?" Anyone who is honest will answer: "Certainly not." Again and again man questions God: "Why all this if you are good?" The question is not unreasonable if it arises from an afflicted heart. But in itself it is foolish, for what is the source of all the evil that embitters man's existence? Man himself is responsible.

When the complaint arises that God cannot be good, or even that there cannot be a God when everything is as it is, then the person who speaks in this way rarely asks or thinks what the reason for all the evil may be. But the fact is that God put His world in man's hands so that man in cooperation with his Creator might construct that existence which the book of Genesis shows us under the figure of Paradise. But man was not willing. He wished to construct not God's kingdom but his own. This brought all that is confused, false, and destructive into the action of man. How then can he rise up and say: "If you, God, were good, you would not have created such a world!" And the disorder which man brings into existence continues and is increased even by the very person who utters the complaint.

And it is a fact that each one of us makes life a bit worse. Every evil or unkind word that we utter poisons the atmosphere. Every falsehood, every act of violence enters into existence and increases its confusion. We ourselves have made life what it is. So it is dishonest if we say that God cannot be good when everything is as it is. We can only say, "Lord, give me patience to endure what we have brought about. Help me to do what I can to make things better where I am." That is the only honest reply.

But we might raise another objection and ask how God can be good when the world of the animals, those beings which cannot be bad, includes so much pain. Many a melancholy person has not been able to handle that problem. How can God's goodness watch over the world when innocent creatures constantly endure so much terrible suffering? I will be honest—I know no answer.

But one thought has helped me and perhaps it will help others. Let us consider what "goodness" means if the term is predicated of God. We have the right—and the duty—to form concepts from the reflection of God's being upon objects and upon our own life, concepts by which we attempt to grasp what He is. So we can say, God is just, God has patience, God is kind, and so forth—all the important statements in which we transfer the magnitude and beauty of creation, freed from imperfection, to Him who created all. But if we look closely, what, for example, does the statement mean, "God is just"? We know what the word "just" means when it is applied to man, for we are finite beings and can be comprehended by finite concepts. But what if we apply the word to God who is beyond all measures and concepts? Do we still comprehend the meaning of the word "just"? Is it not, so to speak, taken out of our hands? Our thinking and speaking of God must proceed in this way: all finite beings receive their nature from Him. So we take one characteristic of these beings, and put it into words, apply it to God and say: He is like that, only in an absolutely perfect manner as the prototype of the finite copy. But thereby the word is in a sense swallowed up by the divine abyss and we can only revere His infinitude. This is the case here. If, for instance, I say of a mother that she is kind and her whole family lives by her kindness, then I know what the sentence means, and no truth more beautiful can be expressed. But what if I say God is kind? At first I seem to know what I mean, but then the mystery seizes upon the word and removes it from my grasp. Yet a direction of meaning remains, like the shining trail left by a meteor when it disappears in immeasurable space. A stillness remains, which perceives the direction, an awe which trembles before the mystery and becomes adoration.

For our problem, this means that God is kind and good even then when we do not understand His goodness.

Understanding

Human society is not an apparatus whose parts are fitted into each other so that they form a smoothly running whole. Rather, it consists of individuals, each of whom, in spite of all similarity of place and time, has his own particular character. Each has his own development, his purposes and his destiny. Each one forms a living entity rooted in itself. Of course individuals are bound together by various relations, by birth, education, friendship, dependency in their profession or work, and so forth. But every person has his own center which relates experiences and activities to itself and so stands apart from the general context. Moreover in each individual there are forces hostile to other living beings, which make association difficult and may even destroy it.

What is necessary in order that an association may become not merely possible, but fruitful? We might name many things; one is understanding. And that is no small matter.

What does it mean? When do I understand? When I notice what the other person, with whom I am dealing, means. When I see why he acts as he does, why he lives as he does, and why he has become the person who now faces me.

In order to see more clearly what is involved we shall look at other creatures who also live in a society, that is, the animals. Do they understand each other? They are bound together by various relations and are dependent on each other in many ways. Let us, for example, consider the birds. They pair off at a definite time, feed and protect their young, and help them to become independent. Do they understand each other? We might think that they do, for each one behaves in the way that is best for the other and for the young. They help each other to live; therefore, we think they must understand each other. But this is far from being the case. A simple fact proves this: as soon as the young are grown they become strangers to each other. Here there is no understanding involved, but the two beings who are mated, and then the pair and the young who spring forth from their life, form a cycle of life, a whole, whose preservation is guaranteed by instincts which otherwise work only for the individual and which disappear when the biological purpose has been fulfilled. It is just because they do not "understand" each other, just because in their relations there is no doubt or time of testing that the whole process takes place with such expedience and security.

Or let us think of creatures that live in an enduring association and for whose conduct we like to employ sociological concepts, such as the ants or bees. Their associations consist of numerous individuals, each of whom performs one function within the whole. They pass each other without disturbing each other; even more, they help and defend each other, and build up a complicated living structure with marvellous cooperation. Do they understand each other? We call their association a "state"—but is it really that? This would assume that within it, at least in certain situations, there takes place a conscious self-subordination of the individual and hence a mutual understanding. But this is not the case, and the whole image of a "state" is basically false. If we wish to express the situation correctly we should rather think of the relation that exists between the cells of an organism. An ant hill is like a single living being, whose cell-animals are not regulated by a mutual understanding but by an instinctively operating general plan, though this expression does not really explain very much.

Where then can we speak of an understanding? Where the situation involves beings in each of whom there is an inner life which is hidden and yet expressed in the exterior activity and so can be perceived by another being of the same kind.

Someone approaches me on the street, looks at me and tips his hat. From this action I can see that his attention is directed toward me, that he "means" me. By the expression on his face I can tell whether the man with whom I am dealing is well disposed toward me or has an aversion to me or feels embarrassed. Someone explains his behavior to me on a certain occasion, which surprised me. I hear his words; their meaning becomes clear to me. Now I know what I could not know before. These and countless other incidents, which constantly occur, indicate that man carries an interior world within himself; that dispositions, conditions, feelings, which are originally hidden, can be expressed in words, countenance, attitude, behavior and actions, and so can be revealed. Understanding, then, means being able to read or grasp the interior meaning in consequence of the external manifestation.

But the external can also conceal the interior meaning. If a person is troubled but does not wish to show it he "controls himself," checks the play of expression, and assumes a quiet mien. The interior processes, conditions, and emotions then lie behind the visible manifestation or beneath or within it, by whatever term we wish to express the relation, depending on the particular viewpoint of our consideration.

What would understanding mean then? We might use the word if the other person were so sensitive that he could tell by the expression of the eyes or some slight movements not wholly controlled, or by details of bodily posture, what is really going on—and also that it is concealed. Understanding could go even farther. We might notice that the other person does not merely hide his feelings but shows something which he does not feel at all; that he wishes to deceive, is hypocritical in his gestures of friendship, pretends interest when he is really indifferent. Then understanding would mean seeing through this whole pretense, noting what the truth really is and also noting the other person's dishonesty. Therefore, we see that understanding is a thing of many strata. Here understanding means to see, to hear, and to perceive how behind a feeling that is manifested, behind an opinion that is expressed, something else is hidden—and perhaps another thing behind that.

But true understanding goes even farther. If someone becomes gruff and surly at a particular moment, then understanding means seeing how this feeling fits into the whole of his nature. A certain way of acting expresses different things on the part of different persons. When a shy person becomes gruff because he wishes to hide his inmost feelings, it is something quite different than when an impudent person becomes violent in order to get his way. He who truly understands also sees the whole context in which a gesture or movement or word acquires its full meaning.

And this holds true not only of the context of disposition and temperament but also of time. Why is one person so timid? Because in the past he suffered violence. Why is he distrustful? Because he has often been deceived. What causes the curious look of sadness and of expectation in his eyes? He has found little understanding in his life and yearns for it. So understanding also means recognizing how the present hour results from a man's life history.

All this is not easy—and yet we have been dealing only with simple things. What if we are dealing with unusual dispositions, morbid conditions, and particular destinies, in the face of which the powers of seeing, hearing and feeling must become positively creative in order to comprehend and penetrate the rare phenomenon?

What, then, is demanded so that we may truly learn to understand?

Many things are necessary. First, there is a talent for this, a keenness of sight, a delicacy of feeling, an ability to put oneself in another's place, which bridges the distance between persons. These are important qualities which establish community between many individuals. They may be highly developed and make the one who possesses them either an artist, a leader, a sage—or else a person who exploits the weaknesses of others and maliciously despises them.

Experience is necessary. This means not merely that something has happened to me in the past, happened perhaps many times, but also that I am capable of learning from it, that I gain from my various experiences a clearer view, a finer perception, a quicker sympathy. "Experience" means also that in the face of other persons' behavior we remember things perceived in the past which are similar to those which are taking place and which, as it were, provide a key to their meaning.

What else is proper to understanding? Let us approach the matter from another angle. Why is understanding so rare? Why do so many persons meet again and again and yet not understand each other? For this is certainly the case, otherwise they would act differently and the atmosphere around them would be clearer.

There are many reasons for this. Let us consider just one. We tend to classify people at once into those whom we like and those whom we do not like. Consequently, people are divided by our self-love into two great compartments and labelled accordingly. This is done so instinctively that a whole sociology has been built upon the relation of amity and enmity.

Understanding is essentially human and begins only when we step out of this relation of congeniality or antipathy and try to accept the other person as he is; when we do not classify him at once according to our likes and dislikes, our purposes and apprehensions, but say: "You have a right to exist; be as you are. You are yourself just as I am myself." Then our view becomes clear and understanding can come about.

For example, what about a friendship? It can prosper only when one does not judge the other according to the purpose for which he can use him, but permits him simply to be who he is; when the relation of amity and enmity, in the sense in which we have spoken of it, does not come into consideration, but two persons stand face to face in freedom and respect. Only then can we see clearly and understand. Or what about a marriage? If one party demands of the other that he should be as he would have him then the two may be married for thirty years and yet not understand each other, indeed, what is worse, may misunderstand each other with a stubborn obstinacy which is incomprehensible to a third person, and each of the two reproaches the other with doing what he himself does.

The beginning of all understanding consists in this: that each one shall give the other freedom to be what he is, and not regard him from the point of view of egotism, prescribing for him what he is to be according to one's own self-interest, but rather regarding him from the point of view of freedom, first saying, "Be what you are," and then, "Now I should like to know what you are, and why."

This is the attitude that brings about understanding. It presupposes that we give the other person the right to be himself, do not regard him as a piece of our own environment which we can use, but as a being who has his own original center, his way of life, his own wishes and rights. Only then can we rightly ask: "Why does he do that? What experiences has he had? What is the history behind his behavior? How are his various attitudes related to each other? Is the gruffness which he shows really violence or only a kind of shame which hides what is within? Is his impatience really such or only the hurt resulting from previous experiences?" And so on. Only then will the questions really find an answer, the answer of understanding.

All this is so indispensable that we may venture to state the paradox that we learn really to understand ourself only when we regard ourself from another's point of view. Would not a physician gain an entirely new insight into his own behavior if he suddenly asked himself: "How do my patients see me?" Not, "How would I like them to see me," but "How do they really see me, from their own point of view?" Not the admirers but the ordinary ones, the poor, those who suffer greatly. Then he would gain a very sober view of himself and this would be very useful to him as a physician. Or if a teacher asked himself: "How do my students see me?" Those students are by no means the stupid rebellious creatures which he often considers them, but they frequently have very sharp eyes and good judgment. He would have to ask himself in very concrete fashion: "How do they see me when I enter the room, when I call on them, when one has done poor work, when there is a disturbance?" Perhaps he would suddenly understand the opposition to him. In a marriage the husband might ask himself, "How does my wife see me on this occasion or on another?" And conversely the wife might ask, "How does my husband see me?" Not, "How would I like him to see me?" but "How does he really see me? How do my attitude, my voice and my demands affect him?" Then each one might suddenly see very clearly whether his love is genuine, when dishonesty creeps in or brutality shows itself.

To do this is not easy. We must often attempt it, must practice this viewing of ourselves from the other person's viewpoint. If we are successful in seeing ourselves without the egotism that distorts the picture, then what we see may be very unpleasant but it will help us to get at the truth.

This also helps us to do something else, to judge others better, and this is necessary in order to live rightly.

The word judge here does not mean that against which Jesus warns us when he says, "Judge not." He who does this, usurps the right to say: "This person can stay as he is, that one must change; this one has the right to be, the other must be removed," and so on. To such persons Jesus says, "Judge not, that you may not be judged." (Matt. 7:1) But we mean that evaluation of another which helps us to do justice to his value, to see his defects as they are, in order to establish the right relation with him, in confidence and in caution. Most judgments of people about each other basically mean only, "I find this person pleasant, that one unpleasant; this person I can use, the other not." A true judgment would say, "This person is suited to the task at hand; that one would mismanage the matter," and so on. But all this is possible only if we have first understood the other person's true nature.

Every genuine virtue extends from earth to heaven or, more correctly, from heaven to earth. Does God "understand"? Indeed, He does, and this understanding transcends all human measures.

God knows every being from its inmost core. This is so not because He gazes so deeply into it and tests it so exactly, but because He has thought it and brought it into existence. Let us think of God's creative power in the right way. His creating does not mean making, fitting something to particular purposes, but with effortless power calling a creature into existence and setting it free. God's creating is so perfect and magnanimously liberal that He not only brought man into real being but placed him in a condition of true freedom. It has often been asked how man can be free if God is omnipotent, whether His boundless might would not overpower the puny freedom of man as the stream overpowers the drifting leaf. The answer is this: My friend, how insufficient is your concept of God's omnipotence! His power is one with His magnanimity and His reverence; it is this that sets you free. Only in God's eye and hand do you become master of yourself. And if you say that is a paradox—no, the marvel is that if there is an Infinite One, finite beings can also exist. But it is presumption if you with your puny intellect claim that you can grasp it.

At this point we might look back. The joy that God takes in every man, the magnanimity with which he sets him free, the pure understanding which is not subsequent to the being of things but establishes it, should teach us, for God has granted us the privilege of being His image.

What would be the purest fulfilment of the meaning of friendship? If friends could feel about each other: In his glance I am wholly myself. His glance does not hem me in, does not reproach me with what I am, but in its light I become entirely myself.

It would be a perfect marriage in which the wife could feel that in the eyes of her husband she reached completeness of being, and conversely the husband found his purest and truest self in the understanding of his wife—if each could see himself in the eyes of the other as that which he was meant to be. Not that vanity imagines a consort such as could not exist, but that love sees the possibilities which are still dormant in the other.

Courtesy

In the twelfth chapter of his Epistle to the Romans, St. Paul writes about the communion of the redeemed and says great things about it. He speaks of the mysterious powers which dwelt in the communities of the early period, and says "Be fervent in spirit"—a sentence which should remind us to what great things we are called and how puny and feeble our response really is. In the midst of these lofty words we find the simple statement, "Anticipate one another in showing honor"; not merely "Honor one another," but "Anticipate one another in showing honor." Perhaps we may translate the sentence in everyday language as "Be courteous to each other."

Now we might ask how St. Paul, who had such noble things to say, could bother about anything like that. But he knew that in our life everything fits together, the extraordinary and the commonplace, the fervor of spirit and the manner of behavior which grows out of reverence for other men. For example, St. Paul himself, who proclaimed the mystery of the "mystical body of Christ," also wrote to the congregation in Philippi that Evodias and Syntyche should stop quarrelling. These were two women who were active in the service of the community, but, as happens today also, evidently couldn't get along with each other.

Various similar things can be found in the Apostle's letters. If he found time, in the midst of his great concerns, to talk about such everyday matters, we can do the same thing.

In these meditations we have spoken of noble virtues: justice, truthfulness, selflessness and many others. But courtesy also is a virtue and worth considering. If I may be permitted I would like to recount a personal recollection: a long time ago, when I was still attending school, a woman whom I greatly revered said to me one day, "Do not forget that there is a great love of our neighbor, but also a small one! The great one has its occasion when there is a great need to be met or when it becomes dangerous to remain loyal. But there is always an occasion for the small one, because it belongs to our everyday life. It is courtesy." I have never forgotten these words.

What, then, is courtesy?

Originally, as we can easily see, the word courtesy denoted proper behavior at the court of the ruler, in a noble environment. Then it lost this particular meaning and took on a more general one, proper behavior as such, the result of a good up-bringing; it is in this sense that we shall use it.

People live together in narrow spaces, within a house, an office, a factory, in conference rooms, in the crowded streets, in traffic, in the limited confines of a densely populated country. Consequently, their spheres of action are always touching each other. Their purposes cross just as their paths do. Here there is constant danger of friction, of the kindling of anger; and every sensible person wishes to encounter courtesy. He will try to find forms which express concern for a proper association of the multitudes, which lessen the violence of antagonism and of cross-purposes, and which move people to be obliging and enable them to receive consideration from others.

This is courtesy. It is an everyday affair, but how important for the whole of life!

Now one might think that this would happen spontaneously. It would—if man were an animal. Everybody has probably at one time or another stood before an ant hill and watched the swarming, teeming activity. Each one of the tiny creatures found its way and did not interfere with the others. Each one performed its task without hindrance. Sometimes a burden became too heavy; then a second ant took hold and helped. And if the observer perhaps gave way to the childish temptation and disturbed the little community, then all ran about in great turmoil at first, but each one set to work and soon everything was in order. We might think that if animals can do this man should certainly be better able to do it. But it is quite the other way. Just because he is man he cannot do it so simply and easily; for the animals live by instinct, which is an expression of organic necessity. But in man mind is operative, and "mind" means that man can recognize truth, but can also err. The animal does not err in matters concerned with the conduct of its life. If it does, it is sick and it perishes. But man can err and is confronted with the task of learning. Man can make mistakes. If an animal does this it is because an obstacle was in the way, either exterior or interior; but man can act wrongly because his judgment may be incorrect or passion may mislead him. Therefore he must be watchful and careful in his association with others, so that it does not become a struggle with every man's hand against every other man. This watchfulness is expressed in ethics and moral education, in law and in the administration of justice. These are the great things. But it is manifested also in the forms of everyday intercourse, in courtesy, and we must say at once that these little things mean much more than one might suppose. A large section of moral life is included in them, just as moral degeneration is quickly manifested in a lowering of the tone of everyday intercourse.

Wherein does courteous behavior consist? If we wish to answer this question and look at the facts we find a great variety of forms. There are some which can be understood at once but also some that are strange and unusual. Many are natural and appropriate; others are artificial, even foolish. Can we discover basic forms on which the manifold varieties are built up? Perhaps we can.

There is first of all the will to give others room. Culture does not begin with obtrusiveness and with grasping; it begins with taking one's hands away and stepping back. Courtesy gives the other person a free space and protects him from oppressive closeness; it gives him air. It recognizes the good in others and lets them feel that it is valued. It keeps silence about one's own qualities and keeps these in the background, lest they discourage others. Courtesy strives to keep unpleasant things at a distance or at least to bridge them. It tries to avoid embarrassing situations, to remove the sting from difficult and painful circumstances, and to lighten burdens. It induces young people to honor their elders, men to honor women, and the strong to defer to the weak. All these are motives which moderate the impulses of insolence and violence and make life easier for others.

These motives lead the person who wishes to associate with others in proper fashion to behave in such a way that the possibilities of tension, of clash, of mutual injury or offence are avoided, so that no evil may result. For man's nature includes all these possibilities.

Naturalism says that the animal from which man has evolved is still present within him. By bitter experience and repeated effort it has been tamed, but it is always ready to break out. But this is too simple a concept. The reality is much worse. It is tragically serious. Within man there lives his primeval ancestor who once broke out and renounced obedience to God. There live in man all the ancestors from time immemorial who disobeyed again and again. It is not only wildness that lives in man, but wickedness. This must be met by the serious and difficult struggle of moral self-education. And courtesy is its simplest form. It lightens the difficulty and assists morality; indeed, it can sometimes substitute for it. Quite frequently moral difficulties are avoided by what we call "good manners," and entanglements which could lead to evil consequences are resolved without much trouble.

Courtesy is very important and very helpful in our life. It is not a great act, such as standing beside someone in great danger or freeing him from some pressing need or distress, but it is one of the little things which lighten the ever perceptible difficulties of life. It is consideration for the mood of our neighbor, sympathy for his weariness, smoothing over a painful situation, and so forth. A constant attempt to make life easier and to obviate the many, and often strange, threats that endanger it—this is courtesy.

Here belongs also that facilitating of life which St. Paul means when he says, "Anticipate one another in showing honor." But why does he use the noble expression, "Showing honor"? Because man possesses what we call "dignity." A thing does not have dignity; it only requires the treatment suitable to its nature—unless we mean that deep, even mysterious quality which belongs to it as an essential structure, and which we perceive so keenly in a noble object. But "dignity" in the true sense of the word is found only in the person. A thing can be bought and sold, can be given and received, used and destroyed. All this is proper, as long as we act according to the nature of the thing. But this cannot be done in the case of a person. The fact that we feel this marks the beginning of culture, as we have said before, and it indicates a great and ever increasing threat that man today is forced more and more into the role of a thing. But man is a person and this means that every man is unique. No man can be replaced. His achievements, his work, and his property may be replaced, but not the man himself. Every man is unique, in his relation to God and in God's relation to him.

This uniqueness demands a special attitude on our part—"honor." This is shown in our daily intercourse, by the forms of courtesy proper to every situation, and we might reconsider what has been said above concerning the basic acts of courtesy, and how honor is shown in each of them.

Finally we might point out that courtesy is a thing of beauty and makes life beautiful. It is "form": an attitude, gesture, or action, which does not merely serve a purpose, but also expresses a meaning which has value in itself, namely the dignity of man. At their highest point these gestures and actions become a drama which represents a lofty mode of being; for example, in the ceremonies of state or in the ritual of liturgical celebrations. Of course, there is also the danger inherent in every symbol; that is, that it may become artificial, unnatural and hence untrue.

But it is a fact that today courtesy is disintegrating everywhere. This is not a criticism of our culture but is meant to bring to our attention something that concerns us all. Our life, influenced by science and technology is largely determined by material objects, and this means that our attention is directed to the demands of the material situation, the work we are engaged in, the end to be attained; and so we are inclined to banish the superfluous, in form and action, and to proceed directly and without any detour toward the matter at hand. This is necessary wherever time has been wasted and materials and work-power have been squandered. It produces a clear, clean style of action and structure which, under favorable circumstances, can attain to an austere beauty. But it is likely to produce an atmosphere in which objectivity become coarseness. And this regards all that we have recognized as the object of reverence—the person, his dignity, feelings and emotions, all the deep and tender things that indicate "life"—as nonessentials, insofar as they cannot be considered as items in an account. And that sympathy for another person, that consideration for his circumstances and his mood in each particular situation, everything that is part of courtesy, is then regarded as "superfluous." The effect is disastrous; existence is impoverished and coarsened.

We must emphasize another point, something that has a direct effect on people's intercourse with each other; namely, the lack of time. Courtesy requires time. In order to exercise it we must stop and wait; we must make a detour; and we must be considerate and defer our own affairs. But all this takes time, and in our age of forced dead-lines, of precisely functioning apparatus, and of the high costs of construction and of fierce competition, the loss of time is something useless, irrational, erroneous, even wicked.

And so, of course, courtesy dies. Sometimes that may be an advantage: formalities are dispensed with; matters that are merely external, and hence unnatural and untrue, such as might easily be bound up with courtesy, disappear. But courtesy itself disappears, and in its place we have at best a terse correctness. It is true that this may lead to something fine, an honesty that rejects whatever is not genuine, an understanding between those who consider the requirements of a task, or a friendliness which requires no words of reassurance. But these require a genuineness of character and a fine upbringing which are not easy to find or to attain. And so that which we call "life" suffers a loss. For life does not go on according to the laws of labor-saving and of the preservation of materials. These are technical standards. Life takes detours, it squanders, or rather, consumes time. Life wants to linger, to delay for the "extra" things. A life deprived of the "extras," of "waste," becomes a mere mechanical process.

So we must be careful that the exigencies of time do not destroy our life. A man who loses courtesy for the sake of material objects becomes poor. And we must be honest and not conceal the fact that much indolence, indifference, and violence may hide behind our boasted realism and objectivity and turn the much-praised honesty into a falsehood far more unpleasant than that courtesy which was accused of being "artificial."

But we can carry this thought farther and then it may help us to a new insight.

How did the old-fashioned courtesy really originate, that courtesy which we who are more advanced in years once learned? It evolved in the course of history and with respect to persons of high degree or, ultimately, the king. The history of civilization and especially the history of religion reveals this. The very origin of the word draws our attention. Courtesy was originally something belonging to the court. It was the kind of behavior demanded by the presence of the king. In the thoughts of the men of old the king approached divinity, was himself something divine. Therefore, he was worthy of special reverence, as a revelation of the sublime, and reverence was also due to the rays of divinity which he shed over the whole of earthly existence. These rays continued downward; in various steps the sublime descended, so to speak, and on each level it exacted suitable behavior. Whenever a person met another with courtesy, something like a reflection of the king appeared and functioned in the particular situation.

This is past and gone. The "divine right" king no longer exists. Where there is a king, he is limited. Our life is no longer in the form of an ascending and descending hierarchy but it is all on a level, democratically structured, and increasingly so. This equality, felt and demanded everywhere, causes the earlier forms of courtesy to disappear. But mere levelling is chaos, and soon a dictatorship replaces the hierarchy and force and violence take the place of reverence. But this is not really an order, it is simply force, and that means hidden chaos. This constantly breaks out in revolt, as long as reverence and a new kind of courtesy do not evolve from the democratic level. But how can this come about?

I believe that it is possible only if we begin with the dignity of man, who must be honored, because there are forces which dishonor him and seek to violate his dignity. We need only recall the various forms of totalitarianism. But man must be honored in relation to Him who created man in His image and who requires us to honor this image. Here there is a reference to a higher level which remains in all equality, indeed, alone makes this possible.

Another point of departure for the evolution of a new courtesy is the vulnerability of man, which requires that we should recognize our responsibility toward each other. What psychology, sociology and biology tell us about man points out the necessity of this attitude. And not only that. They also show us the constantly increasing danger in which man finds himself in consequence of his economic and technical progress. This progress, upon which he prides himself, indicates an increasing artificiality of life and a consequent threat to life, to say nothing of the power which man has acquired over nature and human life. And no one knows how man, who is not wise or well anchored, but rather driven by every kind of passion, will use this power.

Therefore it is to be hoped that present-day man will become aware of a fellowship in danger and will carry out this awareness in mutual responsibility and consideration, which means courtesy.

There is also a courtesy in relation to God. We may consider, for example, that we cannot come to church improperly dressed; that there is a suitable attitude—both external and internal—for prayer; that all thought and speech related to God must be carried on in the proper disposition. Here the liturgy can be our teacher: it is permeated with reverence. All that is spoken, heard, or done, every action is, as it were, veiled in reverence, so that we may ever remain conscious of the mystery which is here carried out.

Then our meditation, if it is properly carried on, reaches a height which constitutes the ultimate mystery. Have we ever considered how God honors His creature? His whole attitude toward man rests upon the unfathomable fact that He created him free.

God, who is all powerful, wills that man should be a free person, self-dependent, disposing of himself and acting from an inner impulse. God does not force us or terrify us, or mislead us, not even when man turns against God and thereby against himself. We hesitate to say that God is courteous. The word must be elevated to the summit of its significance before we can apply it to Him. The fact that He created freedom and continually preserves it is the inconceivable lordly courtesy which He shows to His creature.

But those who have grown into intimacy with God tell us in addition that God here shows a tenderness which is more overwhelming than his very omnipotence—indeed it is perhaps only the converse of his perfect power.

Images reveal much, often more than concepts. Only we must interpret them correctly. How meaningful it is when in the New Testament Christ's admonition that man should receive His message is expressed in this image: "Behold, I stand at the door and knock." (Apoc. 3:20) He who speaks in this way is he to whom "is given all power in heaven and on earth," (Matt. 28:18) and who "with a rod of iron" could shatter every obstacle "as one shatters a [useless] earthen vessel." (Apoc. 2:27ff.)

Gratitude

I f the thought that we expressed at the beginning of our meditations is correct—that every "virtue," in each case with some particular moral value as its dominant, expresses the whole man—then it must be true that history exerts its influence, on the life history of the individual as well as on the cultural development of a country or a nation. The same virtues do not always determine the moral attitude.

We might say that the virtues are like constellations which appear in certain epochs and govern the firmament of values and then gradually fade from our sight, giving room to others. This does not mean that they cease to be legitimate values. They still exercise an influence, because the epochs are not rigidly separated. Nevertheless, they no longer stand in the foreground of moral consciousness. Of course, they may later reappear as a result of the changes that take place in men's souls throughout the ages.

We shall now speak of one of these virtues, which, if I am not mistaken, is now receding, namely the virtue of gratitude.

Naturally we still give and receive whenever one person wishes to give pleasure to another or to help someone personally, but this has become a private matter, and even here we perceive a kind of organization of giving which is bound up with our business and consumer-trade and which destroys spontaneity. We need only think of the mad rush of giving and receiving at Christmastime. No, what determines the general sentiment is not asking and giving but the announcement of rights and their satisfaction by means of organized associations. And the response is not gratitude but a receipt; then, the matter is properly settled.

This has certain great advantages, namely that the matter is handled objectively, according to a properly conceived system, and personal feeling is not brought in where it does not really belong. The growing democratic consciousness of the personal dignity of all men also contributes to this; the feeling that what is a matter of proper economics cannot be left to individual requests and a gracious bestowing, but that social conditions must be met by a common effort. However, this brings with it the danger that the living element, that which the words "ask" and "thank," "give" and "receive" mean, may disappear.

Even worse than this: there is danger that the image of a mechanical apparatus may become the criterion for human relations. Our society and its life appear as a structure of functions in which there is no question of asking and thanking, nor even of proper rights and duties, but merely of appropriate functioning. Insofar as this concept becomes dominant there is, of course, no place for gratitude.

Let us attempt to obtain a view of this gradually disappearing virtue. Let us ask what is necessary so that gratitude may become possible.

Above all there is this: We can be grateful only to a person. Gratitude and petition are possible only between an "I" and a "Thou." We cannot thank a law, a board, or a company. We may do so out of mere politeness when the proper sum is handed to us, in order to keep everything in the domain of good manners, but real gratitude does not enter into the matter, for gratitude is the expression of a personal encounter in human need.

But two persons, one of whom is situated so that he has something or can do something, while the other has not or cannot—these stand face to face. The one asks and the other is ready; the one gives and the other thanks; and the two are united by a human tie. Here gratitude is possible and it becomes a basis for community.

Furthermore, gratitude is possible only in the realm of freedom. For the fact that the sun rises in the morning or, to express it scientifically, that the earth comes into such a position in relation to the sun that it becomes visible, for this I am not grateful. It is certainly true that on a bright morning very lively sentiments of gratitude may arise because something so powerful and beautiful is taking place. But these are the responses of man to Him who has created all, or else they are the after-effects of a time in which the sun itself was revered as a divinity. Otherwise, we know the astronomical formulas, and if we have proper intelligence, we know why the sun must "rise." I do not thank for that, nor for a machine that runs properly. Here too there may be a transfer of feelings. If my car runs well under difficult conditions I may feel about it as if it were a tried and true comrade. But in reality there is no gratitude here. If a machine is properly constructed and properly handled it must function properly.

Nor do I thank when I have a rightful claim upon something. If I have bought some article and it is delivered to me I do not thank, but I give a receipt: "Such or such a thing received in good condition." If I have made an agreement on the basis of which another person must perform some service, then I do not thank him afterwards but say: "It is right"—anything beyond this is mere politeness.

True gratitude can exist only in the realm of the voluntary. The more our attitude toward human affairs approaches our attitude toward mechanical functions—this board regulates traffic, another the conditions of labor, one thing must be done according to the law at this time, another thing at another time—the less room there will be for the free response of the heart which says, "I thank you." Its place is taken by the statement that says one has received his due.

A third condition necessary for gratitude is this: he who gives the gift must do so with reverence for the one who receives; otherwise, he wounds the receiver's self-respect. He must not give with indifference; neither must he play the part of one who condescends; nor must he desire to show his power by the gift. A danger for all in social service is the desire to feel their power, for the person in need is, as such, weaker than the one who helps, and when he thanks for the assistance, he admits his weakness thereby.

All this makes gratitude difficult. If the one who helps lets the other feel his superiority, then gratitude dies and in its place we find humiliation and resentment. How many persons who receive would like to throw the gift into the giver's face.

So there are three important conditions. Gratitude can exist only between an "I" and a "thou." As soon as the consciousness of the personal quality disappears and the idea of the apparatus prevails, gratitude dies. Gratitude can exist only in the realm of freedom. As soon as there is a "must" or a claim, gratitude loses its meaning. Gratitude can exist only with reverence. If there is no mutual respect, gratitude perishes and turns to resentment. Anyone who gives assistance to others should think about that. Only the assistance which makes gratitude possible really deserves the name.

True asking and giving, true receiving and thanking are fine and are human in the deepest sense of the word. They are based upon the consciousness that we stand together in our need. Accidentally here and now one person has something, the other does not; one person can and the other cannot. Tomorrow it may be the other way around.

But human need is not the only occasion which can give rise to gratitude. Gratitude can spring up wherever kindliness perceives an opportunity to bring joy or create beauty or brighten life. Then the one who is made joyful says, "You have done this. I thank you." This is a fine thing, and if it is really true that the structure of our life leaves less and less room for gratitude, then we should want to seek such opportunities wherever they exist, and create them whenever possible with that power which cannot be overcome, because it is the central power of the heart—love.

Here we wish to bring to the reader's attention something which, in the light of what we have been saying, seems like a paradox and perhaps is one. How many paradoxes does life contain! It cannot be reduced to a formula. There are moments when we feel that we must thank someone simply because he *is*—not for doing something or other but simply for being. Actually this is nonsense, because he did not make himself. And yet the feeling is there. Perhaps it is unconsciously directed toward God, because it is He who willed that this person should exist. But perhaps there is something more to it, for "to be" is a verb and denotes action. So the feeling may perhaps be directed toward an "achievement" which cannot be really understood or explained.

This type of gratitude takes on a new and mysterious meaning in relation to God. In the "gloria" of the Mass we say, "We give You thanks for your great glory." Historians tell us that this "thanking," in Latin *gratias agere*, belongs to high ceremonial language and is an expression of honor: "We render homage to You because of your great power and majesty." That may be so, and yet it is more than a mere expression of honor. It is also proper to remember that it is impossible for God not to be, and so we really have no occasion to thank Him for being. On Mt. Horeb, when Moses asked Him His name, God replied that His name was "I am." In the case of every finite being the fact that it is not merely thought, but really exists, is something additional; in God this is essential to His nature, and it would be quite proper to address Him as "You who are." All this is true, and yet—in the unutterable immensity of God's essential glory there seems to be something which we may call the freedom of real being. It is as if He gave us the fact that He is; as if His very being were a grace that He bestows upon us; as if His being were an achievement which lies beyond all concepts, and for which man expresses a gratitude which would ravish him into ecstasy if he really experienced it. We trust that the reader will not be offended by this thought which actually was intended only to indicate something beyond all comprehension.

Giving and thanking, which lift man above the functioning of a machine or the instinct of animals, are really the echo of something divine. For the very fact that the world exists and embraces such inexhaustible profusion is not something self-evident; it *is* because it was willed; it is a deed and a work.

At present there exists a concept which is in one way indispensable, in another a calamity; that is, the concept of nature, and here we use the word in its modern sense. It signifies the sum total of all that is directly perceived, the whole which is governed by universally valid laws as it is investigated by science. But then it transcends itself, stands in opposition to the faith of the past and means the world as that self-evident entity in which we live and search and work, but about whose origin we do not think. "Nature" is simply that which is, which is as it is and cannot be otherwise. When people adopt this view, the noblest things die, because they live by the very fact that they are not self-evident, that they are born of freedom. The world is not "nature" but a "work," the work of God. It *is* because He conceived it in His mind and because He wishes it to *be* in the mystery of the freedom of His love.

Hence the world is the abiding gift of God to us. The fact that we ourselves are is an abiding gift of God to us. That we are as we are and can breathe and feel and work is by no means self-evident, but is worthy of adoring wonder. To know this is part of man's basic consciousness. Constantly to receive oneself from the hand of God, and to thank Him for this, belongs to the essential being of man, of the real man who is as he was meant to be. It is quite possible that I might not be, and that the world might not be. Nothing essential would be lacking, "only I," "only the world"; for God is self-sufficient.

Perhaps this is really the basis of all piety, to know and to accept and to confess: "You are, O Lord, and You suffice. But You willed that I should be and I thank You for it." This is a prayer that always sets us right. Let us try it, perhaps in the morning when we are fresh and rested; when we, as it were, receive ourselves anew after the absence of sleep: "Lord, how good it is that You willed that I should be! I thank You that You have permitted me to be!" Then the false sense of self-evidence will be dissipated; the mechanism of our concept of nature and the presumptions of our pride will disintegrate. Everything between God and ourselves will come to life and things will be right. Later, in the course of the day they will again be hidden by the turmoil of wishes and events. But they *were* there in the morning and they will be there again tomorrow morning and will bring order into our existence.

We may go a little farther in our meditation. What about God himself? Does He thank? We might reply at once: What could that mean? All things belong to Him. But if we want to know the mind of God then we should not sit down and cogitate how "the absolute Being" should act, but we must ask God himself, and there is a place where His heart is revealed and that is in Christ.

Did Christ thank? When he sat beside the well in Samaria and asked the woman, "Give me to drink" and she drew the water and handed him the vessel he certainly would have thanked her. Or when Lazarus and his sisters, Mary and Martha, entertained him in the house at Bethany he must have thanked them, in grace and power. And when the despised woman of Magdala came to the feast of Simon and poured the precious ointment over the feet of Jesus, and in the perfection of contrite humility dried them with her hair, while the self-righteous Pharisee and the hypocritical Judas turned against her, Jesus spoke immortal words about her. (Luke 7:40ff.) How mysteriously his knowledge of her repentance and the pardon of her sins are combined in his words with the fragrance of the ointment and the beauty of the gesture.

In Jesus we find gratitude in weakness and in power, for he had need of all things because he had become one of us and we, presumptuous as we are, have need of the gifts of existence from our first breath to our last. But Jesus responded by looking into the eyes of the one who showed him a kindness and touching his heart. Who can measure how much of this can be referred to God? Who knows, if we may speak in this way, what God feels when we do not merely perform our duty to Him, but give Him love; when our littleness strives to be generous toward Him? Then there is something in God which we may faintly and distantly indicate by the word gratitude, very briefly, and then it plunges into mystery. But some day. He will show us how He received our gift, and that will be a part of our blessedness.

Unselfishness

The name of the virtue which we are now going to consider is curious. If we examine it, it makes us wonder. What do unselfishness and its converse, selfishness, really mean?

How can we seek that which we are, our own self, or get away from that which is the basis of all that we are and do, and even of this very attempt to get away from it? Let us consider more carefully what this curious something is, the self, of which we speak in such strange fashion.

The "self" of a person may mean simply the piece of reality that he is—he, man—in distinction from a tree or an animal. He, this man, in distinction from anyone else and from all other men. That definition of self would be correct, but would still remain something external, statistical.

We must delve more deeply. Then "self" means the particular characteristic quality of the person, his peculiarities, talents, possibilities, and also his limitations, failings and faults, all these gathered into one around a central point—namely himself. So then, self would be what we call "personality." This would be richer and more decided as the qualities are more developed, more clearly defined, more harmonious, and as the whole is stronger and more efficient. From this point of view we speak of a great or mediocre or small personality, strong or weak, genuine or false, and so on.

In an even deeper sense "self" means the curious fact that this being, called a man, not only exists but possesses himself. How does he possess himself? Especially by knowing about himself. No animal, however noble, knows about itself. A man knows that he is. He knows his possibilities and weaknesses, at least some of them, because daily experience presents them to his consciousness. He is able to know them better and better if he makes the effort, because he can observe and understand himself, can examine and judge himself. He can ask: "Why did I do this in this way and not in another? Was it right or wrong?" In doing this he grasps himself and possesses himself in his mind. Sometimes when his work is successful or he feels the surging of life, he rejoices in thinking: this was granted to me; I am allowed to be this.

This involves something more, or at least the possibility of something. "Being oneself" means that man can dispose of himself. We experience this when we reflect in some situation: "What shall I do? This or that?" And finally we decide, "I shall do that." In this decision man disposes of himself, decides for himself. He is not merely moved from without as a stone is moved by a force stronger than its own weight, but he is activated from within. He is not compelled from within as an animal is compelled by its instincts, but he determines himself from some point which lies deeper than all which belongs to his immediate being: organs, urges, talents and dispositions. We could say it lies higher than all these—freedom. Because he is able to do this, he has power over his actions. He can also work on himself, can curtail certain qualities and strengthen others, and in this way change the relations of the different elements of his nature to each other. In short, he can do all that we call the formation of self, or self-education.

It has been maintained many times and is still being maintained that such freedom does not exist. At the moment when we hear the objection it impresses us. But as soon as we come to our senses we know that it is in error. Freedom does exist. We are free. We are not always free; frequently, we are not entirely so; but, basically and potentially, we are often really so.

Certainly various elements influence our decisions: heredity, disposition, environment, the particular situation, urges, physical and mental conditions, and the like. But all these only supply the ground on which freedom makes the decision. And it does really decide. And even if circumstances should prevent the carrying out of the decision it still exists as the basic possibility and standard and gives to the whole event its particular—and sometimes very bitter—character.

Certainly all that happens has its reason, even a free decision. We can always ask, "Why do you do this?" and we receive the answer, "For this or that reason." Therefore, the objector might say, we cannot speak of freedom. But here the "reason," or rather the "motive" is confused with the cause. The motive of the decision is always some particular purpose or intention, but the decision is its own cause. It is the primary power, the "initiative."

Apart from such considerations the freedom reveals itself in an interior echo, in conscience, in the consciousness of responsibility for the action. It is a strange, mysterious phenomenon that an interior feeling says not only, "That was harmful," or "That was dangerous," but, "That was wrong, you should not have done that and yet you did it. Now it belongs to you and you must answer for it before the laws of good and evil; not another, but you." Here, in the sense of responsibility, the self is revealed in its ineffaceable austerity.

Of course, much more could be said on the subject from the standpoint of logic, psychology, sociology and so on. Discussions about freedom are endless. Here our purpose was only to make clear the meaning of the word, so that we might understand what is indicated by the terms selfishness and unselfishness, namely, the manner in which a person is himself and how he possesses himself; what attitude he assumes and what intention directs him.

A man may have a task to do, something demanded by his vocation. He can do it with his eye upon-himself, upon the impression he will make upon others, the advantages which will accrue to him, and so on. Then he has been seeking himself in his work. As far as the work is concerned, it has probably been done badly, or at least not as well as it might have been. And that upon which his eye was fixed, his self, has not fared very well in the process; for keeping our eyes upon ourself makes us crooked, and paying attention to the impression produced deprives us of genuineness. To be unselfish here would mean as much as to be objective, to fix one's attention upon the task and not to think of oneself; to do the work correctly and properly as it should be done. Then the work flourishes, for the person doing it is concerned with the task, not with his vain self. In addition—and this is what concerns us particularly here—such an attitude produces a singularly free mental area in which the person really becomes "himself."

Here we touch something strange that must lead every serious-minded person to deeper reflection, namely the paradox of the person. As soon as the person fixes his eye upon himself, he fills the mental space, so to speak, in which a portion of life is to take place; he gets in the way of his own realization. But if he forgets himself and turns his attention simply to the matter in hand the space opens out and now the person truly becomes himself.

A large number of our daily acts consist in coming into relation with another person; they are "I—thou relations." But these can be carried on in very different ways. Encounters in friendship and in society, collaboration in our profession or business, helping the needy—in all these we can behave in such a way that we play a part, and we often do this. We watch to see what impression we are making, whether the other esteems us properly, whether we shall receive something when we give, and so on. But what happens? The living "I—thou relation" withers; that which should be a clear face to face encounter follows two different lines which interfere with each other; it becomes broken, crooked. And the other perceives this. He thinks, "That person is not really with me; he is always thinking of himself." And this makes him uncertain. He does not reach a straightforward, confident "Thou relation," but he becomes suspicious. But the man who is open in his friendliness, disinterested in showing honor, straight-forward in giving help, departs from himself, but by that very fact his true self arises free and harmonious from its inner depths and calls to the self of the other.

Herein we find the mysterious dialectic of the person: The more a person seeks himself the more he slips away from himself. The more important he considers himself, the more insignificant he becomes. The vain, calculating person who lives only for himself thinks that he is attaining a fuller, stronger self-hood. In reality he is becoming interiorly crippled because he never moves in that free space which only unselfishness creates. As we depart from ourself and give our attention to the other, to the work, or to the task, the true self awakes and grows. A person is more truly himself the more freely he leaves himself for the other person with whom he is dealing, for the task that confronts him.

Of course, he must also pay attention to himself. He must examine himself to know whether he has done the right thing, has been wise in his dealings with others, has served the purpose of his calling or profession. He must make the many corrections which life requires, because otherwise there will be ill feeling, annoyance and harm. But the essential attitude of man is the movement away from himself toward the other person and toward the task to be accomplished.

The same rule can also be applied in religion. There is selfishness and unselfishness toward God. Jesus said "Not as I will but as thou wilt." (Matt. 26:39) This word cuts a sharp line between the will that seeks the self and that which seeks the Father. To the extent to which man seeks God he moves away from himself to the divine "Thou"; but this is not so that he will lose himself; no, he truly finds himself in God. This is the promise that the Lord has given, saying, "He that finds his life shall lose it and he that shall lose his life for me shall find it." (Matt. 10:39) This refers first of all to the losing of one's life in martyrdom. But the Greek word for "life," *psyche*, in the New Testament also means the soul and its eternal life. Whenever a person, in opposition to God, clings to his soul he loses it, but when he gives it to God he finds it. Man gives his soul to God in every act of obedience to God's holy will and, at the same moment, God gives it back to him, and the soul has become more truly itself than it was before.

A mysterious exchange between man and God! The more often man does this, the more his life advances, in this constant giving of himself and receiving himself again from the hand of God, the more he becomes the person he should be or, we might say, becomes the person he truly is.

The mystics speak of the "birth of God in man." This is a mysterious phrase about whose ultimate meaning we shall not speak here, but one thing we can understand immediately: God wishes to enter into man, to find a place in him and assume a human form, here in this person who is generically one among countless others, but personally is unique; that is, is himself.

There is a resemblance to God in all things. Everything expresses Him, each according to its own kind, and this expression of God constitutes its basic created nature. But God wishes to express Himself in man in a special way, in each person according to his particular character. This is the inmost core of what we call "personality," a reflection—if we may be permitted this comparison—of the incarnation of the eternal Son. The real, essential incarnation took place in Christ, but by His grace which confers His image, God wishes to enter into every person and express Himself in him, and in everyone in a special and unique manner. Every believer should be an expression of God. The foundation is laid in baptism, in the "new birth of water and the Holy Spirit" as we learn from the nocturnal conversation of the Lord with Nicodemus. (John 3:5) And every act of the believer in doing the will of God constitutes a step in that direction.

The perfection of the expression can be seen in the Saints. God "appears" in them. But, since man is the image of God, and God is the model of man, this manifestation also reveals the essential nature of man, of every man. He becomes truly himself. How did St. Francis of Assisi become truly

himself? By not seeking himself in anything. If he had remained the son
of Bernardone and continued to play the great role in Assisi and Umbria,
which his father wished him to play, and for which his talents and his
fortune fitted him, then he would probably have been a glamorous and
charming person, but his essential nature would have remained hidden.
But when he took his great step: "Only God and nothing else," then the
beauty of God blossomed in him and he became the man he was meant
to be, the man who expressed the magnanimity of divine love more than
almost anyone else.

Every saint reflects in a particular way the incarnation of God in
Christ. In no longer seeking himself he gives place to God who makes him
the person he really should be, as God's essential incarnation in Christ
manifested what man as such, the "son of man" really is. Of course the
way thereto is a self-surrender, one sacrifice after another, the "painful
death of self" as the spiritual masters call it.

Every virtue has its model in God. All virtues are modes in which
God's goodness is reflected in man in particular respects. This is also true
of unselfishness, however strange this statement may sound at first.

Before and above all God is infinitely Himself. When Moses on Mt.
Horeb asked Him His name, so that His message might be ratified among
the horde of pagan gods of that time, God answered, "I am the I-am."
Thereby He expressed His eternal selfhood, and all who seriously meditate
about God must learn from this word if they are not to go astray. The word
says there is no "name" which can express God from the point of view of
finite beings, that is, classify Him with anything known and created. His
name is "He," or, to put it in another way, "That it is so—this is God's name."

But the Epistle to the Philippians says of the Son of God; that is, of
God Himself: "Let nothing be done through contention, neither by vain
glory, but in humility let each esteem others better than himself; each one
not considering the things that are his own, but those that are other men's.
For let this mind be in you, which was also in Christ Jesus, who being in

the form of God, thought it not robbery to be equal with God, but emptied himself, taking the form of a servant, being made in the likeness of men, and in habit found as a man. He humbled himself, becoming obedient unto death, even to the death of the cross. For which cause God also hath exalted him and hath given him a name which is above all names; that in the name of Jesus every knee should bow, of those that are in heaven, on earth, and under the earth; and that every tongue should confess that the Lord Jesus Christ is in the glory of God the Father."

Something tremendous is expressed in this passage: that the son of God did not anxiously and forcefully cling to his eternal selfhood, as to something unlawfully acquired, but "emptied" himself, or more exactly "annihilated" himself, and gave up his selfhood by becoming a servant although he was the Lord of all. He became a "servant," a bondslave, in bitter earnest, even to the death on the cross which a malefactor had to suffer. But thereby he obtained the new "name," the name of "Christ," the anointed and victorious one, and of the "Kyrios" the Lord God, who is enthroned above all creation; and this brings eternal glory to the Father.

It is an ineffable mystery that God does this, is able to do this and yet remain God. Revelation tells us that God acts in this way and that it is glorious for him to do so. A God who acted and thought and willed otherwise cannot exist. He would be, as Pascal says, a "god of the philosophers," a concept of God by which man seeks to justify his own self-centeredness.

God is sovereignly unselfish, and every act of unselfishness in man faintly reflects this divine mystery.

Recollection

An expression which was familiar to the religious and ethical language of the past, but which is seldom used in our day, is "recollection," the recollected person. And yet that which it denotes is more relevant to us today. Psychiatrists and educators in particular are beginning to understand its significance. So the thoughts of this reflection will find quite a few points of contact.

In order to have a better understanding of what recollection means, let us recall the structure of our existence. It oscillates between two poles which are related to those which are mentioned in the chapter on silence and speech. The first pole is the interiority of the person, his center. It would not be easy to explain what this center is, but everyone who uses the word of himself knows what he means: the point of inward relation, that which makes of his powers, his characteristics, his attitudes and actions not a confused chaos but a unity. That is the one pole.

The other is the connection of external things, events, circumstances, relations; it is the other persons, their way of life and their actions, history. In short, it is the world insofar as the individual has the power to survey it and the ability to experience it.

Between these two poles, the center in us and the world about us, our life moves. I constantly go out of myself to the objects around me; I observe, grasp, take possession, fashion and arrange. Then I return to my center and ask myself: "What is that? Why is it so? What does it resemble and how does it differ? Wherein does its essence consist?" Here, in knowledge, that which I have experienced outside is perfected.

If I want to do something I do not simply work at random, but I consider its purpose and what the situation demands. I make a decision and only then do I have direction and order for my activity "outside."

After I have acted, I reconsider and test my action. Did I do things right? Was I just to the person involved? Have I done my duty?

What we have said simplifies the matter. Actually, the "out" and "back," and again "out" and "back" takes place not only once but countless times. It is a constant play of acts which make up our daily life.

So the two areas are related to each other. What happens outside is guided and judged by that which is within; what is within is called, aroused, and fed by what is without. If we ask ourselves what person is to be considered properly developed in this respect, the answer must be, he in whose life these two poles function in proper relation to each other; the person who does not lose his direction in outward matters nor become entangled with himself, but in whose life the two areas are well balanced and determine and perfect each other.

But in our ordinary experience it is different. Here the objects of exterior life predominate most powerfully. Their many forms, the insistence of their qualities, the tasks which they impose upon us, their value which arouses our desire, their danger, which awakens fear, all these are so powerful that they gain the preponderance and draw our life outward. So we have the "extroverted" person, whose inner self is weak and becomes constantly weaker.

On the whole, this has long been the case and those concerned about the deeper culture of man have long warned us. But the condition has become especially dangerous at present because the stimuli which force themselves upon man have become so strong and so numerous and their strength and number is constantly increasing. Man is in constant turmoil, not only in systems which catch and absorb him but generally in a chaos that he cannot grasp. Moreover the "publicizing" of existence has increased to an alarming extent. Events are announced with increasing speed and completeness, so immediately that one is tempted to say that the account is a part of the event and that the latter takes place from the outset before the lenses and microphones of the announcers. Publicity forces itself upon men's personal lives without the least consideration, so that privacy is plainly disappearing. The boundaries of life's course become transparent as glass, and men move behind them like fish in an aquarium, whose activities one can observe from all sides.

It is very symbolic that the modern house frequently has no wall. Within the house man lives as if he were outside and imagines that this makes him free. Actually the inner world evaporates. And as if this were not enough, the outer world is expressly brought in. We all know homes in which it is never quiet because the radio is constantly blaring away, or television brings the sensation of world events into the hours when persons should be by themselves.

So we have the man who no longer has a living center. The events of life constantly flow through him and carry him out. He feels cramped if he is in his room; he must always be in motion. He cannot manage to stay alone; he must always have people around him. To spend an evening quietly with a book would seem to him a waste of time because he must always be "doing something." The request to consider his own life eye to eye with himself, to think about encounters, activities, responsibilities, principles—this would embarrass him. He would not know how to go about it and, after the briefest reflection, would slip away from himself. Or even worse—he would not want to see himself at all.

The life of such a man resolves itself into reactions to external stimuli. He does not stand anywhere but is tossed about by a thousand influences. He does not possess himself but "happens" anywhere. He has no convictions, only views which have come to him from newspapers and radio. He does not act from interior initiative but only as he is propelled by impulses that come from without.

This has a special significance in our religious life. What is the core of all piety? It is the consciousness of the reality of God; that He "is," is living here and now, and is working, acting, ruling. This idea develops further and becomes the consciousness that actually God alone is primarily and originally real and that all finite creation is only "through Him" and "before Him"; that He alone works and acts in a sovereign creative manner and we can work only in Him. Piety means living in the sight of God.

But there is more. Piety means a dialogue with God, so above all the fact that one addresses Him. But in reality to whom does one speak in addressing God? Usually to a fog—or only to oneself without the consciousness of a "Thou." If we are speaking to a man we look into his eyes, we note his expression, so that we know that our words are addressed to a countenance and beyond that to what is expressed thereby: the mind that thinks, the heart that feels, the person who exists. In his countenance I read what is there expressed, the person himself. For the act of addressing God, the Psalmists use the expression "to seek the face of God," to speak to the countenance of God. But how is that done?

Piety means "seeking the face of God," and living according to His countenance. This is a part of the meaning of creation, as St. Augustine said, "Thou hast made us for Thyself, O God." (*Confessions* I 1:1)

But we can do this only if we are at home with ourselves, masters of ourselves. We can do this only if the inner realm is open and the other person becomes clear, or at least the fact that we are addressing Him becomes clear. In the exterior world in which we usually find ourselves, in the turmoil which pervades our being, God is, so to speak, wiped out. The many images of things, the many countenances of men prevent the countenance of God—this mysterious entity which all who associate with God know—from being clear, from being perceived.

But up to this point we have only an attention, a direction on the part of man, not a dialogue. For this we need the other voice, the voice of God. Indeed,—and only so do we grasp the matter rightly—this comes first. For we can address God only if He permits it; we can speak the word only if He releases it within us.

But how does God speak within us? And how does He enable us to understand His word and to answer it with ours. His voice and our hearing and answering we call "conscience." This is a wonderful thing. Constantly, we are touched by the call which comes to us from "the good," the right, that which is worthy of being and *should* be. This good is all-inclusive and yet quite simple. It constantly urges us, "Do me—realize me—carry me into the world so that the kingdom of the good may come into being." And let us assume a voice within us, our conscience, replies: "Yes, I will, but how shall I do this?" And thereupon follows a silence, for the good is as unlimited in content as it is simple in form, and so it cannot simply be "done."

But then "the situation" takes shape; perhaps it has already done so and waits for us. It is like this: the stream of temporal things constantly flows around us. But again and again objects, relations, events form an image: this room, this person, this conversation, this need—and we are facing it. In this image the good takes form as that which is here and now demanded. This turns to me, regards me, addresses me, "Do this, here, now!" And "conscience" is the ability to perceive the call, to understand and to decide: "Yes, I will!"

All this may be understood in a purely ethical way. Then it means the consciousness of always being bound by the moral law and the ability in each case to understand that law through the concrete situation. But the core of the whole matter is the religious relation. For "the good" in the final analysis is God, His holiness; and the challenge to bring about the realization of the good in the world is His voice. But He demands of us that we bring into existence the kingdom of the good, His kingdom, in the world at the place where we are, hour by hour, according to the situation which always arises through Him, through His action and guidance, through His providence.

The sensitivity to this constant admonition of the good, the ability to recognize the given hour as the elucidation of its commandment and the necessary assumption for its realization, and to grasp it by the readiness of true obedience and by confidence in our own interpretation and decision—all this is possible only as the result of an interior disposition which signifies attention and readiness; that means, a standing before God, and this is "recollection." Only a recollected person recognizes the "hour," whether it has a great significance—the greatest was that of which the New Testament speaks in the words "The time is fulfilled" (Mark 1:15)—or whether it has a simpler one, for instance, that a decision upon which much depends should be rightly made. And there is also the every-day significance, that every hour of our life has its meaning for the kingdom of God. All this is possible only through an interior disposition which we call recollection.

From this point our thought continues: The whole existence of man takes place in the "I—Thou" relation between God and him.

Things were created by the command of God. "He spoke and they were there," says the psalmist of the constellations, and they exist through this command which preserves them in being and reality. With man it is different. The account of creation expresses the special quality of the creation of man by the marvellous figure of God bowing down over the clay that had been formed into a human body and breathing into it the life-giving element. This means that man was created not as a species but as an individual, and was so regarded by God. God created him for the "I—Thou" relation with Himself. So man's life goes on as a constant dialogue. Through everything that occurs, and also through every movement of his own life God speaks to him. We may say that the life of faith consists in learning to carry on this dialogue, in bringing all that happens to us and all that we do into this dialogue, understanding it all in relation to God and carrying it out for Him.

But how can this be possible if man is in a constant state of distraction, always extroverted, pulled this way and that by the impressions that importune him? He can sustain this existence in dialogue only if he is interiorly alive, if he is attentive, listening, and listening in such a way that he goes on to action, to obedience. In truth, man carries out the basic nature of his existence only in the measure in which he is recollected.

What we have said of the "I—Thou" relation to God holds true to a lesser degree of man's relation to another man. For some time the point has been emphasized that our life is based upon a constant realization of the "I—Thou" relation to another. We are conscious of the fact that the great danger of our age of masses and machines consists in making man a mere thing. We notice that the act of recognizing a person is different from that of recognizing a thing. In the case of the thing we say, "that over there," in the case of a person, "you over there." Herein the meaning of what we call the person is revealed: a being that has been given freedom. From the "I—Thou" relation comes the proper attitude of one man to another: reverence, faithfulness, charity.

But this is possible only through recollection. The person who is not recollected treats men as if they were things. He counts them, groups them by catch-words, uses them for his purposes and expends them. Only when the peculiar interior watchfulness, the particular attention which we call recollection comes into being, is it possible to meet man as man. But the danger of not doing this, and hence the necessity of recognizing the problem, grows as the number of human beings grows and as our lives are in consequence determined more and more by machines which treat all that they handle as mere things.

But we must go on once more. Even the work of man—more precisely, the nobler work—can be understood only through recollection. How can we grasp the peculiar nature of a work of art if not by a kind of reflection of the "I—Thou" relation? How does the manner in which a true connoisseur experiences a work of art differ from the manner in which a dealer rates it according to its market value? Evidently in an attention, a reverence, which are possibly only as a result of recollection.

Of course this takes an effort. We need only to notice how people behave at an exhibition or a concert. Most of them do not establish a true relation to the work but they treat it as a thing. We perceive this in the rapidity with which they become critics, comparing and evaluating, and this means that they take the work of art as an object. Here too recollection is essential and we can tell by the face of the observer or listener whether he is capable of it and willing to make the effort.

Perhaps we would need to go a step farther and say that nature also can be met properly only if we approach it with some degree of recollection. How does the glance of a person who beholds in a tree the mystery of silent life without power of locomotion, uniting the depth of the earth, the breadth of space and the height of heaven, differ from the glance of the woodman who looks to see if the tree should be felled, or the glance of the dealer who calculates its price in the market?

We might say the same thing of every form of nature. And the greatest danger of our age, with its mass-tourism and recreation which has become a business, consists in the fact that the attitude of recollection becomes more and more rare.

Let us return to the thought upon which we touched at the beginning of our meditation: the virtue of recollection means that a person has learned through natural disposition, education and experience how life moves between the interior realm of personality and the exterior realm of the world, between the deep center and the far-reaching whole. It means that he has to some extent mastered the distraction and exteriorization of which we have spoken and has learned to set his inner self free and make it work effectively.

This task has at all times led men to construct a definite, very strict type of life, the life of the hermit or the monk. Both of these words mean the same thing etymologically, a person who wants to find the essential thing, wants it so much that he wants nothing else. Therefore he leaves everything else and turns wholly to the "interior realm," either as a hermit, one actually dwelling alone, or as a monk who dwells with others but in a community whose rule guarantees a maximum of solitude. He withdraws his attention, his inclinations and his powers from the world and gathers them within himself. He turns his attention increasingly toward God dwelling within him and accustoms himself to stand before the face of God and to listen to His word.

We cannot do this, for we live in the world and have our tasks. We have various ties and obligations that bind us. But we too must learn to be at home within our interior center, otherwise we are distracted persons.

This cannot be done without effort, without serious and continued practice; it requires asceticism. This word—of which we have already spoken—originally meant simply "practice." But practice means that we arouse a dormant power, develop an organ which is undeveloped, put off a bad habit and form a good one, and so on.

Perhaps we refrain from going out, although we are inclined to do so, and we attempt to "come to ourself" by means of quiet work, a book, or honest reflection. But without artificiality or trifling, soberly and earnestly. And if there is no quiet place at home or we have no room of our own, we go into a church, sit down and find solitude. Or we do not permit the noisy radio to disturb the silence with its blaring, but turn it off. We resist the impulse to turn on the television and to be at its mercy for hours. Instead we read something sensible. The same thing holds true of the newspapers, that mass of sensation, indiscretion and shamelessness. We refuse to be taken over by these, even if only for a quarter of an hour. When we go along the street all the attractions of the age press upon us, traffic, noise, people, advertisements, display windows and their wares on exhibit. From all sides things call us, draw us, take us away from ourselves. What an important practice it is to resist all this, not to let ourselves be torn to pieces, to remain calm and self-possessed—and so on.

Man—and especially in our time—always wants to go to others, to speak, to hear, to participate. He constantly wants to see something and wants something to be happening. This desire has become a mania, and if it is not fulfilled he becomes restless and something drives him out. He who has realized what a valuable thing it is to be recollected must overcome this tendency—or let us speak more modestly, must strive to overcome it more and more. It is really a mania, and overcoming a mania is difficult because the urge has affected the nerves. It takes a long time for it to cease, but it can be reduced to a proper measure.

But at the same time something positive must be done, we must become established in the interior world, must be ourselves and be interiorly independent. What we have been saying must not be taken as a moral sermon, but realistically, as spoken from experience, as pointing out the way to a rewarding life. For distraction, the constant outward motion, makes for an interior emptiness. If we try to imagine the end to which this scattered life leads, the thought occurs to us that the end will be a hopeless boredom interrupted by outbreaks of desperate impatience. So we must resist, for the sake of life itself that it may have meaning.

This can be attained only by constantly examining ourselves: "How was it today? Did I possess my soul? Or was I in a constant state of agitation? Is my life such that I cannot attain self-possession? What must be changed?" And we must do this seriously, not with that dishonest resignation which gives up because it really does not want things to be different.

Then—and above all—we must seek the face of God, must realize what is the basic truth of our existence. God is the eternally existent one, the only one who lives from and through Himself. He is here. He is "the One who is." But we are and exist through Him; we are here before Him; we are ourselves only because He wills us to be.

This "He and I—I before Him—I through Him"; this hearkening to His word, this seeking and speaking, "Thou, God"—this is what makes us interiorly alive and firm.

Such interiority is the counter-balance to the mass of things, the multitude of people and the turmoil of external events; to publicity, fashion and advertising. It is also—and after the experiences of the past half-century we must emphasize this—the only true counterbalance to the violence of the state, the modern, rationalistic, technological state which is always in danger of becoming an ochlocracy and hence totalitarian, and which must deprive man of self and of interiority in order to have dominion over him.

Revelation tells us that man is the image of God. Therefore God is man's original model and His being opens for us—in the manner permitted to our thought—a way to Him. But we can say that He is most perfectly recollected, completely unified, entirely self-possessed, living, feeling, knowing Himself through and through.

In the history of occidental metaphysics we find an attempt to approach the nature of mind or spirit, which states that each being is higher in rank, the richer and yet the simpler it is. The spirit is decisively simple since it cannot be divided, but it is articulated by its various acts and their relation in time, by its relation to the body which it animates and the objects to which it turns.

The sovereign spirit, God, is perfectly simple. He contains within Himself the fulness of life in the pure simplicity of being. He is entirely recollected, at one with Himself and therefore perfectly master of Himself and completely happy.

Silence

The life of man is passed between silence and speech, stillness and the word—two poles which are related to those which we considered in the reflection on recollection.

We sometimes say the word is "spiritual," but that is not the case. It is human. In it that union of matter and spirit which we call man reaches its highest refinement. By the tone which the breath produces through the movements of throat and chest the speaker expresses his interior meaning. At first he has this within himself; he thinks it and feels it. But it is hidden. Then he projects it into the figure made up of tone and sound and thereby it is revealed to the hearer. The latter understands what the speaker means; he can answer and so a conversation ensues. This is a wondrous thing, a great mystery. He who could understand it would understand man.

We must not let this be destroyed by naturalistic platitudes which seek to derive the word from the cry of an animal. This cry may express quite directly fear or pain or enticement or whatever it may be, but for all that it is not a word. This comes into being only when the sound-structure communicates a meaning which was first thought, a truth. But only man is capable of this, for only in him is there a personal spirit. If an animal that lives with man seems to do something of this sort that is a misapprehension on our part. What the animal produces is not a communication but an "expression," often quite complicated. Only a man can put into the movements of the sound a truth of life, of science, of piety.

The word is one basic form of human life; silence is the other, and it is as great a mystery. Silence does not mean only that no word is spoken and no sound is uttered. This alone does not signify silence; the animal is capable of this, and the rock even more so. Rather, silence is that which takes place when man, after speaking, returns to himself and grows still; or when he who could speak remains still. Only he who can speak can be silent. Silence means that he, who would "go forth" by speaking, remains in inner reserve; it is a knowing, a feeling, a living stillness, a vibrating within itself.

The two things belong together. Only he who is also able to be silent can speak meaningfully; otherwise, he talks nonsense. Only he who can also speak can properly keep silence; otherwise, he is dumb. Man lives in these two mysteries; their unity expresses his nature.

To be capable of silence is a virtue. He who does not know how to keep silence does the same thing with his life as a man who would wish only to exhale and not to inhale. We need only imagine this to feel terrified. The man who is never silent dissipates his humanity.

As we have already said, in speech the inner man is revealed. What I think, feel, or intend is known only to me. But as soon as I express it in words, it becomes known. It stands in space between me, the speaker, and the other who hears it. Thereby I give the hearer a share in what I possess interiorly. Many conflicts are resolved by being brought out into the open by means of words. But there are also experiences which should not be revealed. When someone has performed an act of magnanimity or delicacy he knows that if he spoke of it, it would disintegrate. Therefore he veils it in silence and keeps it to himself. And if, in some dark hour, he must ask himself if life is worth while, then the act comes to his attention and justifies his existence.

Through speech we have communion. When two persons exchange views about something the word passes back and forth between them. Question and answer, affirmation and objection move onward toward clarity, and probe more deeply until the moment comes when they know, "So it is!" Now they have communion in truth, a marvelous manner of sharing.

There are also times in which man does not desire communion, does not need another to share the truth that is inwardly beheld. It may be that one enters a church, one of those buildings in which the presence of God may be perceived. One sits down, is conscious of the pillars rising round about, feels the vast space, notes the sacred images, and silence fills the soul. What is brought to our awareness at such times must not be put into words. If we tried to express it, something would be lost.

By speech man enters into history. He faces a situation in which something must be decided and asks himself what should be done. If he decides and expresses his decision, then history begins. For the word has weight; we are responsible for it. It is power; it sets cause and effect in motion and man himself is affected by it.

But if he does not wish to enter into history then he is silent and thereby withdraws into the realm of reserve.

We could mention various other things. The most important events of human life take place between these two poles of existence. But usually there are not two poles, but one, and consequently no "pole" at all, since a pole requires its contrary in order to function. Usually speech is the predominant thing, since man cannot be silent, or rather does not wish to be, for if he is truly silent he comes to himself, and to be with himself is something he finds unendurable. He then perceives all that is stunted, perplexed and spoiled in himself and he runs away from himself into speech.

Only in silence is true knowledge attained. This does not mean cognizance. This too is good and necessary. For instance, it may establish the fact that a certain person is ill and in pain. Then we can act accordingly, can apply remedies or call a physician, and then the matter is taken care of. But the desire for knowledge asks, "What is pain? What does it bring about in our existence when it is interiorly accepted, lived, or rejected? And what of this person? What effect does pain have on his life?" These are questions which do not find their answer in speech. Perhaps they find an external answer but certainly not the answer of an interior understanding which grasps the essential thing. The person who is speaking misses the very point, the interior *vis-à-vis*, the penetrating glance into the existence before him, the understanding of the way in which this one unique existence functions. In order to attain this we must recollect ourselves, must become silent, must bring the matter before our interior sight, must enter into the other person's feelings. Then, at the proper time we begin to understand what is taking place in the person who suffers. This is knowledge, the dawning of truth. He who cannot be silent never has this experience.

What holds true of knowledge also holds true of our associations. Association with others consists largely in giving to these others something of oneself—friendliness, helpfulness, our presence, and finally the joy of complete communion. But can one give something of himself if he does not possess himself? He who is always speaking does not really possess himself for he always slips away from himself, and what he gives to others, when he should give himself, is nothing but words.

And finally this: only in silence do we attain the presence of God. This is so true that building one's whole existence upon silence has become one form of life. There are religious orders which do this. It is a daring enterprise which, if it is properly carried out, leads far into the silent kingdom of God. But it may become dangerous if generosity and wisdom are lacking. We shall not go into that, however, but shall keep to ordinary life.

The beginning of all religious life is the awareness that God is. He is not merely a feeling or an idea, but a reality. He is more real than I am myself; He is the essential, self-based, eternal reality, and all serious religious life leads to the experience that God is, and we are only before Him and through Him. But God is not only real; He is "somebody," Himself. We have already spoken in these meditations of the way in which Scripture expresses this. Scripture speaks of His countenance. "Show us, O Lord, Thy countenance and we shall be healed," says the Psalmist.

Are we familiar with this experience? Do we have knowledge of the countenance of God? Do we know what it means when the Scripture says God turns to me, He looks upon me, He takes account of me? Only then can we properly and meaningfully say, "Thou, God."

Have we ever thought how wonderful it is that I can really say "Thou" to God? That He is even the essential "Thou" for me?—so much so that a man in prayer could be told, "God and thy soul, nothing else in the world." And when he asked, "Lord, what of the others"? the reply was, "It holds true of everyone, God and he, nothing else."

Into this most intimate relation—God and I—we do not come by speaking, but only by silence; when we are recollected our inmost soul is opened and the sacred presence can manifest itself.

This silence must be learned. No virtue comes to us spontaneously. There are predispositions. There is the introverted person in contrast to the one who is predominantly extroverted. But this predisposition does not suffice. It may make a person thoughtful, attentive to the processes of his own mind, serious, perhaps even melancholy—but all this is fluctuating, subject to the moods and experiences of the moment, and can be thwarted and confused by external events.

So we must take pains. We must resist the endless chatter and noise that fills the world, must struggle as an asthmatic person struggles for breath. Otherwise something in us withers and dies. But the external noise is only half the problem and perhaps not even the most difficult half. The other is the inner turmoil, the whirl of thoughts, the drive of desire, the restlessness and worries of the mind, the burden of care, the wall of dullness—or whatever that may be which fills our interior world as the rubble fills an abandoned well.

We must be serious about this. A life properly lived includes practice in silence. This begins with keeping our mouth shut whenever this is required by the confidence of another person, the duties of our vocation, tact, or respect for others. It goes on to include keeping silence at times even when it might be permissible to speak, especially if speaking would create an impression. Not to speak at such times is a good exercise in keeping our mastery over the inordinate desire to talk. We should strive to conquer the mania for constant chatter and idle talk. How many superfluous things we say in the course of the day, how many foolish things! We must learn that silence is beautiful, that it is not emptiness but true and full life.

And then, in addition, we must learn interior stillness, lingering over a serious problem, an important task, the thought of a person whom we value. In doing this we shall make a great discovery, that the interior world of man is spacious and admits of ever deeper penetration. St. Augustine in his *Confessions* has spoken profoundly on this matter (e.g. 10, 8ff.)

But what we have been saying does not transcend the natural, what we call the psychic life. The person who entrusts himself to the mystery of grace and the new birth is given something more. The preaching of St. Paul is interwoven with the message that a new and holy life awakens in the believer. Christ, the risen and transfigured Lord, awakens it in him.

Here there is an interiority, a depth which lies beyond the merely natural, as far beyond the natural depth of soul as the "realm" where God is enthroned, and where our "glory to God in the highest" seeks Him, and is beyond all thoughts and feelings of natural sublimity. This interiority has been given to us by baptism, and now Christian practice must lift it beyond the natural world of feeling and thinking.

Let us strive to become silent so that we may learn to be human. The symbol that warns us is already in our world, the talking machine. It is interesting, as a result of science and an accomplishment of technology, but it betrays—in connection with computers and other machines—a secret desire to deprive man of his dignity. But as soon as man learns really to speak and really to be silent he becomes inimitable, because then the image of God is revealed in him.

What the machine accomplishes is not really speech any more than the accomplishments of the other apparatuses are really thought. In the machine the mechanical forms of speaking and thinking are isolated and placed at the disposal of the operator. They are raised to a degree of speed of which true thinking is not capable and thereby new technological possibilities are created. These are amazing accomplishments of science and technology, but what a temptation to attempt to fathom the real life of man by comparison with the machine and thereby to forget his essential nature. It may help us to understand if we consider that the machine can "talk" but not be silent. It can only stand lifeless. This spectre of silence makes us feel at once that its "speaking" also is only a spectre. To be silent, to live in silence is possible only for man.

Let us try again, by means of human life, which is the image of God, to attain to a view of the original. Is it true that the acts of speaking and of keeping silence mean something in connection with God? Is there something in Him for which they can be a symbol?

It is indeed so, and this is expressed in two statements of divine Revelation.

The first lies in the pronouncement which rings through the whole sacred message, that God alone is God and there is no divinity beside Him. He alone is the Lord, the wholly free and independent one, the eternal, ever-living, who has and is all.

Before this supreme one, who transcends all possibilities of thinking and feeling, all images which imply noise or agitation must fail. It is true that the Psalmists speak of theophanies that are accompanied by storm and lightning and thunder, and these enable man to surmise the meaning of "omnipotence," which transcends all created power. But once and for all God Himself revealed the decisive truth when He called the mighty Elias, the stormiest of prophets, to the holy mount Horeb after the

tremendous exertions of his struggle against Ahab and Jezebel, and there
revealed to the zealous prophet who He was. He commanded him, "Go
forth and stand upon the mount before the Lord; and behold the Lord
passed, and a great and strong wind before the Lord overthrowing the
mountains, and breaking the rocks in pieces; but the Lord was not in the
wind; and after the wind an earthquake; and after the earthquake a lire;
but the Lord was not in the fire; and after the fire a whisper of a gentle air,"
and God was therein. (3 Kings 19:11–12) He was not in the images of crushing forces, but in a gentle breeze He revealed Himself to His prophet. So
we may carry on the thought: the image of the life of God would be the
infinite stillness of an all-embracing silence.

But the New Testament speaks of another image, at the beginning of
St. John's Gospel. There we read: "In the beginning was the Word; and the
Word was with God and the Word [itself] was God." At the end of the
Prologue the thought is resumed and given a mysterious depth: "No man
hath seen God at any time; the only begotten Son who is in the bosom of
the Father, he hath declared Him" (1:18).

Again we see a glimmer of God's mystery. We are told that in the
unicity of God which permits of no comparison there is a community;
His complete simplicity has a *vis-à-vis*; his majesty includes a giving and
taking. The image for this is the uttering of a word out of silence. This
image is then linked with that of the birth of the Son from the Father. The
"Word" is the "Son" and "speech" is "birth"; both are incomprehensible.

The first image, that of silence and soundless simplicity, and the second, of speaking birth and community in love—these include the mystery
of God's life and sacred lordship.

But what a mystery is man also, since in him is reflected, by God's
will, the primal glory! And what a task it is to preserve this in its inviolate purity!

Justice before God

One of the first reflections in this book was entitled "Justice." By this word we designated that virtue which seeks to meet other persons, the events of life and the things of the world in the manner which their nature demands.

But in both the Old and the New Testament another concept is emphasized, justice before God. When is man just before God? When is he such that his debts are remitted before the divine judge; when God receives him into eternal communion with Himself?

The two concepts intertwine. Ethical justice is based upon the truth of natural being, and this has been created by God. This kind of justice is good and is approved by God, the same God who in the New Testament tells the believer that it is insufficient. So the two kinds of justice differ, sometimes so much that our immediate sense of justice objects, for example in the parable of the laborers in the vineyard. (Matt. 20:1ff.)

Here, at the end of our reflections we shall try to make clear what Revelation understands by justice before God, being justified in His sight; and in this way we shall seek to bring all that we have previously said to a definite conclusion.

We are inclined to consider the ethics of the Old Testament "natural" and to say that the "supernatural," the reception of human activity into the activity of God, is made clear only in the New Testament. But this is not true. What is called "justice" in the Old Testament would not, for example, be understood by Plato, since it rests basically not upon an immediate insight into the nature of things, nor upon the seriousness of a conscience which is determined to follow the good, but upon an act of God, the covenant of Mt. Sinai. Hence it belongs to no system of ethics which could be separated from and understood apart from this event. All "merely ethical" judgments of the Old Testament are erroneous.

It is rather like this: God there carries on with men a history which shall build His kingdom on earth. A solemn act, the covenant on Mt. Sinai, establishes the existence of the nation which shall carry on the kingdom. Justice here means the fulfilment of that which the covenant demands. First of all, and basically, it means God's own conduct in granting the covenant and binding himself by it and keeping it. Then it means the conduct of man, which is made possible by God's action—of man who knows that he is bound to fulfil the demands of his divine partner in the covenant.

But the binding quality which this covenant possesses in common with all true ethical conduct, lies in the universal sovereignty of God, who has begun the building of His kingdom with this nation and in this land, but wishes—as the Prophets never wearied of declaring—to spread it over all nations, over the whole earth, even over the whole creation.

So the justice of the Old Testament means a manner of life demanded and made possible by God's grace in the covenant. It consists in God's guidance of history, building the kingdom, and in man's readiness to fit himself into it. Its demands are related to the manifold tasks of life and further developed by the "law," and here they encounter the immediately ethical justice which results from the nature of things and give to this a new meaning.

To fulfil this demand of God required heroic faith and obedience on the part of the people. They renounced entirely all natural politico-social and economic judgment and trusted that God by his covenant had promised that the nation as well as the individual would survive and flourish even in this world; that is, they relied upon a continued "miracle."

Hence the man of the Old Testament was always tempted to distrust the miracle of the covenant and to live "like all nations." The tragedy of the Old Testament consisted in the fact that he succumbed to this temptation again and again. The first book of Samuel tells of the first instance: "And it came to pass when Samuel was old that he appointed his sons to be judges over Israel.... And his sons walked not in his ways; but they turned aside after lucre, and took bribes, and perverted judgment. Then all the ancients of Israel being assembled came to Samuel to Ramatha, and they said to him: 'Behold, thou art old, and thy sons walk not in thy ways; make us a king to judge us, as all nations have.'" Samuel was shocked by this defection. "And the Lord said to Samuel—'They have not rejected thee, but me, that I should not reign over them.'" (1:8, 1–7)

In the course of history the concept of the justice of the old covenant loses its true meaning and turns into that ambiguous pharisaical attitude which Jesus opposes.

In the Sermon on the Mount he constructs his message on the contrast, "It was said to you—but I say to you." (Matt. 5:21, 27, 31, 33, 38) Wherein does the new covenant here set forth consist?

Evidently, it consists first of all in this, that Jesus places all the emphasis on the interior instead of the exterior and on purity of intention rather than on correctness of action. The whole Sermon on the Mount shows this. But could we also say that now God's covenant separates from the single historical instance, that is, the person, the action and the destiny of Jesus and spreads out over the whole of humanity? Could it be that the ethical situation hereafter develops between a general "moral law" revealed by God and a purified but autonomous conscience, and that "justice" means the purity and perfection with which God's demand is fulfilled?

It is self-evident that an attitude toward life of such sublimity and at the same time so realistic as that proclaimed by Jesus must also contain a structure of general norms and values that can be theoretically grasped. But everything is bound up with reality. Now every system of ethics, if it does not limit itself to the merely formal, is bound up with reality. But this consists of the reality of existence as such. In the other case it is a question of something which comes to us only through Revelation and depends upon it, namely God and his kingdom.

But the term "God" is not to be understood as "the absolute being" or "the basic cause of the world" or in any other philosophical terms, but as "the living One," who is hidden, and who becomes known only through Revelation, or, to put it more exactly, as the God who acts and carries out history. And this, too, not in the general sense that He, as creator and preserver of all existence also guides the actions of men, but a very special history which also is based upon a covenant, the incarnation of the Son of God who has atoned for the sins of mankind, and "in his blood" has made of men the new people of God. (Luke 22:20) From this covenant there arises a new, divinely guided history whose purpose is to realize the new kingdom of God.

This "kingdom" does not signify any abstract order of values or a generally comprehensible form of human society, but the world of grace and love of the living God and the transformation which everything human, indeed everything created undergoes therein. The very first message of Jesus announces the approach of this kingdom. In the "fulness of time," in which the history ripens toward its crisis, it is to be realized (Mark 1:14), and renewed admonitions and parables bring it close to man. Right action is faith in the growth of this kingdom and love which serves it in daily activities.

Jesus' message about providence also does not mean something like the hellenistic world order, but rather the divine guidance of history which is directed toward the realization of the holy kingdom, but at the same time the guidance of the destiny of every individual so that the one takes place in and through the other. "Seek ye therefore first the kingdom of God and his justice, and all these things [necessary for life] shall be added unto you." (Matt. 6:33)

The justice of God, then, means that He fulfils His promises to man, and the justice of man consists in placing himself within the covenant, seeking God's kingdom first, putting it before all else and trusting God's holy guidance. (Matt. 6:33ff.) The Lord's Prayer expresses the attitude which should prevail here.

Of course, the admonition to justice is combined with the admonition to follow Christ, which includes "taking up the cross." But this too is not to be a general ethical attitude of stoical or ascetic nature, but rather the personal relation of the believer to Christ, his Savior. (Matt. 16:24) Here again the commandment is stripped of every abstract form and is revealed as the claim of God's love addressed to each individual person.

If we look farther, at the act of God which shall conclude history and give to all existence its eternally valid definition, the last judgment, then we see that love of God is set up as the criterion for each man's judgment. But again this love is not the generally ethical value which results from the character of a human personality as such, but it is love of Christ which expresses and realizes itself in every act of love of neighbor. "For I was hungry and you gave me to eat; I was thirsty and you gave me to drink; I was a stranger and you took me in; [I was] naked and you covered me, sick, and you visited me; I was in prison and you came to me—as long as you did it to one of these my least brethren you did it to me." (Matt. 25:35–40) It is Christ, then, who steps into every encounter of the believer with his neighbor and operates the mystery of relationship.

And finally that event in which everything, creation, redemption and sanctification, shall be fulfilled, namely the birth of "the new man" and the coming into existence of "the new world," is expressed by the revelation of Christ and the eternal consummation of his kingdom: "And I saw a new heaven and a new earth. For the first heaven and the first earth were gone and the sea is now no more. And I saw the holy city, the new Jerusalem, coming down out of heaven from God, prepared as a bride adorned for her husband. And I heard a great voice from the throne, saying, 'Behold the tabernacle of God with men, and he will dwell with them. And they shall be his people and God himself with them shall be their God.'" (Apoc. 21:1–3)

The final conclusions of this line of thought were drawn by St. Paul. In his lifetime the true meaning of the old covenant had largely faded from sight. It was generally considered a kind of juristic action in which two parties undertake mutual responsibilities and acquire rights.

Of course the difference, which results from the sovereignty of God and the humanity of man and which nothing can bridge, was retained. But the nature of the human "achievement," that is, the fulfilling of the law, is emphasized to such an extent that it must lead to the view that by this fulfilling as such man is justified before God and acquires a legal claim to the fulfilment of God's promises. The pharisaical doctrine and practice comes into being, which includes a great seriousness and constant willingness to take pains and make sacrifices, but the decisive thing, the fact that everything which comes from God is grace, moves into the background.

Saul of Tarsus, the pupil of the Pharisees, was a man filled with a deep sense of his own sin and a consuming desire for justice, but also a mighty urge toward sanctification through his own power. His epistles, especially the Epistle to the Romans, show how in such a character this urge becomes poisoned and leads to despair. The immediate expression of this *impasse* was the persecution of the early Christian community of which the book of Acts tells us. (7:58ff.)

The experience on the journey to Damascus, of which the book of Acts also tells (9:1ff.) brought the solution, and in such a way that Paul realized that there can be no justice through our own actions, but that justice and salvation are both of grace. The whole order of the Old Testament, Paul continues, had the task of showing the nature and enormity of sin and the impossibility of justification by human power. Man—both the individual and the race as a whole—is incapable of any action that could please God. Of himself he is capable only of evil.* (Rom. 3ff.)

One only is just, Christ, the Redeemer. Although personally sinless He took upon Himself the responsibility for human sin and atoned for it. This atonement and the justice that issues from it He gives to His human brethren by an act of sovereign grace. It becomes their own through faith and baptism—the sacrament in which the old sinful life is put to death and a new life is born, the man who no longer stands in his own justice but in that of Christ. Thereby of course he is in duty bound and also able to do all of which personal good will and desire for the fulfillment of God's will are capable. The mystery of the saving and justifying action of Christ finds its ultimate expression in the sentence of the Epistle to the Galatians, "I live, now not I [as the natural self], but Christ lives in me." (2:20)

What Paul proclaims is absolute mystery. Justice in the Christian sense is the justice of Christ which is given to the believer in his rebirth to a new life. How this is possible, how, to ask a plain question, the moral character or justice of one person can become the property of another person, this can be answered reasonably only if we understand the whole relation as the fruit of a sovereign divine action, an action in which the

---

* Of course this train of thought must be accepted as what it is: a definite aspect of the whole situation, carried to the extreme. That the Old Testament also had a very positive character, and that a fruitful effort of man in the task of his own sanctification is possible, is shown by the Epistle of St. James and by the whole group of the "silent ones in the land," to which belonged persons like the mother of Jesus, Elizabeth, Zacharias and others.

creative power which was first revealed in the conception and realization of the world, reaches its highest peak.

It is true that the New Testament idea of justice has largely lost its true meaning in Christian thought. Many circumstances have contributed to this. One was the necessity of having general norms for moral life, norms which would be comprehensible even to a non-Christian environment. These norms were found by explaining the biblical teaching by means of concepts which belonged to general ethical thought. But the result of this was that the true meaning of what was called "justice" in the Pauline sense faded more and more. Then theology also required concepts with which to build a connected system of ethics. These were found in philosophy, and this also brought it about that what St. Paul meant by justice was assimilated to the general notion. And finally the whole Christian revelation and the life of faith which was based upon it was included in the history of culture, and Christianity was thought of as one epoch of this history, as the working out of an individualistic or altruistic or social or some other way of thinking.

In the course of these occurrences, which reciprocally affected each other, there came about what we call the "secularization" of Christianity, an event whose disturbing effects are very evident in our day. In consequence of this it becomes more and more necessary to distinguish the themes of Revelation from the philosophic and cultural conceptions which were used to explain them, and at the same time to show that the true thought of Revelation is capable of producing effects for human existence which are quite beyond the power of the vague and faded concepts of general ethical thought.

If we seriously consider the personal implications of these thoughts which Revelation brings to us, must not our deepest self-consciousness rebel?

This tells us—and what it says is true, for the glory of our humanity depends upon it—that we are persons. It holds true for each one of us: My deepest consciousness bears witness to the fact that I am a person. Then is it possible that I can be redeemed by the act of another, that is, freed from my guilt, and justified, that means, declared "just" before the absolute judgment? Can God's eternal Son give me a share in his justice, that is, his own personal ethical character?

Guilt is not merely something which hangs upon me; it is not some characteristic that could also be different, but it is bound up with my self in that closeness which we call "responsibility." I cannot free myself from this, however much it burdens me, but I must accept it. And if my finite ethical force is no match for the greatness of this debt, then I must simply remain indebted. For in this debt—and it is this fact that makes it so profound—there lies not only my misfortune, but also my dignity, misused, it is true; for it is only what is done in freedom, and that means in the dignity of the person, that can be called a "debt." Hence the question arises: is it possible that this debt should be removed from me, as the message of salvation states, by "another"; that is, Jesus Christ?

Likewise "to be just" is a freely willed ethical value belonging to the person. This value is not merely something that is externally, juridically attached to me but it is also fixed by that strictness which comes from responsibility. From this also I cannot detach myself. For example, I cannot say that an ethical value, no matter how much it appeals to me, shall be attributed to me if I have not realized it in the responsibility of freedom. If I have not done this then I must simply admit, in the honesty of an ethical judgment, that I do not possess this value.

All this gives rise to the following question: Is it possible that the debt can be taken from me in the manner of which the message of salvation speaks, "through another"? And also that the value which stands validly before the absolute judgment can be given to me through this "other"? Is there any communion which so bridges the distinction between "I" and "not I" that this substitution can take place?

Here lurks a danger to which many—and no mean spirits—have succumbed, namely the danger of equating "person" and "absolute person."

But the basic character of my human self-experience consists precisely in this fact that I experience myself as person but also as finite, as created, and that means entirely depending upon "alien power." This seems to involve us in a contradiction.

Two definite considerations lead us out of this difficulty. The first indicates that God is not "I," but simply and in absolute majesty "He," yet at the same time is in relation to me not "another" or "the great other," but God the Creator, who is above every category that determines finite creation as such. The second is that we must not think of God's creative act as uniform, no matter to what it is directed but that He, as act, contains the whole plenitude which belongs to his work as such. God creates mere things by commanding "It shall be!"; for example, "Be light made, and light was made." (Gen. 1) But God creates man in "breathing His breath" into the form made of the stuff of earth (Gen. 2:7), and that means, in turning personally to him and saying: "Thou, be!"

This is the basis of created personality, and everything depends on man's understanding himself from this viewpoint.

The personality of man is not absolute like that of God, but it is finite. His freedom is not autocratic but it is a gift. His existence is not based upon himself; it is created. The sin that man commits he commits by a freedom bestowed upon him and he realizes the value of moral integrity through a freedom given to him, not an absolute and original freedom. Similarly, the identity between his own decision and his person is not absolute but finite and that means that it is a gift. So when the love of God for lost mankind is so profound that the Creator intervenes in love for His creature and the eternal Son, sent by the Father, becomes man and takes the responsibility of His brethren upon Himself, he does not deprive them of the dignity of their freedom. He does not place the atonement upon their shoulders like a garment or write above them the verdict of justice like a judicial pronouncement, but a unique identification takes place. The Redeemer bestows His atonement and His justice upon man, yet it remains His own, not man's accomplishment. Herein is consummated that love which has given man his existence as his very own but as finite and bestowed, just as it gave him his personal freedom and responsibility as really his own but as a gift.

When I say "I," I do not say it autonomously, but as based upon that "Thou" which God speaks to me. I say it as truly my own "I," but as coming from God, and so dependent upon the keyword of my existence which is "I through Him," or more correctly and piously, "I through Thee." In this way I am also absolved, but through Christ's atonement; I am justified, but through His justice.

(These ideas are not deductions from a natural philosophical dialectic of the person, but an attempt to follow through premises and conclusions provided by Revelation.)

What we have said leads to a further question: If the justice which is given to me as a Christian, and which alone is valid before the eternal judge, is the justice of Christ, then must not everything that we call conscience, responsibility, and moral endeavor, be wiped out? Must not this bring about an attitude which is as much indolence as discouragement?

The answer comes from the same line of thought which we have developed: Existence is given to man so that he may take it with a sense of responsibility and use it rightly. It is not really given to him, but it is "entrusted" to him, just as the world was given to him in the form of a sacred trust, that he might "cultivate it and keep it." (Gen. 2:15) So also the justice of Christ is not man's possession but a trust, the last and most precious gift of God's love placed in the hand of man's freedom that he may "administer" it. (Matt. 25:14ff.)

Moreover, the doctrine of Revelation, that man is absolved and justified in Christ, means something active. The justice given by Christ is not merely a "juridical adjudication" but a task and a power and it is realized in the believer who rightly understands it as an urge to do God's will in every way and to work for His kingdom. (Gen. and Matt. loc. cit.)

So we can understand that the Apostle who more than all others has proclaimed this mystery, St. Paul, could say of himself, "By the grace of God I am what I am; and his grace in me has not been void, but I have labored more abundantly than they all; yet not I, but the grace of God with me." (1 Cor. 15:10) The whole mystery of grace and its relation to freedom is here expressed, and everything that might be added would only repeat the same thing: as soon as the believer rightly understands the revelation that he exists in the justice of Christ, there awakens in him a great seriousness and he brings forth all the fruits of moral virtue.

Of course, there is also brought about what Christian ethics calls "humility." It is contained in the Apostle's words which we have quoted, "not I but the grace of God with me." And yet he had just said, "I have labored more than they all." This is a continuation of the basic truth of Christian existence which he expresses in the Epistle to the Galatians when he says, "I live, yet not I, but Christ in me." (2:20)

Hence all Christian action has this twofold character: the seriousness, the readiness, the efforts that Christ's justice shall bear fruit; but at the same time that which is expressed in the words of Jesus: "When you shall have done all these things—say, 'We are unprofitable servants.'" (Luke 17:10) These two points are together the basis of Christian action. They are also the basis of the last incomprehensible character which belongs to all Christian action, that it is the doer's own and yet a gift, belonging to him yet the property of Christ.

This thought should be added to all that has been said in the preceding meditations. In order not to endanger the simplicity of our images of the various values, we refrained from working this theme into our account of the virtues. It is left to the reader to do this in his own meditations. The virtues of which we have spoken then become ways in which the justice of Christ becomes fruitful. They receive a new fulness and a new character, that which is meant by the much misused word, "holy."

Perhaps the reader may ask how he is to understand all this. Only human matters can be actually "understood." And unless we are rationalists we know that we are not even wholly successful in understanding those. For man is not simply "man" but he is man created and called, the one into whose hand God's confidence has given the world. Therefore he is the finite being, "man" but he is also created, called, and taken into confidence by God—and who could say that he understands that? And when we add the climax, that God himself steps into the existence of the believer, that He becomes man and without endangering the personality of the believer, is actually, according to St. Paul, the one living in him—how can this be "understood"? But we have been given not only natural reason but believing reason enlightened by Revelation. This enlightened reason understands, insofar as grace and "purity of heart" (Matt. 5:8) enable it to do so.

The Word of God

On Faith, Hope, and Charity

The Word of God

I

"In the Beginning was the Word" (John 1:1–18)

The beginning of St. John's Gospel, more exactly, the first eighteen verses of his first chapter, the so-called Prologue, have always made a particular impression upon the believer. Many of its words touch the most hidden recesses of the spirit—especially the very first—"In the beginning was——." One of the eternal questions of mankind is indeed "What was in the beginning?" In that beginning of time at which we arrive—or believe that we can arrive—if we retrace the hours and years and ages. What was, before anything had happened? What was the first thing that happened, and how was it brought about? And the beginning of being, the roots of things which we reach or believe that we can reach when we grope through the structure of things, the interaction of forces, the tissue of causes? What was, when nothing as yet existed? What was the first thing from which all else came, the essential, which gave its law to all the rest, and from what power did it come?

Our consciousness seems to have two answers to these questions. The first consists in explaining that there is no answer, or more exactly, that none is required, because the question itself is false. There is no original cause and no first or ultimate force, because beyond all that we fathom a new riddle arises. Indeed, everything is in itself a closed cycle. The world is that which has no beginning or end, the whole and the all, the closed cycle, and no question can transcend it. The other answer says: the movement of being is upward, from darkness and chaos into light and form. Hence in the beginning there is voiceless being, blind necessity, unconscious urge, the primitive force.

Revelation replies: there is a beginning and at the beginning stands the word and its creative act. We do not know as yet what this "word" means—for surely it means something special and of that we shall have much more to say—but one thing is clear immediately: it is something bright, extended, free, a clearness of mind and a capacity for responsibility, not "nature" but "spirit."

II

The Prologue begins: "In the beginning was the Word, and the Word was with God [*pros theon*, turned toward God] and the Word was [of its nature] God."

The beginning of which we have been speaking is that of the world, the same of which another passage of Scripture speaks, which also begins with this word, namely the book of Genesis, whose first sentence reads, "In the beginning God created the heavens and the earth." But if we consider it carefully, the beginning of which the Prologue of St. John's Gospel speaks lies even beyond this. He does not mean the beginning of the world, but beginning itself. It is not so named because it is the origin of something that came later, but because it is before all that can ever be. It is analogous to the term Lord as applied by the Scripture to God. He is not Lord because there is something over which He rules, but in Himself and of His very essence, the one absolutely free, powerful, self-possessed and self-sufficient. So this Beginning is prime reality and being, the eternal, fulfilled forever through itself and in itself.

Of this being we are told that an eternal speech goes on within it. That which existed in itself in the beginning is not dumb but speaks—and this means also that it is spiritual, possessing the power of reason, and free.

The word is the fruit of speech. In the word the hidden inner meaning is revealed. The truth appears and becomes a possibility and power in the structure of the situation. With man this word is a fleeting thing: scarcely has it been spoken when it dies away and remains only in the memory. The word of which St. John speaks does not fade away but is essential and real like God Himself. So it is said of this word that it "was" in the beginning, was and is forever, and itself (of its essence) was God.

The history of the word is recounted later, its creating and acting, its coming and dwelling in the world, its dealings and its destiny. Hence it is a being. In the beginning, in the original existence, there is God and His word, the one speaking and that which is spoken.

But what does God speak? That which is alone sufficient for Him to speak: Himself. Himself, the all-inclusive abyss of meaning, the infinite power of being, He puts into the expression of the word.

And to whom does He speak this word? Our word goes to another person, and, when it is perfect, to the one who belongs to us in love, the living "Thou" of our "I." But to whom does the eternal word of God go? There is no one who would be capable of receiving it, only He Himself. But how can He be His own hearer, His own "Thou"? If we correctly understand the Scripture, it tells us: God's word, on its way to Him who would receive it, takes up a position in itself and becomes an ear that perceives. It is not the word that goes to another but that which has arrived in itself. Forming itself from the fulness of what is spoken it becomes itself a "Thou."

So at the end of the Prologue, in the eighteenth verse, the word is called by another name. There it is called "the Son" and He who speaks it "the Father." "No one has seen God (in Himself) at any time. The only-begotten,

God (in essence) who is resting at the bosom of the Father, he has brought us knowledge (of Him)."

But even now we wish to emphasize what should be said after every sentence of what follows; namely, that nothing is explained by what we are saying here, not a fibre, not a nook of the mystery of which Revelation speaks. We can only trace its sentences, call attention to details and draw connecting lines to that which is familiar to us, in order to come closer to its message.

Of this word—let us use the more familiar Greek term, of this *logos*—it is said that it was "turned toward God." The next sentence repeats the statement, hence it must be important.

It means that the *logos* does not depart, as our human word does when it seeks the one who shall receive it, and if it does not find him it vanishes in space. The *logos* does not depart; it remains. The word "remain" is dear to St. John. It means the opposite of parting, of leaving, of desertion and faithlessness; it means union and abiding, intimacy and faithfulness, ful-fillment and eternity. Compare sentences such as this: "Let that remain in you which you have heard from the beginning. If that remains in you which you have heard from the beginning, then you will remain in the Son and in the Father. And this is the promise that He has promised us, eternal life." (I John 2:24–5; similarly 3:14, 17, 24; 4:13, 15–16, etc.) In this way the *logos* remains in God.

Even more: "He is turned toward God." A sacred expression. The word, spoken and sent on its way, as is the nature of all speech, takes up a position, as it were, in itself. It becomes its own ear, is perceived and understood of itself and turns back to Him who has spoken it. It becomes an "answer" (return-word), an assurance of agreement in the common possession of truth. We must again refer to the last verse of the Prologue. There this re-maining and returning is expressed by the phrase that the "only-begotten Son is resting at the bosom of the Father." Now the whole intimacy of the relation is revealed: the "answer" is faithfulness, closeness, love. And when we know St. John a little better, we feel a breath of his own experience passing through the words, for he was "the disciple whom Jesus loved." At the Last Supper he rested on the bosom of the Master, and that was probably not the only time. He knew something of the heart of God.

It is the triune life of God that is spoken of here. The manner in which there is "I" and "Thou" in God, the way in which He is person and yet has community.

Two faces appear, arising together and turned toward each other, the Father's and the Son's. The third, that of the Spirit, is not mentioned here. St. John speaks of Him in another connection, just as solemn as this one, namely in the discourse of our Lord at the Last Supper. There the Lord says, "These things have I spoken to you, abiding with you, but the Paraclete, the Holy Ghost, whom the Father will send in my name, he will teach you all things, and bring all things to your mind, whatsoever I shall have said to you." And again, "But I tell you the truth: it is expedient for you that I go; for if I go not, the Paraclete will not come to you; but if I go, I will send him to you.... But when he, the Spirit of truth, is come, he will teach you all truth. For he shall not speak of himself; but...he shall receive of mine and shall show it to you." (John 14:25–6; 16:7–14)

We cannot here attempt to penetrate these sentences. They would tell us that the mystery of God's speaking is accomplished in the Holy Spirit. That God speaks, and speaks in this way, that His word has this reality, but does not become a second God, that it proceeds living and rational from the Father, but does not depart, turning about, as it were, and turning to Him, that in God there is a true "I" and "Thou", and yet unity and oneness and complete intimacy—all this is possible only in the Spirit. But if we wish to perceive this mystery of the divine intimacy as a living impulse then we must read the close of the last discourse, the seventeenth chapter. It is completely pervaded by the Holy Spirit.

III

"Through it all things were made and without it nothing was made of all that was made."

That of which we have been speaking took place in the primeval sphere of the divinity. Now comes the account of the deeds and adventures of the *Logos*.

His first deed was the creation. In Genesis we read: "In the beginning God created the heavens and the earth," and then the interior progress of this creation is recounted. But how does God create? By speaking. Not by letting the world spring forth from Himself, or by externalizing Himself in it, or by imagining it; but by His word, His command. "God said, 'Let there be . . .'" St. John tells us the deeper secret of that which Genesis shows us at work, for behind the word that turns outward in divine creation, there is the interior word of the divine life. The former is a free radiation of the latter, free because creation is not of necessity but comes from God as deliberately willed action; but a living radiation, because in the *Logos*, the eternal expression of the divine mind, all possibilities of divine creation are likewise expressed. God creates through His eternal word, the Father through the Son—and let us add—in the power of the Holy Spirit.

There is a clear and definite distinction between the world-concept of Revelation and all others. In the beginning we find not that to which the present age reduces everything, mere nature with all the reserve, determinism, stuffiness, even stupidity, which is implied in this concept, but the bright, free, responsive word of the living God. From this everything proceeds.

St. John emphasizes this: absolutely everything. Nothing that was made was made without it. There are no lateral channels of becoming, no other sources of being—nothing that is independent of God. In no sense is there an autonomous world, which by that very fact would necessarily be an evil one. Everything comes from God, everything comes from His word. Whenever we meet something in the world which is estranged from God, denies Him or opposes Him, as a being it also originates from His word and has received from Him the very power by which it rebels against Him. Of itself it has only the evil will, the rebellious disposition. Nor is there a principle of evil, a "force" which of its nature "always wills what is evil," but only the will which was created good and became unfaithful, the power that is capable of good but fell away from God.

Wherever man goes he meets God's property. Nowhere is there a realm which essentially and rightfully belongs to another, nowhere are there enclaves of reality where man could confront what is really foreign. All is the property of God. Perhaps we must undergo certain periods of desolation, certain experiences of merciless wickedness in order to understand what that means. There are moments in which the words: "Everything belongs to God, and what appears otherwise is only rebellion against Him," become the only support of our hope.

IV

"In Him was life and the life was the light of men. And the light shineth in darkness and the darkness did not comprehend it."

So the world was made, God's work through the *Logos*. Of this *Logos* it is now said that He is life and light. The two words belong together. They explain, interpret and fulfill each other. The God who creates the world and whose power everywhere pervades the world is life. He abides in Himself, breathes and blooms from Himself, works from His own beginning, and in working belongs to Himself. This life is not dull, not a mere fermentation, urge, stream, or whatever the present day means by that word, but such that His nature can be expressed by the word "He is light." The first epistle of St. John, the echo of his Gospel, tells us, "And this is the message that we have received from Him and proclaim to you, that God is light and there is no darkness in Him." (John 1:5) "Light" means clearness of mind, breadth of consciousness, freedom and responsibility, brightness and sublimity, grandeur and glory—in a word—"spirit." "Spirit," not as our age understands it, but "life." The light here spoken of is not merely consciousness, hard validity, dry concept, cold order, overpowering law, but warmth, fruitfulness, a streaming and self-giving fulness, intimacy, closeness and love.

Out of this the world was created, and where it seems contradictory, the will of man, into whose hand it was delivered, has spoiled it. So it is, and is it not a joy to be permitted to think this?

This life of the *Logos* "was the light of men." This does not mean the sun which strikes the eyes of man and causes him to be able to perceive objects and go upon his way—yet it is this also. For the sight of our eyes is much more inclusive than the sense-perception of the animals, because it reaches even into the spirit. The renewal of understanding which is the task imposed upon us, the heirs of a dying age of reason, consists largely in rediscovering what the eye is, namely, not merely the beginning but the half of all understanding; in learning once again what true and complete seeing is, namely the grasping of the original reality. Then we shall succeed also in the second half, the right comprehending and naming of the essence of things. When this seeing, which reaches from the surface of the body even into the spirit, is properly carried out, then things reveal themselves therein as truth—that is light. And now St. John says they cannot do this of themselves. Of their own nature they would remain closed. They open to truth only in another which gives them the ability to do so, and this is the true light. The Greeks had a presentiment of this when they spoke of the idea. They said that the understanding of an object did not consist in our perceiving qualities and establishing proportions, but that it meant that what had previously been closed to us opened in the spirit as truth. But this it could do only in its eternal prototype, the idea. When the spirit had properly striven and the time was ripe, then the idea would rise from the object, and in the idea the object would be revealed, and this act of becoming light and transparent they said was the truth. In this way they created a concept which later was ready at hand when St. John wished to explain the eternal nature of his Master, and which he used. The condition of all understanding, the light that reveals all things so that the spirit of man can behold, find direction, satisfy itself with truth—that is the spiritual power of the eternal word, the *Logos*.

It shines in the darkness. To begin with, all is darkness, voiceless being, locked in that which we call earth and time, but everywhere the light of the *Logos* waits, ready to shine forth. But then we read that the darkness did not comprehend the light. This darkness is evidently different from that of which we have just spoken. The former was the natural veiling of that which is not yet known, the darkness which bears the spark in itself; the latter has shut itself up within itself and refuses the light which comes from the *Logos*. This refusal is sin. God created the world in such a way that the light of the *Logos* shall shine out for men from all that exists. Everything should be for them a living revelation and hence a way to God. Then each thing would have become a call, an outstretched hand, a means of returning home, as we read in the Epistle to the Romans: "Because that which is known of God is manifest in them. For God hath manifested it unto them. For the invisible things of him, from the creation of the world, are clearly seen, being understood by the things that are made, his eternal power also and his divinity." (Romans 1:19–20) Men were unwilling, and so a veil came over creation. Everything became rigid. Things shut themselves up and directions were changed.

V

"There was a man sent from God, whose name was John. This man came for a witness to give testimony of the light, that all men might believe through him. He was not the light, but was to give testimony of the light."

The thought of the apostle began in the eternal existence of God, proceeded thence to the beginning of things and their creation, and then turned to the width of this world, the light that comes from the *Logos* and is everywhere. Now he enters upon the history of the explicit revelation in the moment before its final hour, when the precursor, John, appears and points to the Messias.

The manner in which the apostle speaks of the Baptist has a particular character—we notice it again when the text later returns to him (VII). John had come to point out the Messias; that completed his task. At the moment when the Messias appeared, John stepped back. His disciples, however, did not understand this self-effacement, but clung to him as their teacher and master. We perceive the possibility of such solidarity when the Gospels speak of the disciples of the Baptist. After the latter had been executed, the circle seems to have remained as a close community and to have set up the figure of their master in opposition to Jesus. The apostle attacks this attitude. The movement must have been of considerable importance and long duration, for St. John's Gospel was written almost seventy years after the death of the Baptist. In view of this we can understand the peculiar emphasis of the sentences. John was indeed sent by God, a prophet who was to give testimony of the light and teach men to believe in it. But he was not himself the light, was not the essential revelation, as his disciples evidently maintained, but only the herald and precursor.

VI

The following sentences of the text are closely connected with what precedes: "The true light that enlightens every man was He who was to come into the world. (And He came.) He was in the world and the world was made by him, and the world knew him not. He came unto his own, and his own received him not. But as many as received him, he gave them power to be made the sons of God, to them that believe in his name, who are born, not of blood, nor of the will of the flesh, nor of the will of man, but of God."

The light, whose rising signifies salvation, was not John, but He who was to come into the world. Usually the sentence is translated: "He was the true light that enlightens every man who comes into this world." But this changes the meaning. Actually the word *come* refers not to men but to the light, and so contrasts sharply with the claim of John's disciples.

At the same time it expresses something tremendous, which we must take into the depths of our soul. The *Logos*, Who is the eternal light, the expression of God Himself, Whose fulness of wisdom and power has created and preserves all things, Whose original idea stands behind all that is and makes it able to flame out in the spirit as truth—this *Logos* himself appears as such in history. This is something before which we must have stood in amazement and whose enormity we must have felt if we are to have a clear awareness of what Christianity means. That God's power of light lifts His own being eternally into knowledge is a truth that teaches us to adore; that everything in the world comes from it gives us holy confidence; that everywhere in things there waits the divine spark, ready to flame up as soon as a spirit of good will approaches it, fills us with gratitude and with remorse as well. All this is great, but our inner being responds to it with a certain readiness. But now something quite different is stated: not only that this eternal power of light has created all things, pervades all things and enlightens every willing spirit, but that it appeared in history as Someone; at this definite time and no other; in that place, not elsewhere; with this particular nature and quality and not another. This is something of quite another order than that which has been previously recounted. And so the text leaves no doubt about it. The fact that the true light "is he who was to come into the world" is decisive for everything, faith and unfaith, salvation and perdition. This decision is so difficult that the worse alternative seems more probable than the better one. When John was writing, he was an old man. Seventy years had passed since Christ had returned home to the Father—more than a whole life-span. John had proclaimed the sacred truth and fought for it, had penetrated it by his thought, his prayer, his life. But always there remained in him the overwhelming wonder how that could happen which did happen: that the *Logos*, the light itself, the boundless fulness of wisdom and creative power, came into the world, that He stood in the world and shone, that He spoke, associated with men, acted, and yet was not received.

"The world was made through Him and yet the world did not know Him." What the world was, it was through Him; it had received from Him the power to think, to will, to decide—and all this it used to resist Him. "He came to His own and His own did not receive Him." He was the Lord. Things were His property, men the members of His household. There was a close bond of relationship between Him and men, not only by right and authority but interiorly, in that He had created them and loved them. The depths of their being should have yearned toward Him, as a moving object to its proper place, as kindred blood to its like—and yet—when He came they did not receive Him.

What happened is not only incomprehensible but terrible. Not only wrong, but in a horrible way contrary to nature. Something powerful and glorious—freedom—here became perverted. The final perfection of God's creation consists in the fact that He not only places His creature in true being, but sets it free to stand and move, to be the cause of its own activity, capable of decision and responsibility. This means the possibility of turning to God of its own accord, but also the possibility of not doing this. This should never have happened, but it did happen. How that could come to pass no one understands.

But if the *Logos* himself stood in the world, if He had created the world and by His power kept it in existence, if He was the Lord and everything belonged to Him, why did He permit that? Here again there is something mysterious, which, however, belongs to the inmost truth of revelation: He had the power, but—dare we say it—was not permitted to use it.

Whatever is of a low order forces its way immediately: bodily needs, movements of defence and protection, essential communications. The higher something rises, the more it loses the immediate force because it must pass through the spirit and the heart of man. The inmost being must open to it more and more purely. Very great and noble things have no immediate force at all, only their inner goodness and nobility. They appeal neither to natural urges nor to utility, neither to fear nor to ambition, or whatever the forces may be which arise spontaneously, but only to freedom, the depths of the heart, the heights of the spirit. Therefore they are wholly dependent on the responsibility of conscience and are defenceless in the world. Nobility consists in perceiving the voice of that which is lofty and consequently powerless, and in defending it. This is true even in the world, and much more so in God. When the living light came into the world it did not wish to blind and overthrow. It could have done so; that is shown by the mysterious events that punctuate the public ministry of Jesus: for instance, when He, at the moment when the raging mob at Nazareth was on the point of casting Him from the cliff, turned around and "passing through the midst of them went His way" (Luke 4:30); when they wished to destroy Him but did not dare to seize Him "because his hour had not yet come" (John 8:20); when in the garden of Gethsemane He asks the soldiers whom they are seeking and to their reply "Jesus of Nazareth" answers "I am he" and they fall to the ground (John 18:6). We should recall too the incident of the fig tree, when He approaches it in order to find fruit and, not finding any, curses the tree, which promptly withers. (Matt. 21:19) In Jesus we feel an incomprehensible power combined with perfect serenity. He releases this power when there is need of help or of a proof of goodness and truth, and then a miracle takes place. He never uses it to overawe or overthrow His opponents, to win over or stir up the people or even to gain the assent of His audience more easily. It is a tremendous thing to see how He Who possesses all power does not use it, so that the truth may appear only in the majesty of its meaning, and man may speak his "yea" to it quite freely, in no way compelled or even influenced.

The succeeding sentences can be understood only if we take them, not in isolation, but in their varied relations. They tell us what the *Logos* does for those who turn to Him readily. "He gives them power to become children of God." But only those are capable of such turning who are "born not of blood or of the will of the flesh or of the will of man, but of God." Their readiness, their whole disposition comes not from nature or from the powers of the species or of sex, but from above, from God. They have within them a new principle of existence, bestowed by God Himself. But if that is the case, they are already children of God. Jesus Himself says that only that man can perceive the sacred majesty of the incarnate one, can hear His voice, understand His message, receive Him as Savior, who is already "of God." "You are from beneath; I am from above. You are of this world; I am not of this world. Why do you not understand my speech? Because you cannot hear my words.... He who is of God hears the word of God. Therefore you do not hear it because you are not of God." (John 8:23, 43, 47) In this case one thing is not earlier and the other later, but they are simultaneous, and the one through the other. He who receives the incarnate God, to him He gives power to become the child of God; but no one can receive Him who is not already "born of God"; that is, His child. In order to receive the *Logos*, a man must "hear His voice" and "understand His words"; but he can do that only if he has "the ear" for it, and that is equivalent to the new life itself. These sentences seem contradictory but they are not. Neither are they the expression of inexact thinking or pious emphasis. Rather, they express something that cannot be said otherwise. Let us recall the manner in which St. Augustine, who is closely akin to the Apostle John, speaks in the first chapters of his *Confession*. There too one thing is not derived from another, but a whole appears, indeed the whole itself, the new life. Before the Incarnate God, from Him and toward Him, this new life awakens—at that time when it does awaken—when man wills, which he can only do when God grants that he will it. But He grants it to everyone who is ready, for all are to be saved. "Come to me, all," Jesus said (Matt. 11:28). The secret of free will and that of grace here flow inseparably into one.

VII

"And the Word was made flesh and dwelt among us, and we saw his glory, the glory as it were of the only begotten of the Father, full of grace and truth. John beareth witness of him and crieth out, saying: 'This was he of whom I spoke: He that shall come after me is preferred before me, because he was before me.'"

And now, prepared from the eternal beginning, from the origin of the world, from His operation in all of creation, and finally through the messenger who had been sent, the *Logos* steps into history.

The Word became flesh—became man—and set up his tent among us—dwelt among us, according to the expression of an ancient pastoral people. Again and again we must tell ourselves that we are men of a later time; even worse, heirs of an age that has everywhere destroyed the meaning of the sacred words. So if we wish to understand the divine message correctly we must first restore to its words that sacred newness which belongs to them by nature. Never, though men pondered it for thousands of years, could they comprehend and assimilate what God's words express. Always, no matter how often he may have heard or read them, they meet the hearer or reader as coming from God's holy hiddenness, at once judging and saving. They are "new" in their nature. This newness is never removed, but it can be covered by superficiality, neglect and custom, and so receive a specious appearance of familiarity.

The sentence of which we are speaking we have heard very often, so perhaps we no longer perceive the immensity of its message. It tells of the eternal Word, the *Logos*, the sum of all that we call intelligence and being, first of all and originally that of God Himself, but in God also of all that which may exist or be created. This *Logos*, which is perfectly simple and yet immeasurably rich, is no order of forms and laws, no world of prototypes and arrangements, but *Someone*, He the living Son of the eternal Father. We can stand before Him, face to face. We can speak to Him and He answers, indeed, He Himself gives us the power to stand before Him and He can grant our request. We can love Him and He is able to give us a communion which reflects the intimacy in which He lies upon the bosom of the Father, and which St. John experienced when his Master permitted him to lay his head upon His heart. This fact established a contrast to everything which natural philosophy and piety can experience or invent. This *Logos*, this one and all, steps into history and becomes man. He does not merely touch a man, filling him with His life, lifting him in a vision beyond his own limits, creating a prophet who burns and shines for Him, but He Himself becomes man so that we can say, "This is He!" If St. John had been merely a prophet or a mystic his spirit would have risen up in indignation against this thought. He would have sided with the *Logos* and so sided with his own mind, and would have said, "That cannot be. The eternal God, before whose power the world is as a breath, can never limit Himself in this way." At that time there was a powerful intellectual movement which did maintain this—Gnosticism. It is in opposition to this that St. John speaks: that this did happen is the very essence of Christianity. If you remove this, then all depth of thought, all intellectual keenness, all ecstasy that you may have is nothing. Even worse, it is false, corrupt and destructive, for you have "dissolved Christ."

This fact, that the eternal *Logos* steps into time and history, that He does this, if we may say so, for life and death, and remains irrevocably the One Who came, Who became man; that He who shines in omnipotence takes up into the condition of His eternal divine life this particle of reality, the human nature united to Him—when you hear this, says St. John, when you feel what this means, when the danger of indignation rises in your mind, the danger of laughter in your feelings and senses, then you are standing before the decision whether you wish to be Christians or not. If you wish it, if you overcome your resistance to "the scandal and the foolishness" which threaten here, if you stand and confess your willingness, then you have truly "overcome the world," for you have broken the standards of the true and the good, the worthy and the right which come from the world and have received new standards from God's revelation. The first epistle of St. John, which is in many ways an echo of his gospel, makes this decision very clear: "By this you know the spirit of God: every spirit that confesses Jesus Christ who has come in the flesh is of God, but every spirit that does not confess Jesus is not of God. And this is the nature of the anti-Christ, of whom you have heard that he is coming, and he is already in the world. You are of God, children, and have overcome the world, for He who is in you is greater than he who is in the world. They are of the world, therefore they speak of the world, and the world hears them. We are of God. He who knows God hears us; he who is not of God does not hear us. By this we know the spirit of truth and the spirit of error." (I John 4:2–6)

But because St. John is opposed to the Gnostics—who declared that matter, the body and the senses were evil, doing exactly what the calumniators of Christianity accuse Christians of doing—and because he himself is a Christian and so does not despise the body, nor the senses, nor matter, he raises a rampart against all such calumny by saying not merely "The Word became man," but "The Word became flesh."

And now his personal testimony comes forth: "We saw His glory, the glory as it were of the only-begotten of the Father, full of grace and truth."

Seventy years had passed since this happened, but it was as vivid as if it had been only the day before that He stood among them and they perceived His secret and beheld the revelation which He Himself was. At that time they did not yet understand; they had not yet found their way to complete faith. That did not happen until the day of Pentecost. But what shone forth on that day through the power of the spirit, they had received before.

The apostle speaks of the completion of what we call revelation: the epiphany of God in Christ. Christ not only spoke of God, He Himself was God. And the fact that He was God was clearly visible in Him. The spiritual soul in itself cannot be seen, but in a man's countenance it becomes visible. The face is the spirit become visible. God in Himself cannot be seen—John will say this explicitly later on—but in the incarnate Christ He became visible: Christ is the appearing, the manifest God. He had said so Himself and John reports His Word. When the disciple begged that He would show them the Father of whom He had spoken so impressively, the Lord replied, "Have I been so long a time with you, and have you not known me, Philip? He that seeth me seeth the Father also." (John 14:9) We must not soften this word. He does not mean merely that He proclaims the Father or by His disposition reminds us of Him, but that the Father, God, becomes visible in Him. This seeing is very important to the apostle; therefore He says, "We have seen His glory." And this is echoed by a passage at the opening of his first Epistle, which begins: "That which was from the beginning, which we have heard, which we have seen with our eyes, which we have looked upon, and our hands have handled, of the word of life. For the life was manifested; and we have seen and do bear witness, and declare unto you the life eternal, which was with the Father, and hath appeared to us: that which we have seen and have heard we declare unto you, that you also may have fellowship with us." (I John 1:1–3) We feel the insistence of the threefold repetition. It is not mere doctrine, but behind this seeing and hearing and handling there lie the experiences of the life of the disciples, the countless impressions of daily association, the hours upon the Mount of the Transfiguration, the risen Lord's standing in their midst and the touching of His wounds. The words express the solicitous striving to impress upon the hearer and unfold before him the reality of the statement, "He became flesh."

The "glory" of which John speaks does not mean just any glory, but that splendor of omnipotence which belongs to God alone, and which in the course of sacred history blazes up again and again, around the divine figure in the prophet's account or above the ark of the covenant or in the temple at the time of its dedication. This glory, whose radiance the shepherds beheld in the field, and which the Baptist saw gleaming from the opened heavens above Jesus as He emerged from the Jordan, this was in Christ, and his disciples beheld it.

It was "full of grace and truth." Pure grace, sheer mercy and the opening of the heart of God. But also and always truth—both in one. When truth remains alone, it becomes hard. Here it is dissolved into mercy. When mercy remains alone, it becomes arbitrary. Here it is made firm in truth.

But nothing of this was in the Baptist. He only bore witness to it. He confessed that Jesus "overtook" him, although he "came after him." Not because he was stronger or more efficient, but because he "was before him"; that is, from eternity. It is the same expression that we find Jesus using when he replies to the Pharisees who upbraid him by telling him that Abraham, to whom he refers, had lived before him. His staggering statement is: "Before Abraham was, I am." (John 8:58–9)

VIII

"And of his fulness we have all received, and grace for grace. For the law was given by Moses; grace and truth came by Jesus Christ."

Even earlier there was a hint of something which now comes out very strongly: the fulness in Christ. John had said that they had "seen His glory—full of grace and truth." This must have overwhelmed His disciples again and again: the fulness in Him, the profound depth of truth, the inexhaustible strength, the never-failing power of goodness, the divine creativity. What does it mean when He Himself says, "Come to me, all you who are weary and burdened, and I will refresh you"? He about whom the sick and crippled, the needy and abandoned were thronging. (Matt. 11:28) Before Him the disciples must have had the feeling: He can carry everything. From Him one can obtain all things. He knows the truth that can solve every difficulty. His strength is equal to every need. One can trust Him for everything. There is a beautiful expression of this experience, told also by St. John. After Christ's proclamation of the Eucharist in Capharnaum there came the great defection. As this affected even the inmost circle Jesus asked the apostles: "Will you also go away?" Peter in his distress before the decision was quite at a loss and cast himself upon the Lord: "Lord, to whom shall we go? Thou hast the words of eternal life." (John 6:68) "The words of eternal life"—that was the fulness that was in Him.

Of this fulness they "have all received"—constantly—"grace upon grace." The word is important. It expresses what they have received—not mere understanding, virtue, righteousness, but grace. That which comes from the primary source of love, from the heart of God—warm, renewing, creative. That which reaches beyond all distinction of merit and demerit, achievement and feebleness, the pure beginning.

This is emphasized once more. "For the law was given by Moses"; there was no need of a new law. "Grace and truth came by Jesus Christ." Again the sacred union of grace and truth, each in each. Grace comes from the intimacy of God, but this intimacy is that in which the *Logos* is the truth of the Father.

And at this point—a light seems to shine forth as we notice it—the Gospel for the first time uses the name Jesus Christ.

IX

"No man hath seen God at any time: the only begotten Son who is in the bosom of the Father, he hath declared him."

And now the circle of this truly sacred text closes in a wondrous way. The thought returns to its starting point. God [in Himself] no man has ever seen. He is invisible. "Invisible" does not mean merely that He is a spirit—in this way our soul too would be invisible—but that He is holy. This invisibility St. Paul expresses by saying that God "dwells in light unapproachable." This light is His consuming holiness. (I Tim. 6:16) No creature has ever come within its range. Only the Son knows of it. There the holy fulness of God's being becomes a revealed truth. When this occurs God becomes Father and Son. And the latter, as the only one who knows the Father, turns lovingly toward Him. Jesus himself speaks of this knowledge, saying, in St. Matthew's Gospel, "No one knows the Father but the Son and he to whom it shall please the Son to reveal him. (Matt. 11:27)

Into the description of this knowledge flows the thought of what remained for the apostle the most precious thing in his life—the fact that his head had rested upon the bosom of his Master and that he felt the beating of His Heart: "The only-begotten Son, God [by nature], Who rests upon the bosom of the Father, has brought tidings of Him."

It seems that nothing more remains to be said. This most sacred relation belongs to that sphere of which Cardinal Newman speaks when he says, "God and my soul, nothing else in the world."

It is an immense picture that St. John paints in this brief text about Christ, stretching from eternity into time, spreading from the clearly defined actuality of the figure that walks along the streets of Palestine far out into the universe, living in the passing moment, yet cognizant of the beginning of all things, and even of the primeval beginning beyond time.

And it is no mere construction whose component parts are "the *Logos*" and "the flesh," but it is a living reality. No one has so plainly discerned the face of the Lord as St. John, who knew of the eternal fulness of wisdom of the *Logos*; no one has perceived so clearly the voice of the heart of Jesus as he who spoke of the eternal intimacy of Father and Son in God.

He whom Christian symbolism portrays in the form of the eagle because he soared to the height of the eternal mysteries still remains "the disciple whom Jesus loved" and who lay upon the bosom of his Master. Men have charged John—and it is the most severe charge that could be brought against him—with being no true evangelist, no simple messenger of the reality of Jesus, but a "mystic" and "thinker," one who buries himself in experiences and fabricates webs of thought. Some have even dared to say that he betrayed the plain truth of Jesus to the syncretistic learning and piety of the philosophers and the religious concepts of the time.

These statements are based upon a disbelief which does not wish to admit that Christ is the Son of God, and also upon a kind of sentimentality which considers pure Christianity something childish, idyllic and edifying. Those who speak in this way have forgotten what revelation means—the self-revelation of the living God at the moment of its ultimate manifestation—and wish to prescribe for Him what He must be.

God is neither universal reason nor religious mystique. He is *He*, as He Himself said at the moment when He first mentioned His name: "And God said to Moses, 'I am who I am.' And He added, 'You shall say to the Israelites, the I-am has sent me to you.'" (Ex. 3:14) Christ is neither the religious genius nor the intimate friend of man, nor the founder of a religion, but the incarnate Son of this God. And to have faith means to receive from Him the measure of that which He is and to break one's own measure.

It is of this Christ that John speaks. So we must do what the Christian always has to do, change the order of things, give up the old starting-point and seek a new one, put away our old measures and learn to use the new. It is not that John paints a picture of Christ which corresponds to his own nature as a theologian and mystic, and that scholars can now sit down and examine what the "reality" is, but John had met Christ. He had lived with Him. He was overpowered by that which Jesus was. He did not understand, and yet he remained with Him and stood beneath the cross to the end. At the message of the women, he ran to the grave and became aware of the mystery of Easter. He experienced the descent of the Holy Spirit and in that light his eyes were opened. Until the end of his long life he pondered about Who this was whom he had encountered at that time, this man so simple and so immense, so close and yet always remote, Who had gone in and out among them for a short time and yet was the Eternal One. (Acts 1:21) John did not imagine this but experienced it, and then he searched for ways of expressing it—just as the others tried to do, each in his own way, Mark and Matthew and Luke and Paul. To do this he employed not only the thoughts of the Old Testament about the creative word of God, but also those which the Greeks had prepared and expressed. What these had guessed, seeking and never reaching their goal as they spoke of the *Logos*, was now fulfilled in Him. As St. Paul had said on the Areopagus, "As I went about viewing your sanctuaries, I found an altar with the inscription, 'To an unknown God.' That which you worship without knowing I proclaim to you."

This is how it is, and all else is unbelief—unbelief and presumption. We cannot pass judgment upon Christ. We cannot say in this point the apostle speaks the truth, in that he is under Hellenistic influence. If we do this we take away revelation and therewith the foundation of all that is called Christianity. We cannot by our own powers pass judgment upon revelation, but can only receive from it what then becomes the content of our Christian thinking.

But we must let it be a real revelation, let it speak freely and receive all that it tells. The Christ of present-day scholarship is empty and insignificant. We cannot believe in Him and He does not bring salvation to anyone. Yet the Christ of faith has largely become atrophied, grown small and sentimental. But Christ is the figure in whom we shall "conquer the world," hence He must be greater than the world, and that means greater than all. The Christ who lives in the customary thinking, speaking and praying of our day is not so. In him there is not the fulness of revelation, but only certain of its words and events, and, for the rest, the image of a custom.

If Christianity is to be renewed, this can only be brought about by a return to its root, that means to revelation. We must place ourselves before this, must put aside all preconceived ideas, all portraits of art, all habitual attitudes, and must open our souls, perceive with our inner ear, behold with our inner eye what proceeds thence—trait by trait, event after event, word upon word, in Matthew and Mark and Luke, in Paul and John. Then a concept will grow up, of which we can perhaps not even say that it is an "image"—something immense that mocks our every measure. A Being that breaks apart all to which we are accustomed and yet touches our innermost soul. He, Jesus Christ—the Lord—Lord by nature, Who is Who He is, Lord of His being, elevated above all judgment on our part, and by this very fact, our salvation; for what would be the good of a Savior whom we had fathomed and stamped with our approval?

When this has taken place and all that is customary has been shattered, then we may begin to consider how this and that may be, how the picture painted by Matthew is related to that of Paul. Then we shall once again perceive the depths of meaning in the traditional doctrines; the customary formulas will begin to glow, and everything that the Church says will become our own in an entirely new fashion.

Of course, something else is also necessary—prayer. The Christ of whom revelation speaks "was yesterday, is today, and will be for all eternity." The way to Him does not lead merely over books and reports, but immediately from us to Him,—no, rather, originally and essentially from Him to us—passing through everything. So we must call upon Him that He may reveal Himself to us. What He did to Paul before Damascus was in prophetic greatness something that He can do to each one of us according to the measure of our smallness and His grace.

The Yearning of Creation

"The Yearning of Creation" (Rom. 8:12–39)

Deep within man there lives the consciousness that something must happen to him, that this present existence is not the real and true one, that it must become new and different and so attain to its proper reality.

If one should ask him he would not be able to say how this is to be, and yet he waits for it with a hope that he perhaps does not admit even to himself. This hope is often mistaken about its own meaning. Then man thinks that what he is waiting for is the coming day or the spring or some encounter or a change in circumstances. But he is mistaken. The change for which he is really waiting does not consist in this—that he will learn tomorrow to control himself better than today, that his next work will be more successful than the last, that he will rise to success and power or will find the person whose love can wholly rouse and fill him. All these things are fundamentally merely changes within a similar situation. What he desires is the real transformation, the genesis of something entirely new from which man would at last receive his proper self.

But are these not phantasies? Beautiful, profound and ultimately vain imaginations of human longing? No, to appeal to this desire, to interpret it, to promise that it shall be fulfilled, indeed that the fulfillment has already begun and is being consummated through the ages, this is the meaning of the "good news" (the Gospel). We shall learn this from one of the deepest and richest texts of Scripture, the 8th chapter of the epistle that St. Paul wrote to the congregation at Rome.

I

In the preceding chapter the apostle had spoken of the lost state of man, of sin and remoteness from God. Through his own vivid experience he had shown that man cannot overcome these things either through the law of the Old Testament or through any efforts of his own strength, but that only grace in Christ could bring salvation. Then he continues: "Therefore, brethren, we are debtors, not to the flesh, to live according to the flesh. For if you live according to the flesh, you shall die; but if by the Spirit you mortify the deeds of the flesh, you shall live. For whosoever are led by the Spirit of God, they are the sons of God. For you have not received the spirit of bondage again in fear; but you have received the spirit of adoption of sons, whereby we cry: Abba (Father). For the Spirit himself giveth testimony to our spirit, that we are the sons of God. And if sons, heirs also; heirs indeed of God, and joint-heirs with Christ; yet so, if we suffer with him, that we may be also glorified with him."

St. Paul speaks of the flesh and of the spirit, and it is important that these words be given their true meaning. By the flesh he does not mean the body in contrast to the spiritual soul. This has been imputed to him and so he has been accused of being a despiser of the body, whereas he is the very one who has proclaimed the message of the Christian body, of man in his entirety. Flesh means body and soul together, impulse, reason, will and energy, the whole man and all his works, knowledge, art and culture—in a word, earthly existence as it is of itself. By "spirit" he does not mean the disembodied soul or mere reason, but that which had come to men in such a tremendous manner on the first Pentecost, the Holy Spirit with His creative power, and all that which this power brings forth and penetrates. And the "either-or" of which he speaks does not demand that man shall destroy the body for the sake of the spirit. There was even then a heresy which held this opinion and which St. Paul himself, and especially St. John, combatted, namely Gnosticism. But St. Paul's alternative proclaims the struggle between the life which the Holy Spirit produces in man and that which comes from the world and is circumscribed by it.

St. Paul says that through faith in the Gospel we are committed to a new way of life. Herein we shall not serve what is earthly, for in that way we shall die. Here speaks the deep experience of the ancients—that everything passes, even what is greatest and most beautiful. No one becomes completely human who does not in some way reach this experience, that everything passes away and that nothing which is itself perishable can save us from this transitoriness. Man is not saved from death when a child is born to him, for this child in turn must die. He is not saved from perishing if he leaves a great work, for in its time this also shall perish. He does not overcome the powers of annihilation if he is remembered by men for his noble deeds, for in time these men will also forget. We must be honest and not take away the meaning of the words. If transitoriness is to be overcome, this can only be done by means of something which does not pass away—and that not merely in the sense in which poets use the words, but in actual truth. St. Paul says that this "something" exists—it is Christ. When you turned to Him and united yourselves to Him, a new life awakened in you through the Holy Ghost, a life over which death has no power.

In this life you have a new relation to God, a new rank and a new right. You are His sons. No longer merely sons of men, of your parents, your clan, your people, but of God. And the Spirit is the sacred breath which blows from Him through you, and the will that comes from the Father and guides you.

In this way you are raised above the natural order by which everyone is bound. Of course there is the distinction between those who rule and those who serve, the independent and the dependent, and the greater distinction between the liberal and the servile-minded man. Paul, with his strong individualism, would be the last to deny this. But he would add that these differences lie within a great universal limitation, that of earthly existence as such. Every man is bound by this—his body through the laws of nature, his emotions through the impulses, his reason through uncertainty and error, his will through the power of evil, his whole life through death. This subservience also includes fear. Everyone, even the bravest, feels this—the fear of the creature in an existence with which it is fundamentally in disharmony. But the Spirit has raised us to a new status in making us brethren of Christ. As a result of this we have a new disposition, that of children. The new spirit within us speaks directly to the holy, eternal God, and in this face-to-face there is no longer fear but freedom and confidence. The word that we speak in the Lord's prayer, "Abba, Father," is the expression of the redeemed existence. How do we know that? First of all from the word of God, which we receive in the obedience and confidence of faith. But we could not receive and retain it, it would be a "folly and a scandal" for us if there were not something in the depths of our hearts that assured us of its truth. This results from the witness in which the voice of the Holy Spirit joins our redeemed spirit.

The Holy Spirit is a great mystery. He is the intimacy and freedom of God. He is His holy animation. We are told that God, knowing and expressing Himself, generates an eternal "Thou," the Son, and thereby becomes the Father. But that this Son does not separate from the Father, depart and become an independent God—which would cause everything to fall into falsity and destruction—but that he "remains" with the Father, "turns toward Him," "lies upon His bosom," as St. John says, that the unity of God is preserved—indeed, receives in this holy plenitude its peculiar force—this is the work of the Holy Spirit. Again it is He who brings it about that the Father, in keeping the Son with Him, does not suppress Him, that the Son is not immature, unreal, the mere shadow of a greater one, but lives in the clarity and power of a free self, the equal and responding "thou" of the speaking "I." So the Spirit is the intimacy of God. And He is divine humility. He does not seek Himself. He seems to have no content of His own, to desire nothing but that the eternal God may possess the dignity of fatherhood and the beauty of sonship, and that both, Father and Son, may be in possession of each other and be one. He is the selfless one, the lover truly so-called, and therefore He is absolute power.

This Spirit also effects the intimacy of the redeemed life. He makes man to be truly the son, the daughter of God, without blurring the clear distinction. He gives him the true life which comes only from God, pure grace, but by that very fact so much man's own that only now does he become wholly himself. Of this He reassures man in the inmost depths of his soul, so that it becomes a powerful certainty in him and no shadow of doubt remains. Man's own spirit, that which is new in him, comes to a joyous self-realization and says, "So it is." What is described in this way is the particular experience of the Apostle Paul and is not granted to many. But everyone who believes bears within himself the reality of which that experience speaks. Everyone who believes is assured by the Spirit in the depths of his being that he is a child of God. The "own spirit" of every believer perceives this assurance and agrees with it, even though the witness and the answer do not become an open experience but remain hidden in the depths. If this were not the case he could not believe the message; the objection of his earthly reality would be too strong. Without knowing it, he believes from the inner witness of the Spirit.

This being a child of God is a serious thing. It gives us rights. It makes us heirs of God. His property belongs to us—His holiness, His life, His kingdom—and since He is one and completely simple, that means He Himself. The true heir is Christ. He will be the Lord of the new creation and we shall be co-heirs with Him, so that He will be "the first-born among many brethren."

Of course we must also be ready to share His destiny, to experience what He experienced when He, Who had come from heaven, lived on earth. If we are willing to endure the contradiction of "the flesh" against the Lord of the spirit then we shall also receive a share of His glory.

II

"For I reckon that the sufferings of this time are not worthy to be compared with the glory to come, that shall be revealed in us. For the expectation of the creature waiteth for the revelation of the sons of God. For the creature was made subject to vanity, not willingly, but by reason of him that made it subject in the hope that the creature also itself shall be delivered from the servitude of corruption, into the liberty of the children of God. For we know that every creature groaneth and travaileth in pain, even till now."

These sufferings are real and they are bitter, but they lose their weight when the Spirit assures us of the glory which is ripening in us and shall one day be revealed. In these and the following sentences there speaks the triumphant greatness of the Christian message about man. It says that man is a mystery. The part of him that we see and hear is a transitory earthly being, but within him lives something that comes from the Spirit. In all his existing, acting and experiencing, in all feeling, possessing and privation, something else lies veiled, oppressed, contradicted, and yet always there. This shall one day be revealed. It is God who actually reveals Himself, He whose revelation is truth. But He wills to make man so that the concept of revelation applies to him also. He too is a veiled meaning, a fulness of actuality ripening in secret, some day to come forth into life. The Christian too is something that must be believed. I must believe in my own Christianity, and that is often difficult, for everything contradicts it. But one day it shall appear and then faith shall pass away. Everything shall be present and open to our sight.

And now comes the tremendous thought—The whole of creation is turned toward this mystery in man, this interior becoming, struggling and unfolding. It is a waiting, and the attention of this waiting is not directed immediately toward God, but toward man, for the way of creatures to God goes through man. Their hearts and heads should be in him; he should lead them to God, and in him all creation should be blessed. But he turned away from God and dragged creatures with him. So the curse struck them also, together with him, kept them at a distance from God, subjected them to transitoriness and vanity and brought it about that there was no longer an answer to the questions whence, whither, why, for what purpose. Nature itself was not guilty, for it cannot have guilt of its own. It exists for the sake of man and receives its meaning from him; hence it was from him that the disaster came upon it. And now it waits that the blessing of salvation shall come about in him, and that it may share therein through him. From all sides a silent, anxious expectation is directed toward man. It reminds us of some old pictures of the nativity: the child lies shining in the manger and all about him eyes are gazing upon the radiance—the eyes of the Blessed Mother and the faithful protector, of the shepherds and the beasts—and it seems as if the darkness were full of life and were pressing in from all sides. It is almost like that in the present case. In man who believes there is an opening, a beginning; a fire is burning, a light is shining, and the whole wide world presses toward this blessed beginning, hoping that it may also be caught up in it. If the new life triumphs in man, it shall also triumph in nature. Then the "service of corruption," the law of dissolution and hopeless death shall fall away from the world and it shall attain freedom.

This freedom means more than the possibility of doing one thing or another; indeed, it is not a freedom of action, but of being—that freedom which is truth. It becomes actual when that which is hidden comes to light, when the insignificant captive of natural laws, the son of man, becomes the son of God and participates in the glory of his Father. And let us take the word glory in its full significance. It does not mean just any beauty or radiance, but something very definite, the light of the apparition of God upon Mt. Sinai, over the ark of the covenant, in the faces of the Prophets, and finally the fulness of light and majesty of the risen Christ. In this we shall share, as heirs of that which belongs to God. It is for this that creation waits. The condition of man in time is that of a blessed life which waits until it can bring to light that new life which is developing within. This is also the condition of creation. So St. Paul says that we "groan" and are "in travail," and the whole of creation with us. Earthly existence, existence in time, is pain and travail, an urge toward the birth of a life that shall transcend all that belongs to earth and time, because the sacred germ has come from beyond all this.

III

"And not only so, but we ourselves who have the first-fruits of the Spirit, groan within ourselves, waiting for our adoption, the redemption of the body. For in the meantime we are saved only in hope. But hope that can be seen is no hope, for if we see something, how can we hope for it? But if we truly hope for that which we see not, we shall wait in patience."

The thought returns to man. Everything human shall also become the starting point of a new birth. But while creation is without knowledge or voice, we have become knowing through the spirit, the inner light, the inner breath. So "we groan within ourselves" that that may be accomplished which is in process of becoming, our adoption as sons of God. Through faith and baptism it has begun. We are really children of God, but only "children," immature. We have neither attained our freedom nor received our inheritance. That will take place only when we come of age, one day, in the "revelation of the sons of God."

And now another bold step: this revelation will be the redemption of our body. No other New Testament writer has ever dared to say anything like that, to define Christian maturity, the completion of our existence and that of the world, hence the end of all things, as the redemption of our body. It must be an evil desire to distort things that is responsible for regarding St. Paul as the enemy of the body and of human life, whereas he is the very one who has carried the body into eternity. Not only the spiritual soul shall enter into eternal life—one could almost say that the Christian message was not necessary for that, because that idea can be found in Plato—but the whole man. That man shall become eternal, that his body also shall attain to fellowship with God and shine in holy life, this has been revealed to us by Christ. But that is not all: Christ accomplished it by His incarnation and resurrection and made it possible for us all. This is the Christian teaching about man, and St. Paul is the one who really proclaimed it. He is the prophet of the resurrection of the body, of the eternalized man, just as he, more than anyone who speaks in the New Testament, is the prophet of the risen Christ, who appeared to him before Damascus and revealed to him the divine glory of His body. It is this glory which, by a creative sharing, continues its operation in the body of redeemed man.

But all this is still veiled, waiting, and in the process of becoming. Of a woman who has conceived and awaits the time when the life which is growing within her shall come into the light, we sometimes use the phrase "she is expecting." This is the meaning that is suggested by the way in which St. Paul in the following sentences speaks of the expectation of man and of creation. It implies confidence in the promise that has been given and also a silent knowledge of that which is growing in secret. This expectation lives by the word of God, and also from its own deepest inner being, assured by the Holy Spirit.

Christian hope is the confidence of man that he shall attain this new life, shall become a partaker of the maturity and dominion of the sons of God. At present it is contradicted by everything: the ugliness and evil within us, the constant failure, the meanness and misery and hopelessness of existence. In view of all this, confidence seems folly, and for that very reason it must be *hope*, trust in that which is not seen, and of which we are certain beyond all uncertainty, "hope," as St. Paul says in the same epistle (Rom. 4:18) "against all hope."

And it is patience. Thereby genuine hope differs from the fanciful. The latter flares up and collapses, because it comes from the surge of emotion and the fleeting images of phantasy. But genuine hope grows from reality, the interior, new reality based upon the Spirit. Therefore it is strong enough to resist the contradiction of the old reality and to overcome its resistance. For reality has one especial quality—it is tough. It permits only that to grow which maintains itself within it. It accepts only what a greater power forces upon it. This persevering, this overcoming of reality by the power of endurance is patience. How strong and full of conquering power is the blessing with which the explanations of the epistle conclude: "Now the God of hope fill you with all joy and peace in believing that you may abound in hope and in the power of the Holy Spirit." (Rom. 15:13)

IV

"Likewise the Spirit also helpeth our infirmity. For we know not what we should pray for as we ought; but the Spirit himself asketh for us with unspeakable groanings. And he that searcheth the hearts knoweth what the Spirit desireth, because he asketh for the saints according to God."

It is the Spirit who has placed the germ of the new life in us, and it is He who helps it to hope—to hope and even to live. What came into being through Him can only live through Him. The life, at once human and divine, was awakened in Mary through the descent of the Holy Spirit and the overshadowing power of the Most High (Luke 1:35) and in the power of this same Spirit, Christ lived and completed His work. The Christian life is patterned after the life of Christ. It begins through the Holy Spirit, in Him it lives and grows, struggles and hopes.

The first movement of this life, its breath, so to speak, is prayer. Of ourselves we do not know how we should pray. The Spirit teaches us. The meanings of these terms blend very beautifully. The spirit is the "breath." The Holy Spirit is the breath of God. So it is He who teaches the new life in us to breathe; that is, to pray. Indeed, it is He Himself who breathes in us, and since it is the breath of an imprisoned life, oppressed by darkness and closeness and contradiction, this breath becomes a sighing for deliverance and consummation. What was said before about the groaning of creation and our own, in the developing of the new life, here continues in a divine way. It is the Spirit Himself who longs within us for the consummation. The eternal care of His love, of His whole being which is love, is set upon this—that the sacred birth in God, the Father's self-expression in the Son and the turning of the Son to the Father, shall be carried out in the truth of a free personality and the union of an eternal "abiding." After Christ sent the Spirit to us, his care in time is that through the mystery of grace the birth of the new life shall be realized in the brethren of Christ.

How good is the message that the Spirit Himself breathes and prays and sighs in us! It would be a grievous thing if this growing and becoming lay in our ignorant, careless hands. How eternally good, that He, our advocate, our comforter, has made it His own work. Constantly, deep within us, in the growing-center of our being, the prayer of the Spirit goes on. Constantly the breath of His prayer ascends to the Father. And when we ourselves pray, whatever has value in this poor, inadequate prayer, comes from Him. His prayer reaches God. The meaning of His sighs is understood by God even if we ourselves do not yet understand it. We should include it in the conscious practice of our prayer, but it will always be deeper than this. It will always be true that God, the Father, understands it better than we do. He can do that, for He is the one who "searches the hearts." Another passage tells us that "the Spirit searches all things, even the depths of divinity." We see how wonderfully close to God the Gospel brings man. It speaks of the inner depth of man—the new and holy depth, not the natural—in almost the same way as of the inner depth of God. He who lives in the mystery of the redeemed soul and in the abyss of God's holiness is—with the inviolable distinction that exists between God and His creature—the same Holy Spirit. What He desires is known to the Father. For the Spirit is the intimacy in which God lives within Himself. He also becomes the intimacy of man, for Jesus said that He would send Him as our "comforter," our "advocate," the one who brings it about that we are not "left orphans." (John 14:18; 16:7) For us also He is closeness—the language of the Church calls Him "the bond," "the kiss." And it is not accidental that the word "saints" appears in this connection. We use this word of those great and extraordinary ones to whom the Church awards the glory of being invoked and venerated, but the Scripture uses it to denote all those who believe and are baptized—those in whom the Holy Spirit breathes.

V

"And we know that to them that love God all things work together unto good, to such as, according to his purpose, are called to be saints. For whom he foreknew, he also predestined to be made conformable to the image of his Son, that he might be the first-born amongst many brethren. And whom he predestinated, them he also called. And whom he called, them he also justified. And whom he justified, them he also glorified."

What follows is a single confirmation penetrating ever more deeply, growing ever more powerful and more joyful.

The text begins, "We know." Not by our reason, not through some intellectual insight or practical wisdom, not through a mystical sense of security, which can always arise from religious absorption, but through that inner voice of the Holy Spirit of which we have spoken. To know that God makes "all things work together for good to those who love him" is a certainty that endures through all experiences and considerations. The "good" which is spoken of here is the development of the new man. This is aided not only by fortunate dispensations, but by "all things." Even earthly ideas of the development and perfection of the personality can be far-reaching, and can include sorrow as well as happiness, but if they go too far, they become unreal. If they stay with reality they soon reach the boundary where the purely destructive begins. But the certainty of which St. Paul speaks excludes nothing. It knows that absolutely everything that happens serves the inner development.

But again, and the reader must not be annoyed if we distinguish again and again—for it is a question of the very heart of the Christian message and all depends on our making the meaning of the much-misused words very clear—all things must serve the inner development, not because it comes irresistibly from the germ of powerful men, but because God's Providence never fails. But the mystery has two sides. The persons spoken of are those "who love God" and at the same time those "whom He has called according to His will." The first statement alone could mean that it is a question of the human heart's capacity of loving, and this would again reduce everything to an earthly level. The second could give us the impression that it is a question of an arbitrary choice, and would make man the plaything of a divine whim. In fact, it is both a call of pure grace, and, at the same time, the interior readiness of the heart; just as we can translate the Christmas message of the angels (Luke 2:14), "Peace to men who are pleasing to God because His grace has chosen them," and also, "Peace to men who are pleasing to God because they are of good will." From this mystery results the Providence which brings it about that whatever may happen, even what is most incomprehensible and destructive, blends with the inner development.

And now this idea of pure grace, which has no conditions but itself, unfolds to its full power. The mystery is so great that it can become dark and oppressive. We cannot penetrate it, but must take care that it is placed in its proper order. The following sentences are found in the Epistle to the

Romans; that is, in the demonstration of the apostle which most completely demolishes every claim that the law of the Old Testament might put forward to retain its validity, but also every claim which man's own will and accomplishments might make to work out his own salvation. It is true that the Old Testament also rested upon grace and demanded of man cooperation with the living God; but in other respects it consisted largely of regulations about what should and should not be done, namely the law, and the promises were bound up with its fulfilment. Repeatedly the words occur: "If you do this you shall live." Much that was found in this law was a matter of morality and piety, which always retain their significance, but essentially it was directed to the realization of sacred history and prepared for the coming of the Messias, either by opening the hearts of men for Him, or, as the Epistle to the Romans says, by their inability to fulfill it, revealing to them their own helplessness. But living by the law had brought about such a consciousness of righteousness and security that the Christians were in danger of taking over this consciousness together with the obligations of the law. In opposition to this St. Paul says: "All this is past and gone. What matters now is not the law and its fulfilment but the grace of God in Christ and faith in Him, life under the guidance of the Holy Spirit and in communion with the Savior." This renunciation of the law includes another. In itself the law was bound up with sacred history, as brought about by God; but it appealed so strongly to the will and the accomplishment of man that it constantly threatened to slip into natural morality and propriety. This too St. Paul attacks. Not that he places little value upon natural virtue, but he only affirms that the essential thing with which the Gospel is concerned cannot arise from that. It comes from God, grows through the operation of His Spirit, and is appropriated by man in faith, love and obedience. But herein lives all that is magnanimous and strong in him. "I live, yet not I, but Christ lives in me." (Gal. 2:20)

Here all that has previously been said about the new life becomes a living disposition. We can sum up its nature in two statements: He who operates is God, not man; everything is a gift; pride and also the fear of being obliged to bring about the effect oneself no longer have any place. Everything is open and selfless. But at the same time man must cast into this freedom all that he possesses of readiness, of nobility, of power to act and boldness to accomplish; nothing is too good or too much. He who has received all must also give all.

From this point of view we understand the following sentences. What we are concerned with does not come from the inner source of human life, nor from the depths of the world, but from the mystery of the free divine decree, which is impenetrable, because freedom is God's self—God, who depends upon the world for nothing, but is its creator and Lord. That is the source of the hope of which we have spoken—for those whom God has "foreknown" before all time, before all earthly conditions, before all willing and ability and action of their own. These He has "predestined" to that holy becoming whose nature consists in "being conformed to the image of His Son." The new thing is the participation in the living reality of Christ, in His original image, His disposition, His life and His right. He is the new man properly speaking, the ancestor of the holy generation (Rom. 5:12–21). He is the "first-born," who came from the womb of Mary, which is the womb of grace. But we are His brethren, together with Him, children of one father and co-heirs of His heritage. Those whom God has so foreknown and predestined He has called, justified and brought to glory. Step by step the sacred event moves toward its consummation.

VI

"What shall we then say to these things? If God be for us, who is against us? He that spared not even his own Son, but delivered him up for us all, how hath he not also, with him, given us all things. Who shall accuse against the elect of God? God that justifieth. Who is he that shall condemn? Christ Jesus that died, yea that is risen also again; who is at the right hand of God, who also maketh intercession for us. Who then shall separate us from the love of Christ? Shall tribulation, or distress, or famine, or nakedness, or danger, or persecution, or the sword?...But in all these things we overcome, because of him that hath loved us. For I am sure that neither death, nor life, nor angels, nor principalities, nor powers, nor things present, nor things to come, nor might, nor height, nor depth, nor any other creature shall be able to separate us from the love of God, which is in Christ Jesus our Lord."

And now there appears to be a leap in the thought. The feeling changes. After the great confidence one perceives a mood of uncertainty. Something seems to take place within the speaker. In his heart that was so filled with the consciousness of his own insufficiency, in which there burned the unquenchable pain that finds expression in so many passages of his epistles, because he did not deserve to be called an apostle because he had persecuted the church of God, there must have arisen the troubled thought: Is this really true? Are there not too many charges against you? Cannot the "accuser of mankind" rise up against you and say that you are not worthy of the promise? To combat this fear St. Paul casts himself the more passionately and unconditionally into the mystery of the love of God.

The first sentence expresses his hesitation: "What more then shall we say?" We feel the uncertainty beneath the words, and then the complete casting of himself upon God. We recall similar words in the New Testament; for instance, those of the man who had begged Jesus to heal his afflicted son, and when asked, "Do you believe that I can do this?" replied, "I believe; help my unbelief." (Mark 9:24). Or the words spoken by Peter when in Capharnaum after the proclamation of the mystery of the Eucharist men were falling away on all sides, the Jews leaving first, then many disciples. Finally, as Jesus turned to the twelve and said, "Will you also go away?" Peter, surmounting the troubled thoughts that rose within him, cast himself into the arms of the Lord: "To whom shall we go?

Thou hast the words of eternal life." There are moments when faith may no longer investigate and argue. Everything is at stake, and only one thing is possible—to risk all. This is the case here.

"If God is for us then who is against us." Is this true? Has His grace pardoned the wrong that you have committed, so that the adversary can no longer reproach you with it? Can grace so completely overcome the evil in you that it no longer rises against God? And it is not merely clear memory and definite knowledge that asks this question, but the oppressive fear and melancholy that has no reason. How do you know that God is for you? It is an evil question, and woe to him who yields to it. Therefore the speaker does not admit it and above all uncertainty sets up the great affirmation of faith: It is so, for the Spirit tells me. But how can you be sure that it is really the Spirit who tells you? It must be He, for when He speaks we cannot doubt. The interior beginning bears witness of itself, and it is only necessary that man shall join himself for better, for worse, to Him who "bears witness."

From this consideration the next sentences receive their triumphant certainty. God has given His Son for us; that means he has revealed a disposition of which the world can have no conception. For from the worldly point of view there can be no concept of a God who acts in this way. For the world it is a scandal. We have said that the average man finds this idea disgusting. If we wish to attain truth we must approach the thought in another way. The very fact that God has done this thing constitutes the revelation, it shows us clearly who He is—and who man is. We hear that man does not live by his own power and merit but by the grace of God. That is a mystery, but, if we may say so, remains within reach of our religious thought. But when we hear further that this grace means that God delivers His own Son, and that means Himself, into an inconceivable state of strangeness and self-surrender (Cf. the Epistle to the Philippians 2:7–8) then we cannot escape the conclusion that man must be something that makes such surrender worthwhile in the eyes of God. Not because of man's own being and merit but because of what God gave him when He created him. But it is truly his. When God created man, He created him as important for Himself. He created him as His own destiny in a way which we cannot imagine. And if we take seriously the message that God loves man—truly loves him, not just in some way and metaphorically speaking—and if we consider that He is the one who loves, then we can perhaps guess what that may mean.

This love is so powerful and all-sufficient that no accusation can find a place. For a man of Paul's strong and sensitive conscience, who constantly feels that his actions and his character are being weighed, the whole of life is a single judgment. The accuser is his conscience, and beneath his conscience the melancholy of his temperament oppresses him, and still deeper down is the dark fiend who observes the evil in man. It is a dreadful thing if the defender is not stronger—so strong that he can overcome fear. Otherwise fear increases and the darkness is victorious. But the defender is there, Christ Jesus, who in His whole existence is the revelation of that love of God—He who died and rose again and is enthroned in glory.

But again doubt and fear may intrude and cause confusion: Christ is there, it is true, but is He there for you?—He is, faith replies, for He loves me. Fear says: Do you know that He loves you?—Faith replies: I know it, for His whole existence is nothing but love.—But perhaps you have become unworthy of this love, for you opposed Him at one time. He himself cried out to you that day before Damascus, "Saul, Saul, why do you persecute me?" Now the point has been reached again when argument must cease, because every answer provokes a new doubt, and the confusion of fear permeates and rises above everything. Again all is at stake, and so faith becomes a single affirmation: "Nothing can separate us from the love of Christ." Nothing from without or from within; nothing that belongs to the world or to the powers of darkness.

The following sentences are a single crescendo of faith triumphing over the objections that arise on all sides—a single hymn of that same consciousness that we have previously called "hope." The innermost being of man, "the heart of his heart" to use the marvellous word of the poet, unites with the innermost being of God, with His will and His nature as revealed in Christ, with His love. When this happens, when this innermost being of man clasps and clings to the love of God, then the decision has been carried out. This is the center of the world. Then anything may come, misfortune and destruction and perplexity: the essential thing is secure. Even more, even better, "All things work for good." What we have previously called the certainty of the developing new life here becomes a victory.

The Canticle of Love

I n the Sacred Scriptures there are some texts that are particularly precious. There is something of perfection and completeness about them—like a poem. So we read them again and again, discuss them and refer to them. This is a good thing. Such texts form as it were points of agreement in the Christian spiritual life. But by the same token they may suffer harm, may become trite and slip into the commonplace and take on a deficient or incorrect meaning.

In dealing with such texts the interpreter's task is above all to restore to them their greatness and their mystery. The superficiality of daily use makes it seem as if the word of God had become familiar and had been penetrated and exhausted. It appears "old"; that is, dissolved in the composite of the world, in the context of human thought. But the word of the revelation is of its nature "new," because it comes from beyond the world and can never be absorbed by it. Essentially, one generation does not know more than the preceding one merely because men have thought thirty years longer about a word of Scripture. For every generation, for every person, for every hour, God's word exists only in the form of a revelation. And this means that nothing which precedes can make it easier to understand, but that it must be understood at all times and by all men according to the inmost predisposition of faith.

To produce this newness is the first and foremost task of interpretation.

A text that particularly requires such a "restoration to its newness" is the thirteenth chapter of the First Epistle to the Corinthians. It has been called the canticle of love, has been treated from the most widely different points of view, referred to on all imaginable occasions, and so it has suffered a sad fate. It has been taken ethically and in that way it has lost all its living quality. It has been taken emotionally and so it has become sentimental and frivolous. It has been compared with other texts that deal with love, especially with Plato, and in this way it has been brought so close to the latter that Plato became half Christian and Paul half pagan; or else, men have taken the Greek philosopher as a measure and proved how scant and poor were the Christian Apostle's ideas of love.

Therefore we must ask what the text really means. And the first approach depends on a very simple fact, namely that this thirteenth chapter stands between the twelfth and the fourteenth. That sounds foolish, for where else should it stand? But this aspect of the situation appears to be rarely noticed. The chapter is not so much of a unit as it is usually regarded, but it is integrally connected with the other two and only receives its meaning from them. For they deal with the early Christian spiritual gifts (charismata) and it is in reference to these that the nature of love is defined.

I

When the Son of God came to us the event took place in the silent manner of birth. The coming of the Spirit occurred in a different way—as an irruption and a shock. Like a mighty wind He came to us from the remoteness of God. The house was filled with the sound. Flames leaped up. Men were gripped, shaken, overwhelmed. And the power of the event was made manifest in another peculiar way. The book of Acts relates: "And all were filled with the Holy Spirit and began to speak in other tongues, as the Spirit gave them to speak, so that pilgrims who had come to Jerusalem from various countries said in amazement: 'We hear them speak in our tongues the great deeds of God.'" (Acts 2:4–11) If we consider this in connection with other passages, the phenomenon could be explained in this way: the disciples are gripped by the power of the Spirit; they experience an interior transformation; the fulness of the reality of Christ becomes clear to them; the glory of Christ overwhelms them. They are beside themselves, and the tremendous experience overflows in broken words and exclamations, perhaps even in mere stammering. Those of the hearers who are prepared and open their hearts to what is taking place are so far gripped by the same power of the Spirit that they enter into harmony with the speakers and their ears comprehend what is meant; but those who shut their hearts and resist hear only a senseless stammering. They mock and say, "These men are filled with new wine." (Acts 2:13)

The breaking forth of the Spirit is not confined to that hour. When the storm breaks, new blasts constantly succeed each other. The book of Acts recounts that the first Christian congregations were wholly filled with this experience. Whenever an unusual event took place—for instance, if a great danger was averted or men came to the faith in a significant way—or when the apostles laid their hands upon new converts "the Spirit came upon them" and filled them with His power. In the life of the early congregations the most varied effects of the work of the Spirit were manifest. Sometimes these were so strong that the essential thing, namely the quiet response that faith and daily life give to the word of revelation, suffered eclipse in the consciousness of the faithful.

A number of such gifts of the Spirit are named. The most conspicuous was that "speaking with tongues" which we mentioned above. Then there was prophecy, when a believer was so powerfully gripped by one of the saving truths that he proclaimed it in a powerful, overwhelming manner. Then there was the gift of discernment, which revealed the condition of another's soul; the gift of wisdom, which understood the hidden meaning of things; the gift of faith, when faith acquired a kind of power and healed the sick or performed other miracles. These workings of the Spirit made the religious life of the early congregations very strong. They clearly defined the difference that existed between the old and the new, assured the believer, convinced the stranger, and acted as sparks that spread a conflagration. At the same time they contained the danger inherent in all that is extraordinary, that motives of an evil nature, such as vanity, ambition, jealousy, envy would mingle with them, that the Christian attitude would slip into the enthusiastic, the frenzied, one might almost say the Dionysiac; that reality and its order, the faith and action of every-day life, might withdraw and everything might somehow become fantastic and visionary. And as a matter of fact this danger frequently materialized and the apostles had to resist it. In any case we know that this was true of St. Paul in relation to the congregation in Corinth.

The name of this city had a particular significance. Corinth was known to be very cultured, very unreliable, pleasure-seeking and eager for new sensations. When a man becomes a Christian he is converted, but he is not magically transformed. His heart is touched by the message and his will resolves to obey, but in disposition and natural character he remains the man he was. So the congregation of Corinth surely had the good will of a Christian community. It even possessed—and this was the mark of a true religious emotion—the plenitude of the gifts of the spirit. The letter of the apostle proves that. But the people, even as Christians, were Corinthians. So we read, for example, that there were among them very serious moral difficulties, and that they were critical of the apostle and inclined to deride him. Hence there were various unsavory motives connected with the gifts of the Spirit in their case. There seems to have developed a kind of virtuosity of religious peculiarity, and with it manifestations of jealousy and envy in a field in which they are most inappropriate. The Greek tendency toward religious frenzy, toward absorption in the impersonal Dionysiac element also appears to have made itself felt. In consequence a strange situation developed: strong charismatic experiences, of which it was not certain whether they were really Christian and did not glide off in other directions; highly developed religious endowments which, however, did not concern themselves with the simplest exigencies of the life of the congregation and failed in daily duties.

All this St. Paul attacks in the twelfth and fourteenth chapters of the epistle of which we are speaking, and the thirteenth stands between them and forms the core of his whole train of thought.

II

"Now concerning spiritual things, my brethren, I would not have you ignorant. You know that when you were heathens, you went to dumb idols, according as you were led. Wherefore I give you to understand that no man, speaking by the Spirit of God, saith, 'Anathema' to Jesus. And no man can say, 'the Lord Jesus,' but by the Holy Ghost." (I Cor. 12:1–3)

These sentences reveal the whole danger. The congregation was full of religious powers and experiences. But the apostle saw that these were uncertain things and gave the Corinthians what is so important in religious life, a standard by which to distinguish. He says: Religious experiences are not the essential thing—those you have known previously in religious festivals and mysteries. Mere religious experience is ambiguous; it receives its character only in our decision before the word and will of God, that means before Christ. A religious manifestation may be as mighty, as glowing, as convincing as possible, but if it turns against Christ in any way, it is not of God. But if a religious manifestation culminates in the confession of Christ, in the cry, "You, O Christ, are the Lord, the risen Savior," it can come only from God.

These words fall like an illuminating and dividing ray into a religious chaos.

The next verses (I Cor. 12:4–11) give us the most exhaustive description of the early Christian charismata which the New Testament contains. But before the enumeration as well as after it St. Paul emphasizes that "there are diversities of gifts" but that "it is one Spirit who works in all and gives to each the particular gift that He will." The argument is obviously directed against those who use the graces of the spirit for purposes of vanity and jealousy. Thereupon follows the fine passage (I Cor. 12:12–30) in which St. Paul evaluates the graces from the point of view of his teaching on the Mystical Body. The believers are not only individuals externally related to each other, but form a living unity, the Church. A single common life envelops them; in this, each one forms a member, a cell, as we would say today. As every cell has its special function and in that very way serves the whole, so does each believer in the totality of the Christian life. The Spirit is the life-principle of the Church, but also of each individual. He gives to each his particular life in relation to the whole. The charismata are expressions of this, entrusted to the recipient not for his private existence but for the whole, and he perverts their meaning if he becomes conceited about them or envies others or disparages one gift in comparison with another. And even if one gift should be inferior, that would merely be a reason to treat it with greater consideration. The peculiar phenomenon of the charismata in this way is set in an order, namely the totality of the Christian community; the individual recipient of the graces is instructed to treat his fellow-Christian with respect and kindliness.

The fourteenth chapter again takes up the question of the charismata, at least from the point of view of Christian community life. But the image which illustrates it is not that of the body and its members, but of the assembled congregation. St. Paul represents to his audience the faithful individually practising their charismatic powers. Who will be more useful to the congregation—he who speaks with tongues or he who is prophetically enlightened? The former is not understood by the others, unless they themselves are seized by the same Spirit. In him only his inner self speaks, his spirit; his understanding does nothing. (I Cor. 14:14) The rapture remains in his immediate experience and does not pass over into thought and word. The result is that the bystander cannot "speak his amen to the other's praise"; that no communion is established. But the gift of prophecy is concerned with the word and requires thought. So the one who is prophetically gifted is able to announce truth and reveal the secrets of hearts. The effect is that the person concerned "falls upon his face and adores God." But when those who are inspired by the prophetic spirit speak, it should not be done in a disorderly way, so that many speak at the same time, "For God is not a God of confusion but of peace." (I Cor. 14:33) They should "prophesy in proper order, so that all may learn and be admonished." (I Cor. 14:31) But if a word is incomprehensible then they should see to it that "one may interpret." (I Cor. 14:27)

From all this he draws the conclusion: "Do not hinder the speaking with tongues," but "seek after the gift of prophecy": as for the rest, "Let all things be done decently and in order." (I Cor. 14:39–40) The spiritual gifts are good in themselves, for the Spirit bestows them, so they should have a free field. But they should be fitted into the life of the community and promote this life. Their respective value is to be measured not according to the regard which they may bring to the individual, but according to their usefulness to the community. The more clear, helpful and fruitful, the better they are. At the same time it becomes evident that whereas the gift comes from the Spirit, the man has a certain influence, in that he asks for one rather than another, or perhaps checks or promotes their interior development. So St. Paul says, "Be zealous for the better gifts," (I Cor. 12:31) and again, "Be zealous for spiritual gifts but rather that you may prophesy." (I Cor. 14:1)

III

With these two sentences the twelfth chapter ends and the fourteenth begins. Between them stands the thirteenth chapter, on love.

Its meaning becomes clear if we adduce the second half of the preceding verse. (I Cor. 12:31) This reads: "But I will show you a more excellent way." And then follow the words, "If I speak with the tongues of men and of angels, and have not love, I am become as sounding brass, or a tinkling cymbal. And if I should have prophecy and should know all mysteries and all knowledge, and if I should have all faith, so that I could remove mountains, and have not love, I am nothing. And if I should distribute all my goods to feed the poor, and if I should deliver my body to be burned, and have not love, it profiteth me nothing."

Here several of the spiritual gifts—instead of all—are taken up again and their significance and insignificance are demonstrated from one point of view, which was prepared for in the preceding chapter and is concluded in the following one—namely love. A man may have the gift of tongues; indeed—and now the thought leaps in Pauline fullness beyond its starting point—he may have the gift of speaking in the tongues of all men, even of the higher beings, of angels, but if he has no love, then it is all empty noise. Only love gives meaning to speech; without love it is empty. A man may have the gift of prophecy, may recognize hidden relations, behold the secret meaning of things and be able to reveal the innermost recesses of the human heart. Without love it is all nothing. A man may have the gift of knowledge—that probably means a deep insight into sacred truth proceeding from his inner experience. Without love it is nothing. A man may have the charisma of faith—which evidently means that his faith becomes a spiritual power capable of miracles. This too is nothing without love. A man may have, through the working of the Spirit, an enthusiasm for self-sacrifice, so that he sacrifices himself for his neighbor and gives away everything for his sake; or for God, so that he casts himself with fiery enthusiasm into martyrdom as the Maccabees did of old. Even that is nothing if it is done without love. These sentences are very important. They tell us that there are magnificent, heroic, seemingly quite unselfish actions whose significance before God is very ambiguous. They can be forms of folly or selfishness, therefore "nothing" by the proper standard—when they do not proceed from love. Only when they do so proceed are they "something" and of value before God. There are even actions of indubitably religious nature, experiences which, like prophecy, religious knowledge, faith that has become a power, seem to certify their own piety and validity, and yet are ambiguous. Even these can be "nothing," an idle game of self-expression and self-indulgence, if they do not proceed from love. Only from love do both ethical greatness and religious power receive their significance before God.

Here we find repeated, from a particular point of view what was said at the beginning of the twelfth chapter. Spiritual values, such as strength of soul, emotion of the heart, religious experience and power, need not of themselves be good. They share in the ambiguity of the world, and their ultimate quality depends on love alone. Its presence or absence gives to everything its final character. So we eagerly wait to learn how the nature of love will be defined.

IV

"Love is patient, is kind; love envieth not, dealeth not perversely, is not puffed up; is not ambitious, seeketh not her own; is not provoked to anger, thinketh no evil; rejoiceth not in iniquity, but rejoiceth with the truth; beareth all things, believeth all things, hopeth all things, endureth all things."

We must admit that we are surprised, even a little disappointed. Should love, which has been spoken of so emphatically, and which has been recognized as the power that gives its meaning to everything, be no more than that? All that is here said about love, that it is patient, kind, without envy or vanity, not overbearing, but well-behaved, unself-ish, self-controlled, ready to forgive, not rejoicing in evil but ready to rejoice at the good—are these not just every-day virtues? But when we consider the matter more closely we see that just this contains the meaning of the whole argument. The charismata are manifestations of a religious peculiarity which is perhaps connected with natural talents, with geniality or heroism. Love is contrasted with this as being the es-sential thing, love in the form of simple truth, goodness and faithfulness of life.

The unusual phenomenon can belong to the realm of mere experi-ence, of imagination, even of vanity, and on that very account can be "nothing," empty in itself and without power to master reality. With this, love is contrasted, love in a form that has nothing of enthusiasm, glow or original talent, but which is "something," reality. Reality in itself, because it is pure in value and genuine in action, and really powerful in the world because it is capable of mastering life as it is.

Love is actually portrayed as Christian sobriety, but a sobriety which has nothing to do with barrenness of heart or narrowness of mind. If it gives significance to the charismata it must come from the heart of God, from the operation of the Holy Spirit. It must be moderation in fullness, the "sober intoxication of the Spirit," as the old hymn says, an attitude which in its serene self-control, its faithfulness and strength is incompa-rably greater, deeper and richer than all that is unusual.

In the final sentence, the power and universality which were veiled by the other statements break forth. Love "bears all things." Elsewhere St. Paul says that "Each shall bear the other's burden," his need, his weak-ness, his importunities. Love "believes all things." Since this refers to faith in regard to other men, we might perhaps rather say, it believes them capable of all good, encourages with faith and confidence the living po-tentialities in others. It "hopes all things," desires all good things for others and expects all that is fine from them. It "endures all things," all pain that comes from others.

V

"Love never falleth away: whether prophecies shall be made void, or tongues shall cease, or knowledge shall be destroyed. For we know in part, and we prophesy in part, but when that which is perfect is come, that which is in part shall be put away. When I was a child, I spoke as a child, I understood as a child, I thought as a child. But when I became a man, I put away the things of a child. We see now through a glass in a dark manner; but then face to face. Now I know in part; but then I shall know even as I am known. And now there remain faith, hope, and love, these three: but the greatest of these is love."

The first section of the chapter stated that the spiritual gifts, which were so over-rated by the recipients of the epistle, receive their meaning not from themselves but from love. This is the essential core. The second section considered the nature of love as consisting in honesty and the simple realities of daily action, again in contrast to the extraordinary nature of the spiritual gifts. In the third section love is again contrasted with the gifts, this time as that which abides, whereas they pass away, "Love does not pass away."

The spiritual gifts belong to our transitory earthly existence. Prophecy has a meaning as long as our life is carried on within the bounds of time and place, of secret inwardness. Here it is very important if the prophet has the gift to proclaim what shall one day take place, to tell those present in a certain place what is happening at a distance, to reveal in his true nature the man who conceals his real opinions from others and perhaps even from himself. But all this is in relation to sacred history which takes place in time, for the prophet beholds the secret operations by which God ordains events, and interprets therefrom what takes place at any one time. But these accomplishments lose their significance when the end of all things, of the world and of the life of the individual, makes everything eternally manifest.

Speaking with tongues is also bound up with the limitations of earthly existence, with the inadequacy of speech. Man does not know God. Between him and the living Lord lies the dullness of his earthly nature. His earthliness separates him from the mysterious and remote divinity. His sin makes him blind to the one who is all-holy. Hence his experience of God remains inadequate, uncertain and ambiguous. But when the Spirit visits a man, then he comes face to face with God in immediate experience, and knows who He is. But he cannot express it. In speaking with tongues he vainly attempts to break the barrier. "It is speech, but spoken in the air," because no one understands it. (I Cor. 14:9) It is a "prayer," a communion with God, in which "my spirit prays, but my mind can do nothing." (I Cor. 14:14) Everything remains in the inexpressibility of immediate contact and does not succeed in finding words. With our earthly existence this gift also loses its significance.

The charismatic knowledge will also disappear. Man is driven by the desire for truth—but it is a truth which does not consist merely in grasping facts, in beholding the nature of things and understanding their logical connection. He would like to know what is before him, why it is so and where it leads, how it comes from the whole and what it is in itself. He would like to understand the fact from the essence and the temporal from the eternal. He would like to grasp the ultimate which leaves no further question but reveals all things in the openness of truth. But he cannot do this because in this respect also his existence is limited. The gift of wisdom must have had something of this quality, but only in such a way that the spirit touched it and then lost it again. When the hour had passed the man could only say, "I had it, but now it is gone." With the end of our earthly life everything comes into the clear present. Then the nature of things is revealed in their appearance, the meaning is evident in every portion of being; fact and necessity correspond to each other. Truth has become a condition and the charisma no longer means anything.

And now the thought of the apostle proceeds from the charisma of knowledge or understanding to understanding in general. Spiritual understanding is a partial thing; prophecy is a partial thing—all our understanding is partial. It belongs to our earthly existence, just as a child's way of understanding belongs to its age. The child has his way of speaking, of feeling, of thinking; as soon as he is grown all this ceases, and now his ways become those of a man. Man upon earth is but a child. He never reaches that ripeness of truth which consists in seeing the whole and the individual thing in their relation, and both clearly and openly. He always sees only parts, pieces, and he sees them dimly, hidden in himself, because he sees the essential not immediately but in reflection. Things do not exist in themselves but are rooted in another, the essential and eternal. In order to understand them correctly we must grasp them in their essential and eternal root, but this never appears to our eyes. It is as if a man could not view immediately the thing with which he is concerned, but only in a mirror, and a mirror which is dark and uneven, so that the figure appears wavering and broken. Some day it will be different. We shall see "face to face." The phrase is so common that we do not notice at once what a great fact it expresses, namely that the essential which alone is ultimately worth knowing and in which all else finds its truth, is a "face." It is God, He whom we everywhere behold in dark, indistinct mirrors, which conceal rather than reveal. One day He will look at us openly, and the veil shall be taken away from our own face, so that it can freely turn to Him. And in every thing the face of God will shine forth, and from this face each thing will receive its truth—that truth which consists in being the content of His eternal knowledge, and which makes it possible for us to discover and know anything. All our knowledge is contained within the knowledge of God.

The little sentence contains even more; this is shown by what follows. The "face" with which man shall behold the face of God is not his completed possession. It is not as if he must look into the mirror here on earth and then simply turn around and behold the sacred countenance. Considered as a face or an eye, man is just as dark, confused and interiorly broken as the mirror of things. But if on earth he has had faith in the self-revealing God and has persevered in the dimness of his earthly existence, then he will be given that face which can turn to God, and with those eyes he shall "know as he is known." The foundation of all truth is the knowledge of God. The beginning of all knowledge lies in Him. It is the presupposition for the thing's being knowable and makes it possible for men to know it. The fact that God knows all things, that every being is from its very root known by God, is now hidden. We say it over to ourselves, try to realize it, but do not experience it. Things stand before us as unrevealed riddles, dark lumps of being. Knowledge only seems to begin when man faces them; they themselves in their own being seem to have nothing to do with this. For our feeling, the world could exist even if no one knew it, just as the silent wastes of ice around the poles exist even if no eye beholds them. But one day it will become clear that before the being of things comes their being known; that they were never unknown because otherwise they could never have existed. The being of things is a fruit of God's knowledge. And that they shall dawn upon us in their reality and essentiality is only possible because they stand wholly in the knowledge of God. Everything exists in consequence of the knowledge of God, but we do not perceive this. Herein lies the hiddenness of existence, the illusion that the world is a beginning and exists in itself, a beginning of mere existence, followed only later, perhaps after endless effort and slow progress, by its being known by man. This illusion is a part and parcel of sin. One day it shall fall away and it shall be revealed that the world exists only in consequence of its being known by God—the world and we ourselves also. I shall realize that I exist only because God knows me. My being known by God is my reality, and I become real in the measure that my life and action are in harmony with the knowledge of God. And my knowledge is true in the measure in which it agrees with the divine knowledge. Now we understand the immensity of the sentence, "One day I shall know completely, even as I myself am known." I shall share in the glance which God casts upon me, and shall return this glance to God. From the knowledge of God I shall know His holy countenance, and therein all things.

This will be eternity, the essential and unending. All else shall pass away, even the spiritual gifts which seem so powerful, so glowing and so great to him who receives them—to him and also to the one who envies him. One day there shall be nothing but pure brightness, quiet genuineness, the perfectly fulfilled presence of this "face to face."

The final sentence has a blended meaning. "Now there abide faith, hope, love. And the greatest of these is love." We do not see at once what the words "Now there abide" mean. St. Paul thinks passionately. His thought ferments and overflows, so that the same word at times has one meaning and suggests another. Primarily "abide" signifies the contrast to the transitoriness of existence. Everything earthly passes away, even the charismata. But faith, hope and love are forces that extend into eternity. They are gifts of the Holy Spirit, like the others, but not given merely to help within the boundaries of time and to disappear with time, but they are an already beginning eternity, which shall one day be perfected. But then another thought slips in: even faith and hope are bound up with time. Of the latter the Epistle to the Romans says: "We are saved by hope. But hope whose object is seen is not hope. If it is seen, why should we still hope? But if our hope is directed toward that which we do not yet see, then let us wait in patience." (Rom. 8:24–5) The same God who gives the charismata is He who produces the power of this hope, namely patience. But one day that will no longer be needed. Faith too shall disappear in an existence in which we see "face to face," and so shall the mirror and its riddle. And so, from the trinity of those gifts which in contrast with the charismata prove "abiding," St. Paul finally selects one as the greatest—love. Its greatness consists in the fact that it never passes away, as he said at the beginning of the passage, but is in the final sense of the word "abiding." Now it becomes clear what the ultimate criterion is by which St. Paul measures the manifestations of the Christian life. It is their power to resist transitoriness; it is their closeness to eternity. The charismata are quite transitory. They belong to time and its limitations. If he had been questioned on the subject St. Paul would have admitted that they were not even essential for the progress of historical Christianity as a whole but were bound up with a definite period. They are expressions of an eruption and its exuberance; phenomena of the youthful Christianity which disappear as soon as mature age with its severity and commonplace begins. This spiritual condition can recur in times of historical crisis, but in as fleeting a manner as in the beginning. By contrast faith and hope have an essential character. A man can be a Christian without the charismata, but not without faith and hope. These have an eternal content even now. Eternal life is already present. Death and God's merciful judgment do not bestow it but set it free and perfect it. Eternity is not a space into which man shall one day step, but it is the character which the redeemed life within him possesses from the beginning. It is the manner in which God lives and the manner in which man through the grace of God shares in the life of God. But at present it is enclosed in the transitory, and only through the interior assurance in which, as the Epistle to the Romans says, "The Holy Spirit bears witness with our spirit that we are children of God" do we perceive it. But one day it shall come forth, open its eyes and become self-conscious and joyful. Then faith and hope shall pass away. But not so love. It shall only then awaken to the fulness of its power and its freedom. It shall be the very act of our eternal life.

This is the last thing that St. Paul says about it here, and by which he contrasts it with all else: love is eternal.

VI

But let us not permit this word to be used carelessly as has happened to so many of the sacred words. The meaning of the word "eternal" has nothing to do with its use in popular language. Its real meaning is not made clear in the thirteenth chapter of the First Epistle to the Corinthians. If we look closely we see that the question, what love in itself is, is not asked here, but only how does it conduct itself and how does it last. What is it then?

In order to answer this question we must refer to other texts. If we consider only the chapter of First Corinthians which contrasts love with the over-rated and misused spiritual gifts, love appears as something ethical, even with a certain inclination to the bourgeois, as moderation and consideration. But this does not completely express the thought of the apostle. He holds that the love which is demanded of man does not originate in man himself, but in God. Of the love of God we read in other epistles, for instance in the one to the Romans. In the passage where St. Paul, as it were, casts his anchor in the love of God as the centre of Christian life, we read: "What shall we then say to these things? If God be for us, who is against us? He that spared not even his own Son, but delivered him up for us all, how hath he not also, with him, given us all things. Who shall accuse against the elect of God? God that justifieth. Who is he that shall condemn? Christ Jesus that died, yea that is risen also again; who is at the right hand of God, who also maketh intercession for us. Who then shall separate us from the love of Christ? Shall tribulation, or distress, or famine, or nakedness, or danger, or persecution, or the sword?...But in all these things we overcome, because of him that hath loved us. For I am sure that neither death, nor life, nor angels, nor principalities, nor powers, nor things present, nor things to come, nor might, nor height, nor depth, nor any other creature shall be able to separate us from the love of God, which is in Christ Jesus our Lord."

Here that power breaks through which our text appears to lack. But we must mentally supply it behind every sentence of the chapter of First Corinthians, so that it fills and animates its self-controlled sobriety. The love of which St. Paul is speaking is not the force of human passion or affection or kindliness which the word expresses in popular parlance, but it is a power and disposition of God. And we must not, as generally happens, think of it after the manner of our own love, only very pure and great, but we must, in speaking of the love of God, first of all forget what the word means in our language and remember that we are here concerned with revelation. We must listen to its words and receive its meaning purely from its own expression. That God loves may be self-evident, as an expression of perfect and complete existence; that He loves man is by no means self-evident. Natural religious experience does not perceive the divine merely in the form of goodness and kindness—witness the gods of hatred and horror of which we hear in the history of religion, the references to the indifference, the envy, the anger of the gods, to the incomprehensibility of the dispensations of fate, and other such things. Even the experiences of divine goodness do not mean at all what the New Testament means by love, but merely indicate that the divine ruler is gracious, takes pleasure in His creatures, is rich and inclined to share His riches. But the New Testament reveals to us in the love of God a seriousness which, if we remove the dulling effect of custom that lies upon all Christian concepts, must affect us more and more deeply.

This love is not something which God, as would be in accord with our ideas, hands down to His creature, man, not a radiation of His favor which does not affect Him, but it is something unheard-of which we can express only if we speak quite recklessly. The fact that God has created a world and men in this world would not in itself need to touch Him in His own existence. It would simply be a creation, separated absolutely from Him, the Creator, by the very fact of its having been created. He would take pleasure in it, behold its perfections, the work of His creation, desire its welfare and its consummation, and guide it to that end by His governing providence. But, for all that, it would not need to touch His heart in any way. He would not have to be interiorly concerned with it. What the Greeks said about the Olympian repose of their gods who sit enthroned above all earthly turmoil hints at this idea. This is as far as the concept of divine love which we could reach by ourselves would go, unless we went to the other extreme and conceived it in Dionysiac fashion, as a kind of universal intoxication of the divinity, as it appears in the case of a number of gods in the history of religion. But that this has nothing to do with the chaste God of revelation goes without saying.

What revelation says about the love of God breaks down, as it were, the barrier that His divinity erects between Him and the world. It tells us that the world means something to Him—far beyond all that we could deduce from our ideas of God and His creation. He is Lord of the world in inviolable freedom, but he has given it a meaning for Himself, has drawn it close to Him, and in a kind of closeness which we can express only by saying that He has let it become His destiny. If we wish to conceive of this we must be on our guard that we do not violate the absolute lordship of God or veil the inexorable createdness of the world. This is the first and fundamental truth about the love of God. But it is equally true that He has drawn the world into the depth of His own existence in such a way that it establishes between God and us a relation which from a human point of view is incomprehensible and impossible. This forms the essential content of the Christian message and is "the love of God."

What else can it mean if St. Paul says that God "did not spare His own Son but delivered Him up for us all"? And immediately thereafter: "Christ it is who died for us, and who also rose again and sits at the right hand of God and intercedes for us." What else can the word of St. John mean: "God so loved the world that He gave His only-begotten Son"? (John 3:16) Let us not take such sentences as self-evident. If God wished to receive us back into His favor after we had fallen away from Him, He could have done so without involving Himself. He is God; an act of indulgence or of newly-creating forgiveness would have been sufficient, and that would have been mysterious enough. It would be presumptuous and foolish as well to try to maintain that a greater price was necessary for the redemption of man. But now we hear that God "gave His Son," that is, Himself. Gave—for what? And to whom? This is the decisive thing. To be seized by something from which He was exempt by virtue of His divinity—namely destiny. But what could deliver Him up to this destiny, which of itself had no power over Him? What can "destiny" be for God? Only a power which would rise up in Himself, in His own inviolable freedom—a power of honor and of love. Let us leave the former aside; it would bring up the whole problem of God, as the great doctor of the Church, St. Anselm of Canterbury did. Let us stay with the second point, the love of God. It is that incomprehensible will with which He permitted the creature to approach Him in such a way that He "must" now solve the problem of its destiny not through an aloof and omnipotent Providence but through the "giving" of Himself; by entering into history, living among us and rising victorious over death and sin. This is the work of that love of which the New Testament speaks.

And now St. Paul says: This love is still in operation as that disposition with which Christ stands before God for our sake. It is the one and all, the beginning and the end for us. Our new existence is rooted and grounded in it as the reality of creation is grounded in the almighty will of Him who created it.

This love by which we live as Christians should also be the disposition and the strength in which we deal with other men. From it there shall grow a new life-relation, a new order of things. This is presupposed by all that has been said about Christian love. If St. Paul opposes the sobriety of Christian love to the enthusiasm of the charismata it is not in order to draw it into the ethical or sentimental or earthly but to contrast it as the truly real and lasting thing with phenomena that very easily slip into the fantastic, and in any case are transitory. But he would say of this same love that it is immensity itself, so far surpassing all our concepts that it can be known only through revelation and must constantly be grasped and held by means of this. How sublime are the thought-processes underlying St. Paul's doctrine of love is shown by the twelfth chapter of the Epistle to the Corinthians, in which the relation of the individual believers to each other is indicated by the figure of the mystical Christ. Let us consider what it means when he says that all are members of one body, and that this body is Christ. But if we wish to hear how the simple teachings of the thirteenth chapter would sound if St. Paul uttered them from their real depths, then we must look at the epistle to his favorite congregation, the Philippians. Here we find sentences like these: "God is my witness how I long for you all in the heart of Jesus Christ." (Phil. 1:8) It is the loving intimacy of Christ Himself with which he loves. That core of love, of which he says in the Epistle to the Romans that no power of the world "can separate us from the love of God which is in Christ our Lord," here becomes active. Only from this point of view do the simple sentences of the Epistle to the Corinthians receive their true magnitude. Now they are an expression of that holy moderation of Christianity with which it expresses matters for which no word would really be sufficiently fervent.

THE WORLD AND THE PERSON

Preface

The essays in this volume deal with the question of the nature of man. This question is far more common today than it has been for a long time. We cannot here set forth all that has contributed to its popularity. That would require an analysis of the most intimate happenings of the last century. In any case, the present age once more thinks of the existence of man as something enigmatic. Not so long ago there were two definitive answers to the question of the nature of man, the humanistically philosophical and the scientifically technical. They contrasted sharply in many ways but had one thing in common: both claimed to know what man is. Their questions moved in the realm of the known. This conviction that they knew man, and the resulting security and the consequent narrowness in dealing with human affairs, has been shattered. The feeling, which was never openly admitted but crept surreptitiously through the 19th century, that the conditions of humanity might be different than the official opinion maintained, has now forced its way into the open. Man has realized that he is different than he thought, that he is unknown to himself and a problem which he must solve. The point of humanity once more lies in darkness and in the future. Hence comes the openmindedness of which we spoke. The question of man is again a real question. Therefore it has become possible once more to seek that answer which Christian revelation gives to the problem—really to seek it, for the Christian milieu has also suffered from the restricting force of a presumed knowledge. The Christian has also, to a great extent, lacked the courage to place man in that realm of the unknown in which he belonged, and the answer which he gave to the question of man's nature was, though limited and changed in tone, no other than the common one.

To give the complete answer to this question of the nature of man, would be the task of a Christian doctrine of man. The author has been working at this for a number of years, but cannot anticipate when it will be completed. Therefore on the advice of friends he is publishing a few treatises which show how the questions should be handled, and he hopes to learn something from the responses to these which will be of value for the larger work.

These treatises are called essays. This word is used in the modest yet confident sense which it possesses in Michel Montaigne's courageous book. These essays are not dissertations, setting forth completely envisioned and elaborated matters, but experiments in which certain ideas are brought to bear upon very complicated conditions in order to find out their usefulness. Fundamentally, it is one idea that shall be examined—that man does not exist as an enclosed block of reality or a self-sufficient figure evolving from within, but rather exists for that which he encounters from without. In the opinion of the author this concept sets forth not only the strongest motifs of the New Testament and important ideas of the past which have today found particular expression—especially the ideas of St. Augustine—but also the experience of the present, since individualism and evolutionary doctrines are more and more clearly recognized as outmoded.

That the word "essays" also indicates that the work takes account not only of all kinds of insufficiency but also of various possibilities of error, need not be particularly emphasized.

The section dealing with the person represents an outline of the Christian portrait of man. The preceding chapters, dealing with the world, investigate the relations of man with reality and the tasks and problems confronting him. The final chapter, dealing with Providence, is intended to show in one particularly important point, how one can conceive of the Christian unity of man and the world, Christian "existence."

Part I: The World

Nature and Creation

I

Nature, Subject and Culture

How does man perceive the being of the world in which he lives? In what way does it exist? In what concepts is the manner of its existence expressed?

Even at the close of the Middle Ages, but especially in the Renaissance, a word appears which gains ever-increasing importance: the word *Nature*. It indicates the totality of things, all that exists. More accurately, it indicates all that exists before man does anything to it. The constellations, the earth, the landscape with its plants and animals, but also man himself, insofar as he is given to himself as an organic and spiritual reality. This totality is experienced as something profound, mighty and glorious, as a fullness of experience ready for man's use, and also as an assignment which man must understand, take possession of, and mold. The emotional quality of the language shows the deep involvement of feeling and circumstances which it expresses.

The concept of nature is the concept of an object which signifies that which presents itself to our thought and action. But it is also a concept of values, and signifies a valid norm for this thought and action: that which is proper and healthy, wise and perfect—the "natural." Opposed to this is the unnatural, the artificial, abnormal, unhealthy, spoiled. This standard of values produces pictures of an existence according to nature: the correct man, the natural society and government, the fruitful education, the noble art, and so on—pictures which correspond to the concept of the "honnête homme" of the 16th and 17th centuries, the "natural" man of Rousseau, the rational life of the Enlightenment and the naturally beautiful in classical and neo-classical art.

The concept of nature expresses something final. One cannot go beyond it. As soon as something is derived from it, it is definitely understood. As soon as something can be shown to have a natural cause, it is justified. As soon as something is recognized as being according to nature the problem disappears. This does not mean that nature in the last analysis and as a whole can be understood. On the contrary: it is perceived as something so profound and rich that the consideration of it is infinite. It is creative, hence it cannot be captured in any system. It is mysterious and "will not be robbed of its veil"—mysterious not only in the sense that its problems are too complicated, but fundamentally so; it bears the mysterious character of beginning and end, of the primary cause, that which is in its very nature impenetrable. And for that very reason it represents the ultimate that can be interrogated. Insofar as it vouchsafes an answer, this answer is final, because it is "natural," because it is immediately evident and because it implies an answer from the ultimate cause inasmuch as it comes from nature.

Into the experience of nature flows another: that of antiquity. For the feeling of the Renaissance which thereafter permeated the whole modern period, classical antiquity is not one of many historical epochs and so, like all others, limited, but it has the character of a norm. It represents the expression of man as he should be. The nature of man, and his feelings, the language and art, the forms of state and society in the ancient Graeco-Roman world are felt to be the valid interpretation of truly natural existence. The concept of the classical in the last analysis signifies the same thing as that of the natural, only in the form of an historical culture. Classical culture is "natural" culture, and the experience of nature is justified by the experience of a culture of the highest quality.

From this point of view the problem of religion also reveals itself in a new form. Very soon two possible solutions appear. The first finds a numinous depth in nature itself. There arises the idea of the mysterious, all-creative, holy nature which is itself God; so it is in Giordano Bruno, Spinoza, Goethe, Hölderlin, Schelling. Nature itself is conceived as the primary religious fact and relation to it as the root of piety. The natural is at the same time the holy and pious, and that which is unnatural or contrary to nature is regarded as in itself sacrilegious.[1] Or else the religious feeling suffers a kind of inversion and becomes a hidden, pious impatience, which regards the immediate existence of things as the only substantial reality, and consciousness of facts and faithfulness to reality as the only criterion of rightness. This is particularly true in positivism, which runs through the whole modern age.

Insofar as man is a primary psychosomatic reality he himself belongs to this nature, but insofar as he contemplates it, investigates it, takes possession of it and shapes it, he stands in opposition to it. That a real opposition is involved, becomes clear from the caution expressed in the concept of the unnatural. The unnatural can exist only because man does not remain in the immediate order of nature. He releases himself from it, thereby bringing it into a crisis and then has the task of rebuilding it through knowledge, action and production. From the experience of this opposition comes a second basic form of the interpretation of existence, that of the subject. This concept, like that of nature, is not found in the Middle Ages. Of course, men knew nature as reality and also as a norm. Medieval man also saw objects, the order of their structure, the regularity of their behavior, and in this way reached a notion of the ultimate unity. In addition, Medieval thought adopted the Greek, particularly the Aristotelian concept of nature, and carried it out in all directions. But this concept does not have the character described above. Rather, it becomes the means of explaining the creation of all things by God. Medieval thought likewise knew of the subject as the unity of individual existence, the bearer of intellectual acts and the point of accountability and responsibility. But this concept had something selfless about it, a quiet objectivity, which is manifested in the way in which the individual recedes before the total structure of existence. This character changes toward the end of the Middle Ages and especially in the Renaissance. A subjective experience begins to predominate which determines the whole succeeding age. Man experiences himself in a new way as something important and interesting. Above all, the exceptional, gifted man attains an importance never felt in the Middle Ages. The fact that the Renaissance abounds in original and magnificent personalities is not enough to account for the impression made by its humanism. The Middle Ages also relied upon exceptional persons, fighters, rulers, creative artists and religious geniuses, but, it was not until the later period, that the great man received that emphasis which gave him his peculiar character. Only then did he become important to himself, to others and to the whole age. Personality becomes a new criterion of value and determines the whole range of life, as may be seen with special clarity in the case of a great personality.

There arises a new feeling for humanity, an interest in its manifold qualities, a consideration for its genuineness and originality. Just as nature appeared as the beginning of things, beyond which one could not reach, so also did personality. Above all, the great personality bore the law of its existence within itself. It demanded to be understood from within itself and justified its actions by its own creative power. That which proceeded authentically from it was valid. Beginning with the consideration of unusual persons, the same standard was applied to mankind in general. Man becomes a beginning as valid as nature. Proper existence consists in man's living and acting from the original basis of his personality. In opposition to the ethos of the objectively good and of truth there arises that of genuineness and actuality. That which had previously been based upon the primary nature of the living, now received its formal expression in the concept of the "subject." This was the bearer of acts which possessed value and was also the unity of the categories which determined these values. We find its most definite exposition in the philosophy of Kant. This philosophy conceives of the logical, ethical, aesthetic subject as something final supported by the world of the mind. One cannot reach beyond this, since every attempt to do so could be carried out only by means of the categories of this very subjectivity. The "subject" is the logical expression of the "personality." Both represent different forms of the nature of man, which is opposed to the nature of things. With a passion which also indicates a shift in existential feeling, this philosophy claims the quality of autonomy for the logical, ethical, aesthetic subject. Autonomy means an existing in itself, the primary nature and absolute validity of the subject; hence it is the same claim which, when applied to the living and creative, is expressed by the concept of personality, and, in the realm of things and objects, by the concept of nature. As soon as something can be derived from the personality or the subject, it is definitively understood. Anyone who has in some way freed himself from "the modern age" and delves into the works of Kant has a peculiar experience. He wonders how the possibility of knowing, of passing moral judgments, etc. is supposed to be guaranteed by the process of rooting the whole system in subjectivity—"transcendental" as this may be. But in the very feeling that this was so lay that "new" thing which Kant, after crossing the intellectual water-shed, cannot follow through. To the modern way of thinking an act of knowing or a moral judgment really appeared valid because it was based upon the autonomy of the subject—corresponding to that which was said above concerning knowledge from nature and the natural standard of values. This was not to maintain that the subject itself was fully comprehensible. Kant himself, for example, reads into the experience of the interior moral law the deepest mystery, a mystery which he significantly connects with the numinous impression of the starry heavens, that is, of nature. Personality and subject are fundamentally as incomprehensible as nature, but that which is understood from their point of view is validly understood. It is as impossible to go beyond them to metaphysical principles as it is to go beyond nature. Personality too continues into the realm of religion. The genius is conceived of as numinous. The poet, the artist, the man of action appear as something mysterious, and there is a tendency to connect them with the image of the gods. The new concept of fame expresses the superhuman radiance which great personalities reflect in history. Subjectivity goes beyond the concept of the subject in itself and is connected with the World-spirit, becoming the immediate expression of the latter. From this point of view thought itself receives a religious character, and this flows into the image of "science" and gives it an unprecedented importance.

Nature and subject—the latter term including personality—stand face to face as the final facts. Existence is posited as nature and subject. One cannot go beyond them. Between them the world of human acts and human works comes into being. It rests upon these two poles: they are its pre-requisites and it is characterized by them. But on the other hand it has a peculiar autonomy. It is determined by a third concept which is also peculiar to the modern age, that of culture.

The people of the Middle Ages had a culture of the highest kind. They strove for knowledge and in their *Summas* constructed a lofty world of understanding. They created mighty works, accomplished bold deeds and established orders of human society which had ultimate value. But all this was done in a spirit, which, if it had become self-conscious, would have described itself as a service in the completion of God's creative work in the world. Man was striving to accomplish the work, not to reflect upon the work itself, because it was the object to be created that interested him, not he himself as the creator. In this respect too there was a change in modern times. The work of man received a new significance and so also did man as the worker. The work of man appropriated the meaning which had formerly belonged to the work of God. The world lost its character of "creation" and became "nature"; the work of man lost the spirit of service determined by obedience to God, and became "creation." Man himself who before this had been the adorer and servant, now became the "creator." All this is expressed in the word "culture." In this word also there lies the claim to autonomy. Man grasps existence in order to shape it according to his own will. In seeing the world as nature, he takes it out of God's hand and makes it independent. In seeing himself as personality and subject he frees himself from the power of God and makes himself the master of his own existence. In his efforts toward culture he attempts to build the world, not in obedience to God, but as his own work. As a matter of fact, the concept of culture then begins to coincide with the foundations of modern science, and from this proceeds technology. This in turn becomes the total embodiment of all the means and methods by which man frees himself from the bounds of organic relations and becomes able to establish his aims as he pleases and to re-shape what is before him. What is involved in this effort is revealed in the doctrine of the autonomy of culture which progressively releases science, politics, economics, art, education, etc. from all connection with faith and also from any connection with universally binding ethics and makes them wholly independent. This culture also takes on a religious character. In it is revealed the creative mystery of existence, whether this be conceived as the primary basis of nature, or as the power of personality or as the world-spirit. This culture also appears as something final which guarantees for man the meaning of existence.—"He who has art and science already has religion."

It then becomes a question of psychological structure or of the particular situation in the history of the mind how the basic realities of nature, of the subject, and of culture subsisting between the other two—existence as the object, as the self and as a task—shall be brought into relation with each other. The emphasis may be placed upon nature and the subject may be regarded as the organ of nature, as it was in the naturalistic philosophy of the Renaissance and of Romanticism. Then culture is also considered as an expression of nature, as nature transcending itself and constructing itself by means of the connecting link of the reflecting subject.

Or the emphasis is on the self and nature appears as a chaotic mass of possibilities, out of which the subject, by an autocratic moulding, produces the world of culture. This is the method used in the philosophy of Kant. Finally, nature and subject may be considered equally important bases of the relation, between which the supra-natural and supra-personal event of the production of culture takes place. This is Hegel's idea.

The matter of religion is also variously interpreted. The divine is drawn into nature and equated with its creative depth; or it is taken up into the interior of the personality, the emotions or the quality of genius, and appears as their mysterious source; or else it is regarded as the creative spiritual principle of existence as such, which unfolds in the process of the production of culture. But the relation can also be dealt with on the principle of remoteness, as is the case in deism and rationalism. Then "God" is moved to such a distance from the world that He cannot interfere with nature and the subject in their autocracy or with the self-development of the work of creative culture. A last possibility tends to conceive of religion as dangerous for the freedom and purity of the world and to remove it entirely. This is what positivism and materialism in their various forms attempt to do.

To the question asked at the beginning of this book, in what way that which exists does exist, the modern mind replies: as nature, as subject and as culture. The structure composed of these elements signifies something final beyond which one cannot reach. It is autonomous, requires no proof and permits of no norm above itself. This answer comes from the age as a whole and does not depend on the individual. It expresses a general attitude into which the individual is born and with which he must come to terms. In one way or another, as a given manner of feeling and an accepted common property, it affects the consciousness of every individual, even when he contradicts it.

The manner in which religious reality, God and His kingdom are experienced and made the content of action is also influenced by this attitude. Its influence can destroy every positive relation to revelation, but it also makes itself felt even where faith is maintained. It works its way into the thoughts and feelings of the man who is willing to believe, and produces the specifically modern religious difficulties which may be summed up in this question: Can the Church, the Incarnation, Revelation, and, finally, the personal and holy God who is presupposed by all these, really exist if the world is such as it is here thought to be?

II

The Created-ness of the World

To assume a proper attitude toward this situation and its meaning is not easy, since it is not only very complicated but is determined by various viewpoints which limit and neutralize each other.

The first question would seem to be: what is correct in the concepts of nature, subject and culture which we have set forth? The immediacy with which the Middle Ages saw the absolute reality of God and the promised eternal life as the essential thing, threatened—on principle, and without detriment to a great vitality and creativity—to depreciate the finite and temporal. The finite appeared merely as the shadowy reflection of the absolute, and time as the antechamber of eternity, without any reality of its own. The symbolic character of creation was so strongly felt that creation itself was not looked upon as having sufficient reality. Beginning at the close of the Middle Ages, the power of religion became constantly weaker. The impulse toward transcendence which had made itself felt at every point of existence, now ceased. The religious atmosphere which had surrounded everything, the immediately felt religious tendency which had permeated everything, vanished. The world, to use the expression we have coined, lost its enchantment. Finite reality stood forth in a new way with its harshness and urgency, its wealth of meaning and its value. The finite as such penetrated into man's consciousness and with it the seriousness of creation. For this seriousness can be resolved in different ways, either by veiling the fact of created-ness and moving the world into the absolute in some way or other, or else by regarding the religious absolute so immediately as the essential thing that the finite loses its density of reality and meaning. This very density now forced its way into man's consciousness, posed its questions and revealed its problems.

All this was expressed in the concepts of which we have spoken, and, to this extent, they are good. Truth remains truth, no matter what the price. And it was indeed truth which the modern consciousness recognized in opposition to the Middle Ages: the genuine, meaningful reality of finite being, which demands our action. In all our admiration for the greatness, the unity and the fervor of the medieval concept of the world we must not forget that it contained, at all points, the religious short-circuit. The absolute was so strongly felt that the finite and its own meaning were not given proper and proportionate consideration. The questions which were asked concerning the nature of the world were only partially formulated; the answers were only partially given. The bold and pious structure of medieval existence had been able to arise and endure only because the eye for the reality of things was often blinded, the heart was protected from the possibilities of the world and the decisions were transferred to the realm of ethical and religious life. Medieval man adored God and obeyed the authority which the Lord of the world had placed within it. In this way he satisfied the ultimate truth, but often overlooked the penultimate: yet this also is truth and must not be crushed by the weight of the other. Consequently, his answers to the questions concerning the nature of the world were often prejudiced and uncritical and reduced it to a mythical, legendary, artistic form. And since the world could not present itself to his view as that which it is, even his faith did not attain its proper confirmation.

In the concepts of nature, subject and culture we find expressed that duty which the modern age has discovered and taken upon itself: the duty of being honest and fair to the matter in hand. The modern age decided to accept the world as reality and not to thin it out by an immediate transition to the absolute. It realized that this world has been handed over to man in a great and terrifying manner, and it took it upon itself not to weaken this responsibility by reverting to religion, but to consider this duty itself as a religious task. Modern science with its inexorability, technology with its exactness and daring, the specifically modern spirit of world conquest, planning and organizing are all true progress. Not progress in the superficial sense, which would infer that the period of history which they characterize is absolutely better than the preceding one. For, to speak here of better or worse is a dubious matter—even apart from the fact that every gain at one point is paid for by loss at another, and that we today, as the modern age is approaching its end, see ever more clearly how much the transition has cost. That which characterizes one epoch of history as compared with another is not that it is better, but that it is timely. To that extent it is good and constitutes progress. The concepts we have discussed express that new spirit which was timely. Perhaps we must go so far as to say that even what is false in them is in some way connected with modern accomplishments and achievements. If a work of such magnitude in science, mastery and organization were to be accomplished, as it actually was, perhaps in some way this passionate turning toward the world was necessary. Nevertheless, this whole structure of concepts, of nature, subject and culture, which we have developed, and which confronts us in the modern consciousness, stands in profound contradiction to Christianity, not only because it carried out the aforementioned new tasks with an exclusiveness which necessarily destroyed the unity of existence, but also because that which was correct in these concepts was dominated by a way of thinking on the subject of existence which was opposed to the meaning of revelation.

Above all, it was opposed to the statement which is basic to the whole of Scripture; that is, that the world was created. But in order to understand all the implications of this statement we must have a clear idea of the meaning of the term "Divine Creation." For the term has changed its meaning yet still contains traces of its original significance and emotional connotations which obscure the change. When the 19th century speaks of creation there is an echo of the Biblical meaning, but actually it means the creative work of nature, which itself, as a whole, was not created, but is eternally independent and evolves from within itself; or else it means the creative power of the great personality which carries its own form and law within itself and accomplishes its work from its own initiative. Various transitions led to this change of meaning, and they can be demonstrated by a careful examination of philosophical, poetical and religious language. Even if the man who believes the Bible speaks of creation, it is uncertain how he conceives of this creation. Usually he has no definite conception of it but refers to it as something mysterious to an endlessly remote beginning. But as soon as he must really think about it, when, for example, he reads the account of the creation or represents to himself the meaning of the first article of the Creed, he will probably imagine the divine creation as the operation of an immense cause which is more or less patterned after the model of nature—a kind of prolonging of the processes of nature into the absolute. His concept of God is influenced by the concept of nature and he is inclined to think of God as that stage of the proceeding which causes nature to be what it is, as, so to speak, absolute nature. The concept of nature serves as a category which shapes all thoughts; the feeling for nature becomes an unconscious but determining attitude which turns even his understanding of the account of creation, of the Psalms, of the statements concerning God's providence in a definite direction.

Here the consciousness of the believer must make a fundamental distinction: the world is not Nature, but Creation, creation in the plain sense of a work brought forth by a free act. It is not something "natural," self-evident, self-justified, but it requires a reason, and it is given this reason by the power which created it in its being and reality. And the fact that it was created does not depend upon the coming into operation of a cause constructed after the model of natural energy, but upon an act which—taking this word in a broader sense—has the character of "grace." To put it in another way: the world does not have to be, but it is, because it was created. The act by which it was created did not need to take place, but it took place because it was willed. It might not have been willed, but it was willed because it was willed. This means that the world is not a necessity, but a fact.

This is the distinguishing characteristic of the Biblical view of existence: the world is based upon an act. This act is no extension of the operation of world forces beyond the beginning of the world but springs from a freedom which is completely master of itself. It does not enter reality as does a physical or biological effect, as soon as its causes exist, but like the action of a man when he has made his decision in freedom.

It has been said that this concept of a personal Creator is the result of the Semitic way of thinking, according to which God has no living relation to the world but is only the builder and ruler approaching it from without. We may leave aside the question how far a divine being, completely apart from the world and merely constructing and governing, can be the object of thought. In any case, such an idea has nothing to do with that of Genesis. A purely transcendent divinity would be the exact opposite of a merely immanent one, which does not reach beyond the world, merely representing its interiority. The two concepts would involve each other, and both are equally foreign to that given by Revelation. The concept of the true Creator runs straight across all those encountered in different religions. Creation is neither transcendent nor immanent. It cannot be grasped by these concepts, but it is the manner of working which is reserved to God alone—to that God who is really God and not "a divinity."

The motive of the act of creation—this is clear from the entire message of Scripture—is love. But this love also must not be defined by the category of the natural. This was done at one time with typical consistency by Neoplatonism. The Neoplatonists maintained that God had created the world from the over-abundance of his compelling love; but they thought of this "love" as a natural condition, a physical consequence, an expansion of soul, the irresistibility of a spiritual drive. Since the supreme Being is rich, it must love, and, because it loves, it must create—just as a spring must flow because it is a spring. This kind, of "love" has nothing to do with that of which Revelation speaks, and which refers to the disposition of the God who is free, and beyond the reach of any "Why" that can be determined by the world, even of that "Why" which the reflecting mind could deduce from God himself as the absolute being, and on the basis of a pattern of perfection. In creating, God is the Lord, in the face of not only finite reality but of his own absolute reality.[2]

In consequence, the concepts of Nature, subject and culture, as developed above, are abolished. Their factual content, however, is not abolished. That which exists in them prior to a good or evil interpretation by the will of man, and which expresses the knowledge that was attributed to a definite stage of history, remains. In so far as the concept of nature signifies the reality of the existent and the stringency of its objective certainties it keeps its validity; what is abolished is only its alleged "naturalness." In so far as the concepts of "personality" and "subject" signify the possibilities and limits of man they are henceforth indispensable. It is only the claim of autonomy which is abolished. Insofar as the concept of "culture" means that the world is entrusted to man in a frightening way, it belongs to the basic content of our consciousness. Only the falsity of an autocratic and independent work of man is abolished. In so far as these concepts indicate that western man at the beginning of the modern age took a step which cannot be retraced, a step toward a new responsibility for the world, a responsibility which is founded upon the psychological and historical situation, and that he must accept this, the concepts remain valid. What is abolished is only an image of the measure, the right and the duty of this responsibility, which seeks to deprive God of His power.

The world rests in the free act of God. Perhaps the reader thinks that we are here emphasizing something that is found on every page of the Bible and that we have heard ever since our school-days. Of course, it is found there and we have heard it and we know it, but do we know it as that which it really means? As a matter of fact, we need a conversion in the very roots of our self-respect and our disposition toward the world if we are to perceive what is meant by the statement that the world is not autonomous but proceeds from the action of God, that it is not necessary but is based upon an act which transcends all known freedom. The world does not have the character of nature but that of history accomplished by God. Man does not have the character of "subject" in the sense explained above, but he is himself because God has called him and continues to call him. Existence as a whole, things, man and action, come from God's grace. The distinction between nature and history, which we use in classifying and interpreting existence, moves only within that all-inclusive history which is originally free and which God accomplishes. The distinction between grace and nature, which our religious thinking employs, has its place only within that all-embracing decision of grace from which the whole of existence proceeds and to which it was pleasing that the world should exist at all, The creative work of man is not culture which has meaning in itself, but a service performed by the order of God to lead the world to that place which it can reach only through its encounter with man in his freedom. This fact is closely connected with those elementary reactions with which our feeling responds to existence: gratitude and protest. A world existing in the form of "nature" could not make that impression which awakens gratitude, gratitude because it exists. Here we cannot permit any lyricism to confuse our categories. I can give thanks only for that which I receive as a gift. To maintain that existence is a gift, if nature is the final cause, would be nonsense. Hence, if I respond to existence with gratitude, this proves that I perceive that it proceeds from action and liberty; i.e., is "given." This attitude can decline into the "natural" and assume a vague lyrical or Dionysiac form, but, as soon as it is critically purified, it speaks clearly. The same thing holds true in the case of protest. This also exists intrinsically, both in a clearly evident form—against the disorder of existence, suffering and confusion—and also in a hidden form—the protest against the very fact that existence is such as it is. This too would be impossible in a "natural" existence. In "nature" one can suffer, even be annihilated, but one cannot raise any objections against it.[3] The fact that the system of thought which we have discussed is rejected and that existence is based upon the freedom of the act of God, is not meant to take away the seriousness expressed in those concepts. This seriousness contains the true meaning of that false matter-of-factness of which we have spoken.[4]

Nature simply is that which is "given," around us and in us, and man should see it as it is. Our faith in Creation must not take on the nature of a fairy tale but within the hand of God's freedom the world must retain the serious strictness which appertains to it. But this is possible only as a result of a penetrating comprehension of the concept of Creation itself. The creative activity of God is true creation. Objects are not merely the concepts of God's consciousness. The world does not exist as the play of the imagination of an infinite Being. The Hindu idea that the world is Maya, the unreal play of divine phantasy, is very superficial. It takes from the world that very character from which its true depth results, namely the seriousness of reality. Whatever God creates he creates absolutely in its entirety. He dismisses what He has created and grants it its own nature, position and activity. The figure which a mortal artist creates exists in his mind. As soon as he works the stone, that which he produces is not the figure itself but a system of signs by which he communicates with the beholder so that the image may also rise up in *his* mind.

The figure exists only as a concept in the mind of the artist and of the comprehending spectator. The reality which stands between them, the block of marble, only brings about the *rapport*. So it is misleading to compare the creative act of God with that of the artist, for the latter is unable to accomplish the decisive fact—really to make that which he has beheld. But this is what God does. He releases that which He has conceived in His thought so that it may stand and act freely. Herein lies the supreme quality of creation. From this results its mighty force and its inevitability. This is the very thing which is misunderstood and misused by the idea of autonomy. In this way, creation possesses that complete seriousness of validity, that inevitability of fact and law which determines the experience and the character of modern science, for it was created by Him who not only knows truth but establishes it. The general opinion is that the view of the world which is held by science, since it depends on the consciousness of autonomous nature, is the one that is really mature and serious, while the view presented by faith is something childlike, edifying, legendary. Even the believer has largely accommodated himself to this opinion, if not in express statements, at least in involuntary feelings and unconscious attitudes. Often the achievement of his faith consists in believing in spite of all this and persevering in the contradictions which result from it. As a matter of fact, that which science has experienced and worked out, is a property of God's work and must be appropriated by faith. This faith, as such, must become mature in accepting and adopting that seriousness.

Only because divine creation is true creation can that which exists be understood as "Nature"; that is, as something existing and comprehensible in itself. The will of man makes illusion of the seriousness, the honesty and the perfection of Creation. If a garden is laid out by an unskilled gardener, the unskilled hand is discernible everywhere; it takes a great artisan to give it that self-evident harmony which is perceived as a higher nature. If the world were the work of an imperfect being we would notice its imperfections everywhere and so recognize it as something made. It would never have that convincing and satisfying quality, that intrinsic value and beauty which can be misinterpreted as the autonomy of the natural. Only because man originated in answer to the call of God and is maintained by that call, because he is the "Thou" called forth by Him who gives His name as the "I am," does man have the possibility to know himself as an autonomous being. Only because the creating God really placed the created world in man's hand can the latter come upon the idea that he must create an autonomous culture. A basic law of all theories of value states: the higher the value the greater the danger. The gift of existence is filled with the value of true createdness, but carries with it the terrible possibility of perverting this true createdness into the self-satisfaction of autonomy. In relation to this concept of creation, that which we have described above as the positive content of the modern development takes on its proper meaning. The world is created: it is entirely the work of God. But as such it has reality, has a fullness of being and of meaning in its created finiteness. It has been put into the hand of man, who is also finite but real and powerful. Man's responsibility for the world is much greater than the Middle Ages could perceive, greater because he can know and handle it in far greater measure than that age could possibly foresee. Into man's relation with the world there has come something which we can only designate as maturity. This word does not connote anything ethical, but rather something that comes with the fact of advancing time, of greater age. The man is mature in relation to the youth. That does not mean that he is morally better, but that he sees the world more clearly, perceives its reality more keenly, has a more definite idea of the possibilities and limits of his strength and a clearer consciousness of his responsibility. This structural maturity, however, becomes at once a moral obligation which he may fulfill or not. But the structure remains, because it follows from the simple fact of a mature age. Something corresponding to this is encountered here. Modern man, as compared with medieval man, is mature. The comparison, indeed, may be to his disadvantage, from the point of view of his humanity and his accomplishments, of ethics and religion. Nevertheless, the fact remains that from the outset and irrevocably he sees the world in a different way.

This also imposes an obligation on the Christian; namely, the responsibility for the world before God. This is also connected with the modern phenomenon of the laity. The nature of the layman cannot, as is so often done, be defined negatively, by the statement that he has no *ordo*—(is not ordained). Actually, he represents the first and basic form of believer. Whereas the priest serves revelation immediately, the layman is in a particular manner related to the world, and the world is God's creation. Responsibility for the world has been given to him as his Christian task. As a Christian he must not only guard against the dangers of the world and "save his soul," but he saves his soul in providing that the world becomes right before God. But in order to do that, he must see it as it is, and maintain himself in accordance with its possibilities. The will of God does not hang above the world, but lies within it, lies in its being as it is.

III

God and "The Other"

The situation we have described leads to a decision: Will man accept himself by a sovereign act and live his life within the limits of this act?

This problem confronts us at many—or we should rather say—at all points of our existence. We shall try to understand it in connection with the experience described in the 138th Psalm.[5] There a man is completely overwhelmed by the recognition of the fact that God sees him. God sees everything about him—his body, his actions, his thoughts. God sees him at all times—at present, in the past, at the first beginning of his life and on to the end. He sees what is manifest—gestures and actions; also what is hidden—plans, intentions, states of mind. God even knows what is not but shall be—the future. As man was formed in the womb, God already knew his whole life, not a day of which he had as yet lived. Every attempt to hide from God would be vain, for He is everywhere and sees everything. And so the Psalm raises the enormous problem of this complete exposure to the eye of God.

Is this endurable? We do not mean the fear that an evil deed or an embarrassing thought may be revealed, nor the reluctance to have something delicate and deeply personal exposed. Rather, it is the much more essential question whether existence is actually possible beneath an eternal and all-seeing eye. To accept oneself from the hand of creation means to know that one stands before the gaze of the Creator. But in order to live, man needs the sphere of reserve. So he must defend himself against this gaze of another. He may act as if the one beholding him did not exist. He will try to escape, to turn to the external, to diversion. Or he may rebel, deny God, and try to bring the self to that state of autonomy in which the observer automatically disappears. Of this we spoke in our discussion of the concept of nature and the subject. Then there is a defection, in the manner in which such things always happen, based upon what is half true and half right. One cannot dismiss it with the sentence that man is disobedient. This would only reduce the problem to silence, not solve it. We make progress only if we posit, as the person who is undergoing this experience, not the proud and disobedient man but the well-intentioned, suffering man entangled in an average existence.

Against what is this man defending himself when he does not wish to be seen by God? Against the other—the *heteros*. He does not wish to be heteronomous, and in this he is as much right as he is wrong when he wishes to be autonomous. In relation to God, heteronomy is just as wrong as autonomy. My self cannot subsist under the power of another, not even if this other is God. Indeed, then least of all. This is so, not because my own person is perfect and therefore cannot endure the ascendancy of the other, but just because it is not perfect. Just because my self is not securely and truly poised in itself, the force of the other's presence becomes a danger. This may manifest itself as insecurity, fear, constraint, but also as the opposite of these, which is rebellion. There arises the feeling, "He or I!" It would not help this feeling if we said to the rebel, "You cannot resist God, he is almighty and you must submit." On the contrary, this would only make the situation worse. It would bring about a condition like that of the engineer Kirilloff whose fear is portrayed by Dostoievski's "Demons." Kirilloff is not terrified for any particular reason, such as a sense of guilt, but what he feels is the fear of the fragile, finite existence which yet thirsts for a fullness of life, liberty and dignity, before the all powerful "Other." It is the feeling that he is being forced out of his own dignity, his life, his very being, and this, not because God has inflicted any particular harm or even is unkindly disposed toward him, but simply because He exists—exists as the omnipotent and omnipresent one, before and above the finite creature. This fear on the part of Kirilloff becomes the more torturing because he is a deeply religious man, who basically loves God. But he loves Him as he would love another human being, and does this so immediately and violently, and he himself is so sensitive and yet so inexorable in his sense of honor, that everything forces him to the alternative "He or I." The same problem returns in the case of Nietzsche—whose situation is actually in many respects revealed by "The Demons." In Nietzsche's feeling also, God deprives man of the space of his existence, of the fullness of humanity, of the honor of being. This results in the "postulatory atheism": "If I am to exist then he cannot exist. But I must exist, therefore he cannot be permitted to exist." How elementary and vulnerable the thing concerned here really is, is shown by Nietzsche's message: "God is dead." Not, "there is no God," but "He is dead." And behind this statement lurks the deeper idea: "I have killed Him. I have come out the victor in the battle with the great 'Other.'" In the case of Kirilloff too, it is not a matter of a simple denial of God, but of an act which extinguishes Him. God is the one who frightens man. God is himself man's fear. This fear is removed if the man proves his courage at the decisive point. But the decisive point is his life. If man dares to kill himself, fear expires, not only because there is then no one who could be afraid, but in a deeper sense because in this way "complete freedom is won and fear itself is conquered." Then God dies. This is primarily the train of thought of a lunatic, but the pathological borderline case reveals a tendency of normal feeling, that feeling upon which the philosophy of Nietzsche and the whole of the tragic modern finitism is based.[6] This difficulty would not be solved even by pointing out that God is the Lover. Even as a lover the eternally present "other" is unbearable. Indeed for the proud man, and the noble person is perhaps usually proud, the "other" who loves is perhaps most unbearable. For the fact that he loves would give the most vital nearness to his presence but the fact that he is the "other" would make of this love something degrading.

On this level of the situation man is right. He cannot live beneath the gaze of the ever present "other." From this point of view, rebellion is self-preservation. But beneath this there is something deeper. The thought, the feeling, that sees in God the overpowering "other" indicates primarily an error in thought and a mistaken feeling, which disguise, however, the real rebellion against God, in order that this may appear as justified self-preservation. By the very fact that man placed God in the role of the "other," the rebellion took place. For God is not "the other" but He is God. Man's understanding of creation and his own self-knowledge depend on his realization of this fact. God is the only being of which I cannot say, "I am this," which is the final goal of all desire of autonomy—but of whom I cannot say either that he is the "other" opposed to me, wherein all

heteronomy ultimately consists. In regard to every other being the statement is valid: this is not I; therefore, it is another. In regard to God the
statement is not valid and the very fact that it is not valid expresses God's
nature. In the situation of which we have spoken, God is turned into the
"other," the greatest of all, the absolute "other." If He is that, then man must
undertake the terrible battle of liberation and Nietzsche would be correct.
But God is not the "other," just because he is God. God faces the creature
in such a way that the category of being-the-other cannot be applied to
Him any more than that of being-the-same. When God creates a finite
being, He does not set another beside Himself, as, for example, the mother
brings forth the new human being in such a way that it now exists beside
her. This happens only because the basic cause of existence for the mother
as well as for the child does not lie in her, but both belong to an existence
which embraces both and through which both come from the same ultimate beginning. The mother does not create the child but serves the order
of life and the will of God that operates therein. But God creates man. The
creative energy of His act makes me to be myself. Because he turns to me
with the evocative power of His love I become myself and exist as myself.
My special character is rooted in Him, not in myself. When God beholds
me it is not as when a man looks upon another man, a finished being
regarding another finished being, but the glance of God creates me. The
concept of the "other" has no meaning here. True, we cannot dispense
with it in our thinking. If we do not wish to identify man with God then
we must think of their relation as expressed by the concept of the "other."
This gives us the logical guarantee that we shall not fall into the wicked
absurdity of making them identical. But at the same time we must be
conscious of the fact that the concept of the "other" must really be put
away. The concept of creation which expresses God's relation to man signifies two things. First, that man is really given his own existence, and then,
at the same time, that God is not "another" beside him, but the absolute
source of his being, and closer to him than he is to himself.

A surmise of this lies in every true religious experience. We might express its meaning logically by saying: The principle of contradiction according to which A, since it is A, is not B, is not absolutely valid in relation to God and man. True, we cannot do without it in speaking of this relation, for it keeps us from monism, but in reality the relation is different. This very special and peculiar thing which cannot be expressed logically is the meaning of createdness, in which the principle of contradiction is kept intact according to its true meaning and yet is transcended in an inexpressible way. Thereby the statement that creation has the character of grace receives a deeper meaning. Creating means that God places man in a relation to Himself in which reason first says "God is not I" and then adds "but He is not 'another'" either, by this seeming contradiction pointing to something inexpressible which is beyond conceptual thought. But this inexpressible something can be immediately apprehended by the religious consciousness. Indeed it is likely that religious consciousness consists in this very apprehension. This relation then attains its ultimate clarity and fulfilment in the concept of actual grace.

From what we have said we can draw a conclusion in regard to God's love. God loves man in giving him all, being and nature. He makes him into that which alone can be really loved, a person. God, who is the absolute Person, makes man His "Thou." He does this not in an illusory or partial manner but in complete seriousness. Man is really a person. But then the love which God bestows upon him must be such as is fitting for a person. To put it more correctly: man is a person only because God's love for him is such as it is. But that means that God esteems man. What we expressed above, by saying that God is for man not the "other" but, in creating him, presupposes and guarantees man's self-hood, this may be conceived as follows: by calling him in love God makes man a person—but in esteem. He does not create him as he does a star or tree or beast, by a mere command, but by a call. In the account of creation this is expressed very clearly. Of heaven and earth we read merely "God created." In regard

to the shaping of things in the world and also the origin of plants and animals we read that God said, "Let there be." But of man the account relates
that God formed his body of the earth and breathed a soul into man, and
then that God named this man. But naming means addressing a person.
In order to make everything clear the account goes on to tell how God
brought the animals to man, and this shows that in his essence man is
different from them all. So God is not "another" facing man, for man lives
by the power and the breath of God. Yet this same God adopts an attitude
toward man which makes him a person and gives him his proper sphere
of value; that is, an attitude of esteem. The statement "God esteems man"
expresses a certain distance; the statement "God is not another" annuls
the distance. The two aspects of divine creation, of which we have spoken,
combine and indicate the nature of God's love which differs from human
love just as divine creation differs from human creation.[7]

The Poles of the Sphere of Existence

I

Above and Within

The concept "sphere of existence" is meant to designate not merely external juxtaposition of corporeal things but the totality of all those relations and areas in which our life, more precisely the life of the one thinking and speaking at any time, takes place. How is this sphere arranged?

The basis of every arrangement is the law of identity and contradiction. In regard to space, in the general sense of the word, this law states that every place within it is only itself and no other, so that anything which is located in this place, by that very fact, cannot be in any other place. The place so differentiated is characterized both in itself and in its relation to other places by reference to a system of measurements, the coordinates. This system is abstract, it can be applied anywhere in space, even so that its point of intersection is located where the person is who asks the question about the arrangement of space. Is the sphere of existence—which is always that of a definite existing person, the one concerned in each case—arranged by this system of coordinates? Let us put the question more concretely. If we call "direction" the tendency of a movement toward its accomplishment, then, in external space, a direction is determined by at least two points, and further by the fact that one of these is fixed as the starting-point, the other as the end. Direction also is related to the system of coordinates. Its axes form the measure of every movement possible in external space. Are the movements of the sphere of existence aligned in this way? Can we say that the person in each case relates his movement of existence to the three axes of the system of coordinates, upward and downward, forward and backward, to the right and to the left?

Let us take the one which in view of our physical organization is especially prominent, the vertical. Is my sphere of existence arranged upward and downward? An arrangement upward and downward is immediately suggested by the fact that my body can raise itself up and stand and keeps this position for a considerable portion of the day, sometimes with a very noticeable effort. Then "above" would be where the head is; "below," where the feet are. Or more exactly "above" is the direction in which body and head extend, and "below" where the feet are propped; "above" the direction in which the burden of the body is lifted, and "below" the direction in which gravity draws it. This order is determined by the center of the earth. "Below," as such, lies in the center of the earth; "above" turns away from this center in all directions, like rays, to the infinite. The farther away from the center of the earth anything is, the higher it is.

This arrangement and manner of speaking is adequate as long as it concerns only the body, and that in the sense of an extended and weighty mass, but not when the body is taken as a living organism. The relation of above and below which we have developed does indeed determine this also; since, for example, stature, growth and movement of the body do depend upon the force of gravity and upon the overcoming of this force. But it is taken up into another which belongs to the process of life. The nature of this can best be seen if we start from the expression which mythological imagination has given to it. Here the above and below are heaven and earth, more precisely, "Father Heaven" and "Mother Earth." In the purely physical realm we were dealing with a formal system of relations, which determined the possibilities of the structure and movement of bodies. Here we are dealing with areas of life having particular meanings, possibilities and powers, the area of light and darkness, of range of movement and of enclosure, of the vault above, lofty and open, and the countervault below, hollow, deep and hidden. The experience of life takes over the image of these cosmological areas and connects them with the image of the basic forces of life: the male and female principles, the paternal and the maternal, the power of active begetting and the receiving and fostering womb. In the general course of the annually recurring seasons of nature which take place between heaven and earth, light and darkness, this unity of the sphere of life, of its zones and directions is experienced anew and unavoidably each year. Its image forms the pattern according to which we instinctively think of a living existence. Between these two—to speak cosmologically: on the borders of the solid earth and the atmospheric space—lies the zone of that life which is born, grows and moves toward individual existence.

This situation is repeated in the personal experience of the individual life. The middle zone in which this life is encountered is the known and available area of consciousness governed by daily activities. This too has something above it and something below it. And here the "above" appears as the zone of the form, of the transparent, of that which can be conceptually penetrated, of the intellect, of freedom of choice, of the ruling and ordering will, of ideas, norms and classifications. The "below" appears as the zone of impulses and instincts of survival, as the sphere of the organic and psychic inevitabilities of destiny, of the common life that courses below the individual, of the subconscious and the unconscious. Between these two zones runs our conscious and individually willed daily existence. This is aware of both as helping, protecting, supporting and stimulating forces but also as fraught with danger. Both give life, but also bring death. There is a death from above and a death from below, just as life comes from above and from below.

These classifications suffice to determine the region of bodily qualities, of natural life, but not that in which spirit and person subsist. When we pass from the sphere of merely corporeal space into that of life, the categories are changed. In the first case they were physical, here they are biological and psychological, finding a characteristic expression in a myth. Now the categories change again and the break is noticeable as soon as we release, in our concept of above and below respectively, that element which is perceptible from the beginning, but now becomes urgent: namely that which is the goal of mental striving—the element of value.

The significance of value becomes particularly plain in the intellectual "above." This is different from the merely corporeal, but also different from the merely vital, which was mythically explained. And yet the perception and the concept of value are connected with the vital and bodily notion of height. This seems to have some relation to man's upright stature, which is at once perceived as something important, distinguishing man from other living creatures. It expresses strength, defensive power, beauty, dignity. It gives the impression of freedom and must be maintained by an effort. It can also bring danger and destruction; a height is exposed; fear bows the head. So this loftiness is not merely a direction of the vertical coordinates of space, nor yet that which is strong and vital and strives toward the realm of light, but it indicates that which in a special sense possesses value. This becomes the more plain the more the realm of the spirit is concerned. But a consequence immediately obtrudes itself here: we cannot oppose a "below" to this "above" which coincides with the element of value; we cannot oppose a depth to this height. For, if this is done, there immediately arises the dualistic polarization which wishes to save the zones of the evil "below" for the whole, by making it the necessary counter-pole of the good "above," equates both with spirit and matter, takes value and absence of value as essential complementary forces of the whole, falsifies the arrangement by giving it an esthetic slant and abolishes anything that can be called a judgment.[1]

If we are to deal with truly mental and personal space, then the points of orientation must signify alignments of existence which are indeed of different kinds but equal in value. This can be the case only if we define them not as above and below, height and depth, but as above and within, height and inwardness.

The directions of the sphere of existence are immediately perceived as having value. As we have already said, we are considering only that case in which the positive value is attributed to the "above." If the basic directions were upward and downward, men would necessarily interpret them as good and evil respectively. But then they would no longer be constructive forces of the sphere of unfolding existence, but contradictory values demanding a decision. Man would have to choose each moment between the good "above" and the evil "below," and existence would become impossible. Or men would evade this decisive character, would conceive of good and evil as poles of existence and so betray value itself, which does not stand in polar-constructive contrast to absence of value, but is its direct contradiction. But, as a matter of fact, evil is not a counter-pole to good— as little as "no" is to "yes" or nothingness to being. The good is that which is categorically valid and has a right to exist; evil on the other hand is that which ought not to be under any circumstances, which of its very nature signifies non-sense. As soon as something becomes a "pole," the "counter-pole" becomes dialectically necessary. But the good is not a pole and does not demand a counter-pole. The good is that which ought to be, the evil is that which should not be and, in the metaphysical sense, does not need to be—the absolutely superfluous. But the sphere of existence clearly has poles, between which the intellectual, personal life moves; therefore they must be defined differently. They are called "above" and "within," and as such are in the first instance indifferent in regard to value. They supply the conditions under which value can be affirmed or denied. So there is a good height and a good inwardness, but also a bad height, for example, the haughty person as contrasted with the noble-minded; and there is a bad inwardness, for instance, the taciturn, cold person in contrast to the thoughtful person. The intellectual-personal sphere of existence lies between the "above" and the "within." Somewhere between these two lies, at any moment, the position of the person, which contains the moral situation.

From this point of view, we must once more examine what has been said about the areas of immediate life. If we look more closely, we see that even there we are not dealing fundamentally with an "above" and a "below." The zone from which life originates is first of all the womb, then biological interiority. Birth and growth take place from within; and the mythological depth lies not below but within.

Even for inanimate being, the concept of "above" and "below" becomes questionable as soon as one considers the whole situation. "Above" and "below" presuppose as their criterion the level surface. But gravity is related to the earth as a body, more exactly, to its center. From this the relations of "above" and "below" in each case radiate outward, so that, when considered as a whole, even for the orientation of lifeless objects, "below" at least indicates a "within."

II

Christian Inwardness

What is meant by Christian inwardness? Or let us first ask: What is really the meaning of inwardness in general?[2]

There is an interior of the body. We speak, for example, of the inner organs in contrast to the outer, of internal injuries as opposed to those of the outer surface of the body.

Another interior region consists of the psychic in contrast to the organic. In regard to inflamed tissues we can determine the length and breadth of the area affected, but the pain caused by the inflammation has no extent, only qualities of intensity and character. The inflammation is corporeal and in so far "external"; The pain has a physical cause but is itself psychic and therefore in a special way interior as opposed to the body.

Now if we compare a pain of this sort with an emotion, such as anger, another difference of depth appears.[3] Anger at an injustice is in a new sense "deeper" than the pain caused by a burn. In the latter, it was the physical injury that reached the person's consciousness; in anger it was the significance of the injustice experienced. Anger itself can again have different degrees of depth. It is something different, something deeper, to be angry at the squandering of a noble gift than to be angry at the impudence of a person. The difference depends on the degree of value of the object. But it can also lie within the emotion itself. Every feeling, whether anger or joy or kindliness, has degrees of depth. We cannot analyze more fully what the "depth" of kindliness is as distinct from its breadth or tenderness. Here it is taken to mean a primary character, according to which the trend of life inclines inward, all the more so the more highly developed this character is. There are also degrees of depth in the relation of different layers of emotion to each other. So I may discover that "beneath" the anger which I feel toward someone, there lies a sympathy which perhaps is really the main thing and induces the anger.

Finally there is the true spiritual depth. The spiritual quality of our behavior lies in its intention. I may benefit a person by an instinctive action—such as a protective gesture—but also by an action of which I am aware and which I deliberately will. In the first case we have a psychic phenomenon; in the second a spiritually determined one.[4] Merely as such, the latter lies "deeper" than the former. And then there are degrees of depth within the spiritually determined actions. First of all, according to the quality of the determining value. I can benefit a person out of calculated self-interest, or out of sympathy or out of true selflessness. True selflessness is "deeper" than the sympathy which feels discomfort at another's distress, and this in turn is deeper than calculated expediency. Besides this the act has its degrees according to the direct quality of depth peculiar to it. So a love may be deep but without power, superficial yet passionate. Accordingly, there is also a false and evil inwardness. It reveals itself in its lack of feeling for an important, noble, urgent value and also in the degree of consciousness and interest with which the good is rejected and the evil willed. Psychologically, it is expressed in the act of becoming immersed in one's own inner feelings and in silence, in taciturnity and hardness—a condition described with frightful clarity in Kierkegaard's book *Der Begriff der Angst (The Concept of Dread)*.[5] Ontologically, it consists in falling away from God, in hurling oneself into the depths of evil, which are also the depths of nothingness.[6]

Much more could be said on the subject. In any case we have made it clear that the existence of man is constructed from within outward—but one could also say inward into the interior. Everywhere, whether in the order of the different areas of existence or within the areas themselves, this dimension of inwardness is significant.

Is something of this sort meant, when Jesus speaks of the kingdom of God being within us, or St. Paul, of Christ dwelling within the Christian? Some have thought so. They have said that through Christianity mankind became "interiorized." The youthful, barbarian people were led from a primitive condition to one of greater depth; the nations of antiquity were brought from a state of hyper-sophistication and preoccupation with externals to interior recollection. This development of the interior world continued through the course of the Middle Ages and modern times. The modern age, they maintain, then brought a new phase of inwardness, as man discovered the meaning of the individual, and, as a result, there arose an "interiorized" religiosity, ethics, interpretation of law, etc. According to this idea, the inwardness of the New Testament would be a step on the path of general human development. This would have as its purpose an increasing realization of the dimensions of depth in our being, and what Jesus meant would be something particularly significant in this connection.

Is this true? Evidently not. But we must be careful. Naturally the whole phenomenon of Christian inwardness does contain elements of this kind. Persons whose life is governed by the consciousness of the Providence of the Father and the eternal destiny of our redeemed nature will also become more interior in the psychological or cultural sense. Faith in Providence, carried out in one's life, will also awaken the natural depths in man. So the gospel of Jesus really does mean a definite impetus in the course of that general development. Nevertheless, what Jesus really means is something else, not the unfolding of the psyche, the deepening of the heart or emotions, the progressive realization of spiritual inwardness through work and action. Nor does it mean that among the hitherto known areas of inwardness a new one is opened—as, for instance, according to the opinion of many, our consciousness, as a result of our new psychological knowledge is supposed to gain an increased quality of depth, which in turn will set in motion interior powers of judgment. The inwardness of which Jesus speaks, does not come from man at all, but from God.

But now we must distinguish again. There is such a thing as religious experience, the awareness of the mystery that lies behind things and events, the surmises of the first beginning and the last end, the feeling of an all-embracing unity, etc. All this is in some way connected with God and concerned with Him. So we might think that interiorization means a deepening of religious experience, a development of religious acts and conditions in regard to power, recollection and fulness of meaning. But this too would not be correct. What Jesus means is not an unfolding of the naturally religious predisposition, such as takes place in the course of the history of religion or such as the mystical and ascetic systems of various religions strive for. But He came to reveal the God who is sovereign in relation to the world and unknown to it; He came to tell us what our condition is before this God and to announce what He is willing to do for us. Jesus does not teach higher possibilities of religious development but accomplishes man's redemption, establishes the beginning of the new

creation and announces the judgment. Here we have primarily and fundamentally not a matter of human experience but of a divine action according to a sovereign decree. And to become a Christian means to take
this action as a foundation and criterion of one's own existence through
faith in the word of Christ, unconcerned about one's own experience, and
whether one is "deepened" or not whether one becomes harmonious or
discordant, perfected or fragmentary.

So the inwardness which Jesus means, is, to begin with, neither psychological nor spiritual, but something which God creates in us; not a dimension
of depth as yet unopened and waiting within one's religious disposition, but
it is absolutely the gift of God. But, of course, when God gives it, it immediately becomes psychological and spiritual as well, for it operates in man's
actions and is appropriated in these, and so the given dispositions necessarily
develop, and historical processes continue. Christian inwardness is not a
space within us that is prepared and into which God can come, but the God,
who comes to establish His kingdom, Himself creates the interior depth and
breadth in which He wishes to dwell. It depends upon God and can only be
received from Him. But when God gives it then it is actualized in our so-
matopsychic being, and that signifies at the same time an expansion of the
concrete individual, a strengthening and deepening of acts and conditions,
an emergence of an inner world in which man really becomes that which the
creator willed him to be.

But we have not yet reached the essential. In the last analysis, what is
this inwardness? The "where" of God. But where is God—really and essentially, that is—even if there were no world? In Himself. The importance
of God—that is the place where He is. The perfect fathoming of His eternal
greatness—that is the place where God is. God's whole being consists in
act. All that He is He thinks; He measures His own value; what He has He
accomplishes. Nothing is merely present in God; everything exists in pure
activity. This fact—that He possesses Himself in act—this is His place and
so also is His absolute un-approachability, for He alone has this power of

action. God's own inwardness is His place and also His hiddenness. The very thing that makes Him wholly manifest to Himself, His absolute brightness, conceals Him from all that is not Himself. "He dwells in light which no created being can approach" (1 Tim. 6:16).

This God, with His self-comprehension, comes in Christ to the believer. Christ says, "If anyone loves me he will keep my word and my Father will love him, and we will come to him and make our dwelling with him" (John 14:23). And his apostle says that "By his divine power all things which appertain to life and godliness have been given to us through the knowledge of him who hath called us by his own proper glory and virtue. By whom he hath given us most great and precious promises: that by these you may be made partakers of the divine nature" (2 Peter 1:3ff.).

If then God comes in Christ to the believer, God's inwardness comes to him, for God is Himself His inwardness. If He gives man the privilege of participating in His nature He also permits him to share His holy inwardness. It becomes the believer's own. In the form of grace he is to share in its life. This, finally and essentially, is Christian inwardness.

Therefore, Christian existence contains a mystery which can be grasped only by faith. Here is a man, a creature, a piece of the world. But in him arises the living God. He is not world, not creature. God is God and lives in His own interiority. But He grants to man the privilege of participating in it. Not of himself or as his own, but by grace and as a grace. When a man steps into this relationship, believing, loving, hoping, then there awakens within him a life that does not come from himself. But it is realized in him and so he becomes the man his Creator intended him to be. Faith, love, and hope are the divine and "infused" virtues, by means of which man shares in the divine life. Beneath them lies the inexpressible unity of the Christian existence of which St. Paul speaks in his epistles.

This is the inwardness that Christ means. It runs diagonally across all other areas of inwardness. All natural forms of inwardness that are current in the world are met by that which Christ meant and which comes from "heaven" from the intrinsically "other." One cannot approach this by means of deepened emotions or a nobler spiritual understanding. To delve within oneself psychologically or spiritually does not pave the way for it. No interiorization which comes from the world—and the world in this sense comprises all that man is of himself—leads to the Christian inwardness. Only faith leads to it, only the willingness to go where Christ stands, a transformation in Christian action and suffering, the "becoming the child of God" (John 1:12). And all this is possible whether the believer possesses psychological inward depth or is simple and objective, whether he is spiritually developed or undeveloped.

But is this really so? Or is it just another fabrication stemming from man himself? Is this divine interiority not a psychological phenomenon after all, only transferred to the metaphysical or spiritual realm? The answer to this question does not come from theoretical discussion. Here, if anywhere, lies the darkness of possible scandal. There is a possible answer to every question of doubt, but every answer can again be questioned—there is probably another "natural" term for every aspect of our existence which is claimed by faith. This becomes ever more clear the more our knowledge of the universe progresses, and the world of the antichrist is that which seems so complete in itself that by it, if this were possible, even the elect would be led astray (Matt. 24:24). Ultimately, faith must stand alone. To believe means to dare to make a new beginning. One can be led to a true beginning but it cannot be proved. It is only reached by being carried out. This beginning means stepping into a new, holy existence. But how could this existence force one who is not within it, who rejects it, to admit that it is there and is right? It can only be there and maintain itself, and, for the rest, await the final judgment.

And yet there is something in the Christian consciousness which can make plain, to him who wishes to see, what is occurring. To the extent to which a person develops his faith, permits the reality of the living God to dominate his life and submits to His will, he becomes free of himself. Not that he advances more deeply into his own inner being and sees more clearly from that vantage point, enabled by the psychical inwardness which he has achieved to judge external things or through a deepened spirituality to evaluate the things of the soul, but within him there arises something that cannot come about in any other way: the true Archimedean point from which he can survey himself as a whole. To the extent to which a man realizes the Christian inwardness, he is enabled to see himself and becomes capable of Christian self-knowledge. This—speaking on principle and not with the intention of making any statement about individual Christians—has a clarity of vision, a depth, an inexorability and creative power of renewal superior to any other. It can do what is otherwise impossible, grasp its own being as a whole, see its own self and judge it objectively. This is possible only because here the human self is no longer simply judging itself; it is not only that the psychological fact of a division between the self as the examiner and the self as examined is carried out and deepened, but the believer shares in God's view of him, the man. Christian self-knowledge in a man is the grace-given participation in God's view of him. So, on principle and in the measure in which he takes the matter seriously, his self-knowledge is complete; there is no remainder of a reserved and hidden self.

III

Christian Height

As we have seen, the "within" is contrasted with the "above," interiority with height. The phenomenon of Christian height shall be developed in the same way as the former topic.

Everywhere in the existential sphere we meet the "above," the height. First of all in a spacial sense: the second floor of a house lies above the first, and one mountain is higher than another.

These concepts seldom remain purely spacial; as soon as they are really experienced, an element of value obtrudes itself. A tall figure gives the impression of power, and a towering summit stirs the feeling of the distant and wonderful. The character of value grows stronger in concepts such as the "climax of an experience." The course of experience which in itself has nothing to do with "high" and "deep," but consists of feelings, tensions and relaxations, acts and the content of acts, here appears in the form of a curve, which represents the strength or importance of a psychic process as a rising, its maximum as a climax, its lessening as a descent. The same figure recurs in the general idea of heightened life. Strength, courage, and joy become a feeling of elevation and are expressed in a more erect posture, a lifting of the head. More subtle do we find the concept of height in such phrases as "I am intent," "The situation grows more tense," "These are exaggerated notions."* The feeling that the dynamic quality of the event in question is growing—"rising," we say involuntarily—and its significance is increasing, is transformed into the idea that life is a chord or a bowstring. Both figures are probably one in origin. The first thing that sounded was the bow. If the string is drawn tauter the arrow darts higher and has greater force. In the case of the string of an instrument, the tone then becomes clearer, "higher," and reveals greater energy.

The idea of height is found again in the realm of the mind. So we speak of "elevated thought." The height of a thought is something different from its extent, its depth or its intensity. It is a primary quality. A thought is not necessarily high if it is correct or richly developed, but if it is noble and difficult to reach. Therefore, the more daring its execution demands, the greater the existential effort it requires, and the higher it lies.[7] The element of mental

---

* Translator's note: It is impossible here to keep the parallelism of the three German words. They all come from the word "*spannen*," to stretch or strain. The word "uberspannt," which has here been translated "exaggerated," suggests something akin to our word "hypertension," but is common in German for the idea of excess or too great pretension.

and spiritual height comes out very clearly when we speak directly of value. A proper hierarchy of values and their realization cannot be carried out in any other way than according to a system of degrees of height.[8] Of course, there is also the distinction of qualities: wisdom is not the same as boldness. And there is the distinction of areas of existence: the values of knowledge are different from those of action. But in every comparison, the consciousness of scale and degree immediately manifests itself, and this scale goes upward. We speak of higher and deeper values, of laying foundations and building up, of rising and falling, etc. The fact that a value as such is superior to another is immediately expressed in terms of height, just as the effort to secure more excellent values and to realize more perfectly a given value is perceived as an upward striving. It has already been brought to our attention that this feeling is connected with basic facts of our existence, especially with man's upright stature which is felt to be significant and valuable, the human as distinguished from the animal, something which must absolutely be maintained even though it should take a great effort. An upright stature is the immediate expression of bravery, defensive strength, beauty, power of domination, preeminence in the rivalry of the species, etc. Added to this is the equally important fact that the sun and the vault of heaven are above. The meaning of this height is also immediately evident. It comprises the values of light, air, freedom of motion—primary values whose meaning extends from the physical to the spiritual.

This general gradation of height also appears within human affairs. It makes sense if we say that the life of consciousness or of artistic creativity is higher than that of mere feeling or of physiological processes—though it is self-evident that these things cannot be separated from each other. For instance, in the case of man, the physiological is determined by the psychical. This hierarchy cannot be disputed. It must not be disputed, and he who does not see it is not only blind, but does wrong. Similarly, there are degrees of value in the particular area. As a bodily organ, the heart is instinctively thought of as "higher" than the stomach. In the psychic sphere, the instinct of cleanliness signifies something higher than that of seeking shelter. In the intellectual sphere the striving for absolute truth is above practical expedience and experience; the knowledge of essences above that of mere facts; the contemplation of the idea above mere cognition. The powers of useful accomplishment are higher than those of enjoyment, the brave deed is higher than work from which one derives profit; pure creativeness free of all ulterior motives is higher than anything which pursues its own purposes. And evident as it is that man as such possesses inalienable dignity, no matter what his character may be, so that the lowest of men is intrinsically superior to the highest animal,[9] it is also plainly evident that men are not equal, but that there is an immeasurable gradation from lowest to highest. And to recognize the higher person, to honor him and be able sincerely to rejoice in him, is almost the same as being higher oneself.

What is the relation of what we have said to Christian "height"? That there is such a thing is evident. The New Testament is filled with revelations of value and with their distinctions, and with admonitions to strive and choose. It is equally evident that this Christian height cannot be simply a continuation along the line of that height of which we have spoken. Certain schools of thought have understood it so; for instance, Pelagianism and the Enlightenment, and every rationalistic manner of thinking. According to these, Christianity would be a clearer reasonableness and a nobler system of ethics than any that preceded it. Let us recall, for example, the line so frequently drawn from Socrates to Jesus. On the other hand, it might mean a purer and more differentiated image of man—like the concept of the beautiful soul to which Goethe gave expression. But all this is not correct. The point toward which the hierarchy of height in Christianity is directed is God. And that does not mean simply the highest and wisest being, nor yet the numinous reality of religious experience, but that God who "dwells in light inaccessible," hidden in himself and only appearing in Jesus. We have defined Christian inwardness as that place where Christ is "in" the believer. In a corresponding way, we shall now say that Christian height is that place where Christ is "above" the believer. "If you be risen with Christ seek the things that are above, where Christ is sitting at the right hand of God. Mind the things that are above, not the things that are upon the earth" (Col. 3:1–2). Expressed pragmatically, the Christian "above" is there where Christ went when he returned home to heaven.

This "above" has nothing to do with the directions of height previously described. It is independent of them and runs athwart them all. It even brings the "heights" to which they point into question. The New Testament is very clear about this reversal of the natural conditions of height. This is shown by the Beatitudes, or the statement that he who exalts himself on earth shall be humbled by heaven, or the word about the wise and the simple, about the folly of the Cross, etc. From this conflict spring the strongest objections to Christianity. Our immediate feeling protests when told that Christian height can also, and indeed, under certain circumstances, must reveal itself in what is lowly from the worldly point of view. Let us imagine for a moment that someone made such abatement in the classical Greek world; a man of noble nature who heard it would ask if the speaker were a slave. A resolute leap into the dark is necessary to understand this. Then one recognizes true height, that before which the worldly distinctions disappear. Christian height is not something that simply exists either as a layer in the stratification of reality or as a degree in the hierarchy of values or as an objective spiritual or metaphysical place where Christ places himself and his own. Rather, this height depends on Christ. "Above" is where he is. He himself is the height. The starting point of Christian love in the believer is directed toward this height. But that also does not exist of itself, arising above the other starting-points of human upward movement, but it only awakens as the answer to the appearance of Christ. It is given by Christ and it dies away as soon as the relation to Him is broken.

Of course as soon as all this is explained, it also becomes clear that the degrees of Christian height, its realization in thought, values and aspiration, its operation in the building up of the personality which is directed toward it, at once take into account all those natural forms of height of which we have spoken. It must necessarily be true that the spiritual height grasped in faith proceeds to dominate the concrete reality of the person and develops his corporeal, emotional and intellectual responses to all heights.

IV

The Summary

The two poles of the Christian sphere of existence lie within and above. Let us re-examine them.

In order to see the interior and that which is within as clearly as possible, we must start from that which is outermost. We could, for instance, begin with the spacial limits of the universe and seek its center, an attempt which resulted in the ancient view of the world, whose center was the earth. But this undertaking would be hopeless, since we know of no attainable astronomical center. Besides, we are not concerned with the astronomical but with the existential world, whose center is always the person who inquires about it. Where I am, is the center of the world.[10] Therefore, the movement should proceed from the limits of the external world toward me and then into me and into the depths of my being. It goes through the different layers of the physical, psychical, intellectual and rational inwardness which we have described. It is doubtful whether this movement really comes to an end, for, as it takes place, ever new depths of inwardness open up. If the movement is to end, then something new must happen, a radical qualitative change. The movement undergoes this change, enters, so to speak, a new dimension, when it passes from the realm of the corporeal, psychical and intellectual into that of the religious. In the act of religious experience, we become conscious of the boundary. Not the boundary between one existing thing and another, but the boundary between the whole and nothingness. In order to experience the totality of existence, I do not need to traverse and measure its entire content. That would be the case only if it were not a true whole but a mere agglomeration. The totality of existence penetrates through every place somewhat as the fact of its being an organism is present at every point of the body, and there is a specific act which experiences it. This totality of existence is bounded, not by a surrounding empty space, which would of course also have to belong to it, but by nothingness. But true nothingness is ascertained only in a religious act, as that which God set between Himself and every creature and "out of which" He made the world. Only in our experience of God does it become definitely clear that the world is bounded.

The way into the interior is, as we saw, infinite. The immediate movement goes on and on upon it. If limits appear on this way they are only accidental: either one does not find anything more within or one is unable to penetrate that which is not clear. I reach the true boundary only when I become interiorly conscious of the totality of my self standing within the totality of existence as such, and this is possible only religiously; that is, in such a way that I am reduced to my own limits, and defined as a finite being by the adjoining completely "other," the holy God. This is the limit of inferiority and at the same time the end of the world in the inward direction. Here appears the nothingness that rises from within—and also the hand of God upholding from within. We express it psychologically by the term the depth of the soul, or the spark of the soul. From the point of view of the totality of existence it may be called "the inner desert" or the "emptiness" in which God watches.

How far the last step can be taken by mere "religious" experience—in which all stages of "common" mysticism would be included—I do not know. Probably this experience not only comes to a standstill at a certain point, but is indefinite from its very beginning. There are realities which in themselves belong to the "world," to the whole of immediate existence and hence should be able to be grasped through a clarified and deepened experience, but in actual fact are grasped only when they are encroached upon by the corresponding realities of Revelation. Probably the inner boundary and the God who watches beyond it are experienced only when the "Christ within us" is grasped by faith. It is the risen Christ who actually draws the inner boundary line and directs the world into its boundaries from within, the Christ who after he had "departed," again returned to us (John 13:33; 14:18). This directing means that he tells man not only that he is finite but also that he is a sinner. It means a verdict: the judgment.

Christian interiority is the place where Christ is with us, and not in a static, inactive manner, but operating. And this is true even of the form of his coming, for he rises up from there, in the realization of the Christian existence. The formation of the believer by Christ, the constantly renewed self-expression of Christ in every believer is a real coming, from that depth into the openness of expression. The moment of real emergence will probably be death.[11]

Thus far we have observed the first pole and the first direction. The second lies in the opposite direction. In order to sense it we start from that "below" which is formed by the level of that average which is the theatre of our daily existence.

There is, first of all, the ascent to a spacial height, which is undertaken—unless some particular purpose compels—only when spacial height is experienced likewise as mental height. The Philistine does not climb a mountain. Then there is the ascent in life, to the different levels of its tension and of quality. Then the intellectual ascent to the truth, the moral ascent to the good, the creative ascent to pure production, and so on. Basically these fines also continue indefinitely. Their end is determined in each case by the strength of the individual. Basically there is above every spacial height

another height, above every tension of life a greater one, above every degree
of knowledge and creative action another more noble and daring.

Here too the movement reaches an end only when it changes from a
merely spatial, psychic or intellectual one into a religious one, that is when
in the encounter with God who is absolutely "other" in relation to all that
is human and pertains to the world, the limits of existence as such are
experienced, insofar as it extends upward and meets the nothingness
which embraces it from above and from without. Here too there is a place
of God. Considered in regard to the totality of existence it is that sphere
designated by the ancient concept of the empyrean, that outer space which
is expressed for our immediate experience by the vault of heaven, or at
least becomes perceptible in the vault of heaven: that loneliness in which
God is enthroned above the world or embraces the world.[12] For the individual, it is that region which is expressed by the terms, "the blade of the
spirit," "the edge of the spirit," "the fine point of the spirit."

The inward movement, as soon as it becomes religious, manifests
itself as a passing over into immanence, the upward movement as a passing over into transcendence. But here, just as before, we must doubt
whether this immediate transcending, which actually should be possible
for mere self-movement, is successful if it is not led by that other movement which is manifested only through revelation. In itself, it should become clear in immediate religious experience that God is the Creator and
Lord of the world, and in creating and preserving it, keeps it within its
bounds, that the world is not infinite but finite, hence surrounded by
nothingness; that it reaches only to a definite point, which He has fixed,
and that beyond this "there is nothing more." But this is something that
we do not seem to succeed in comprehending; our notions become confused and indefinite, either leading to the view that considers the world
as actually infinite and does not recognize the boundary that God has
drawn for what is created; or else we incline to the view that overempha-
sizes finiteness which then claims autonomy and rebels against God. Only

when we accept from revelation the fact that the world is judged by God and is lost before His holiness, does the "natural" boundary also become clear through this revealed boundary.

The revealed "above" and the boundary set from there is again Christ—there where he "sits at the right hand of the Father." This sitting is not a static boundary even as his "being within" is not static. The place is viewed as the end of a movement, namely the ascension, and as the starting point of another movement, namely the second coming of the Lord. And the purpose of his second coming will be to assign to the world its final, definite boundaries in the last judgment. The coming from above, from the edge of the world, from the end of time refers also to the individual, just as does the coming from within, for there is a judgment at the end of the life of each individual. This "coming" of the Lord is death.

These are the two poles toward which Christian existence is directed. God stands at both of them—more correctly, God in Christ. Ultimately, both places are one. The "within" and the "above" are the same remoteness of God from which He approaches the world as the Lord. They are only experienced in different ways, because existence still extends inward and upward.

Christ comes from both poles, for the individual as well as for the whole. Indeed, he comes for the whole even in each individual. On the other hand, the destiny of the individual is fulfilled only in that of the whole. The consummation, the new man and the new creation, is not constructed in this way. There no "within" or "without," no "above" and no "below" shall exist. Therefore there shall be no tension between "within" and "above," but only a simple present. All that is within shall have been expressed; all that is hidden shall be revealed; all being shall be true. The exterior shall be full of depth which lives within it. Concealment shall become a free soaring in that which lies revealed and open. Mystery shall be changed into simple preciousness. All that is "above" will have been exhausted because the movement toward it will have been accomplished, the striving fulfilled. All that is "below" will have reached the height, become itself high and noble. This whole condition we call transfiguration and it exists in the Holy Spirit. It is of him that the conclusion of the Apocalypse speaks. In Him there is no longer a boundary. It is assumed into love. Mere finiteness is abolished, for all things are in God. We could say much more on this subject and it would give rise to a phenomenology of eternal life.

The World—Its Enclosure and Openness

I

The World as the Whole of Existence

I t is part of the problem of the world that it is possible not to see it, although it bears our existence, and that a certain effort is required in order to have sight of it. What, then, is the world? The answer may proceed from immediate experience and one may say that the world is that immeasurable something which extends around us, embraces, bears and threatens us, which is felt as permeated by our vital spirits or else as something strange. Or the answer may start from scientific consciousness and then one could say that the world is the totality of that which is given, which may be divided into the realms of the physical, the psychical, the intellectual and cultural, and the personal, whose arrangements can be understood and expressed in concepts. Or the answer may be based upon action whereupon one could say that the world is the endless profusion of tasks, including that of the questioner in each instance, and that it contains this task but does not reveal it, so that it must be discovered; that it possesses the means to master it, and yet interferes with our use of these; that it is assistant and enemy at the same time. Other definitions could be given, but none of them would be basic. Rather, they would be derived from reflections about the various ways of encountering the world. If we permit that which is meant by the word "the world" to be expressed fully in feeling and perception, and inquire about its primary meaning, the answer is: the world is the totality of existence.

Above all, the world is not this thing and then that, and so on. In this way we would not reach a totality, nor even a proper coherence. For the latter does not come into being by patchwork, and, in the case of the former, our method would be endless. The world is a whole and a structure, the entirety of all being, but in a meaningful form. It is an all-inclusive totality which expresses something radical and absolute. In order to grasp this, we do not need to take in all that is, for we encounter it at every point. The law of a curve lies in its smallest segment and the total structure of an organism lies in each of its organs; if that with which we are dealing is really the world, we must be able to grasp it at every point.

Furthermore, the world is not present in an objective way. This does not mean that there is no independent reality. There is. There is the "thing in itself" and the mass of things in themselves. But the world is more than the things. It is that whole, in which I—at this point everyone who entertains these thoughts says "I"—am present. Furthermore, I am present not only in the way in which anything else is present, but essentially. The world is a whole of a particular kind. It consists in tension. One of its two poles lies everywhere in objectivity, diffuse as it were; the other "pointedly" in me.[1] And not only as a matter of fact, since, when one wishes to speak of the world, the seeing, feeling, acting subject must be there, but it is essentially so. The world is not only being in its fullness which must be seen, perceived and grasped because otherwise its reality would lack a dimension of its development, but from the outset, it is as a whole related to the person and his destiny. So there takes place in every person a decisive judgment on the meaning of the world, and that not only as one instance among many, but absolutely, for a person is always and in any case irreplaceable. The fact that one person loses his salvation, and thereby the meaning of the world, is not compensated for by the fact that another person attains his salvation.

This quality is what we mean when we say the world is existence. The words "existence" and "world" mean the same thing, only, in the case of the former, it is regarded from the point of view of the person and his decision about his salvation, and, in the case of the latter, it is regarded from the point of view of the whole and its involvement in the risk.

There seem to be two characteristic forms of world experience; first, that in which I perceive the whole as opposed to myself, in fear of its magnitude and power, in the feeling that I must defend my being and my welfare against it, and in an admiring and yearning awareness of its glory. This experience implies that I stand apart from the world and withdraw into myself, delivering up to the world all those aspects of my concrete existence of which I can say I "have" this—property, qualities, powers, destiny, joy, sorrow, etc.—until I reach that which I ultimately "am," that which is distinct from the world, which is threatened by it and contradicts it, the naked self. It stands opposed to the essence of that monstrous whole which menaces me. This process is especially evident in the philosophy and self-assertion of the stoics who experienced the world at a time when it began not merely to grow monstrously large, but to disintegrate and at all points to take on a menacing character.

Opposed to this there is another form of world-experience. Here the person experiencing it stands within the world, takes part in it, and shares in its activity, perhaps in such a way that he extends himself sensitively in all directions, as in the universal sympathy of the romantics and the Buddhist practices of benevolence. Or else, he perceives the whole as concentrated in the living here and now, as in the case of Faust's invocation to the moment of fulfillment, or he may contemplatively grasp the meaning of the world and realize his responsibility for it—even to those final religiously-mystical experiences in which the person experiencing them becomes aware that he is standing in the center of the world or that the axis of the world lies within him.

The color of the experience also varies. The person may be drawn into a venture with the world in a spirit of calm joy, or in excitement or seized by its power or in union with it. In every case, however, he is what he is because he stands in the world, participates in it, and cooperates with it. And the world is what it is because it becomes present in him, and has its center of meaning in him.

Both forms of experience take the whole as an actuality. Not as a sum of its parts, but as the one, to which all parts are related and which subsists in all the parts. It exists at every point. More correctly stated, it exists there where the person concerned is present.

II

The World as "the Whole," "a Whole" and the Mighty

This world is "the whole." In my experience there is, to begin with, nothing besides the world. The question how far it is possible that a particular experience of something immediately given may show that there is a real "other" which does not belong to the world-whole—namely religious experience—may for the moment be left aside.

For the time being, we may assume that all that can be grasped is "the world." All space is filled with the world. In exterior space, one object crowds another, event follows event. Nowhere do we find a gap. I myself am fitted into this context from all sides. I may become conscious in an overpowering manner that the world is a continuum without a break and that I cannot penetrate it anywhere, that it fills "all" and I cannot reach around it. The same thing holds true of the interior space of consciousness. This also is entirely filled with concepts, feelings, tensions, movements of the will and has neither boundary nor gap. Even experiences like the lack of thought of the dull or methodically emptied consciousness merely indicate a different condition. This is probably one of the decisive insights of modern man; that is, that there is no free space around the world in which the supra-mundane could exist, nor gaps within the world into which, as such, the extra-mundane could enter. Earlier religious consciousness always worked with the concepts of boundary and gap; that is, a space empty of the world which surrounded the limited world, and gaping empty spaces between the units of substances and events in the world. For these concepts God appeared in the emptiness surrounding the world and in the spaces within the world. From these, for instance, resulted the answers to prayer; in these, the miracles took place. Modern consciousness is aware of the fact that there is no space around the world nor gap within the world. The world permits nothing beside it or in it.

It possesses the intolerance of the "all." The world is the All.[2] The concept "world" indicates also that it is "a whole." Its immense abundance forms a unity, and that not only through an external unifying power, but through a form that is operative throughout and a universally pervasive order. Usually the world is experienced in such a way that it forces us to assume that it has a single ultimate center.[3] We find within it many kinds of centers, everywhere where constructive and dynamic forms of meaning are realized. These are always related to greater ones and so tend toward a final unity. We are unable to reach the center of the whole, but, nevertheless, we have the impression that everywhere the lines, even through endless complications and intersections, through situations of equivalence and symbolism, run toward an ultimate center. Viewed from this center, the world is a whole, a unity. This unity can perhaps not be proved, but it is so evident that we may say the burden of proof rests upon him who denies it.[4]

Up to this point we have spoken of something that concerns the form—extremely important however. We have said that the world is the whole and a whole. But the concept of "the world" also expresses something referring to content; namely, that it is powerful. The world is a monster of actuality—in materials and powers, structures and events, tasks and deeds, tensions and arrangements, marvels and horrors. The world is something triumphant, violent, abundantly bestowing and mercilessly destroying at the same time. The world is such that it not merely fills all space but obtrudes upon all powers. It is the object absolutely. It also attracts to itself the powers of the impulses, of the heart and the mind. It prevails by the might of its being. It claims universality not only in being but in experience as well. It presents itself as a task, a deed and a work for our powers. But this demands a decision, and we do not satisfy this if we disparage the world. The experience of the power of the world breaks forth in the Renaissance[5] and then constantly increases.[6] Of course we must not forget that in modern times the opposite attitude also develops—scepticism, loss of the sense of reality, an inability to experience something unconditional—all that which, according to Nietzsche, leads to nihilism.

The nature of being regarded as a world may be viewed according to different patterns. The Greeks conceived of it as an objective cosmos in which everything has its own structure through the natural forms of being and action, entelechy and *telos*, through the idea and the movement of the soul which strives toward it, through reason dwelling within being itself and the order of the world's course, *nous* and *heimarmene*. The consciousness of victorious creative power which the Greeks tried to express through science and art, the Romans attested to through government and law. For them also the world was something objectively organized into which man with his particular nature had to fit himself. The philosophy of the 19th century liked to look upon it as something objectively formless into which man introduced order; that is, his mind by forming it in thought, as in the idealism of Kant, and his will by constructing it into a world as far as its power reaches, as in Nietzsche's philosophy of power. But the world can also be experienced in such a way that its essential nature emerges only in the encounter with things and persons. Then, of course, there is already order in the things as well as in the interior of persons. But this is not sufficient to establish the world in the proper sense; it arises only in the realm of encounter. "The world" in this case is not something complete and existing once for all. Rather, it is something that constantly flares up and comes into being. This seems to us the proper view.[7] This world-character of being can have various kinds of dynamics. Its power can increase so mightily that it floods everything that can be called boundary and measure and finally extinguishes the very counter-pole of objective reality, the heart, in its own feelings. Herein consists the Dionysiac experience in its various forms. The force of the world breaks through and overwhelms consciousness. The whole rises up and crowds out the individual. The "it" prevails and extinguishes the person. The world triumphs. But in that very fact, the experience of the world breaks down, for this consists not only in the experience of the mightiness of the world but in its wholeness. And wholeness is form and tension. The world is outside, in all that we call distinction, order, opposition, and architecture; it is within, in the conditions of interior areas and powers; and it is in the relation of the two, growing up between the two poles. In the Dionysiac experience the objective pole prevails to such an extent that it destroys the other, but thereby it ceases to be a pole and the world disappears. In its final consequence, the Dionysiac experience is that experience of the over-powering force of the world which is followed by ruin.

The dynamics of our world-experience can also be shifted in the other direction, so that the element of limitation permeates our consciousness. Then distinctions are emphasized everywhere and boundaries are more sharply defined. The measure grows more exact and stringent, and the criticism becomes more penetrating. Relativities are more closely observed. Everything that can be called form develops and intensifies. Control and reserve increase. The world is deprived of its power. It is less and less able to penetrate as a force. It is deprived of its enchantment by reason. Its secrets are revealed, its objects, powers and relations are rationally examined, calculated according to utility and arranged according to expediency. This attitude which is first experienced as a sense of reality and the mastery of reality then likewise reverses; it becomes empty of the world. Rationalistic thought becomes scepticism. Behind the tendency to

grasp things there stirs the feeling that these are shadowy. The consciousness of its own sovereignty and responsibility, which is the basis of all its
planning, the hidden presumption, the tendency to take over those operations which faith held to be the prerogatives of God—creation, providence,
the government of the world—these gradually lead to the feeling that one
is no longer anybody (depersonalization). In this way also the excess of
world-experience annihilates itself.

III

The Boundary and Nothingness

The true consciousness of the world seems to depend on this; that is,
that its power is experienced but at the same time is successfully restrained.
This is expressed particularly in the experience of the boundary. In order
that the boundary may be perceived there must be something—blood,
impulse, *elan vital*, expansion of feeling, boldness of will—which presses
upon the boundary and gains its form through that which opposes it.

There are boundaries of various sorts. First, the boundary between
object and object; one thing stops and another begins. This is the relative
boundary which lies within the world, and which is identical with the
qualitative and quantitative distinction between existing things. But as soon
as it is rightly understood, there emerges from it the perception of another
boundary, which does not separate from other measures or qualities but
from that which is wholly different, a boundary which radically negates
all—nothingness. This nothingness indicates absolute limitation. It does
not cause a being to end in order to make room for another being, but ends
it simply and absolutely. Nothingness does not mean that there is a neighbor or predecessor or heir in being, but indicates aloneness. This cessation
and isolation is the other side of qualitativeness, of character. A being which
is really something thereby stands ultimately "before nothingness"; that is,

in isolation. "Character" in its deepest sense means just this; that is, to stand by what one is and by that very fact to be alone.

But not only the individual thing, but also, and above all, the whole, is experienced as thus characterized and bounded. The real boundary concerns the whole; in the case of the individual, it appears only as a representation. The nothingness, which lies on the other side of the characterizing boundary, really encircles the whole. If I am to represent to myself this whole, the world, it can only be by becoming conscious of it as finite, limited, and surrounded by nothingness.

But the location of this nothingness must be determined more exactly. It lies where the poles of existence are, above and within. More exactly, it lies beyond these poles, over the "above" and inside the "within."

We do not immediately attain to a clear consciousness of these two places. In regard to the upper boundary, we are inclined to think of it as an outward one. The reason for this is probably our concept of the upper surface of a body and the surrounding air. Only when we realize that of which we have spoken before; that is, that ultimately the boundary is not a natural phenomenon but one of value, that we are not dealing with the boundaries of the cosmos but of the world of existence—only then do we see that it is not determined from without but from above. It is of this that St. Augustine speaks when he says in his Confessions that he had seen above his soul the absolute light, but that this "above" was not like that of oil above water or the sky above the earth, but like the relation of the creative power to the created object.[8] This boundary is fixed by the power which is "higher" than the world because it has created the world.

Equally indistinct is the other boundary which lies within, because this interior is conceived of as a center. Only gradually do we become conscious of the fact that there is an indefinite continuation inward, just as there is an indefinite continuation upward, and that the practical impossibility to reach an end within does not indicate a real infinity anymore than such is the case as we proceed upward, and that there is also an inward boundary. This boundary, moreover, as soon as it is discovered, is particularly impressive because it coincides with the inner boundary of the whole of existence. There is a "center" within, but it is not absolute and self-based. Rather, it is finite and conditional. It is, so to speak, perforated; that is, it has a passage inward and there, adjoining it, is the power that carries all—God. "Between" God and the world, above and within, is nothingness. The world is bordered, overlapped and traversed by nothingness.

It is only in this way that we reach a concept of the world which makes us conscious of the nothingness above it and in it. As the boundary becomes a force, that which it surrounds becomes permeated by feeling. We become conscious of the power of existence as we experience its crisis. Heidegger showed this through the experience of dread (Angst). In contrast to fear, which is always fear of one thing or another, and that means a feeling of differentiation within the world, dread is not related to anything definite but to being as such. In it nothingness is revealed as a power, finiteness as a menace. But herein the whole also appears, and—if we could carry on the thought—then the opposite feeling awakens, that of the power and reality of the world.

The true "not" and "nothingness" comes from the reality of God. He "reduces the world to its limits," by making clear that the world is not He. Rather, that He is above it and within it, that He is the self-existent, the truly existing one, "the Lord" in the ontological sense, and that the world is created and exists only "before Him," existing ontologically in obedience. But by this very fact, the world is itself and is real as a world. God is the one who is really the absolutely other, who is able to create, and thereby to fix, the true boundary between Himself and all creation. The true "not" and "nothingness" is what is meant by the statement that the world was created "out of nothing" and this other, that the world always exists as a creation, that means, that it is "not God." Only by proceeding from God can one really experience the world.

But it seems that this too cannot be accomplished simply and immediately. That limitation which consists in the creation and preservation of the world and in the differentiation between God and it continually becomes blurred and reveals itself clearly only when another explicit limitation take place—through Revelation. Therein God reveals himself as the Lord whose being has been denied and whose law has been broken, and the world is exposed as one that has overstepped its boundaries and arrogated to itself a right that belongs only to God. He reveals Himself as the Holy One and the world as sinful. This is a new indication of limits, through the fact that God steps into the world, becomes man and in the God-man shows the world its own disposition. This is the judgment, the word, in the sense in which Jesus uses it in St. John's Gospel (John 3:19). Only from this point of view does the whole situation become clear, so that, considered in a Christian way, "the world" enters our consciousness only as a result of the judgment of God.

IV

The World's Enclosure within Itself

A true boundary encloses, but since it "has another side," it also opens. A true boundary is like our skin: it breathes, feels, transfers from one side to the other. The world—not the objective system of nature, but the world of experience, in which my will to live operates—shows a tendency to put something else in the place of a true boundary, a breathing finiteness. The will of man strives to lock it in itself and around its own being, to make it autonomous and self-sustained. This means, however, that the boundary in the true sense disappears.

This can happen in such a way that the boundary is pushed out by the sensation of an ever expanding space, a never-ceasing vital urge, a constantly continuing effort. And not only in degrees, as for instance through the concept of the increasing size of the world, but absolutely, decisively, as the boundary is forced from our consciousness and so declared to be nonexistent. From the fact that the world extends ever farther, the fact of finiteness is removed, and for the concept of "ever farther" there is substituted the concept of the "boundless," even the "infinite." The concept of the infinite is then based upon that of the absolute, and a world is conceived of which is not only "a whole," not only "the whole" for our immediate consciousness, but simply "the whole," the ultimate, the absolute. The whole no longer has any boundary. Such boundaries as are found within it are only structural elements and have lost their true meaning, which is to point to the absolute boundary. This transformation takes place in modern Pantheism beginning with Giordano Bruno and extending throughout the 19th century.

How questionable this concept of the infinite and absolute is, is plainly shown by the fact that at a definite moment it changes into another, that of radical finiteness and factualness. The concept of true infinity, which is possible only on the basis of true absoluteness, could not change; only a complementary concept can do that, changing into the one on which it is dependent. More exactly expressed, the concrete living thing in its self-determination can change from the place of one complementary phenomenon into that of the other, from the range of one pole to that of the other, because it was originally related to both. But the true absolute and infinite is not a complementary phenomenon. It has no counter pole. It rests completely in itself. In the line of thought of which we have been speaking, the two concepts are taken as the expression of complementary phenomena which are dialectically related to each other: infinity to finiteness, the absolute to the factual. They are centered upon life which exists in both. And when this life, in order to establish itself as autonomous, first uses the phenomena of "ever farther" and carries them on to the dialectical "infinity" and "absoluteness," there comes the moment when it drops them and uses the contrary phenomena for the same purpose. As long as the feeling prevails that something can subsist in itself only if it is absolute and infinite, the will to autonomy seeks to prove that existence is of such a nature, both the world without—the universe—and the world within—the subject. As early as the Renaissance, however, the feeling arises that the very factuality and finiteness of existence is able to support the will to autonomy. That finite existence is only "this," passing, exposed and endangered, gives it particular intensity and preciousness. Note, for example, the spirit of adventure in the Renaissance. In this way, there grows up the idea of an existence which is neither infinite nor absolute but in every respect finite and factual, yet as such takes all risks completely and exclusively on its own. This idea comes out in Nietzsche. The insufficiency of the finite is over-compensated by the feeling of honesty, of daring, of defiance, and there comes into being the tragically finite world. In this the boundary is also destroyed, only in the opposite direction. In the "infinite" world it was, so to speak, made to evaporate; here, it is drawn most sharply, but in such a way that it no longer has an "other side." It becomes, according to the emphasis given it by emotion, a kind of clamp—either brilliant, and tense with defiant force, or despairing, locked in rigid loneliness—enclosing the world, which not merely "is suspended" in nothingness, but is "cast" into it. And it remains only a question of inner consequence when the surrounding nothingness becomes a demonic reality, the ghost of the rejected and displaced God which drives man to despair.

Finally, there is a third conceivable way in which the world becomes restricted to itself; that is, the view which considers it as fundamentally illusory. Here there exists the consciousness that the world is not capable of providing its own meaning and of being really self-subsistent; however, the step to the idea that it is God who gives it meaning is not taken. So there arises an autonomy of meaninglessness, which is carried out radically in Buddhism. Here the illusory quality is so complete that there exists no one who produces it nor one to whom it appears. The world is a delusion, self-moving, appearing to itself, the phantom subject, as a phantom object. Of course, it is doubtful whether Buddha himself desired the autonomy, or whether he was not rather concerned with a definition of God and a relation to God, which he could express only in a negative way. In this case, the illusory nature of the world, as set forth by him, would become a real form of autonomy only if an "unbelieving" man of the West should detach from its true meaning the world-structure which Buddha intended in a "believing" sense, and should make it the means of his own will to autonomy. The true experience of absolute illusion is probably possible only for the oriental. In the West, it is found only in scepticism, and not in dialectical scepticism, in which the doubting thought hovers suspended over a basic mystical, metaphysical fundamental experience, but in bare scepticism which arises from weariness and the experience of meaninglessness. Something similar appears in the pathological experiences of depersonalization and unreality, of which we have already spoken. There the experience of illusion becomes the basis of a desperate autonomy of an existence locked in its own meaninglessness.

In all these cases the world is locked within itself. There is no way beyond it either inward or upward. Above it as well as in it all is closed.

This self-sufficiency does not indicate any denial of the religious aspect. Only pure positivism, whether it be materialistic, biological or sociological seems to go so far. And it does this not in its earliest, enthusiastic phase, which uses the positivist formula as the means of a piously intended liberation of the world, but later, when it unites with the attitude of the bourgeois, the man of expediency who is cold and sluggish of heart. Then the autonomy of the world appears in its contemptible form, as the self-sufficiency of an existence of profit and enjoyment duly running its course with no purpose beyond itself.

Otherwise, the autonomizing of the world involves the religious feeling. This does not coincide with a definite view of the world—nor with a definite religion—much less with the Christian faith which rests upon revelation. The experience of the autonomy of the world originally has its source in religion. It turns against the concept of the biblical, supramundane God and the order of existence proceeding from him, which seems to deprive the world of content, and it maintains that the world itself is penetrated by religious power, depth and beauty. This is evident in the pantheistic, monistic images of the infinite world, but is also applicable to the finitistic concept. That nothingness into which finiteness has ventured is given an entirely numinous character. It is a nothingness replete with mystery and basically a pseudomorphosis of the concept of God.

The feeling of the preciousness of the finite, the death-daring defiance with which man risks this handful of existence, is also filled with religious energy. The religious mightiness of the absolute world is turned around, and the place of the streaming infinity is taken by the intensity of the finite as experienced in the sense of "nevertheless." The comforting security of necessity is replaced by the glory of the venture. The feeling of the limitless depths of the world is replaced by that feeling in which finiteness, as soon as it is accepted with religious fervor, will send forth from itself a divinity of a new kind, finite divinity. This we see in Nietzsche's doctrine of the super-man.

A religious quality is even necessary if man's will to autonomy is to take the risk of living with himself and the world. Setting oneself up as autonomous is itself a religious act, a religious revolt. The autonomy of existence can be willed only if existence is carried by a religious current. Otherwise, it would be like a planet without an atmosphere, on which no life can develop. Only the religious quality gives it that weight and fulness of meaning as a consequence of which the spirit feels it possible and worth-while to base the world upon itself alone.

But how can this be? The objectively religious, the numinous, is a radiation of God, the fact that all being has been created by Him, exists through Him, and has its ultimate meaning in Him, the fact that He permeates everything and all vibrates with Him. How can this be attributed to the world? But this very thing constitutes the ultimate nature of the declaration of autonomy. It attempts something monstrous in the way of sacrilege and deceit. The will to autonomy detaches the wealth of mystery, which God imparts to His work, from Him the supra-mundane, the free, the sovereign, the Holy One, and transfers it to the creature. That which should, like a ray, lead to its source is changed by this desire for autonomy into a depth-dimension of the world itself. It is an undertaking which is incomprehensibly great in regard to subtlety, dexterity and the organization of all the required processes.[9]

In the measure in which this is successful, religious feeling becomes the means of locking up the world in itself. The religious quest, which really tends toward that which is other than the world, is, by the usurpation of the numinous, led into the world itself and locked up in it.

This locking up the world in itself—and here we approach very delicate relations—does not even have to mean that a "beyond" is denied.

The point from which the phenomenon of the "beyond" is most plainly grasped seems to be death. "Beyond" is that which stands behind death, the manner of being, powers, values, meanings which concern this "hereafter." Then when the modern consciousness attempted to base the world exclusively upon itself, it could not deal with a "beyond," for, when it was mentioned, the Christian concept immediately came to mind. But this concept is not determined simply by death, but by that death which is followed by the judgment of the Holy God, who really Himself constitutes this judgment. The Christian "beyond" means God's sphere of being, which is fundamentally inaccessible for the world, because He is the Creator, the Lord, the Holy One, and the world is a creature, subject to Him and opposed to Him in sin. From the Christian point of view, death is something which results not only from man's nature but decisively from God. Death is not something "natural" but appointed by God as a consequence of sin. In death God approaches man in judgment. This is the complete death, that man's life ends because God has fixed its term and carries out the judgment. Therefore as soon as one said "beyond," it was this "beyond" that men thought of. Consequently, it was not spoken of at all. Existence was here and that was all. At death, that which was real in man was dissolved in the primal flow of world-matter and forces. But the spirit, not as a personal and living reality, but as the sum-total of thoughts, strivings, ideas, emotions, intentions, lived on in history, in remembrance, in fame and in the after-effects. Then the situation changed. The Christian concept ceased to be the general norm. An un-Christian world of thought and feeling grew up which could be appealed to immediately, and the feeling began to emerge that the world was not complete without a "beyond." The positivist view in its various forms still maintained that the world needed no "beyond" and it controlled the official consciousness, supported by the attitude of science and the evaporation of the concept of the "beyond" in idealism and the like. But beneath this and in opposition to it, a new concept of the world came into being.

Hölderlin seems to be the first to make the attempt to win over the hereafter, the dead and their realm for the existence of the world. He was supported by religious experiences and worked with concepts which are definitely not Christian.[10] The dead and the realm of the dead, he maintained, are real. They do not sink into that nothingness into which modern thought would consign them. Rather, they remain united with the family, the people, the country. They are not shadowy but real and powerful, not meaningless, lost to life, but quite positive. They belong to existence and influence it. They even return, expressly, historically. Where Christian conviction sees the returning Lord and his kingdom, Hölderlin places the returning dead—not as ghosts but bright and meaningful—those of the dead that is, who were positive in their thinking. On the other hand, the wicked, or rather the despicable, the "slavish" sink into nothingness, into "Orkus." The good return however, and are gathered about that form of the past which represents the center of values of all earlier history—Greece. The mediator between them and us is the seer. He feels and proclaims the unity and teaches us how to celebrate it in religious solemnities. It will be realized at that future time when the greater world, which includes both realms, is revealed.

The connection may also be seen from another point of view. Death then appears not as a simple end. It is that only in the weary or evil life; in the worth-while life death appears as the climax. It emerges from the life which approaches its culmination. While the life in this world reaches its final intensity, the life beyond heralds its approach within it, as the abyss into which the over-opulent earthly life "becoming too beautiful for itself," plunges. This is evident both in the individual life, as seen in the poem "Heidelberg" and also in the life of the nation, as seen in "Stimme des Volkes." Or else it may appear from the logic of blasphemy and expiation, as in the "Empedocles."

In this way the realm of death, of the "beyond," becomes real and meaningful and an addition to the world. It appears as the other side of "life," of this world. The world is then conceived of as the greater whole which extends through this life and the hereafter. The two sides are its two aspects. Existence is carried out through both. For the positivist and the bourgeois, death is something unpleasant; it embarrasses them. So they eliminate it, even in ways of speaking that appear to indicate faith. The idealist resolves it in an absorption in the objective spirit, the pantheist in the stream of the universe. For Hölderlin, death and the hereafter constitute a real form of existence whose other, equally real and meaningful form is the life of this world.

This feeling was given a sharp definitiveness by R. M. Rilke.[11] He set it forth solemnly in the *Duino Elegies* and in the *Sonnets to Orpheus* and explained both of these poems in an authentic commentary, the letter to his Polish translator, Witold von Hulewicz (*Briefe aus Muzot*, p. 332ff.). There he says:

> The affirmation of life and of death prove to be one in the *Elegies*. To admit the one without the other, would be, as it is

there experienced and glorified, a restriction that would ultimately eliminate all infinity. Death is that side of life which is
turned away from us, not illuminated by us. We must attempt
to attain to the supreme consciousness of our existence, which
is at home in both of these undemarcated areas, nourished
inexhaustibly by both.—The true structure of life extends
through both realms; its blood circulates through both in its
· greatest dimension. There is neither a here nor a hereafter, but
the great unity in which the beings superior to us, the "angels"
are at home. And now, what is the situation of the problem of
love, in this world expanded by more than half, this world
which is only now whole and healed?

All this is a

tending more toward the center of that realm whose depth and
influence we, unbounded on all sides, share with the dead and
those to be born. We, the men of here and now, are not for a
moment content in the world of time, nor bound to it. We
constantly pass over to those who preceded us, to our ancestry
and to those who appear to succeed us. In that greater open
world all are—we cannot say contemporary—for the very dis-
appearance of time implies that they all are. Transitoriness
everywhere plunges into a depth of being. And so all confor-
mations of this life are not only to be used according to the
limits of time, but, as far as possible, to be adjusted to those
superior meanings in which we share. Yet, not in the Christian
sense (which I reject more and more passionately), but in a
purely earthly, deeply earthly, blissfully earthly consciousness
we must introduce what we have seen and touched into a
wider, the very widest circuit. Not into a hereafter whose

shadow darkens the earth, but into a whole, the whole. Nature, the objects of association and use, are preliminaries and incidentals, but as long as we are here, they are our possessions and our friends, sharing our grief and joy, even as they were the intimates of our ancestors. So it is necessary not only to keep from slandering and depreciating these earthly things but because of their very preliminary character, which they share with us, to comprehend and transform these phenomena and objects in an intimate understanding. Yes, transform them, because it is our task to impress upon ourselves this preliminary, transitory earth so deeply, so painfully and passionately that its being is resurrected in us in an invisible manner. We are the bees of the invisible. We are passionately gathering the honey of things visible, to store it in the great golden hive of the invisible (p. 333ff.).

And again he says,

The elegies set up this norm of existence, they affirm, they glorify this consciousness. They insert it carefully into its traditions, by employing for this conjecture ancient traditions and reports of traditions and even surmising a premonition of such relations in the Egyptian cult of the dead. If we make the mistake of comparing Catholic concepts of death, of the hereafter and of eternity with the elegies or the sonnets we depart completely from their starting-point and prepare for an ever greater misunderstanding. The "angel" of the elegies has no connection with the angel of the Christian heaven (rather with the angelic forms of Islam)—The angel of the elegies is that creature in which the transformation of the visible into the invisible, on which we are working, is already accomplished. For the angel of the elegies all towers and palaces of the past are existent, because they have long since become invisible, and the existing towers and bridges of our life are already invisible, although still remaining (for us) in bodily form. The angel of the elegies is that being which guarantees the recognition of a higher degree of reality in the invisible (p. 336ff.)

The realm of the dead is here as real as that of the living. That they are "dead" does not mean that they are less "powerful" or "existent" but that they are so in a different way. They even have a greater degree of existence than the living, because they are more quiet, more recollected, more truly themselves. To speak more exactly, they have attained rest and recollection in a decisive manner, although, as Rilke says in several places, they are not yet consummated.[12] Here Rilke goes a step beyond Hölderlin. The latter explains the relation of the hereafter to the here on the basis of a cosmic, metaphysical concept, Rilke on the basis of an anthropological one. For him the sphere of death does not lie in the mysterious realm of the cosmos, but in the "invisible," whereby he means the interior of the spirit, or rather of the heart. The invisible is the place which an object reaches when it is experienced with the intimacy of loving sympathy. Hölderlin's concept of the hereafter is of a Dionysiac kind; it is based upon the dialectic of life and death and upon the spreading of this experience in the world through cosmic enthusiasm. Rilke's, on the other hand, has an Orphic nature and is based upon the power of the soul and its ability, by loving and appropriating them, to transfer external objects into the sphere of life. But what exists there is not simply a concept of consciousness, but it is completely existent, even, as the conclusion of the passage quoted indicates, more truly existent than the visible.

So the realm of the dead, which actually includes not only those who have lived in the past but also those still to be born, and hence "being" as such, free of before and after, free of all time—this realm constitutes not only the sphere of existence which begins beyond death, but penetrates life everywhere. As for Hölderlin, so for Rilke, the realm of the dead is even now a force, and the transition is in the sensitive interiority of the heart. There things are transformed and lifted into the realm of transfigured purity.[13] Only now is the world "whole and healed." The realm of death is added to that of life, the invisible to the visible. Existence extends through both. At the point of transition stands Orpheus, the transformer. And the angels are those mighty beings which are not confined to either sphere. Their relation to the world is not that of a man awakened to understanding, who must painfully "feel himself into" the other sphere, in order to achieve the experience in which the whole and healed existence reveals itself, the "opening." But they are related to the world as a whole, so essentially that they "often do not know whether they are moving among the living or the dead." To them the world is always "open," because they themselves are so.[14]

Actually these notions of the hereafter do not open the world but lock it more tightly within itself.

Thereby Christianity is confronted with a critical decision. "The world" develops more and more completely. One area after another, which faith had considered the absolute preserve of God, is drawn into the world. At the same time, this world closes in upon itself more and more completely; it appears substantial, functional, a unity which meaningfully moves by its own power and is sufficient unto itself. Not so long ago, the decisions seemed to be as follows: a materialistic world or one determined by spirit; a world following after profit, pleasure and power, or one determined by conscience and prepared for moral control; an irreligious, secular world or one filled with piety and religion; a world purely temporal and ended by death or one that knew a hereafter and was determined by it; a positivistic world in which only calculation and technology mattered, or one in which religious enthusiasm, ritual, mystery and miracle played a part. And the second of the two possibilities in each case was immediately equated with a Christian concept of existence, the first with a world that was without revelation and faith. But we are beginning to see more and more clearly how wrong this view was. The world is growing more and more complete, and is developing aspects which used to be considered the special property of Christian existence. At the same time, it is rejecting Christianity more and more decidedly.

To overcome this, to show wherein true Christianity consists, in contrast to all this, by faith to "overcome" the world, but in such a way that the latter retains all its proper rights, this is the task of Christian existence, a task which grows increasingly difficult.

V

The Situation of the World and the Redemption

For the Christian consciousness the concept "the World" has a manifold, even contradictory meaning. And it is St. John above all who sensed the problem—evidently because he had to come to terms with gnosticism which was the first to question the Christian relation to the world and carried this question to the point of heresy.

The prologue of St. John's Gospel says, "Through him (the *Logos*) all things were made and without him nothing was made of all that was made.—He was in the world and the world was made by him and the world knew him not. He came unto his own and his own received him not" (John 1:3 and John 1:10–11). This is the first time that the most lofty statement is made about the world: namely, that its meaning was based upon and its being realized by the *Logos*, the second person of the divine Trinity. So it is filled with the validity of the *Logos*, supported by his power and subject to his sovereignty. But of this same world it is said that it did not receive this very Logos. To that extent it is his adversary, something that closes itself and does not receive him when he appears in it as the redeemer. In this way it is actually called "the darkness."

In another passage we read, "For God so loved the world that He gave his only-begotten Son that whosoever believes in him may not perish, but may have eternal life" (John 3:16). So the world is dear to the Father, to such an extent that he risks "His Son," and that means "Himself," for it. This "risk" is a very definite one. The Son comes into historical existence, becomes "man," "flesh," a reality within the world as John also emphasizes in the Prologue of his Gospel (John 1:14). In his discourse at Capernaum, Jesus said, "I am the living bread that has come down from heaven. If anyone eats of this bread he shall live forever, and the bread which I shall give is my flesh, for the life of the world" (John 6:51). If man receives this God Who gives Himself, he experiences a new birth into a new existence, and receives "the power to become the child of God" (John 1:12). But Jesus also says to his adversaries, "You are from below, I am from above. You are of this world; I am not of this world" (John 8:23). He says to the disciples, "If the world hates you, remember that it hated me first. If you were of the world the world would love its own. But because you are not of the world, but I have chosen you out of the world, therefore the world hates you" (John 15:18–19). And in the prayer at the close of the Last Supper he said, "I have given them thy words, and the world has hated them, because they are not of the world, even as I am not of the world. I pray not that Thou shouldst take them from the world, but that thou mayst preserve them from evil. They are not of the world, even as I am not of the world. Sanctify them in truth. Thy word is truth. As thou hast sent me into the world so have I also sent them into the world. And for their sakes I sanctify myself, that they also may be sanctified in truth" (John 17:14–19). And before this we find what is perhaps the most severe statement: "I pray for them; I pray not for the world, but for those whom Thou hast given me, because they are thine" (John 17:9). Here emerges the concept of the "below" of which we have spoken before; not the living counter-pole of the "above" which would be the "within," but the evil contradiction of it, the realm from which "the evil ones originate," whose "father" is Satan, the realm in which Satan "reigns" (John 16:11), the lost world, for which Christ does not even pray, and whose revolt is described in the Apocalypse.

Christ is God and man.[15] Everything depends on our accepting this fundamental concept of Christian thought in its entire force. God not merely filled a man with religious power, seized him prophetically, bound him to Himself by a particular destiny, but He "became" man, formed with him an existential unity, so that the "I," which is here spoken, is His own in the strictest sense, the life that is here lived and the destiny which is here fulfilled are in the simplest sense His act and His destiny. But not in a "private" way, in a sphere of exclusiveness concerning only Him and the chosen creature, but as the redeemer of all Creation. In this way Creation itself is drawn into this unity of existence with the Son of God and the condition of its existence is fundamentally changed.

Christ lives in pure obedience to the will of the Father. His human nature joins in performing the eternal act of love of the Son. But through this human nature creation itself abides in love. The revolt and apostasy of sin are here fundamentally overcome. In Christ, the world is oriented toward God in the way in which He willed it in creating it. "As the Father hath loved me so I also have loved you; abide in my love. If you keep my commandments you will abide in my love, as I have kept my Father's commandments and abide in His love" (John 15:9–10).

Christ says of himself: "I am the truth" (John 14:6). Truth is that which falsehood contradicts: recognition of that which is and witness to that which is valid, higher in degree and more decisive in meaning the more important the being to which they are directed. Ultimately, it consists in the adoration and praise of God. It is the Son himself who gives to the Father the glory of truth, recognizing and confessing Him. The myths of the revolt of Son-divinities against their fathers give us a hint of what that means. With divine seriousness the Son recognizes and confesses: the

Father is, and it is right that He should be. This act of truth penetrates the human nature with which it has united. The human nature of Christ performs this act also. Everything in him gives glory to the Father. This is the truth that decides the destiny of the world, for in Christ the world has been taken up into this truth and so redeemed from the denial and revolt of falsehood. Truth is also that which disguise and concealment contradict, the openness of being, which comes about when, in the understanding spirit, that which is comes into the light of the divine original and into the transparency of the word. The *Logos,* that which is spoken, is the fullness of being of the *legon,* the speaker. As he is uttered by the Father, he, the hidden and unknown, comes into the openness of the eternal word, which has been spoken and has arrived and at the same time returns as an answer. This word contains the fullness of the prototype of all finite things, the ultimate meaning of the world. In its brightness appears also the humanity of Christ, and thereby the world. In Christ, it is redeemed from muteness and concealment; it has become open and true.

The final word must be spoken from the viewpoint of the existence of Christ. In St. John's Gospel, He makes the awesome statement, "If you do not believe that I am he, you shall die in your sins" (John 8:24). This statement signifies the appropriation of that most special of all statements of God about Himself, which we find at the beginning of the covenant: "And God said to Moses, 'I am who I am.'" And he continued: "Thou shalt say to the Israelites, 'The I-am has sent me to you' " (Ex. 3:14). The Son exists as the one begotten and spoken by the Father, but equal to Him in the holy autonomy of divinity. The consciousness of this is expressed in the Gospel passage. The human nature of Christ is taken up into a participation in this existence, for the whole Christ utters this "I am." Thereby creation is rescued from the power of nothingness, lifted from its state of abandonment into the eternal protection of God's existence. This fact is the root of the Christian consciousness of existentiality and the Christian doctrine of existence. In the human nature of Christ created being "is" in a manner for which there is no category from a natural point of view. Theology expresses it by the doctrine of the *communicatio idiomatum*, the community of expressions which exists between the divine and the human natures in the one Christ. In him—only in him, but in him really—we may say that God experienced a destiny, suffered and died, and also that the humanity of Jesus is holy and eternal, stands in the glory of the Father and is equally "worthy to receive power and riches and wisdom and strength and honor and glory and blessing" (Apoc. 5:12 and Apoc. 4:11). The special character of this existentiality is expressed by theology in the concept of "*gratia unionis*" the "grace of the union of the divine and human." The fact that the believer is given a participation in this existence and that he is rooted in its triumphant freedom (cf. the Pauline promises of the freedom of the children of God and their reigning together with Christ)—this is "grace" in its ultimate sense.

This fact remains in the world; it is eternal and cannot be annulled, for the Son of God who became man remained man. After his death, he arose and "sits at the right hand of the Father," Lord for all eternity. And this takes the form of redemption. The world is redeemed not only in the immediate personal environment of Christ, but his influence is dynamic and reaches out. He is proclaimed and must be believed; he is set up as the norm and must be followed and imitated; in the mystery of the Eucharist he gives himself as food and must be received. The whole world must be drawn into him and transformed into a new creation. It must be renewed as a whole. St. Paul and St. John proclaimed this message and laid the foundations of the structure.[16] But as this is done a division also takes place, to which St. John refers again and again, especially in the last discourse of the Lord. In the response of Yes or No to Christ there is a separation of two "worlds," as different as good and evil, holy and unholy, God and the contradiction of God. They are not originally separate realms, like the relation of spirit and matter as viewed by the gnostics. In this sense, according to their being, there are not two worlds, but only one, created by God, ontologically good. It is judged by him, but retained and finally redeemed. In Christ there came a new beginning. This now stands in the old world as the new one which has already begun and summons the other to itself. To make this clear was the purpose of St. John's struggle against dualism. The old world, by means of man, who is free, can change its disposition and turn to the new beginning, can open itself thereto, accept the Redeemer, and through the Redeemer pass over to the Father and itself become a new creation. But it can also shut itself up within itself, turn away from the Father and so become ultimately the old world and hence the kingdom of evil.

In Christ, God comes to the world. In him its nature becomes clear. Its tendency toward self-enclosure, toward sin, is revealed. It is confronted with the final limit of which we have already spoken. In his judgment God rejects it as unholy. But He does this in love, while he, through whom the judgment takes place, the son of God, places himself on the side of the world, takes its guilt upon himself, and becomes for it the living "way" to God.

That the world is directed to its limits, but therein opened to God; is convicted of its sin, yet redeemed in love; is shown to be not only finite, but also callous and occluded, and yet is drawn into union with God in grace—only this again restores the world to that state which God intended it to have.

The Christ, who has consummated his work now stands at the "edge" of the world, down from above and up from within. He is the mediator and as such its living boundary, a breathing boundary, divinely breathing in the Holy Spirit, the "breath of God," and so accomplishing the constant transfer back and forth.[17]

This—"the new heaven and the new earth" of the Apocalypse—signifies the totality of things insofar as they become the realm of existence of the believer, who himself in faith accomplishes the constant change and transformation into the "new man." It is St. Paul who prophetically experienced and proclaimed this process of becoming. He says in the Epistle to the Romans: "The expectation of the creature waits for the revelation of the sons of God. For the creature was made subject to vanity, not willingly, but by reason of him that made it subject in the hope that the creature also itself shall be delivered from the servitude of corruption, into the liberty of the children of God. For we know that every creature groans and travails in pain even till now" (Rom. 8:19–22). Similarly, in the Epistle to the Ephesians, where he speaks of the "mystery of his will, according to his good pleasure, as he has purposed in him, in the dispensation of the full-ness of time to reestablish all things in Christ, both what is in heaven and what is on earth" (Eph. 1:9–10). And more powerfully in the Epistle to the Colossians: "Who is the image of the invisible God, the first-born of every creature; for in him were all things created in heaven and on earth, visible and invisible, whether thrones or dominations or principalities or powers; all things were created by him and in him. And he is before all and by him all things endure. And he is the head of the body, the church, who is the beginning, the firstborn from the dead; that in all things he may hold the primacy. Because in him it pleased the Father that all fullness should dwell; and through him to reconcile all things unto himself, making peace through the blood of his cross, both as to the things that are on earth and the things that are in heaven" (Col. 1:15–20). But in man there is also the evil. Redemption does not mean that it is abolished—that would be magic—but that a new beginning is established in man and thereby the possibility and the strength for the new existence is given. But in the same man there is the old beginning and hence the possibility that he may constitute himself the center for the preservation of the old evil world. And these two things do not exist side by side as compartments of being, but the same existent person can put himself at the disposal of one or the other beginning. Nor is it true that man, if he transforms the world to his existence in faith and so brings the new world into being, stands once for all in the good order. There exists constantly the evil possibility, and he can slip back into it. So he becomes a kind of battlefield, upon which the two orders fight an inexorable ultimate battle. Not in the sense that the two are equally matched, but, since the new world can come into being only through freedom, and freedom in our temporal existence is a choice between good and evil, since man is inclined to evil and God cannot force him but only call him and set him free in grace, there is a true side-by-side. Again it is St. Paul who experienced and proclaimed most powerfully the force in history of that which is in itself unreal and deceptive. The 7th and 8th chapters of the Epistle to the Romans tell of this.[18] But St. Paul also knows the blessedness of the victory, as we see in the wonderful hymn of victorious hope at the end of the 8th chapter:

> For I reckon that the sufferings of this time are not worthy to be compared with the glory to come that shall be revealed in us. For the expectation of the creature waits for the revelation of the sons of God. For the creature was made subject to vanity, not willingly, but by reason of him that made it subject in the hope that the creature also itself shall be delivered from the servitude of corruption into the liberty of the children of God. For we know that every creature groans and travails in pain even till now. And not only it, but ourselves also, who have the first fruits of the Spirit, even we ourselves groan within ourselves waiting for the adoption of the sons of God, the redemption of our body (Rom. 8:18–23).

Preface to Part II: The Person

C onfronting the world—the given totality—there is man, or more correctly, I. Every man at any time confronting the world, says "I." This confrontation does not mean that a particularly important individual is lifted from the totality of being and opposed to the rest, but is something more fundamental, more absolute. In each instance, the man concerned, precedes the whole. He does this not as an animal might do, for which likewise its own existence is the one and only thing that matters, but in a "decisive" manner. Man knows that he is not merely compelled to this confrontation by the self-assertion of the living creature or enabled thereto by a superior power but that he is entitled and even obliged thereto by a particular quality of meaning. This is of such a nature that it maintains itself through all the differences of ability and of conditions, and survives all disturbances and distortions. It remains, even if the man becomes ill, incapacitated or wicked, even though the man forgets it or acts contrary to it or does not wish to think of it. This quality we call the person. And it is of this that we shall speak in the following sections.

In carrying on our investigation we shall start not from the problem of the abstract nature of the person, but from that of the concrete, personally existing man. In this entire phenomenon we can distinguish several layers. We shall describe them in order from the bottom to the top; that is, not so as to derive the higher from the lower but to progress from the supporting element which is in its nature less important, to that which is supported but is decisive and meaningful.

The Structure of the Personal Existence

I

Person and Form

To begin with, "person" signifies about the same thing as form or structure. The statement that something possesses form means that the elements which compose it, such as matter, powers, attributes, acts, events, relations, are not in a state of chaos and confusion, nor are they merely cast into an external shape or mold. Rather, they are related in structure and function in such a way that the element exists and must be understood from and through the whole and the whole from and through the elements. In this sense all things that can be named are forms: crystals, organisms, psychic processes, sociological structures, geometric figures, logical connections, works of art, etc. The statement means further that what exists is differentiated as something proper and particular from the totality of things and also from every individual of this totality and that it maintains this particular quality.

In this way we determine the lowest stratum of being and meaning for that which is called personal existence. Inasmuch as man is a structure he stands as something formed among other forms, as a unified process among other processes, as a thing among things.

II

Person and Individuality

The next stratum of the phenomenon we call a person is individuality. "Individuality" is the living being, insofar as it represents a definitive unity of structure and function. In this way the living being is distinguished from the sum total of things as such. It requires the world, its matter and energy, and it also forms a part of this totality of matter and energy, but at the same time it differentiates itself from this totality and defends itself against being absorbed by it.

This self-demarcation and self-assertion of the living individual take place especially in two ways. First, it reduces the surrounding world to a structure in relation to its own existence. It creates an environment for itself. This comprises all those elements of the universe which are of vital importance for the individual in question. So it is a selection which is made particularly by the organs of sensation and activity. Whatever—qualitatively or quantitatively—escapes these organs does not belong to the environment in any case; whatever they grasp belongs to it, and in the way in which it is grasped in each instance. The selection also depends upon the relations of the individual to other individuals, as they are determined by nature, those individuals which are required by its existence, such as parents or the animals that form its prey, or those creatures with which it is in some way connected by the purpose of its life, and conversely, those which on their side have need of it. The selection is also related to the particular organization of the individual in question, its means of attack and defense, its "technical" abilities, such as the construction of nests or webs, etc. All this results in a reduction of the universe for the purposes of the individual. The central point of this world of its own is the vital urge by which the living creature makes its own way in the universe. The universe extends in all directions around the environment, as a background indefinitely continued.

The individual is further distinguished from the totality of life as such—or rather the totality of the species as represented by its own kind. The individual is produced by parents and itself produces offspring. Thereby it is placed in a continuous line. It is directed to this by definite urges, so much so that at times, such as the period of procreation or as long as the young require care, it is completely monopolized by these needs. And yet the individual is not identical with the lineage but maintains its separate existence even against this. This separation is also secured by natural urges, and their force appears to increase with the biological rank of the particular species. The lower the living creature, the more it is absorbed in the demands of the species; the higher it is, the stronger becomes the urge to maintain its individuality. The characteristic qualities become more numerous, the special accomplishments are more clearly defined, the number of offspring decreases, the claims of the young to greater care increase. In this way the individual, as opposed both to the species as a whole and to other individuals, acquires an ever increasing importance. By that very fact it is also imperilled, for, the more sharply the individual stands out from the species and the multitude, the less it is protected by these. The instincts become less imperative, the possibilities of a break-down increase. The pre-requisites of development become more numerous and qualitatively higher. "Value" does not mean matter-of-factness. Whereas it gives meaning it also imperils and the higher the meaning that it imparts the greater the peril. Individuality is a value; the more it develops the more insecure is its duration.

The individual is determined by its milieu. This milieu is not spacial but living. It does not mean a place which can be determined by measurement and reached by simple penetration—as, for instance, in a crystal—but it lies beyond a qualitative boundary and is attained only by crossing this. The living milieu is interiority. The passage between the interiority of the living creature and its proper environment is effected by sense-perception and self-activity. When an external stimulus causes a sense-impression and the stimulating object brings about an interior effect, in awakening a sensation—for instance, a flame is perceived as a form of light and movement, as heat or as a rushing sound—then there lies between the beginning and end of the process a change of sphere. This change does not proceed immediately from the area of a physical stimulus to that of the sensation of light or pain—as the process of kindling leads to the reduction of the wood to ashes—but the two areas are separated by a boundary which is overcome only by a "passage." The "boundary" and the "passage" compose a phenomenon which cannot be further explained. It belongs to the primary and intrinsic quality of life. The same is true of the self-activity of the individual. If its metabolism requires a supply of nourishment and hunger arises, this drives it to external acts of seeking, grasping, etc. But the stimulus of hunger does not proceed immediately from within outward into movement, as when a substance is heated, disintegrates and so causes an explosion. This latter process goes on in the same qualitative area, that of physical and chemical causality, but in order that the impulse of hunger may lead to the act of attack, the boundary must again be crossed, but this time in the opposite direction, from the interior into the exterior world. The same character of a passage of the boundary between the interior and the exterior belongs to the processes of nourishment and growth. When a crystal forms in a solution and continues to increase in size, this is a process of accretion which takes place in the same qualitative area. But when an animal eats a fruit then this is decomposed by the organism which receives it, its matter undergoes a structural change and is applied to the process of growth which, in its turn, proceeds from the spontaneity of life. The growth of the organism proceeds from its interiority which is as distinct from the exterior world in which the objects of nourishment are found as the sphere of sensation is from that of the stimulating object. Between the two spheres there lies a boundary which must constantly be crossed in the process of growth and which determines this process in contrast to that of simple accretion.

This interior sphere establishes the living individual in itself. On this basis it distinguishes itself from the world and constructs its own environment in opposition to it. On this basis it also distinguishes itself from the species and maintains itself against it as an intrinsic value.

In the total being of the personally existing man there is also the stratum of living individuality. By this he is a living being among other living beings, an individual as opposed to the species and also to the other individual members of the species.

III

Person and Personality

A third stratum of the total phenomenon of the person consists in what we call personality. It signifies the form of the living individuality insofar as it is determined by the mind. We have already spoken of the sphere of interiority. This is found even in growth and in the relations of a plant to its environment. In the animal it receives a new character through sense-perception and self-movement. It receives its ultimate definition as life motivated by mind.

There it becomes above all an interiority of self-consciousness. We cannot really give it this name as yet when perception awakes and self-activity is guided thereby. This takes place also in the animal and forms the psychic side of organic life. True consciousness is found only when the perception is penetrated by the spirit and leads to the grasping of the meaning; that is, when it is from the beginning ordained toward the attainment of understanding. Naturally, there is likewise a meaning in the perceptions of an animal, one that is determined by the objective organization of its life and serves the play of responses to stimuli, of memory, etc. But it is entirely ordered to the immanent purposes of the particular living being; it is carried out but is not grasped and understood as meaningful. In a life determined by mind we are dealing with the grasping of the meaning as such. An animal may note the events around it with most delicate sensitivity, may remember infallibly, may find its way most exactly among the various perceptions, and so fulfil perfectly the meaning of the totality of circumstances for its own life—but it never grasps this meaning as such and in itself. But it is this very thing which is the basis of true interior consciousness and forms a boundary which is not crossed by any of the adaptations accomplished by the higher apes. Consciousness in the true sense is found only when the process of perception and the succession of acts that it involves are determined by the value of truth. This interiority perceives the claim of existence to be grasped for its own sake, to be "understood." It possesses the will to construct the externally existing world in the realm of "knowledge," as a truth that is understood. No road leads to this point even from the most highly developed biological interiority. In any case where such a passage is claimed to exist, we find errors in observation and reasoning. A true consciousness becomes possible only by the fact that man possesses not merely "psychic qualities"— which are found also in the atom, in the crystal, in the plant and in the animal—but a concrete reality of the mind, an individual mind which has its center of activity and the place of its historical responsibility in this particular organism.

The interiority of the person (not as yet of the personality!) is furthermore an interiority of the will. Of this we may say the same that we have said of the consciousness. It is not a will in the personal sense when in a living individual there arises an urge which leads to organic and psychic acts and has the purpose of preserving the individual's life. A true will is found only when an organ of evaluation is affected by the character of value possessed by the object or by the meaning of the situation, and when it grasps this value as something valid in itself, takes up an attitude in relation to it, and from that point proceeds to action. This characteristic appears with special clarity in a situation where it is not value as such, something precious in itself, that is concerned, but an obligatory value, the moral duty involved. Here too there is an absolute boundary between the initiative of the animal and the will of man. All pretended proofs that an animal selects or decides, perceives value or even acts morally, are also due to errors in observation and reasoning, insofar as we are not dealing merely with sentimentality. They confuse the mechanisms of functions in the psycho-physical complex of life, which are present even in the animal, but which are dominated by an entirely different standard of meaning, with this standard itself.

The interiority of man is, finally, one of action and creation. The objects of perception and evaluation are taken as the starting-point in order to construct a second world from the materials of the first, a world of work and action from the world of nature. This is shown most plainly in those accomplishments whose intention is to produce something so that it may exist. Not in order to attain some purpose but in order to reveal meaning, not in order to construct something useful and practical but in order to create a form which expresses meaning.[1] This takes place in the production of a pure work of art or a true symbol. Here too a qualitative difference distinguishes human creation from every kind of animal production. The latter is a function of the whole organism, the former is determined by the meaning which proves itself through itself. An animal may be beautiful, may move gracefully, may sing delightfully, but it never creates a work of art; it is and lives as nature.[2] Behind the work of art there is the interiority determined by the mind which experiences the meaning and gives it form by means of its creative power.

It is in this form that the nature of creativity is most clearly revealed; but from it we can see that even in a work that has an ultimate purpose and which at first sight appears as the result of the immediate urge to construct which is a part of life—even in this there lies something more. If we call the totality of actions that are determined by purpose "technology," we find on closer examination that this also proceeds from a true will to create. Mere expediency and desire for survival would never drive man to the risks of technology. This is ultimately directed to something different in its nature from the building of a nest by a bird or the weaving of a web by a spider. The activity of the animal, regarded from the point of view of its purpose, produces excellent structures. They are perfect from beginning to end, but this very perfection shows that they have nothing to do with true creation, for their perfection is that of mere nature. The powers here in operation belong to the same kind as those which produce the organism itself. What they produce is, as it were, continuations of the organs. No human work attains this perfection, not because it is inferior, but because it is more. It proceeds from the mind, its tensions and its risks. By that very fact, it is less certain in the immediate natural sense. Its certainty is of another, a spiritual kind; it lies in meaning, not in immediate existence.[3] Technology does not mean merely that the inner purposes of life are externalized. Even the simplest measures which apparently lie upon the level of mere animal behavior are aimed at the production of a work. And if we actually consider the phenomenon of technology as a whole and do not permit our vision to be deceived by imperceptible transitions, then we see that it proceeds from the will—which is by no means "natural"—to destroy the existing state of things in order to construct a new one, to create a world-form which expresses a meaning born of the mind. Thereby the world does not gain a greater natural security and well-being. To relate all activity to wellbeing may be permissible in the case of the animal; however, in the case of man, something else enters into consideration, something that has an entirely different meaning, and may sharply oppose his immediate physical needs and requirements. A man who has only stone weapons finds it beneficial at first to receive an iron spear or a gun. But as soon as the gun develops in accordance with its innate meaning, and also is viewed in connection with all the other questions and consequences which it presupposes and brings about, one can hardly say that man is really and generally benefitted by it; rather, the gun ultimately becomes more dangerous for man than any beast of prey. But the ultimate meaning of the weapon is really not to remove danger or to enable man to attack more safely. This is only the penultimate meaning which sets in movement the whole process of the invention of weapons. Ultimately it is a question of bringing about a new world of forces and structures in which the phenomenon of battle recurs on a new level. On the whole, and in the final analysis, technology is not concerned with usefulness but with work. By this work life is as much, if not more, endangered as it is benefitted, and no one knows whether its enormous adventure may not end with a catastrophe.[4] A technology which was merely the continuation of a natural urge to construct could never bring the being which develops it into such a contradiction to the meaning of its own existence, a contradiction which breaks down all the logic of nature. Only if this being carries within itself from the first moment the possibility of bringing about the dissolution of nature; that is, if it is determined by mind, can it undertake something so tragically paradoxical—and so great. Through the spirit that determines it, personal interiority becomes, on principle, immeasurable. Only its expressions are measurable, and these depend upon conditions which are also measurable. But the interiority cannot be measured. The expressions can be analyzed logically and psychologically, but only up to the point where true creativity begins. This is itself beyond all analysis.

Because of the spirit this interiority also escapes all domination. Its expressions can be governed, but only those processes which are accessible for habit, suggestion, etc. The spiritual core remains free.

A synthesis of all that we have said lies in the concept of personality which the modern age has developed. It signifies the living basic form of the individual human being as distinct from all others. This combines the individual elements of its contemporary existence into a perceptible totality, and the separate acts and events of its life into a structure of development and destiny. This concept is revealed most clearly in the case of a great creative person—it was first studied and developed from this point of view—but it has become the norm for the modern view of man in general.

Through all this the personality accomplishes its differentiation from the totality of things and also from the species—indeed from everything else. For through the spirit it knows about itself and all besides. Not only in such a way that it could, if the conditions were given, encounter and grasp all things, but in a decisive manner, so that it has a consciousness of the whole; and that not through an enumeration or abstraction, but through that primary experience, by means of which the totality of existence at every point becomes perceptible to the concrete spirit which, as such, stands poised in itself and confronting the world. Through this experience, the personality is able to encounter existence also—is able actually to "encounter" anything that exists, instead of merely running against it. And so it can also encounter itself, instead of merely being and living that which it is.

IV

The Person in the True Sense

Form, individuality, personality—these do not yet tell us what a "person" ultimately signifies, but in a sense they prepare us for an understanding of the term. Our previous discussion was based upon the question: "What is this?" The answer was, "A structural being, based upon interiority, spiritually determined and creative." But if our question is: "Who is this?" then the answer must be "I," or, if we are speaking of another, "He." Only now do we touch upon the person. And it is indeed the structured, interior, spiritually-creative being, insofar as it stands in itself and is self-determined. "Person" means that in my being myself I cannot ultimately be possessed by any other authority, but belong to myself. I may be living in an age in which slavery exists, in which one man buys another and disposes of him. But the buyer exercises this power not over the person, but over the psycho-physical being—and that under a false category, namely in assimilating it to an animal. The person itself escapes from the condition of ownership.[5] "Person" means that I cannot be used by anyone else but am my own purpose. I may be caught in an economic system in which the leader treats me as an element in a machine-like whole. But then it is only my labor that he uses, not me as such. And this use is based upon a manner of thinking which saves strength, and, to a certain extent, is proper from the practical point of view, but which really puts in the place of man a highly developed machine. This error, then, of course takes its vengeance in dire consequences. The account does not balance and the economic and social structure built upon it does not ultimately operate properly, because what it deals with are human beings and not tools.[6] "Person" means that I cannot be penetrated by another but in relation to myself am alone with myself, that I cannot be replaced by any one else, but stand on my own, that no one can substitute for me, but that I am unique. All this remains valid, even if the sphere of reserve is disturbed most profoundly by encroachment and publicity. What is lost is only the psychological condition of being respected and at peace, not the solitude of the person as such. The significance of the person would be lost if I existed in duplicate; that is, had a double. Every hint of the possibility of such a phenomenon stirs a feeling of horror. The same thing happens if we consider the possibility that I might not be ultimately at one with myself, might be not a single person but several, not known to myself as a self, but really a stranger (split personality). A third form of this experience would occur if I began to feel that I no longer had power over myself but were in the power of another. (Compare the folk tale motif of a man selling his shadow or his reflection or even his soul). All this is impossible in view of my immediate existence. The person cannot exist in duplicate, cannot disintegrate, cannot lose its power over itself, though this is possible for the mere individual whose unity has originally a different character. The phenomena which psychiatry observes in this connection are not disturbances of the personality itself but of the psychological functions which support the personal consciousness. And yet these experiences have a significance for the nature of the person. The horror which they inspire is the fear of the possibility that such disturbances could really take place, and so it reveals something essential about the nature of the human person.

The fact that such experiences can occur shows that the person is not evident or certain. This fact is revealed by the very way in which men conceive of a person. If I am not mistaken, antiquity did not have a true concept of the person—indeed one does not seem to find it outside the realm of Revelation. The modern intellectual development tends to disintegrate the concept of the person, to equate it with that of the form or individuality or personality—or else to exaggerate the finality of the person and to speak of it in a manner permissible only in the case of the absolute person.

But here the question arises again, whether the person cannot, after all, be endangered. It can, indeed, but only from that direction where the source of its being lies. Let us ask another question first: Can the spirit become diseased? Certainly not in that way which our ordinary speech refers to as "mental illness." This really involves disturbances in brain-functions, in the life of the instincts and urges, in the course of the imagination, in the experience of reality, etc. Such disturbances do not touch the spirit as such, but only its organic and psychic bases. They hamper its activity, but also constitute a test, and by overcoming them the spirit grows. Yet the spirit does not exist absolutely, independent of its contents. It cannot live as it pleases without having its actions exert an influence upon its being. The life of the spirit—and this is characteristic of its nature—is determined not only by that which exists, but also and ultimately by that which is valid, by the true and the good. If it slips away from these its spiritual quality becomes dubious. The simplicity and indestructibility, which men generally attribute to the nature of spirit, do preserve it from such damage as the composite body may incur, but not from the consequences of its attitude toward value. If it falls away from truth, it becomes diseased.[7] This falling away does not take place if a man falls into error, but when he renounces truth; not if he tells a lie, even though he do so frequently, but if he no longer accepts truth as binding; not if he deceives another, but if he directs his life to the destruction of truth. Then he is spiritually diseased. This state does not necessarily have to produce psycho-pathological effects; indeed, such a man may even be very strong and successful. Nevertheless, he would be diseased and an observer who had not merely psychic but spiritual insight would perceive this. But the condition could also become a psychic one and bring about disturbances that could be clinically determined. Mere psychiatry would not be able to heal him of this disease, but he would have to undergo conversion. This conversion could not be accomplished by a mere act of the will. It would have to consist in a true change of heart and it would be more difficult than any therapeutic treatment.

From this point of view it also seems possible that the person as such may be endangered if the man breaks away from those realities and norms which guarantee the person—from justice and love. The person becomes diseased if it falls away from justice; that is, not if it commits unjust acts, even commits them frequently, but if it renounces justice. Justice means the acknowledgment that things have their intrinsic character, and a readiness to preserve the right of this character and the laws that spring from it. As a person, man has been set free to stand on his own feet and to act from his own initiative, without being God. The condition for the reasonableness of this manner of being is that he should take his place in that order which is based upon truth, namely in justice, and that he should even make justice his real life-work.[8] The finite person is significant only if he is oriented toward justice. In forsaking justice the person becomes endangered and dangerous—a power without order. And by that very fact the person, as person, becomes diseased. He is no longer in harmony with himself.

Equally decisive for the health of the person is love. To love means to behold the structure of value in another being, above all in a personal being, to perceive its validity, to feel that it is important that this should exist and develop; to be moved by concern about this realization as if it were one's own. He who loves moves forth into freedom, freedom from his real bonds—himself. And by the very fact that he banishes himself from his own sight and feeling, he fulfills himself. A space is cleared around him and he has room for his truest self. Everyone who knows anything about love knows this law: that it is only by departing from oneself that one obtains that openness in which the self is realized and everything flourishes. It is in this space that true creation and the pure act also take place, all that bears witness that the world is worthy of existence. In renouncing this love, the person becomes diseased. Not if man sins against love, wrongs it, falls into selfishness and hatred, but if he denies its seriousness and bases his life only upon calculation, force and deceit. Then existence becomes a prison. Everything is locked. Things become oppressive. All becomes in its essence alien and hostile. The ultimate revealing significance disappears. Existence no longer blossoms.

The horror of which we spoke shows wherein the essential quality of the person consists: that I am at one with myself, stand firm in myself, have myself in hand. This fact unfolds itself in the conditions we have set forth: the completeness of the form, the interiority of the life, the spiritual basis of knowing and willing, of acting and creating. But all this is not yet the person, "person" means that in all this the man stands in himself.[9] Is it a question of form then? Certainly, but not merely form, although it is decisive. Hence the peculiar elusiveness of the person. To the question "What is your person?" I cannot answer "my body, my soul, my reason, my will, my freedom, my spirit." All this is not as yet the person but, as it were, the stuff of which it is made; the person itself is the fact that it exists in the form of a being which belongs to itself. On the other hand, this "stuff" really exists in this form and so conforms wholly to its character. The whole reality of the man, not only consciousness or freedom, belongs to the realm of the person, is its responsibility, and is stamped by it with the mark of dignity. This of course does not indicate how far it has actually attained the truly personal attitude.

This form makes itself felt in the whole course of life. The structural quality of the personal human being is different from that of a crystal; his individuality is different from that of the animal; his personality is something different from what scientific study means by that term—different in that it is the "person" that is realized in all this, the fact that it can and should stand in itself. Our preceding considerations have separated the various "layers" in order to distinguish them more clearly; as a matter of fact they are interwoven; each one is taken up into the higher relation. The form exists only as something living,[10] the individual only as something penetrated by a concrete spirit, but the whole is infallibly characterized by the fact that it stands in the unicity and originality of the personality. The form and fulness of a human existence is realized only so far as the personality prevails.[11]

The person is that fact which again and again elicits existential wonder. It is the most self-evident of all facts—in a verbal sense: to understand that I am I is for me the self-evident purely and simply, and imparts its character to every other fact in a situation. But, at the same time, it is enigmatic and inexhaustible that I am I, that I cannot be forced out of myself, not even by the most powerful enemy, but only by myself, and even that not entirely; that I cannot be replaced, even by the noblest person; that I am the center of existence, for I *am* that, and you also are that, and you yonder, and all the lights which this globe of mystery emits as it revolves in the spirit.

Again and again doubt presses against this concept, objecting that the fact of the person cannot be taken as referring to content but only "formally," as a mere category of self-knowledge. This doubt resolves the fact psychologically, seeing in it only the unity of consciousness and of initiative. It makes the concept ethically questionable, as being presumption, self-deceit, the breaking up of the community. It depreciates the person because of its powerlessness since its actual being and ability appear to be in constant contradiction to its claims, so much so that the supposed person becomes actually comical; indeed, it has been maintained that herein lies the root of all comedy. This doubt urges the person to renounce its claims and become modest and simple like the plant and the animal. The person itself becomes weary of itself, feels the burden of responsibility for the inadequacy and the evil of its being, and seeks to be dissolved in the combination that relieves it of its burden. It becomes bored with its definitiveness, the ennui of always having to be itself and it seeks to escape from itself in masks and dramatic roles. It fears its loneliness and presses toward the releasing union of species and nature. It seeks to forget itself, casts itself into transience and mutability, into the stream of continuous coming into being and passing away. It betrays and sells itself, to pleasure, to mere work, to what is base and evil—And yet the tremendous fact remains: "I am I." Hard, glorious, terrible, creating destiny and establishing responsibility. It gives to all its radiance and its gravity. Even if I say, "The idea must triumph, not I; the beloved one shall live, not I," these words of self-abnegation contain the fact that it is I who utter them. Only the self can be unselfish. Indeed, the fact that it is just in unselfishness that the self rises not merely to the fulness, but even to the reality of its selfhood, is a basic principle of human existence and shall be discussed at length hereafter. It has been said that being is ultimately a mystical fact, and that is true. As soon as we are really conscious of it we see clearly that it consists of a mystery. Decisively—for it decides the meaning of man—deeper does the mystery become if we say, not, "Something is," but, "I am." Mere philosophical hypotheses would not suffice to analyze it; its analysis would lead to the roots of religion.

In all this we are not constructing a myth of the person. The argument we have developed does not mean that the person stands alone as a closed, self-sufficient monad; the next section will have as its task to show how essential for the person is the relation to another person. But here also, at the end of this section, we wish to emphasize strongly that the definite character which we have assigned to the person does not set it apart from the relations of materials and forces nor yet those of the species and of history.

The personally existing human being stands within the unity of all the structures and processes which compose objective Nature. The body of man consists of the same materials and obeys the same laws as that of the animal. He too is dependent on the processes of nature and is related to an environment. But through him the whole situation comes within the sphere of the person and so receives the character of self-centeredness. This does not mean that, for example, moral self-determination is actually attained or even attempted. Man may succumb to instinct and so to the natural condition. But then it is a succumbing, not the self-evident absorption of the animal, and hence it is personally determined, even though in a negative manner. Inevitably, the fact of the person is a concomitant in every bodily process, even though it be in the form of a failure or a forgetting. The same thing is true of the other circumstances; e.g. the psychic, all that we call inheritance or family connection, or what psychology calls the collective: geographical, national, sociological and historical conditions. None of these are overlooked or curtailed, but all receive from the fact of the person their true human character. And if this character is consciously recognized, willed, lived and practiced, then all these conditions are brought under a real control which comprises within itself all that signifies personal culture and maturity.

The Personal Relation

I

The Limitation of the Person

In the preceding sections we have attempted to construct the inner system of the person. Now we must consider whether and in what way this person is limited externally.

According to the statements we have made, the relations of the substances and forces of the material world will evidently limit the person only in so far as these compose the basis of things and processes upon which the person rests. The biological nature of the species will limit it only in so far as it produces the organism which gives the person its position in existence. The person as such does not come from physical or biological facts but stands on its own. Only as a consequence of this independence can it take upon itself the responsibility for things and for the species. So we might ask further whether the person is limited by the world of the spirit, by morality and so forth. The answer would in each case become more difficult but in the last analysis it would always affirm that the person needs all these circumstances of reality and of meaning in order to subsist and to maintain itself, but in itself and as a person is not limited by them.

The situation seems to change if we ask whether the person is limited by another person. This is certainly not the case in the sense that one

343

person produces another. It is only the organism that is produced. That this, because of the personal "Form," stands on its own is something different than when a young animal has left the maternal organism and walks by itself. The manner in which the child grows in the womb and proceeds from it—in spite of all that it has organically in common with the young animal—is determined originally by the fact of its previously outlined personality. This personality is already presupposed. The same thing is true of the different methods of caring for the child. The person who feeds, protects and educates the young personal being helps it to develop, brings to it the stuff of the world and teaches it to maintain itself in its environment. But all this does not produce the person but presupposes it. Every aid to advancement given by one person to another is given on the basis of the fact that he is a person. But does the possibility of the existence of a person depend on the existence of other persons? More exactly: can there be a person unless it is related as "I" to another person which constitutes its "Thou"—or unless at least the possibility exists that another person may become its "Thou?"

II

The Relation of "I" and "Thou"

What do "I," and "Thou;' really mean? When one kind of matter is brought to another then we have two substances with definite measurements and qualities which exert definite mechanical or chemical influences upon each other. When one animal meets another then we have two biological systems with their respective centers and purposes, which are either strange to each other and run apart or else have some natural relation and seek to draw each other into their own teleology. A man may also meet another man as in the first instance, if they happen to collide. It can also happen as in the second instance, perhaps if they are fighting for food.

In both cases the other is not the man's "Thou," and he in turn confronts the other not as "I," but as the subject of definite tendencies. The situation need not be essentially different even if the two subjects strive and act with the keenest reason and the most skillful technique. It is always possible that in a particular case the one sees in the other not his "Thou" but only an object: resistance, matter, a constructive contrast or the like. This attitude considers the other not as that being which stands in itself and forms the center about which everything that exists arranges itself in the unique form which composes the "world"; it rather relates him to oneself as the only center concerned and considers him a tool in the accomplishment of one's own purposes. Consequently, it confronts the other not in the attitude of the "I," but only of the perceiving and acting subject.

The other becomes my "Thou" only when the simple subject-object-relation ceases. The first step toward the "Thou" is that movement which means "hands off" and clears the space in which the person's capacity of serving as his own purpose can be realized. This is the first exercise of justice and the basis of all "love." Personal love begins decisively not with a movement toward the other but away from him. At the same moment my own attitude also changes. In the measure in which I release the being which at first I regarded only as an object, and consider it as a self meeting me from its own center, permitting it to become my "Thou," I pass from the attitude of a using or fighting subject into that of the "I."

This process involves a risk. When confronting an object a man is only objectively interested. His personality is at rest. His interior countenance is not revealed. His hands are free for any desired movement. It is only what he possesses or can do that is involved, not his own self. But as soon as he confronts the "Thou" as an "I" something arises within him. Not as if a man who hitherto had been able to hide his true nature suddenly becomes transparent for a keen observer; not that mask and mimicry cease and "expression" takes place; but he loses the protection which consists in the "objective quality" of the situation in which he is acting. When I glance at another as

"I," I become open and "show" myself. But the relation remains incomplete unless the same movement begins from the other side and the other lets me become his "Thou." But it must be the real "I," not some other identified with me; "I" as I really am, not as he would like me to be. If this does not take place the whole relation remains incomplete and tormenting. Indeed there arises a feeling of betrayal, for in really becoming "Thou," one shows a willingness which must receive a response of some kind if it is not to forfeit its honor. But if the movement is returned, then the protection of objectivity falls away on the other side also. The countenance is revealed in the glance, and there arises that relation in which eye meets eye. Only now the complete condition of personality comes into being, and also in connection with it, destiny in the personal sense. This does not result merely from the meeting of a subject and an object—whether this be a thing or a human being in an "objective" attitude—in such a case the self is armored and what results is only profit or loss, growth or decay. Personal destiny springs only from the unprotected openness of the "I-Thou" relation—or else of that "I" relation which is denied fulfilment on the part of the "Thou."

This "I-Thou" relation can be realized in various ways and at varying depths. It lies even in our taking another seriously, in the respect shown by a greeting, in a stirring of sympathy, and then, as trust, comradeship, love, it continues to grow stronger, more meaningful and more definite. The true *vis-a-vis* toward which the "I" activates itself, is also an "I." But there is also a quasi "I-Thou" relation, namely where I place an object, a tree, a landscape, or the world itself in the attitude of a personality which can be addressed. This happens to a certain degree in the true mythical attitude for which there are behind things and processes not matter and forces, but active beings.[1] It occurs in a different manner in the case of the poet, when in his lyric emotion he beholds the tree or the landscape as if it were a face. We find it also in another way in the feeling of love, when a man takes an object, a country or the world into his relation with the beloved person or sees this person as revealed in the object.

III

The Person and the other Person; Language

Does the person then require the other person in order to be itself? We have shown that the person activates itself in the "I-Thou" relation, but not that it arises from it. Actualistic personalism maintains that there is no such thing as the person at rest, that the person exists only in the act of self-activity and can be conceived of only as sharing in a condition of sympathy. This view is opposed to that other which equates person with individual, taking it only as an object. Both views are dialectically inter-dependent and both destroy the reality. In actual fact the person is not only *dynamis* but being, not only act but form. In the meeting with another it does not come into being, but it is only activated thereby. But it is dependent on the fact that other persons do exist. It has meaning only when there are others whom it can encounter. Whether the meeting actually takes place is another question. A man might be shipwrecked on an uninhabited island and be obliged to stay there. Nor is it necessary that he should meet that person which grants him the fulfilling relation. There are many forms and degrees of meeting, including the tragic, from which only renunciation and wisdom can glean a personal meaning. Here we are dealing with the ontological fact that basically the person does not exist in a solitary state.

We can also express the situation by saying that man by his nature is in a dialogue. His mental life is ordained to be a communication. This does not mean that he has social talents. There are whole periods which have an individualistic character, and there are also phases in the life of every human being during which he must shut himself up within himself if he is not to suffer harm. The statement refers to something that lies within the very nature of mental life: the fact that mental life is carried on essentially in language.

Language is not only the means by which we communicate conclusions, but mental life and activity are carried on in the process of speech. Thought is not a pre-verbal act of the mind which only later, as a result of some decision or for some particular purpose, is formulated in words, but it takes place from the first moment in the form of interior speech. Language is not a system of signs by means of which two monads exchange ideas but it is the very realm of consciousness in which every man lives. It is a connected whole of forms of consciousness determined by supra-individual laws, into which the individual is born and by which he is formed. It is an entity independent of the individual, of which each one constructs something according to the measure of his talents. In this world of consciousness man exists. Language offers, as Heidegger says—"the very first possibility of standing amid the openness of being."[2] Through language, truth becomes an objective thing.[3] But speech, in the true sense of the word, is possible only with another and not with oneself. So complete speech, which is carried on in the common responsibility for truth and the common bond of human destiny, tends toward the realization of the "I-Thou" relation. In this way speech becomes the objective plan for the construction of the personal encounter.[4]

The Verbal Character of Things

This situation receives its ultimate meaning from a revelation which runs through the Old Testament and is completed in the Logos doctrine of St. John's Gospel, and according to which things actually exist in the form of the word.

God is not only the one who knows and has power to reveal, but He is the one who speaks. Indeed, He himself is a kind of word. "In the beginning was the word and the word was with God. And the Word was God. As such it was in the beginning with God" (John 1:1–2). If the Son is here called the Logos, this statement tells us something about God himself. The Word forms the core of the divine existence. God is in himself the speaker, the one spoken, and the loving comprehension of the eternal speech. He is this by nature, independent of whether a creature exists which could hear Him. From all eternity God is the prime reality and the ultimate mystery, but also the one who expresses himself. So there is in Him the Word, through which reality communicates itself and the mystery is revealed—the Word in which the eternal reality is received and returned as the answer, the revelation is accepted and preserved in the intimacy of mutual understanding. In the beginning—here we take this term not as the starting point of a succession of things, but as eternity, eternity as it appears when it is reached by taking one's way back through time. In the beginning, then, there is not the blind urge, not "mind," not "the deed," but the clearness of the Word. "Through the word all things were made and without it nothing was made that was made" (John 1:3). God is not mute. His life, of its very nature, bears the word within it. God lives in speaking, and in such a way that in Him the word does not presuppose the person but establishes it. God is a person in relation to the word. He utters His infinite mystery and thereby exists, as the one who speaks, in relation to the one who is spoken—and who is also, we may say in addition, the true hearer. It is the completely fulfilled, completely arrived word of which we are here speaking. Completely arrived because the "Thou" to which it turns is not a strange and independent self, but this "Thou" proceeds from the very act of speaking. The word passes over and at the same time takes up, as it were, a position in itself. It is both speech and ear, a speech perceived and also a reply. So John says that the Word was "with God," "turned toward Him," receiving itself as it hears, and as a consequence existing in itself. But then it does not depart elsewhere but gives itself back to the Speaker in the assent which says, "It is so, and I am Thy truth," "abiding in Him," as St. John likewise says. But it is the Holy Spirit in whom that which is hidden reveals itself in the Word and that which is revealed preserves its intimacy, for the Holy Spirit is love. Only in love can the mystery be truly revealed; only in love can the revealed mystery be preserved, just as it is possible only in love that the inner depth comes out into the freedom of personality but does not "depart" in self-seeking, but "abides" in the original unity. And this it does, not in such a way that it loses itself, but, secure in equality, turns as the spoken Son in love toward the speaking Father.

Now, all things come from the Word in God and hence have the character of words. They are not mere realities. Neither are they mere mental facts standing in silent space. They are words of the One who speaks creatively, addressed to him who "has ears to hear." The world proceeded not only from power and not only from thought, but from speech. Its structures are words by which the creating God utters his full-ness of thought to finite being; words which go forth to seek him who will comprehend them and who in praising, thanking, and obeying, will enter into the "I-Thou" relation of creature and Creator with the one who speaks. The 18th Psalm reads:

> The heavens declare the glory of God and the firmament shows forth the work of His hands.
>
> Day unto day utters speech and night unto night shows knowledge.
>
> There is no speech or language whose voice is not heard.
>
> Their sound has gone forth into all the earth, their words unto the ends of the world (Ps. 18:2–5).

The doctrine, according to which things are words is deeply imbed-ded in the Old Testament consciousness. Only this helps us to understand what the providence of God in history really means, how providence is related to creation, the kingdom of God to the world, and things to man. The Johannine doctrine of the *Logos* is rooted primarily and decisively in this, and only secondarily in the Greek concept of the *Logos* and of the idea. The fact that the world exists in the form of speech is the reason why speech is possible within it. The possibility of speech lies not merely in the fact that man possesses the gift of language and that things are objective structures of meaning which can be expressed in words; it lies also in the fact that the world itself has a verbal character, proceeding from speech and existing as spoken. If this were not so, human speech would not be assimilated by existence. The words would wander about within it like phantoms.

But this train of thought would carry us too far afield. For the point of our discussion they simply mean that the person exists in the form of the dialogue, related to another person. The person is destined by his very nature to become the "I" of a "Thou." The fundamentally solitary person does not exist.

The Person and God

I

The Human and the Divine Person

The person, then, is dependent on the condition that other persons should exist. Not this or that person, though they might be the most important or outstanding at any time, but just persons as such. It is different in the case of the absolute personality, God. Without Him I cannot exist. This is so, not only because God has created me and I ultimately find the meaning of my life only in Him, but because I exist only in relation to God. My personality is not perfected in humanity, so that it may perhaps set its "Thou" in God or refrain from doing so, refusing to do it and yet remaining a person. My being "I" consists essentially in this, that God is my "Thou."

The person has a significance which transcends the importance of its being. In a certain sense, its significance is absolute. As this person, not as the bearer of certain qualities and talents, it is unique. As such it has an irreplaceable dignity and responsibility. The loss of a person cannot be actually compensated for by anything else. This does not mean that the human person may not sacrifice himself for another, or be replaced by another at the will of someone in authority, since it belongs precisely to the nature of the person that this can be done and in certain cases should be done. But it is only the physical life, possessions, or work that may be sacrificed, not the dignity of the person itself. To surrender its integrity for any purpose, even the highest, would prove to be not only sacrilege but sheer waste, if we had eyes to see aright. The person has absolute dignity. But this it can receive not from its own being, which is finite, but only from the absolute. And not from an abstract absolute, such as an idea, a value, a law, or the like. These could only determine the content of its concrete life, not its personality, which it derives from the fact that God has brought it into existence as a person. The statement, God created the person, means something else than the statement that he brought an impersonal being into existence. Whatever is impersonal, whether living or lifeless, God creates simply as the immediate object of His will. He cannot and will not create the person in this way, for that would be unreasonable. He creates it by an act which presupposes its dignity and thereby establishes it—by a call. Things come into existence by the command of God; the person by His call. And this means that God summons it to be His "Thou"—more exactly that He destines Himself to be man's "Thou."

God is the absolute "Thou" of man. The created personality subsists in the fact that this is so. If it were possible for man to step out of this relation to God, that means, not only to forsake God but to bring it about that he no longer stood ontologically in this "Thou"-relation but only in the relation of a created being to its creator as the norm and realization of its existence, then man would cease to be a person. He would become— it is a nonsensical notion, but illustrates the point—a man-thing, a spirit-beast. But this he cannot do. In creating him, God made him His "Thou," and this he is whether he wishes to be or not. He is a man to the extent to which he, in understanding and obeying, realizes his "Thou"-relation to God. If he does not do this, however, he does not cease to be a person, because through his very existence, which is not in his power, he is an answer to the call of the Creator. Nevertheless, by his will, he contradicts his own nature and so becomes an absurdity whose ultimate end constitutes damnation.

This is the intrinsic "I-Thou" relation which cannot be abolished. The world is also drawn into it. We have said that the world itself has a verbal character. Here we have the points of reference for our argument. The world is addressed by God to man. All things are words of God spoken to that creature which by its nature is destined to stand in the "Thou"-relation to God. Man is the one who is meant to be the hearer of the world-word. He is also meant to be the one who answers. Through him all things should return to God in the form of an answer.[1]

II

The Christian "I"

The nature of the person, then, lies ultimately in its relation to God. The Christian consciousness bases this relation not on a religious encounter which takes place in the open space of the world and of history but upon the person of Christ.[2] The basic statements of the Christian's personal consciousness are found in St. Paul's Epistles. St. Paul is the New Testament writer who experienced most profoundly the conversion to a Christian existence and who as a result of his experience investigated the nature of this existence.[3]

In Paul's Epistles we find, with variations, a peculiar statement, which develops the theme: Man is in Christ; Christ is in man. So, for example: "Therefore there is no longer any condemnation for those who are in Christ Jesus" (Rom. 8:1). "If any one is in Christ, this is a new creation" (2 Cor. 5:17).

The meaning deepens in statements which regard Christ as present and operative in the believer just as the entelechy is in the natural man: as the prototype of his divinely willed being and as the power which seeks to achieve this type in a concrete existence. In certain connections we may say that the soul of man is the entelechy of his empirical existence and expresses itself in its various utterances. According to St. Paul's view, the human whole, soul and body, spirit and matter, becomes the material in which a new kind of being, not given by nature, expresses itself. The natural man—St. Paul says the "fleshly man," but does not mean thereby the body as distinguished from the spirit, but the natural whole, body and soul, environment and actions, in contrast to that which comes from grace—is taken over by a new kind of being which will prepare him for a holy existence, the "Christ in us." "Those whom God foreknew he also predestined to be made conformable to the image of his Son" (Rom. 8:29). In every believer, throughout all his actions, his experiences and developments, something deeper is to take place, the "mystical" life of Christ, which forms the Christian. Christ, who lived upon earth and fulfilled his destiny as the Redeemer, has entered into eternal glory and become "the Lord." He has become "spirit," pneuma, not casting off that earthly life but taking it with him into the eternal form.[4] This pneumatic (spiritual) Christ, who bears within him the whole fulness of reality and destiny of the historical Christ, forms the theme that is repeated in every believer, and not only the theme, but also the power which carries it out, for its accomplishment is grace. So the believer undergoes beside, or rather in, his natural development a second one, that from spiritual childhood to full maturity. The Epistle to the Ephesians says that what ultimately matters is that "we all attain the unity of faith and of the knowledge of the Son of God," which is to be gradually perfected to perfect maturity, "unto the measure of the age of the fullness of Christ; that henceforth we be no more children" (Eph. 4:13ff.). These statements receive their final point in words like: "I live, yet no longer I, but Christ lives in me" (Gal. 2:20).

These Pauline statements tell us the decisive truths about the Christian concept of man, and it is of supreme importance that their meaning should not be weakened or twisted. The statements are not casual remarks which may be disregarded, nor are they the expression of an ecstatic experience of Christ, nor yet the manner of speaking of the religious teacher who

wishes to bring Christ as close as possible to his hearer. Rather, they are
the foundation of St. Paul's knowledge of man and are intended to be taken
exactly.

But, if that is the case, they pose great difficulties for our thought
which begins with the natural experience of personality. They seem to
endanger even simple logic, which depends after all on the principle of
identity and contradiction; at any rate, they threaten the unity of psychological life, whose various elements must gather around a uniform center.
Finally, and above all, they seem to endanger the unity of personal existence, which, whatever may be the power of the "Thou" relation, presupposes that the "I" be wholly and exclusively rooted in itself. Therefore, we
must try to find out whether the condition referred to by St. Paul cannot
be explained in a way which clears away these difficulties.

For instance, there is the bond between the adolescent educable person and the older one whose character is already formed, the disciple and
the master, the follower and his model. A vital training involves not merely
the acceptance of the instructive word but also the valid figure. By this the
pupil measures right and wrong; through it he constantly experiences
stimuli toward instinctive behavior; from it he receives his confidence in
a meaningful existence. This relation may extend beyond the individual
and embrace a closely-knit group or a whole epoch. We may think perhaps
of the founder of an order, or of the standards of valid existence which,
first molded by individuals, later dominate a whole class, like that of the
knight or the gentleman. This would give us an example of the powerfully
molding figure of the master becoming effective in the person influenced.
As soon as we take St. Paul's ideas exactly, we see at once that he means
something else, namely a real indwelling of the real Christ. There is no
question of such a thing in the pedagogical relation.

Another relation is perhaps closer to what is meant. If the physical
likeness or the character of a father or an ancestor is clearly visible in a
man, we may say that the father or grandfather lives again in him. This

impression may become very vivid, especially when there is a single trait which is particularly conspicuous or one of those strange repetitions of good or evil fortune which gave rise to so many legends about families. One may explain the situation in different ways, perhaps by saying that the formative power of an individual is so great that it causes the plastic substance of a whole family to produce constant repetitions; or the formative will of a family is expressed so sharply in one individual that he becomes as it were the type which thereafter constantly recurs. But the fact remains that it is the psychosomatic structure of the grandfather or ancestor which returns in the descendant, and not he himself. But this is just what Paul affirms of Christ.

A real parallel seems to lie in the experience of religious possession or indwelling. In certain oracles, for instance, the process is regarded as the god's entering into the priest and speaking through him. Or as the Bacchantes felt, they were so filled with their god, Dionysus, that it was he who lived in them and drove them to actions which they would not otherwise perform. The situation has a certain relation to a split in consciousness, in which a personality lives not in one but in two forms of character and conduct. These are relatively independent of each other, at times so much so that the consciousness does not reach from the one to the other, the initiative of the one does not bother about that of the other, and may even be opposed to it. From this point of view, the total personality, insofar as it exists in one form, could say that the other is "in it." The experience assumes a new form and also a religious character when "the other" is felt to be a mysterious being entering from without, that is, in possession and its related forms, such as spiritualism. The "other being" then acts according to its own impulse and in a manner that causes great difficulties for the one harboring it. In the previously discussed phenomena it was immediately evident that there no real indwelling was involved; that which met our consciousness or feeling was an image or motif. But St. Paul's statement maintains that "the other" dwells within the person himself. So far as the experiences of divine visitation are concerned, they seem, according to the accounts, to be passing manifestations, not lasting situations which determine the whole of existence. Therefore we may dismiss them from our consideration. We may do likewise with those conditions of split consciousness which are characterized as pathological. That would leave as the one serious parallel experience that of inhabitation or possession. But in this the person affected knows that it does not in any way serve his well-being, but rather threatens the very thing with which we are here concerned, namely the freedom and dignity of personal existence. What Paul means is evidently something else. He speaks of a real indwelling of the pneumatic or spiritual Christ in the believer, but describes the relation in such a way that it cannot be either an ecstatic or a pathological condition. Rather, it appears as a permanent basis of a personal existence of perfect clarity and most lofty seriousness.

In order to understand this we must delve more deeply into the Christian experience of St. Paul.[5] The decisive event of his life is that which his disciple, St. Luke, recounts in the ninth chapter of the Acts of the Apostles: the occurrence before Damascus. It presupposes a passionate, strongwilled character with a deep longing for salvation, but interiorly restrained in many ways. In the long discipline of Pharisaic piety this man had become a stern zealot for the ancestral law but had thereby fallen into the deepest interior distress. Convinced that he must attain his salvation by the fulfilling of the law, he had discovered that he was incapable of doing this. The violence which he imposed upon himself only submerged the evil and did not remove it; indeed, it poisoned his conscience more and more. He sought a way out of this distress by external action for the cause of the law, by cooperating in the execution of Stephen, and by persecuting the new church. In this state of hypertension—perhaps he had already been struck by the spiritual power of Stephen—he underwent the experience referred to.

And Saul, as yet breathing out threatenings and slaughter against the disciples of the Lord, went to the high priest and asked of him letters to Damascus, to the synagogues, that if he found any men and women of this way, he might bring them bound to Jerusalem. And as he went on his journey it came to pass that he drew nigh to Damascus, and suddenly a light from heaven shined round about him. And falling on the ground he heard a voice saying to him: "Saul, Saul, why persecutest thou me?" And he said, "Who art thou, Lord?" and he, "I am Jesus whom thou persecutest—Arise and go into the city and there it shall be told thee what thou must do" (Acts 9:1–6).

And again:

Ananias went his way and entered into the house. And laying his hands upon him, he said, "Brother Saul, the Lord Jesus hath sent me, he that appeared to thee in the way as thou earnest, that thou mayest receive thy sight, and be filled with the Holy Ghost." And immediately there fell from his eyes as it were scales, and he received his sight; and rising up, he was baptized. And when he had taken meat he was strengthened. And he was with the disciples that were at Damascus for some days. And immediately he preached Jesus in the synagogues, that he is the Son of God. And all that heard him were astonished and said, "Is not this he who persecuted in Jerusalem those that called upon this name, and came hither for that intent, that he might carry them bound to the chief priests?" (Acts 9:17–21).

This experience signifies first of all a tremendous liberation. Paul had been convinced that he must achieve his salvation by fulfilling the law through his own power. At the same time, he knew enough of the holiness of God to surmise what it means to be just and whole before God. So his experience was not the experience of a violent, self-contained character which needed redemption through human kindness. Of course, it was that also, but only as the natural prerequisite which enabled him to experience in a typical instance that no man, not even the noblest, can escape from his predicament, since, from the Christian point of view, it is not a question of man's rising higher in his actual existence but of the redemption of this existence as a whole. This Paul experiences in his meeting with Christ, who places him in a relation to God which man himself cannot attain. Christ releases him from his bondage to self in making Himself the content of his existence. And not merely so that Paul was to appropriate this content in thought or in love, but really, in that Christ, who as "spirit" is lord of time, of space, of things and persons, enters into him. Thereby Paul obtains a new center and form of existence, which is more really his own than the former one. All this is a whole from which no element can be removed. It is "existence," in which object, subject, power of realization and relational area determine each other in turn.

The point from which this whole can be understood lies in the concept of the Spirit. The first thing said about Paul in connection with the event is that he should "be filled with the Holy Spirit." The meeting at first brought about a condition of profound disturbance—he was blind for three days and neither ate nor drank—but then it caused him to stand up and bear witness to Christ. The intervening conditions are indicated in passages like: "But even until this day, when Moses is read, the veil is upon their heart. But when they shall be converted to the Lord, the veil shall be taken away. Now the Lord is the Spirit, and where the Spirit of the Lord is, there is liberty. But we all, beholding the glory of the Lord with unveiled face, are transformed into the same image from glory to glory, as by the Spirit of the Lord" (2 Cor. 3:15–18). The expression "the glory of the Lord" presupposes first of all the Old Testament vision of the divine radiance, and then that light which Paul saw before Damascus, and it signifies the condition of divine glory in which the risen Christ exists. This condition is spiritual. "Spirit" does not mean the spiritual as opposed to the corporeal, but rather the living spiritual power of God which seizes man and recreates him.[6] Of this Spirit St. Paul says that Jesus existed within Him even while He was still on earth. From the Spirit Jesus drew His power, taught and worked. Permeated and activated by the Spirit He lived out His destiny. But this power of the Spirit and of glory was enclosed in the confines of the "form of a servant" (Phil. 2:7) during His earthly existence. When He died it broke through, raised Him from death to life and transformed His whole being. In Romans 1:3–4 we read: "Who was made of the seed of David according to the flesh, predestinated the Son of God in power, according to the Spirit of sanctification, by the resurrection from the dead." The "Spirit of God," which is the "Spirit of sanctification," transformed the humanity of Jesus and brought it into a spiritual condition, so completely that we can actually say "The Lord is the Spirit." This spiritual Christ becomes the life-principle of those who believe in Him. Again, it is the Holy Spirit who bears Him into the believer. We recall that according to the Biblical concept the soul is a breath coming from God and animating the body. Here a new breath proceeds from God, that of which Christ speaks in His conversation with Nicodemus (John 3:3ff.). This breath enters creatively into man and raises him to a new life which is to penetrate not only the body but the whole human being. Now we are at the center of St. Paul's experience at Damascus. Paul experienced the approach of Christ whose humanity had been transformed by the Spirit and had become glory. As the glory of the Lord shone upon him he felt himself seized by the spiritual power of Him who is "the Lord of the spirit"; the spiritual form of Christ entered into him and became the "entelechy" of his existence.

If we investigate man's experience of the Spirit—especially in the Old Testament prophecy—it appears that the pneuma abolishes the enclosure of earthly-historical existence. The personality is enclosed within its own limits, and admittedly also secure therein. The other person is not immediately accessible for me. I must deduce his inner qualities from their various forms of expression. Insofar as that is not possible he remains closed to me. The attempt to force an immediate entry would be phantastic or magical, in any case a delusion. But for the one who is seized by the Spirit the other becomes open. In the prophetic condition interior and exterior are changed to pure presence, without detriment to the dignity of the person. Of course not at anyone's arbitrary will, but in connection with God's action in the history of our salvation, in the manner which the situation requires. The same Spirit also brings about the new birth. Thereby another quality of our earthly-historical existence is abolished, that rigidity through which I am really myself, but must also remain "I-alone." The attempt to escape this law would again be phantastic or magical and in any case vain. The Spirit alone brings about a true renewal, and in such a way that it does not touch the dignity and responsibility of the person. It is a renewal coming from God the Creator, but also from the personal responsibility of man.

This throws a new light upon the situation we have developed. Paul experienced how he, who previously had been closed to Christ, became open by the Spirit. And not only in the sense of understanding Christ, but in such a way that the Christ who had become Spirit entered into Paul's sphere of existence and Paul was lifted into that of Christ. Thereby he became another man but also truly himself. As Christ arose in him and began to dominate him, Paul awakened to himself. He could say, "I live, yet no longer I, but Christ in me." The way to this was neither phantasy nor magic but the association in the redemptive existence which was afforded by the Spirit and realized and carried out in faith. All of St. Paul's Epistles proclaim the doctrine of this process, in which the believer dies with the crucified Christ, is, as it were, annihilated with Him in burial, and becomes a new man with the risen Christ: "Do you not know that we all who are baptized in Christ Jesus are baptized into his death? For we are buried together with him by baptism into death, that as Christ is risen from the dead by the glory of the Father, so we also may walk in newness of life" (Rom. 6:3–4). It is the doctrine of the new birth. Gal. 6:15 demands expressly that the Christian become a new creature. St. Paul sees this fulfilled in the relation of which we have spoken. He says, "Where anyone is in Christ there is a new creation," old things "are passed away, behold all things are made new" (2 Cor. 5:17). The seriousness of this renewal lies in the fact that it comes through dying: this distinguishes it from all phantasy. The birth of the new man presupposes the death of the old: "For I through the law am dead to the law, that I may live to God. With Christ I am nailed to the cross. And I live, now not I, but Christ lives in me" (Gal. 2:19–20). The old man is not extinguished; Paul himself experiences his reality in a most distressing way. (Cf. Rom: 6–8.) But the security of the old existence is fatally damaged. By faith there begins a process of dying which then must be carried out in the course of one's earthly life and in the death of the body at the end, in order to lead to the ultimate renewal. "I count all things to be but loss for the excellent knowledge of Jesus Christ my Lord; for whom I have suffered the loss of all things and count them but as refuse, that I may gain Christ and may be found in him; not having my justice which is of the law but that which is of the faith of Christ Jesus, which is of God, justice in faith; that I may know him and the power of his resurrection and the fellowship of his sufferings, being made conformable to his death, if by any means I may attain to the resurrection which is from the dead" (Phil. 3:8–11).

Now the statements of St. Paul about the structure of the Christian self have attained a distinct form. According to these statements man is not a being which stands enclosed in itself. Rather, he exists in such a way that he transcends himself. This transcendence takes place constantly even in this world in the various relations to things, ideas and persons, as we explained before; actually, it takes place beyond the world, toward God. The redeemed existence is based upon the fact that the "Thou," which is

God, and which approaches man in Christ, draws the "I" of man into itself, and itself enters into this "I."

Here a new clarification becomes necessary. Until now we have simply spoken of the personality of God. But this, according to the clear sense of revelation, has a special character. God is not the absolute One-Person, as modern thought—insofar as it conceives of God as personal at all—and Islam and post-Christian Judaism imagine. This mono-personalism is not Christian. The core of the message is rather the revelation of the mysterious and super-abundant way in which God is personal. This revelation is given in explicit statements of Jesus, but especially in the manner in which he relates himself to God and carries out the work of salvation. That there is only one God is not questioned. This is certain from Old Testament history. What is newly revealed is the manner in which this God says "I." Christ, who shares human existence in every respect, separates himself from all other men in his religious consciousness. He is related to God in a different way. He teaches them to say "Father" through faith and grace; he himself says it from his own being and power. This consciousness is already manifest in the synoptic Gospels, but decisively in St. John.[7] Here Christ openly claims divinity, and not in such a way that the one divine self unfolds in him in some form of spirit-dialectic, but that within the one divinity a definite *vis-a-vis* becomes plain. This relation—the unity of divinity and the *vis-a-vis* of existence, the identity of life and the true polarity of "I-Thou"—has two explanations in the New Testament. The first is taken from the relation of father and son, a representative expression of the more inclusive relation of parent and child. According to this, God exists as father by the fact that He begets a son; He exists as son by the fact that He comes from the Father and faces Him. The other explanation is found in St. John and is connected with the relation between a rational, living man and his word. According to this, God is the speaker by the fact that He speaks a word which has true being; He is the one spoken by the fact that in God there is a mouth which speaks. He who is called "the Son" is also "the Word." The child and the word have a natural relation. Life, which in itself is hidden, becomes manifest in begetting and speaking. Here this process appears in its absolute prototype. Within it there unfolds the perfect "I-Thou" relation, so perfect that the "I" is not only actualized by the "Thou" but only comes into existence through it—that Thou which it does not find and address but itself brings forth.

This expresses an absoluteness of unity and also of liberation, an intimacy of closeness and a reverence of distance, which are of a special kind. We find it in all the passages in which Jesus speaks of the Spirit, especially in his last discourse. As St. Paul says, it is the Spirit that "searches the depths of the divinity" (1 Cor. 2:10). He brings it about that God carries out in the Word a self-revelation in which He surrenders himself wholly, even to the point of giving personal self-hood to his expression in the person of the Son. This liberation does not constitute a losing or severing, but, on the contrary, is the way to an equally perfect communion, in that the Son turns back to the Father and abides with Him. St. John says in his Prologue that the Word was "with—or toward—God" and "in the bosom of the Father." All this signifies love, whose very nature consists in liberation and union. In God this love also becomes creative. The divine mutual love produces a person, the Holy Spirit. We are well aware that what we have said explains nothing. The Blessed Trinity is absolute mystery. We have made no attempt to deduce it either from a dialectic of absolute life or of the absolute person. We have done nothing but follow the immediate expressions of New Testament thought. And we were concerned with showing where the prototype of what we call the human person lies, not that the human person would be the original and evident thing and the personality of God its immense and mysterious elaboration. Rather, it is the other way around. The manner in which God says "I," is the real and fundamental thing. If it were possible to take the step into faith purely and simply, the answer to the question "What is personality as such?" would be "God's Trinity." This answer would of course not be evident, in the sense of being comprehensible, since it is absolute mystery, but it would be familiar in the sense of reality, since its mystery constitutes the expression of its blessed absoluteness. The human person and its "I-Thou" relation are the faint and scattered imitations of this absolute personality.

The "I-Thou" relation to God, of which we have spoken, and which imparts to the human person its ultimate destiny, is not a relation to God simply as such but to the Triune God. It is interwoven with the relation in which Christ stands to the Triune God. The "I-Thou" relation of man consists in his participation in the relation of Christ to God.

The real and ultimate "Thou" is the Father. He who really says "Thou" to the Father is the Son. To become a Christian means to enter into the existentiality of Christ. The one who is reborn says "Thou" to the Father, as he is given a share in Christ's pronouncing of His "Thou." In the ultimate and definitive sense the Christian does not say "Thou" to Christ. He does not confront Him, but goes with Him, "follows Him." He enters into Christ and carries out the movement with Him. Together with Christ, he says "Thou" to the Father and says "I" of himself. In this way he realizes the Word of the Lord, who calls Himself "the way, the truth, and the life" (John. 14:6). But it is the Spirit who brings man into the intimacy of the personal relation. He inserts him in Christ and so summons him to become his true self. He sets him before the Father and so enables him to speak the essential "Thou."[8] This is the final word about the Christian personality and gives the ultimate significance to all that has been said before.

Now someone might object that the statements of St. Paul, as well as those of St. John, proceed from an experience which transcends the general Christian consciousness. The latter knows nothing of such depths. We might reply first of all that St. Paul is the prophet of Christian existentiality and so experiences clearly and openly what the Christian ascertains by faith in a veiled manner. But apart from this, the same experience is simply an element of Christian faith and between it and the consciousness of the Apostle there is ultimately no essential difference, but only one of degree. Our interpretation of Christian existentiality—according to the rule for grasping any phenomenon—must proceed, not from the vague average, but from the most highly perfected supreme instance; just as Christian action is not to be determined by our immediate perceptions, but by the supreme instance, the content of Christian hope. Therefore, St. Paul's view of the person constitutes the ultimate criterion of that which the Christian experience of personality actually is. And finally, if we consider instances of more intensive Christian life, the structure of its consciousness of personality and the manner in which the one who really believes acts toward God, then the situation described by St. Paul appears more frequently than we might suppose. The clarity of the phenomenon portrayed by St. Paul sharpens our sight and enables it to perceive a similar phenomenon by glimpses and traces even there where it is still dim and undeveloped.

Christian Personality and Love

I

Grace

In continuing our line of thought we should now develop that relationship which we call "grace." We should ask in what way man is to be a person according to God's intention. Here we see the paradoxical situation that something may be a pure gift and at the same time, indeed for this very reason, most intimately personal to the receiver. We may even say that here the matter reaches its extreme significance, perhaps more correctly that here its real essence is revealed. For that very thing is given which enables us to speak of personality at all: the self. Not a possession, a condition, a portion of my personality, but the focal point of every statement about existence, the fact of the person itself is in its essence a gift.

This does not mean to say that a person is "heteronomous." That word is as empty of meaning in this connection as the word "autonomous." We are dealing with something quite different: with the meaning of grace.

Seen in its full strength, as proclaimed by St. Paul and developed by St. Augustine, grace does not mean something added to man's perfection, but the form in which man is ultimately himself—provided, of course, that we understand by "man" what St. Paul and St. Augustine understand by this word, not an artificially extracted "purely natural" man, but that man whom God means and of whom the Scriptures speak. Grace means the category of Christian existence and cannot be expressed more plainly than by the statement in the Epistle to the Galatians: "I live, yet no longer I, but Christ lives in me" (Gal. 2:20).

But, like all revelation, this statement also tells us something about the nature of being as such. Revelation cannot be interpreted from the point of view of the world, but it comes from the pure liberty of God; yet, after it has been given, we perceive that it throws light not only upon specifically Christian relations but also upon the world itself. This is the case here also. The world is such that autonomy in the modern sense of the term not only would exceed its possibilities but actually destroys its essential meaning. The meaning of grace is already outlined in the world. In the Epistle to the Romans we read, "The expectation of the creature waits for the revelation of the glory of the children of God" (Rom. 8:19). The world is such that it can ultimately possess itself only as a gift. Herein alone does freedom—the "blossoming of being" as Hölderlin calls it—become possible.

II

The Nature of Christian Love

It is said—and the New Testament seems to confirm it—that Christianity is the religion of love. This statement is disturbing. We feel that there is a contradiction. In one way it is evidently true: certain personalities, certain conditions of the hierarchy of values, the characteristic traits of Christian psychology seem to bear witness to it, but other things contradict it. The Christian attitude, present and past, does not give us the impression that "love" is its criterion. It has even been maintained that the Christianity we know—that is, Western Christianity—has practiced greater violence than any other religion, and we are not able to reply to this charge with a flat denial. This indicates that the concept of Christian love is not a simple one.

Does the statement that Christianity is the religion of love mean that the Christian is a man of kindly disposition, and that the Christian ethos is one of consideration and appeasement? Evidently not. Such statements relate to a definite form of feelings and attitudes which may be found in the Christian milieu but also occur outside of it; for example, in the South Sea Islanders or Burmanic Buddhism. On the other hand, there are doubtless Christian personalities which by no means possess this form of natural friendliness and peaceableness. We might recall at once St. Paul himself, or the one in whose case our understanding of him depends definitely upon our not attributing this nature to him—St. John. He is called the disciple of love, and his first epistle constitutes the most urgent proclamation of the commandment of love in the New Testament, but it is wrong to think of him as belonging to this mild and gentle type, for by nature he was hard and fiery, and if Christ had not redeemed him he would probably have become an intolerant fanatic. Can the statement mean then that the Christian is an essentially altruistic person? That is to say, someone who immediately sympathizes with the existence of others, at once considers their interests also, indeed, places them above his own. We incline to this view but soon notice that here too we are dealing with a disposition, and one that cannot even be equated with ethical selflessness. For there is a selfishness of altruism and an enjoyment of absorption in another. Natural altruism as such still stands on this side of good and evil, and so does egoism, as soon as we take it not ethically but as a form. Both can become morally positive or negative. So there exists in Christianity the altruistic type, in whom practical service of the neighbor plays a great role, as in St. Vincent de Paul. But there is also the opposite type. We may think of those men who carried out the first break with the ancient pagan culture and its enslavement to the senses—the early ascetics. Finally, can the statement that Christianity is the religion of love mean that the Christian is a person in whom the will has the primacy over the intellect, the heart over the mind, value over truth; that is, a man in the economy of whose life acts of appreciation of value and the eros are basic and decisive? Again we must reply that this manner of perception is also a disposition. It was reasoned out and expressed and applied to practical life, long before the coming of Christ, by Plato. It is found—consider St. Augustine—in Christianity and constitutes one of its noblest possibilities, but not the only or the authoritative one.

The statement we are considering cannot then mean that being a Christian consists in an attitude that can be determined psychologically. Christianity is not a "disposition." As soon as we recognize something as a disposition we also recognize that it is not Christianity as such. Every disposition exists in Christianity but also outside of it. Every disposition constitutes a possibility for Christianity but also against it; a basis from which the decision in regard to the Christian Gospel is made. So we must go deeper.

First of all, we may call Christian that attitude and scale of values which clearly subordinate the categories of "the thing" and of "life" to that of the person, and consider the latter as the really decisive one. But thereby the values of love at once receive the primacy.

However, we must distinguish again. We defined "person" as the fact that man stands in himself, acts from within, is responsible for himself and in his dignity is his own purpose. But this plainly does not suffice to determine what is Christian, for every man is a person, whether, by his conviction and his attitude, he stands within or without the Christian sphere of existence; although the person, if we carry out completely a theological study of its nature, reaches fulfilment only through grace. Therefore the primacy belongs to the personality and so to love as such, apart from Christianity. An admirable anticipation of this is found, for example, among the Stoics with their severe doctrine of independence. They undertook the task of making the personal prevail over the material and also over that which is biologically and psychologically normal.[1] The attitude is truly Christian only when the finite person stands in the "Thou" relation to God revealed in Christ. Its essential nature consists in being called, that means being loved by Him; its realization consists in carrying out this vocation, that means loving Him. This is what the statement that Christianity is the religion of love fundamentally means.

Up to this point our investigation has dealt with principles. These alone give the real meaning to the practical question what "love" is in a concrete sense and to what extent Christianity is actually the religion of love. First of all it becomes clear that the personal attitude of love is something else than that which is immediately perceived as love; namely, kindness, altruism or eros. It may penetrate these other attitudes and then becomes immediately evident. But it may also attain its realization in the opposite, psychologically hard, matter-of-fact, self-centered characters. Then it is more difficult to recognize but is not for that reason less pure. Indeed, it is perhaps true that the dignity of the person, its spiritual quality and chastity emerge here with particular clarity and genuineness.

But if person means the "I" of man which realizes itself in its "Thou" relation to God, the selfhood which is born as soon as the spiritual Christ arises within it and brings it into the relation of son or daughter to the Father,[2] then this signifies something which has a special rank and dignity not comparable to any phenomenon within the world itself. By that very fact, it is correspondingly endangered and difficult to realize. Consequently, that which at first comes to our attention will not be the results but the failures. From this point of view, wherein does concrete Christian love consist?

Let us seek it there where it appears in its original purity, in Jesus himself. How can we determine the nature of Jesus' love if we do not reduce it to an attitude—either those attitudes which are congenial to the beholder or those which are repugnant to him; if we do not interpret it as gentleness or altruism or desire for value, or cosmic eros or anything else? As soon as we endeavor to see the form and attitude of Jesus in their original quality, and from that point to express what love means in Him, we become discouraged. We meet attitudes, acts, values which do not coincide with our concepts of love. His love is revealed as something which cannot be determined from man's point of view, but which comes from God and appears to be as beautiful as it is terrible, as intimate and protective as it is strange and destructive. It 'does not fall under any ready-made psychological or philosophical category. We cannot say, "Christian love, which is also found, and in its perfection, in Christ, is that attitude which—" but only, "Christian love is the manner in which Christ conducts himself." It begins with Him. It does not exist before Him or without Him. It is not determined by a concept, but by a name, His name. Only in proceeding from this name and within the standard which it sets do the concepts begin.[3] If this attitude is recognized in any way, carried out and applied in the world, then something happens: all the phenomena of love which are dependent upon forms of disposition are disturbed. The same thing happens which always happens when a higher element breaks into a lower one which had previously been undisturbed: there is confusion. From this point of view, the statement of Jesus, "I have come not to bring peace, but the sword," becomes all too-plain, especially in the most self-evident relationship, the family. The love which is dependent on biological and psychological elements, natural philanthropy and unselfishness and the eros, protest. We have the impression that the natural friendliness of primitive races, for instance, is much purer than the Christian attitude, and when the latter is brought to these people it destroys a paradise. One may feel that the goodness of oriental wisdom and its attention to the soul is purer, humanly and spiritually more cultivated, than the Christian, and in many cases this may be true. An order of the soul previously unshaken, which could develop according to its nature, is seized by something which is absolutely of higher value, but for that reason different in its economy.[4]

To go more deeply: through the new Revelation the very passions are affected in a new way. Evil, for instance, will acquire, on the level of the new personality, a consciousness, an edge, a seriousness which were previously impossible. Not every man can be evil in the same degree. The evil receives its weight from the existential level on which it is willed. Only in the Christian sphere does it become quite plain what kinds of evil exist: the decidedly evil quality of the person who is master of all his possibilities; the evil of wickedness which only awakens when the magnanimity of God reveals the glory of His kingdom; the Satanically evil which only becomes evident when the holiness of God steps openly and defenselessly into the world. As long as the personality remains in the context of things or in the entanglement of life, because the call to a holy self-realization has not yet come, evil remains in a certain sense harmless. But in the sphere of the emerging Christian personality, this harmlessness becomes impossible. The evil is now determined not only by an urge or a passion, not only by the mind and its overweening arrogance, but by the very person who has been called and awakened by God. Even if a man or a family or—as it began with the Renaissance and progresses ever more rapidly in the course of the 19th and 20th centuries—a whole epoch departs from the ethos of Christian love and retrogrades into mere worldliness, their condition in this worldliness is not the same as it would have been before the Revelation. They have brought with them a soul, a capacity for action, a scale of values in which all that we have explained was at one time awakened. They possess an attitude which could only come into existence by the fact that it was aroused and practiced by many generations of Christian influence. Possibilities of freedom, of seriousness, of decision were released which are not found elsewhere, but also possibilities of revolt, of hatred, of destruction and of blasphemy. Compared with these the evil of immediate existence with all its dreadfulness appears naive. Only in the sphere of Christianity and in man's encounter with it does mature evil become possible, which is to earlier evil what the wrong-doing of a man is to that of a youth or a child. As soon as God entered into history in the Incarnation, ready to take on a destiny from man, there appeared a possibility of evil which we can only speak of "in fear and trembling" and must define as the will to destroy God—and together with God—that which comes into man from Him.

All this must be taken into account when we ask about the nature of Christian love. Christianity is really the religion of love; but to say what love means here is very difficult. First of all, this is so because the phenomenon is psychologically and philosophically so complicated. Secondly, because the negative aspects, disturbances, shocks and resistances are always plainer than the positive ones. Also, because the existential risk required for the understanding of the problem is extremely great. Finally, and above all, because we are dealing with Revelation; that is, a phenomenon of existence which is not derived from the world but comes from God, and which, in order to be known, must itself give the requisite conditions, namely the grace of understanding.

The task of setting forth the nature of Christian love from the person of Christ himself, from the figures of the Saints, from the inner structure of meaning of the Christian existence, while proceeding not from psychological or ethical attitudes but from the original phenomenon itself, has not advanced very far. There is still very much to be done in this field.

Providence

I

General Remarks

The doctrine of Providence is at the core of the Christian message. It sums up all that Jesus, by way of parables, teaching, direction, and through the Lord's Prayer, proclaimed about the Father in heaven, the world and the life of man in the world. So it is important to understand exactly what it means, all the more since the idea of Providence has also been corrupted by a worldly point of view and has thereby taken on an indefinite and even false meaning. So it must be distinguished from similar yet essentially different concepts which have become associated with it.

The idea of Providence is connected with the more extensive concepts of the new man and the new creation—a world in the process of becoming. Now the "world"—and this ties up with the inquiries of the first part of this volume—does not mean only the sum of that which exists, but a whole which is constructed between two poles, one of which lies always in the individual person and the other in the multifariousness of things and events. The world of whose coming into existence the New Testament speaks is also constructed in this fashion. It is realized as the believer encounters things, experiences and recognizes them, evaluates them and assumes an attitude toward them, overcomes their power, masters, orders

377

and forms them. However, a man does not come into contact with all things, but only with definite ones, relatively few. Is this encounter a matter of chance or does it take place as part of a whole? According to Christian thought, the fact that of the incalculably numerous and manifold happenings, which in themselves would be possible, only certain ones touch a person, indicates a guidance in the direction of his new existence.

This guidance is already present in the beginning of every man's history. The fact that he himself and everything about him is as it is forms the first sketch of what is to follow. Here is the root of all that we term "vocation": physical and mental structure, talents, environment, nation, country, historical situation and the like. In this way the individual receives his appointed place in the whole sphere of existence and the basis for his later relation to reality. But this matter has its questionable aspects, as can be clearly seen in a limiting case, when, for instance, an individual, through birth, education or environment is brought into a situation which makes it impossible for him to give a meaningful form to his existence; it may be through destructive tendencies or insufficient mental endowments, a corrupting environment, paralyzing sociological or historical conditions, etc. Up to a certain point we can in such a case speak of a tragic situation in which the will is to be purified and the character is to develop. But there is a limit to this. The individual does not stand alone but in relation to a whole; yet the relation of the individual and the whole world cannot be brought into a satisfactory formula. Therefore the doctrine of Divine Providence must be combined with another: that there is a consummation of meaning even for such destinies which appear meaningless from the point of view of the world as it is. Important as talents, health, heredity, education, social environment and one's role in the world may be—the ultimate for man cannot be confined to these. A fulfillment is promised which transcends all the immediate possibilities—without and in spite of these—from the pure creativity of grace which is beyond the reach of any judgment.

Providence then must begin at the very beginning, in the condition of the world as a whole and in the place of man as an individual, combined to form that projection of personal destiny which we call birth. It then continues in the manner in which at various times events take place around the person, and things touch him and he acts upon things. What interpretation shall we give of this term, "Providence"? Let us ask a preliminary question: What interpretations of it could be given?

II

Inadequate Interpretations

The word "Providence" could have a mythological meaning; perhaps that a higher being was favorably disposed to man, watched over him and saw to it that he prospered. Such, for example, are the old ideas of the tutelary spirit of the clan or the family or the individual. This being is the more dependable in its protection the more closely it is bound up with those under its patronage. The totem-animal is in some way identical with the tribe that it protects. The "genius" is the "double" of the hero whom he strengthens; the favoring "manes" are the deceased and hence numinous members of the family who guard the present living members. The protecting powers are in the last analysis identical with the one who is protected. They are in some way his most intimate forces asserting themselves to maintain his existence. Or, to put it in another way, the invisible powers and the visible earthly man, tribe, etc. together form the whole and essential human reality.

These ideas can then pass into the nature of a fairy tale, perhaps in the theme of kindly spirits, benevolent ancestors, or the grateful dead. They can also descend to the level of superstition, as in the various notions of magic objects and signs, animals, times and places.

Also connected with these concepts is the idea of luck. Here it is not a higher being or magic sign that makes things prosper, but existence itself. The lucky person is born so—or has later received it as a gift—that existence in its mysterious core is favorable to him. Hence things arrange themselves for his advantage; people are well disposed toward him; he easily does the proper thing. This phenomenon has appeared in great figures of history, sometimes so decidedly that the conviction of the man's luck or his "star" became a regular matter of faith. Of course this luck could abandon him as unaccountably as it had come. Then his own efforts availed as little to save him as they had previously been necessary for success.

This phenomenon also can pass from its original depth into the world of the fairy tale, for example, in the tales of the Sunday-child or "Lucky Jack," and it can go farther into the realm of superstition, as in the countless notions of favorable constellations, omens, talismans, etc.

Ideas such as all these cannot really be used to explain the Christian concept of Providence. No one would seriously say that Providence means something of this sort. But the ideas are very ancient; they are planted deep in the domain of the unconscious and form the most elementary means of expressing the way in which destiny is shaped and moves from these sources; and, consequently, they affect the interpretations of the concept of Providence, even where the actual thoughts are of an entirely different nature.

A more serious meaning lies in the attempt at an interpretation proceeding from the experience and idea of order. This means, first of all, the order of the physical and biological sphere with its unchanging facts and recognizable laws. There everything is as it should be and moves as it should move. Whatever stands within the structure of this order is protected by it. Necessity means also dependability. And the structure gives it its reason for being. Necessity means also correctness. Then there is the order of the psychological sphere. Its facts and relations are of a different character than those of the physical and biological sphere. The element of creativity which we can explain only partially, both as to its origin and its course, is here very strong. Yet this also reveals regularities in the structure of its phenomena, typical forms of activity and laws of recurrence—all those things upon which a practical knowledge of man may be based and which psychology scientifically investigates. Then there is the sphere of the spirit, the ideas and values and their relations as they prevail in the construction of human existence. This order likewise gives support and security to the extent to which the individual is receptive toward it. The greater the importance of goodness, truth and meaning for any man, the more he feels supported and safe in his spiritual and personal existence in consequence of these values. We may think of the eternally classical example of Socrates. Finally, there is the historical sphere in its proper sense, the realm of actuality which comes into existence as a result of the fact that the freedom of man exercises itself in the various aforementioned areas, human activity on the part of the individual and the whole. This contains first of all—and thereby it differs from the others—an essentially inexplicable element, this very freedom with its consequent "initiative." But it is the freedom of a concrete individual and therefore has a given place within the whole and receives from it more or less definitely determinable presuppositions of a psychic, physical and social nature. Its acts are purely its own only in that moment of the innermost "so be it" which cannot be concretely determined. From the first moment of realization they take their course in the various orders of empirical reality. So there arise within this freedom also relations which may be foreseen and which constitute the prerequisites of new activity. They are of a particular personal character which is expressed in the concepts of historical succession, fate, destiny, establishment and organization, tradition, morals and manners. We could mention other forms of order: the forms of symbol and language, of creation and production, of religion with its objective and subjective structures. These and all the others that have been mentioned

evidently combine to form a whole, which cannot be proved or theoretically derived, but can be everywhere perceived and regarded as a necessary
counter-value to the individual.

This totality of order with its subordinate areas which continue to an
immeasurable extent; this manifoldness which is everywhere ordained
toward unity; this abundance of qualities which cannot in themselves be
attributed to any cause but which are all bound together in the fact of a
constant, meaningful and dependable regularity—all this could be called
Providence. Then "Providence" would be the ordered structure of existence itself, as soon as it is experienced as a fact of numinous character, as
a meaning and a power which come from the divine, upon which man
relies with religious confidence, and which on their part are commended
to man's faith.

According to this interpretation, a man is in the domain of Providence
as soon as it has become clear to him that everything in nature proceeds
according to necessary laws and recognizable rules and he has assented
to these laws and rules. He perceives that they are the expression of reality
and meaning and hence are inexorable; that they can be neither changed
nor avoided; that they permit nothing specious and give to everything as
much weight as it really deserves. He discovers that they receive and bear
him as soon as he sincerely submits to them. If he acts wrongly, they let
him feel it and he is warned for the next time. If he does not heed the
warning, then he must pay the price. The same thing is true of the psychological laws. They support the one who recognizes them and acts in
accordance with them. All that is in harmony with them becomes sound,
strong and fruitful. What is opposed to them does not succeed. Deficiency
in reality becomes suffering in experience. So anyone who follows the laws
and rules of existence, whoever, even instinctively, through a fortunate
disposition, or consciously through knowledge and experience, is wise,
he is under the care of Providence. The laws of the spirit likewise cannot
be altered. He who respects truth and acts according to it is supported by

it. He who strives for justice is protected by it. He may of course come into conflict with other systems of order. He may find himself in a situation where he must pay for higher values with lesser ones. If he does this, he has attained a loftier height, and that too is order. If he does not do this, but clings to the lesser value, then the higher is denied him, and this again is order. Whoever recognizes and desires this, not as a mere law of being and of occurrence, but as the expression of a divine meaning and a sacred primary power, lives in the care of Providence.

We may become conscious of this in a more superficial way, perhaps in the optimistic feeling that everything is wisely ordered and will somehow turnout well. But it may also become a progressively deeper experience. Man recognizes the order, accepts it sincerely and places his confidence in its meaningful nature. He is convinced that as soon as his desires are opposed to this order they are wrong. All that cannot be realized in being and activity is inadmissible. Here we have an attitude of the amor fati which assents to that which must be and knows itself secure therein. Such a man regards the order as divine. The order of being, which he conceives of in the manner of the Stoic nous, and the order of occurrence which he conceives of in the manner of the Stoic heimarmene, appear to him as different forms of a final meaningful force, which is incomprehensible for man but must be revered in its manifestations. To recognize it and place oneself in harmony with it is true piety. This act of assent and self-harmonization is also the way in which, as we see in Stoic mysticism, the final unity itself may be experienced. It is this which gives everything its proper meaning. He who has attained it knows that everything is best for him as it is. From this experience, practice, and renunciation arises the Stoic ataraxia which cannot be shaken from its security by any stroke of fate.

On the basis of certain historical or individual assumptions this attitude may assume a new character. Whereas in the preceding statements the emphasis was on the great order, behind which stood the all-ruling divine unity, the emphasis is now placed upon man himself. The orders exist so that he, knowing them and knowing himself, may shape his life within them. Now it is not the order and behind it the divinity which "provides," but the man himself in his maturity. He knows the facts and laws of existence. On the basis of the past and of the necessary he anticipates what can and will happen. He sketches his plan, shapes his work and his life. The basic note here is a confident energy and joy in accomplishment, sure of the dependable nature of the order of being. The dominant character is the consciousness of responsibility for the world of act and deed which is to be constructed. The religious aspect lies in the mysterious magnitude of this responsibility and in the courage to take life and work into one's hand and in good fortune or bad, in success or failure, to answer for oneself.

This attitude however can move another step in the direction of activity. Then we have the opposite of the first type, which presupposed that things were in a state of order and events occurred in a meaningful connection with each other. The wisdom and activity of the individual consisted in conforming. For the opposite type there is no "order" subsisting in itself and resulting from the nature of being. What there is only a chaotic jumble of forces and matter which the will must shape. From this point of view every concept of a supposedly self-subsistent order is only an excuse for cowardice and laziness. A mature person must recognize that there is just so much "order" as he is able to provide and maintain; that he is, moreover, not protected by anything, but stands upon his own finite bit of being and power in the midst of a meaningless chaos. Now "Providence" becomes something else. It really no longer means anything objective. Existence itself is in no way provident; still less can we find in it a wise and kindly divine power. Indeed, reality is just the opposite of this; it is chaotic and indifferent. If there is any intention perceptible, it is that of malice and cruelty. Providence can hence consist only in the keen-sightedness of man himself. It means that the strong man "provides," watches, is always alert and ready to act; that he struggles incessantly to preserve his existence in the eternal flux. It means that he understands clearly what he wants, projects the image of his will on to the space of time allotted to him, and, relying upon nothing except his own strength, carries it out exactly, carefully and obstinately. If he is able to do that; if, as a result of his interior freedom, he is in harmony with the indifferent and pitiless quality of life; if he is sufficiently resolute and persevering; then the stuff of reality obeys him, and his providence and prevision are justified. The religious element here is the very boldness with which he acts, the creative quality of the advance, perhaps supported by the secret command which existence addresses to him hoping that it may be compelled by the strength of his will to produce something higher.[1]

If we compare the attitudes which we have described we find in them a dialectic of typical adjustments to the world. On the one side, there is the attitude which places the emphasis wholly on the law and order which prevail throughout existence, and holds that the proper behavior of man consists in relying upon these. On the other side we have the attitude which denies all objective order, and places the emphasis on the free initiative that shapes the chaos of existence; it maintains that man is behaving correctly when he relies upon nothing except himself and pure possibility.[2] Between these two is the other attitude, which recognizes objective laws and regulations but makes them the basis of its own activity, and which attains within their compass as much as is consonant with its knowledge and strength.

As soon as the phenomena are clearly seen, it becomes immediately evident that the Christian doctrine of Providence means something else. The sober-minded man will notice especially the implications of the various interpretations of the term "providence" which have been given.

So far as nature is concerned, it is immediately evident that she does not concern herself with man if he is considered as an individual or as a person. Nature cares only for the species. The individual as such has no meaning for her. Values, such as a good deed, a meaningful work, personal fulfilment and a noble life do not exist for nature. But if we look at the whole situation, nature does not really "care" even for the human species. Even on the comparatively tiny space of the earth and during the even more minute phase of its history which makes life possible, nature shows only a very limited interest in mankind. Consider all the things that we call unfavorable circumstances, catastrophes, etc. In momentary moods of joy or times of physical well-being, stimulating encounters or the like, a man may be of the opinion that he is protected and supported by nature as such. Otherwise, this view can be maintained only if he considers whatever nature withholds from him at any time as unnecessary or worthless, an attitude which is not only difficult to preserve but is basically unworthy as well.

But even the order of the world of man—of thought, of shaping and creating, of communities and of totalities, of culture and history—does not ultimately concern itself to any extent with the individual. Historical events, sociological structures, collective cultural phenomena obey laws for which the individual is only the material or the prop, at best a certain dialectical counter-part; rarely is he himself, as an individual, their purpose or meaning. When, for example, a theoretical problem arises, the attempts to solve it go their own way, as though they had an initiative of their own, without concern for the consequences that they may have for the person who may be involved. When a technical or sociological situation begins to change and shift, this takes place regardless of the good or evil effects on the individual concerned. Even institutions of social service are not ultimately accommodated to the existence of the individual but arise from the relations of the whole and have its continuation as their purpose. In the general order of human existence, the individual flourishes insofar as his qualities, requirements and efforts coincide with those of the whole. Otherwise he is passed over. At certain moments he experiences the general progress as an expansion of his personal existence;

sometimes it appears as something which demands his devotion and self-sacrifice and thereby contributes to his spiritual growth; often, when viewed as duty, it becomes a prerequisite of his moral maturity. But, very often, it is felt to be something essentially alien, the center of whose meaning lies elsewhere than in the individual and which simply uses him.

It might be objected that these considerations make the prosperity of the individual the basic criterion of existence, whereas the important thing is that the aims of the whole and the general good should be realized; that the individual must submit to this, and if he does so the very difficulty of this service leads to his personal fulfilment. We do not need to affirm that we are not dealing here with any kind of individual hedonism. We too share the conviction that a selfless commitment to supra-personal service is the way to genuine personality. But here the question is a different one—the nature and meaning of the term "Providence," which refers to the individual as well as the whole; indeed more particularly to the individual since he is weaker than the whole. It is a question of the personal pole of that which we call "world" and "existence" and of the way in which divine "care" for the person, which is always felt to be the most comforting element of the concept of Providence, can really exist. It is clear that a condition in which the course of universal reality coincided with the teleology of the individual life would be pure fairy-tale. Here the fruit-bearing tree would really be concerned about man's hunger and the beast would help him in his distress. But, even in this case, it would not be the person who had passed the test of character, but the person who was born lucky, the Sunday child, to whom this happened. Only later do personal values enter in. But in this way man is again brought into an attitude which is somehow natural; the unity is brought about at the cost of true personality. Moreover the Providence of the New Testament does not mean something on the order of the fairy tale; it is not comfort in dream or phantasy, but it is reality. Indeed a mythical interpretation does the New Testament message a greater harm than the plain statement that the doctrine of Providence is unacceptable, since it contradicts the actual state of the world.

The interpretations hitherto recounted either depart fundamentally from reality and transfer the phenomenon into the realm of fancy, or else they look upon reality with half-closed eyes, clinging to what agrees with their view and concealing what contradicts it, and they call this attitude piety. The New Testament message however is based upon reality and means something very definite. As for those interpretations in which man himself takes over the functions of Providence, they depart so plainly from the simple concept with which we are dealing that they do not even enter into the consideration of the Biblical doctrine of Providence. They do not give it a mature instead of a childish sense; they absolutely and completely negate it.

III

The Biblical Concept

If we wish to see this, which is the essential thing, then we must turn to Revelation. The classical example, which is supported and developed by other passages, is the following: "You cannot serve God and mammon. Therefore I say to you, be not solicitous for your life, what you shall eat, nor for your body, what you shall put on. Is not the life more than the meat, and the body more than the raiment? Behold the birds of the air, for they neither sow nor do they reap nor gather into barns, and your heavenly Father feeds them. Are not you of much more value than they? And which of you, by taking thought can add to his stature one cubit? And for raiment why are you solicitous? Consider the lilies of the field, how they grow; they labor not, neither do they spin. But I say to you, that not even Solomon in all his glory was arrayed as one of these. And if the grass of the field, which is today and tomorrow is cast into the oven God doth so clothe, how much more you, O ye of little faith! Be not solicitous therefore, saying: 'What shall we eat or what shall we drink, or wherewith shall we be clothed?' For after all these things do the heathens seek. For your Father knows that you have need of all these things. Seek ye therefore first the kingdom of God and his justice, and all these things shall be added unto you" (Matt. 6:25–33).

At first glance, this seems to deal with fairytale notions, or else the fanatical or idyllic thoughts of a harmonious, pious and extremely unworldly person. But this impression soon disappears when we see the key to the meaning of the whole passage, which lies in the sentence, "Seek ye first the kingdom of God and his justice and all these things shall be added unto you," and when we also consider the attitude of the speaker, which has no dream-like qualities but is realistic even to a degree unknown to the ordinary "realist."

Then the message of Providence seems to be as follows: "Believe in the God who discloses Himself to you in the Revelation and is quite different from the nous of the Stoics or the world-spirit of some religious experience, the God who is the Father in heaven, hidden in His own nature and only revealed by Christ. Take into your thought and mind, as the thing of supreme importance, the new possibility of existence which He offers, His 'kingdom'; and place yourself in harmony with Him in concern for this kingdom, as it is expressed in the petitions of the Lord's Prayer, 'Thy kingdom come,' 'Thy will be done.' Then this kingdom will take shape around you and you yourself will receive what you need for your life." We see that it does not say: "Depend on the course of events; they move in a favorable way and will prove favorable to you also," to which it would be necessary to add the note of resignation, "If anything does not turn out as you think it should, you will simply have to accept it." Rather it says, "Make God's interests, your concern for His kingdom, the central point of your life; then the world around you will be transformed. The laws of existence will put themselves at your service; events will happen and things will turn out as it is good for you." The promise is not merely that the believer, if he endures hardships and perseveres in suffering, will be purified and elevated but that he will receive what he needs for his life. For this he does not need to fight about things and cling to them; on the contrary, he should not do this, at least not as "the heathen" do; that is, those who know only the World and worldly powers. Things will take shape around him, and what he needs will come to him. All this becomes a fairytale if we lose sight of the condition on which it depends—the concern for God's kingdom—together with the decision of which the preceding sentences speak, "No man can serve two masters. For either he will hate the one and love the other, or he will sustain the one and despise the other. You cannot serve God and mammon" (Matt. 6:24). What is spoken of here is something entirely different from a fairytale attitude or a pious unconcern. It is rather a difficult decision for the true Master and against the false one; an effective decision, one from which proceeds an entirely new concern and purpose in life and therewith a new hierarchy of values very different from the natural one.

Moreover, Providence is not something ready-made, not a hidden order of the course of the world, difficult to reach yet nevertheless presented and therefore capable of being grasped by man, an order to which he may then accommodate himself. It is something in the process of becoming, something directed to man who presses on to the purity of faith and of love for God's kingdom. But perhaps we must be more explicit. Providence is also something which goes on without the person in each case. It is the totality of world-events, which is really the governance of God and is ordered by Him, the creator and director, toward the salvation of men. But this is only the beginning of Providence. It is free to attain its true nature and fulness when man, toward whom it is directed, takes on responsibility in faith and places himself in that harmony with it which the Sermon on the Mount demands. Then there takes place in his regard that transformation of existence of which Jesus speaks. Things about him behave differently than they otherwise would. They are "applied" to him by God in a special way. The world about him assumes a meaning and form of activity whose motive is the love of the father for his child—let us say less lyrically, the love of the father for his son or daughter. In the events of existence the movement toward the new creation begins to prevail—that new creation in which the new man dwells under the new heaven and upon the new earth, more strongly and purely as his faith becomes purer and his love more bold.

IV

Providence and Environment

But what do we mean by this transformation of reality around the believer? Isn't this after all another fairytale?

Perhaps we might find it helpful to ask another question which we asked once before: What is the nature of the world around the individual man? It is not simply a piece of the world in general but a structure, that which we call the environment, to distinguish it from the whole world. This environment is something which is selected from the world and given a form. It is that part of the whole world which influences this particular person and also that which results from his activity. He is influenced by it and influences it in his turn. Taken as a series of events this environment is man's destiny. This too is a selection—a selection of events ordained toward a particular person, a selection of events in general, or more exactly, of all that which could happen to this person. Not everything that could happen to him actually happens. But what happens to him is not accidental—taking this word in relation to the logic of this individual, integrated existence—but it is, on the contrary, determined by this very logic. Of course we must not, in this connection, consider the man from the point of view of that which is visible on the surface, but also of that which is hidden—hidden even from himself and buried in the unconscious.

The environment consists of the objects and events of the whole world which are related to the individual. It is the result of a selection carried out first of all by the instrumentality of the senses, both those of man in general and those of the particular person concerned. What I do not perceive does not belong to my world or affects it only by its physical operations. The selection is further made by the urges and the impulses of the will. What does not interest me does not exist for me, or is less effective, or effective in a different way, than that which interests me. The selection is also determined by the qualities of character, the prevailing temperament, the powers of arrangement and organization. All these sift the totality of objects and possibilities. One thing is rejected, another accepted, and what has been accepted is rearranged. A center of purpose is established according to which things are evaluated, a perspective according to which actions are carried out. At its borders this environment fades into the general world of the strange and unknown. And it is constantly endangered by this. To ward off the encroachment of the world in general upon one's own environment and to preserve the latter from being overthrown by the former is the marvellous task of the individual, constantly interrupted and constantly resumed. It succeeds according to the measure of a man's strength. The environment is greater, richer and more definitely constructed according as the self-assertion of the person in question is more decided, his will more clear and calm—even and above all his unconscious will—and his vital force more composed. The environment also has a varied character in its effect on the person. If a man is greedy and insecure in the depths of his nature, things about him behave differently than they do about a strong and unselfish person. If a man is always driven by personal motives, always intent on doing and attaining something, existence takes on a different character around him than around a person who is disinterested yet living intensely. The person who loves has a different environment than the hard-hearted or envious one; the sincere and honest person a different environment than the liar and the cunning man; the magnanimous and candid person has not the same environment as the narrow-minded or tyrannical one. Different talents also produce different environments. So, for example, if a person has manual dexterity, the instrument accommodates itself easily to the form and movement of the hand, the arm, the whole body, and proves very effective. In the case of another man, the relation between the instrument and the moving body is not established; the work is not successful; the instrument breaks; and the object is spoiled. But since the environment of man consists in large part of his relations with instruments, it receives a very different character according to the kind and degree of his "touch." It becomes right, friendly, fruitful, easy, or else obstreperous, hostile, full of trouble and failure. Similar statements could be made about the presence or absence of the artistic sense, or about the relation to living beings, plants, animals, children, the sick, the poor, etc. All this is not a fairytale. It is not that in the case of one man the hammer resists, while in the other case it cooperates. The hammer has no initiative, but it does have a law of being, a truth, and this truth, according as it is released or hampered, becomes either an assisting or a disturbing force. To say the thing "wants" something would be a fairytale, but the thing is something, and when we say this we express what is real. The thing is not only an object but it has a meaning of its own and to that extent a power which works out in one or the other way according to the attitude which determines the structure of the environment.

So destinies too are different in the different environments—indeed destiny is nothing more than the environment in the form of events. Destiny is primarily that which happens. But what happens is conditioned not only from without but also from within, not only by things but also by the person involved. When lightning strikes, this is the result of atmospheric conditions which cannot be influenced by man. Here there is no question of his determining the environment. Yet even here what happens is not purely "objective," for the lightning does not strike the house of "a" man but of "this" man, strikes it under particular circumstances, with the inhabitants in a particular situation, and so the event takes on a particular character. Then there are those events which result from a combination of objective causes which are independent of man and subjective ones which lie in himself—accidents, for instance. An accident may happen like a stroke of lightning, but even then the attitude and condition of the person, his powers of resistance or his inclination toward that which destroys, plays its part. But usually, as psychology shows, the accident happens largely because of the attitude of the victim himself, which is influenced in a very definite way by interior urges, unknown to himself. But these urges constitute that state of mind which determines the environment of events. Or what do we mean when we say one man is lucky and another not? What is the meaning of "streaks" of bad luck and a succession of lucky events? Why does something succeed at one time and not at another? Why is it that today, when I "got up on the wrong side of the bed," things behave differently than yesterday, as if it were not the same world? It isn't the same, for the world which concerns me is not the general physical or "objective" totality of things, but my environment, and that comes into being only in part from without. Half of it comes from within, from my own attitude at any time and receives its character from me. I am really "the artisan of my own fortune," taking this phrase in a much deeper and more effective sense than rationalistic ethics usually gives to it.

At first sight, the idea of "destiny" seems to mean that its course is inevitable. But this view is in part erroneous. It is perhaps a result of the fact that the whole delicate and complicated structure works properly only when we are unconscious of it. It is a fact that some of the sources of destiny cannot be influenced, but others, and probably the majority, can be, at least to a large extent, inasmuch as man influences himself. Not his original nature as such, which is fixed and is in the strictest sense his destiny; but his attitude. Of course we must understand this term in its deepest sense. It does not mean simply that which we consciously will, or even the recognizable basis of this willing. Neither can we take it merely in a moral sense as an affirmation of the good or the evil. "Attitude" is rather the condition of the depths of the personality which precedes all conscious willing, the interior receptiveness or unreceptiveness, narrowness or magnanimity, fear or readiness, weakness or strength which determine the first willing and direction of life and so represent its basic predisposition. To the extent to which this attitude changes—and it can change; here the real metanoia (repentance) takes place—the destiny also changes.[3]

What then will it mean even from the point of view of the structure of his environment and his destiny if a man is oriented toward God in the way of which Christ speaks and if the concern for the kingdom of God is of primary interest for him? We must think what magnanimity, what security in that which is the ultimate and what tranquility in regard to all lesser values will result from this. Around a man who is so disposed, things even in this world must behave differently than around a man who is the slave of the world, worries about it and fears it, clings to it and flees from it, is too intimate with it and for this very reason is blind to it. Wisdom says that existence serves the man who does not need it; that the world bestows itself upon the man who is independent of it, and that happiness is found only by him who does not seek it. This also applies to the relation of which we have spoken, but with a depth and strength unattainable by mere worldly wisdom. And since it is neither a matter of expedience nor of ethics it touches the inmost impulses, determines the powers that give direction and so changes one pole of the world of existence. Thereby the other pole also is drawn into a new relation and all things are transformed.

However, we have not yet reached the essential thing, but only cleared the way. The essential thing is found in Revelation. A man with the faith of which we have spoken forms as it were a portal of entrance for the creative power of God which is directed toward the world.

The world is not something ultimate but lies in the hand of God which shapes it. It is not, as modern man conceives of it, simply existent and normative, so that it supplies the only criterion of possibility and cannot itself and as a whole be called in question. The world constantly exists as a work of God's creative will; it is in a state of potentiality in relation to this will and obeys it.

When matter is informed by life it behaves differently than when it obeys inorganic laws. Regarded from the point of view of matter, this behavior would be a fairytale; in the sphere of life it is natural. As soon as a biological organism is moved by mind it acts differently than when it is determined simply by instinct and growth. Every deepening of the emotional nature, every moral advance, every self-conquest calls the biological organism to higher accomplishments which are not the consequence of its own immediate nature, but which now become natural. Now Revelation tells us that the possibilities of the world are not limited by its natural condition or confined to effects which the world can produce as a result of impulses lying within itself, but that these possibilities immeasurably transcend the world itself.

Things have, as scholastic philosophy says, a *potentia obedientialis*, a potentiality of obedience in relation to every power which is really able to command, whose possibilities cannot be measured beforehand. Existence gives up as much as this power—principle or will—forces it to give; and what is extorted from it in this way is not a fairytale, but quite in order. Now existence as a whole is receptive of the creative will of God. This will may enter where it pleases, for God is the master of the world; and then there results a miracle, in the sense of the extraordinary. But He himself has mentioned one place at which He will enter surely and regularly, as soon as the required conditions are present: namely, the existence of the person who believes and who loves the kingdom of God. Here God grasps

the world and it obeys. Around this person circumstances assume a new
character. The world behaves as the Sermon on the Mount describes it,
not symbolically or by a subjective impression, but in reality. At this point,
the world takes a step forward to a possibility which as *potentia obedien-*
talis was latent within it but which it could never realize by its own efforts.
It becomes that world which is appointed for the child of God, a new
creation. God wills that existence become holy, but this can come about
only through freedom. If that resists, God is bound, if it becomes open
and receptive then we have that breadth of capacity in which God's will
has a free hand, and the second creation, the *recreatio* of the old theology,
begins. This is the constant miracle, whose proclamation was the most
intimate concern of Jesus, the miracle of Christian existence, the development of the new world around the child of God. It has no connection with
fairytale or legend, neither in an objective way—because it does not ab-
rogate the laws of nature, but calls them into the service of a higher, legitimate order of events—nor in a subjective way, because the attitude which
it presupposes is no pious phantasy or carelessness in leaving everything
to God, but a wholly serious faith.

This faith is to be seen most plainly in the figures of those who hero-
ically and unconditionally risked everything for it, the saints. And here
the judgment implied in the derogatory use of the word "legend" must be
corrected. There are playful legends which indicate merely a taste for religious romanticizing or sheer sentimentality, but there are also serious
legends which express a genuine experience of Christian existence, such
as the *Life of St. Martin of Tours* by Sulpicius Severus or the *Dialogues of*
Gregory the Great about St. Benedict or the *Fioretti* of St. Francis. These
stories are absolutely serious, and they are true. How far they are true in
the sense that the recorded miracles actually happened in this way we may
leave unsettled; and that really is not the main point. The thing that matters is the character which existence as a whole assumed around this holy
person; we may say more properly, around this person who had been given

the charisma to set forth in a supreme and revealing way that which takes place in the existence of every believer. The manner in which things behave around him, the character which the world assumes, the fact that here there is familiar reality, yet with a difference, the constant coming of the kingdom, the powerful, disturbing yet blissful penetration of the new creation within the space of his existence—all this the legend expresses by the recounting of miracles. Whether the individual miracles actually took place is not important; what is important is the whole miracle of this existence, the accomplishment of Providence in the development of the new creation. The saint is not a private phenomenon; his significance lies in the whole of Christian existence. He reveals what takes place everywhere in varying degrees of power and purity, and especially, in a hidden and inconspicuous manner. In individual instances it would probably be impossible to show that a certain turn of events or arrangement of things depend on anything other than the inner calm of the person concerned or upon his gift of accepting reality—more impossible the more sincere and genuine the person is. One can always mention "natural" conditions which "explain" these happenings, especially if one holds the preconceived opinion that only "natural" conditions exist. As a matter of fact, the natural conditions always do exist, for that which is new does not consist in miracles occurring in empty space, but in the way in which the "natural" conditions are formed into an environment by the forces proceeding from the living center of a personality open and responsive in faith. These forces are often imperceptibly delicate influences of guidance, moderation, deepening, the changing of perspective and purpose, etc. Hence a seeing eye is required to discern them, and in this matter no human eye sees with complete clarity. Ultimately, everything depends on faith.

This faith—both in the person concerned and in the beholder—is most severely tested when the promise is apparently not fulfilled, and that "which man shall eat and drink and wherewith he shall be clothed" is not supplied. To comment on this is difficult. The first answer might be that the promise is given on condition that "the kingdom of God and His justice" is really sought, and the questioner must first of all direct the question to his own conscience. The second answer would be that the bestowing of food, drink and raiment is involved in the mystery of the Father's wisdom and He "knows what we have need of." But we also have need of trial, so that Providence may consist in denying us the immediate necessities. Scepticism will reply that this invalidates the whole argument. But it does not. Providence means the Providence of that God who knows not only what we think we need but what we really need. Our existence is safer in the care of His judgment than of our own; indeed in His wisdom is all our good and all our safety. His standards are divine; that means that the course of our destiny takes ways which are incomprehensible to us. Criticism will reply that this puts everything into the realm of the uncontrollable. If "uncontrollable" means trivial and fantastic—no. The basis of the idea has been shown to be a very serious matter. But if it means that the total structure of what Providence signifies is a mystery and therefore cannot be fathomed by man, then the statement is true. The act which grasps it is not calculation and examination, but faith and confidence. And that this "faith" has no connection with what the thinkers of the past century understood by that term when they described it as a pious feeling, a subjective glimmer, a fantasy of immature childishness or some such thing, to be distinguished from the one thing to be taken seriously—science—that we have probably made clear.

All this indicates also that the question of Providence is ultimately an eschatological one. It looks toward that which is to come. St. Paul says in his Epistle to the Romans: "For I reckon that the sufferings of this time are not worthy to be compared with the glory to come, that shall be revealed in us. For the expectation of the creature waits for the revelation of the sons of God. For the creature was made subject to vanity, not willingly, but by reason of him that made it subject in the hope that the creature also itself shall be delivered from the servitude of corruption into the liberty of the children of God. For we know that every creature groans and travails in pain even till now" (Rom. 8:18–22). Providence is directed to that which is to come, inasmuch as events here are still veiled in the darkness of the status viae and shall be revealed only in the final judgment which is also the last word of the Revelation. Moreover, the content of the Providential dealings of God is the formation of the new creation. The true purpose of Providence is not that man may prosper in time, but that "the kingdom of God" may come and His justice may be fulfilled; that the new creation and the man of eternity may be perfected.[4]

THE CHURCH OF THE LORD

On the Nature and Mission of the Church

Preface

I t seems proper to begin by calling the reader's attention to the fact that this book consists of reflections.

Hence it does not attempt to provide a systematic treatment of its subject, nor to examine all aspects of the problem; still less does it attempt to deal with all the questions that have arisen in connection with the work of Vatican Council II. The following chapters seek only to provide a deeper insight into those aspects of the Church which seem particularly important to the author.

Between Two Books

I n the year 1922, on the threshold of my academic activity, I published the book, *On the Meaning of the Church*. It seems to me that a spiritual cycle is closing as I am now permitted, immediately after my eightieth birthday, to present this second work about the Church. Between the publication of the two books lies a history.

But in order to do justice to it I must go farther back, to the time of my theological studies in Tübingen; that is, from the autumn of 1906 until the spring of 1908. (I know that it may seem unfitting to introduce personal matters when dealing with an objective question. However, since I believe that the objective matters to be discussed may be better expressed in connection with these personal reflections, I hope that the reader will have no objection.)

At that time it first became clear to me what "the Church" is, and two lines of thought, whose significance the intervening years have not been able to take away, have made this insight ever clearer.

The first line of thought ran as follows: The Church is a structure which reaches into all areas of existence and is operative even to the inmost depths of humanity. It questions the natural security of man and makes heavy demands upon his reason and his will. This structure stepped into history almost two thousand years ago; it was shaken by all the conflicts of this history, and all human problems were thrashed out in it. Nor is that all. With imperturbable consistency, the Church worked out and maintained for more than seventeen centuries a divine Revelation transcending all imagination; the doctrine of the triune God, as well as the message of God's love, which, when understood in its fullest sense, breaks asunder all natural intelligibility. According to all the laws of nature such a structure should have disintegrated after a short time. But the Church did not disintegrate, and so something took place in it which, from the point of view of all history and knowledge of life, is impossible. This fact indicates that the Church is based upon and supported by something that is more than human.

The second line of thought was this: Long preoccupation with the composition of living things had taught me that everything human is arranged in typical structures and can be determined by these. As long as one does not from the outset limit the Church—historically, sociologically or in some other way—this is not possible here. Of course we find in her all types of human life, but she is not confined to or identical with any one of them. Again and again the danger has threatened that some type would grow too luxuriantly and would dominate her. The history of the heresies delineates these processes one after another. But they were unable to overpower the Church in her essential nature. Sometimes they narrowed or impoverished her, but anyone who knows her true history knows that her essential nature always remained complete and unified. That means that there is something in her that is above all structures and their contraries. Adolf V. Harnack expressed this by speaking of the *coincidentia oppositorum* in the Church, though he thought of this as a mixture of contradictions. Actually there is something living in the Church which, like the energy that holds together the component parts of the atom, overcomes the tension between the structures and combines them into a whole in a way which, according to all sociological theories, is impossible on any earthly basis. It is the operation of the Holy Spirit which makes the Church

"Catholic" and enables her to be the Church of all nations "all days, even to the consummation of the world." (Matt. 28:20)

These reflections taught me to understand the Church as she is; that is, the constant realization of something which cannot be derived from natural assumptions. She was willed by Christ, born of the Holy Spirit and she will endure, have a destiny, suffer and be renewed, again and again, until the end of history, and then she will be transformed into what the Apocalypse calls "the heavenly city." (Apoc. 21:2)

And now I return to the book of which I spoke at the beginning. It designates the moment in which "the Church awakened in the souls of men."[1]

Before that time, the Church had been generally looked upon only as something objectively given, as "the house that stands in glory," in which the believers dwelt and found refuge, as the religious authority established by Christ, which was often felt to be a dominating power. But then the situation changed, and the Church was experienced as something that lives in the believer. It is that which is expressed by St. Paul's concept of the *corpus Christi mysticum*, of which the individual is a member, or, as we would say in modern parlance, of which every believer is a cell. (I Cor. 12:12) The individual felt that he lived by the Church, that the Church lived in him, that between her and him there existed a relationship like that between a living part of the organism and the whole. Every believer stood in this relationship and so lived in a communion which was more intimate and rich than that which had been expressed by the ecclesiastical concept of membership in the "perfect society."

I.

But then history went on. I remember well how in the midst of the joyous experience of "the Church in us" there were opinions that this was not sufficient.

It was a part of the common experience during the German Youth Movement that not only was the individualism of the nineteenth century overcome and a living communion attained, but also that it proved possible to communicate with people holding other ideologies—for instance members of communistic societies—and to do this in a way that clearly recognized the differences of conviction but at the same time entered into a community of dialogue and responsibility in a matter-of-fact way. Men realized that the force of a lively conviction did not shut one off from men of other opinions but, by the very clarity of the distinction, cleared the way to them. Why should not similar conditions prevail in regard to the Church and those who did not belong to her, since both appealed to the same Christ?

Indeed, the idea went further. What of the pagan? Was he merely one who was "outside" and to whom our only relation was the possibility of converting him? Or did he share with the member of the Church a common interior quality which we might conceive of as the community of those who pray? And could this not be maintained without any blurring of "Yes" and "No," of essentials and distinctions, into a vague and meaningless fog?

This vital assumption of the Church into the life of the individual resulted in another question: Why was "the world" so often regarded only as alien or even hostile?

It is true that the Apostle John in his first Epistle said, "Love not the world, nor the things that are in the world. If any man love the world the love of the Father is not in him." (I John 2:15) But John himself gives to the word "the world" another meaning, clearly indicated by the warmth of the statement, "God so loved the world that He gave his only-begotten Son (for it)." (John 3:16) And the book of Genesis recounts how God gave man responsibility for the world that he might "dress it and keep it." (Gen. 2:15)

Here too a kind of reserve seemed to prevail, not definitely expressed but perceptible in men's attitudes. The predominant concept was that the

Church stood in the world like a fortress, and its relations to the world should be only those that were inevitable. But did not this reserve indicate a lack of confidence in the inward power of truth given to her through the Holy Spirit?

And again, was there not a kind of reserve evident in the Church herself when, for instance, the believer, during the celebration of the Eucharist, saw the priest performing his function far up at the altar, facing the wall and speaking in a low murmur, while he had to occupy himself with some "devotion"? Was this the great openness and unity which the experience of an interiorly awakened Church demanded?

II.

We might speak of many other points. These feelings of restlessness, the questions and wishes that proceeded not from a lack of confidence in the Church but from the newly recovered interior relation to her, from the demands of love and trust, found their answer in the figure of Pope John XXIII and the event of the Vatican Council. As a result of this Council, many have experienced what is meant by "charisma," the life-giving action of the Holy Spirit which transcends reason and legality.

No one would have expected that the quiet personality of this pope would supply the initiative for such an event, tremendous even when viewed externally, because it required a gathering of representatives from the whole world. Not only did this take place, however, but there was also a creative outburst of understanding and declaration. A consciousness of the living power of Christian truth was manifested, which may have troubled many who were accustomed to old and familiar ways of thinking and speaking. And the certainty of the lasting validity of faith was expressed not in approximations and attenuations, but in the confidence with which eternal truth has been proclaimed to this present moment of history.

As a result of this conviction there came about a great "opening." The Church began to speak to all who know that they are bound in duty to Christ, although they may not be in the Catholic community, and to speak to them without fear or harshness, in order to be heard.

Nor was that all. Rather, the way to those who are religiously inclined, yet do not believe in Christ, was now open, as was the way to those pagans who are receptive to divine matters. Here too, however, there must be no false adaptation or relativistic weakening of the truth.

But the matter extends still further: are non-believers merely "outside"? Could not their lack of faith be caused by the faults or even by the indifference of members of the Church?

And again we must continue to extend our view and to ask: Does the statement of the Church Fathers that the Church is the "heir of the pagans" mean only that she takes over truths which the thought and the lives of unbelievers have worked out? Or does it also mean that Christian theologians recognize that truths require their own soil in order to develop, and that values require an atmosphere for their discovery? Here too we might discern a kind of division of labor, by which, for example, certain truths and values became clear in India whereas Europeans had not yet grasped them. Hence we might find in the spiritual realm of the Vedas some insights which could be useful for a deepening of the doctrine of the Trinity,[2] or it might be that in Buddhism—the strict Buddhism of the south—experiences emerged clearly which might be valuable for the problem of the "negative" knowledge of God?

And what of the matter of mythology; indeed, the whole question of the myth? Shall we simply reject it, and shall those who are concerned about the purity of the message confine themselves to freeing this message from its mythical elements? Or is it not possible that a way of experiencing and thinking, in which all people have lived for a time, should contain images, experiences and insights which could contribute to a deepening of the Christian faith?

An "opening" is also taking place within the Church herself; for example, in the relations between priest and laity. The new practice of celebrating the Eucharist facing the people and also the increasing use of the vernacular, appear to symbolize the fact that the congregation has become conscious of itself and enters, as a congregation, into the liturgy. What we call "liturgical renewal" means that the performance of the sacred functions does depend upon the priest by virtue of his office but should also be a common concern. And now we are watching with great expectation the efforts that are being put forth in order that the promise may be fulfilled. We hope that the difficulties encountered will not result in discouragement, and that too great haste and a passion for innovation may not confuse and hinder true growth and development. The Church has come to regard "the world" as something that is not only profane and dangerous, but also, and above all, the work of God, a work which He loves and has entrusted to men. It follows then, as a logical consequence, that the Church should respect and give a hearing to the one who is responsible for the world, namely the layman, and that she should turn over to him what is his affair.

All this gives us a reason for joy and great hope, and it is no indication of doubt or a desire to belittle if the writer of these pages expresses a wish. He has lived a long life and from the study of history and of human nature has learned something of the tendencies in accord with which given impulses work out in actual human affairs. He wishes therefore that the events of the present age may not lead to a weakening of the Church or her stagnation but that men may always remain clearly conscious of the fact that the Church is a "mystery" and a "rock."

The Church is a "mystery" because, in her essential nature, she did not arise out of psychology or sociology or any historical necessity, but was founded by Christ and born through the descent of the Holy Spirit. She is permeated by all that we term the world and history, but in her essence she lives by the Cross of Christ and the action of the Spirit. She proclaims the truth of the Holy God, which leads man to salvation but "passes all understanding."

The Church is a "rock" because Christ willed it so. (Matt. 16:18) She is not the effect of experiences, changing as these change, nor is she the expression of psychological needs and cultural situations at any given time. Rather, over against all which is merely subjective, she is the objective message from God. In spite of all her relations to the times, she is firm and unshakeable in her distinction between truth and error. She despises neither history nor the individual, but respects man and his conscience. For only truth and the demand for truth imply genuine reverence, whereas permissiveness and carelessness constitute weakness, which does not dare to expect of man the recognition of the majesty of the self-revealing God. Indeed, these are fundamentally a contempt for man whose dignity consists in the very fact that he exists by truth.

The Church cannot be resolved into merely natural concepts. Her actions cannot be prescribed for her merely in view of natural demands. On the contrary, she lives by her mission and she must fulfill this—even though it may be at the price of giving scandal.

The Will of Jesus

T he period of history in which we live will some day be referred to as that age in which man became definitely conscious of what the "world" is and of what he is in the world. It is also the age in which the Church is becoming aware once more of what she is and of man's relation to her. The Council will ask the second question with full consciousness of its meaning, and, in consequence, the first question will naturally present itself, and each will cast light upon the other.

The answer given to these questions and their relation to each other will determine future history for years to come. Therefore, the meditations contained in this book are meant to share in this awakening, to assist in carrying it out and so perhaps, as far as they can, to contribute a little to the great event.

It is not easy to say what the Church is. Evidently she is something that cannot be immediately grasped. Some see in her the self-evident basis of their religious existence, and are conscious of being nourished by the strength of the Church and borne up by its order. Others consider her the embodiment of spiritual intolerance and the means of dominating men through religion. This is a strange contradiction, for the Church has been in existence for almost two thousand years, manifest among men. She has revealed herself, developed and defined herself. So there must be something peculiar about her.

Let us suppose that we met someone who is an authority on historical affairs and asked him, "What do you think of a social structure which proclaims to men doctrines that trouble them, and make demands on them which do not accord with their immediate wishes and needs, and yet is recognized and even loved by innumerable persons? A community with a very definite organization and a single head, extending through the most diverse countries and cultures, everywhere drawn into the tensions of political life, yet maintaining its position in the midst of all disturbances; touched by all the currents of the ages, all the changes of the centuries, yet in its essential nature unharmed by all of these?" The answer would probably be, "Such a structure is impossible."

And yet it exists in reality. Therefore we may well ask what it is, how it endures and what forces operate within it.

A more definite question will show us the way. What did He whom we reverence as "the Lord," Jesus Christ, wish to be the means of continuing His teaching and His work throughout history? He said that it would continue to spread to all nations even to the end of time. (Matt. 28:19ff.) How did He intend this to be done?

Jesus knew that the message He was bringing possessed absolute value: "Heaven and earth shall pass away, but my words shall not pass away." (Matt. 24:35) And again: "I am the way and the truth and the life." (John 14:6) He opposed His authority to that of the old covenant, the law, the prophets and the sages: "You have heard that it was said to them of old...but I say to you."

And at the close of St. Mark's Gospel He says, "He who believes and is baptized shall be saved, but he that believes not shall be condemned." (Mark 16:16) He that believes—whom? Him and His messengers. What a claim! One who speaks in this manner must have asked himself in what way that which he had done and spoken would continue through time and space.

And what was His answer to the question?

How would we, men of today, with our modern historical sense, answer such a question? We would say that everything must be written down; events, doctrines and prophecies must be carefully authenticated. The documents thus obtained must be securely preserved, carefully reproduced and made accessible to all. But what does Christ say? Does He command that His words, deeds, and regulations shall be recorded? Does He refer at all to a written document? To a book?

He might have done so. It was indeed a book, the "Old Testament," that formed the basis of the religious world of His time. And He recognized it as such. Again and again we hear Him say, "It is written." His reply to the tempter at the beginning of His public activity takes the form of an appeal to Scripture. (Matt. 4:4 and following) When a man came and asked, "Good Master, what shall I do that I may receive life everlasting?," Jesus referred him to the Ten Commandments that are recorded in the book of Exodus. (Mark 10:17–19) When another wished to embarrass Him and asked what was the "greatest commandment in the Law," Jesus replied with the sentence taken from Deuteronomy: "Thou shalt love the Lord, thy God, with all thy heart and with all thy soul and with all thy mind." (Matt. 22:37)

Jesus knew the Sacred Scriptures and recognized their divine authority. Would it not be likely that He would entrust His own message to a similar book? He might have said to His disciples, "Write this down." We can even conceive of the possibility that He himself might have written, and how wonderful that would have been! We must not interpose the objection that the Son of God could not be associated with such an action, for we read in the book of Exodus that God commanded Moses to hew out two tables of stone and then continued, "And

I will write the words [of the Ten Commandments] upon the table."
(Exod. 34:1) In whatever way we should interpret this "writing," it still
means that God ties up His revelation very closely with something written. Jesus certainly could have written down His important doctrines, or
He could have done what God did in the Old Testament when He spoke
to the prophets, "Take a great book and write in it with a man's pen."
(Isaias 8:1) The prophet wrote and the written message was handed down
through the ages. How easily Jesus could have said to His disciples, "Pay
attention to what I say. Write it down, so that you can read it later and
your children may receive it from your hands, and their children from
them, and so on through all generations."

But He did not do this. No word of Jesus refers to a written document
about His work and His doctrine.

Of course, such documents were composed later. Soon after His departure "sayings of the Lord" were collected and later incorporated into
larger treatises. In this way the Gospels came into existence, four of them,
by Matthew, Mark, Luke and John; precious texts of equal authority with
the oral message of the Apostles who composed them or vouched for
them. Letters of instruction, which reported and developed the thoughts
of Jesus, were also written, by Paul, James, Jude, Peter and John. And Luke
wrote an account of the early days of the young church, the Acts of the
Apostles. And finally there appeared the last book, the Apocalypse of the
Apostle John, which shows us the figure of Jesus in eternal glory. All these
were collected at the end of the first century and set beside the Old
Testament as the New Testament, forming together with it "the Sacred
Scriptures."

All this was done, but not at the express command of Jesus. He did not
insist upon a book or written record as the authoritative standard for the
transmitting of His message, but, as we shall see, He sent forth messengers
who were to proclaim and teach it. For these, the written word was a supplement to the spoken word, as the circumstances required it. So the New

Testament Scriptures came into existence "by chance," as a result of particular situations, insofar as the term "chance" means that they came about
without a definite plan, but rather as incidents within a comprehensive and
basic whole. The books of the New Testament are the word of God, the
message of salvation. They permit us to hear, more or less immediately, the
speech of Jesus Himself and of His apostles and put us in touch with the
life of the early church. This is of great significance for the awakening and
the subsequent growth and deepening of men's faith, for the development
of Christian ideas and for the self-criticism of Christian thought. But the
message of Jesus would have made its way through history even if the authors of the Holy Scriptures had not written these.

This is not meant to depreciate them, but to point out the place where
they stand and the function which they perform. As a matter of fact, some
of these messages were lost, a letter of St. Paul to the Laodiceans and two
to the Corinthians. But this did not detract from the completeness of the
message to be proclaimed. In other words: the New Testament is not independent or self-explanatory. It stands in the context of a whole which
bears it, and includes it and enables us to understand it, and that whole is
the Church.

But what is the Church? We shall not begin with concepts, but consider what has taken place.[1]

At the very beginning of His activity Jesus gathered men about Him.
Indeed, we may recall the fine accounts of these vocations at the beginning
of the Fourth Gospel; how John came to him, then Andrew, Simon Peter,
Philip and Nathanael. In a solemn hour, Luke says, after He had long
prayed in silence (Luke 6:12), He chose twelve of these. (Mark 3:13–19;
Matt. 10:1–4) This number is an actual one; that is, the names of twelve
men are given. However, it also has a symbolic value, the twelve tribes of
Israel; that is, the totality of the redeemed people of God. The number is
so significant that it was retained even after there came to be thirteen
apostles. When Judas, the betrayer, had taken his own life, Matthias was

chosen in his place, and then came Paul—but we still speak of the "twelve apostles," the sum total of the messengers sent to all mankind.

Of this group one stands out particularly, Peter. He expresses the thoughts that stir in the minds of all the disciples; for instance, in regard to the reward for following Christ. (Matt. 19:27) At decisive moments he steps forward and speaks, as in the critical hour in Capernaum when there was the question whether "the twelve" like "many of the disciples" would also leave Jesus in consequence of His statement about the Eucharist. (John 6:60ff.) The manner in which Peter acted at the Last Supper, at the time of Jesus' arrest and after the Resurrection, clearly shows that he was in the habit of expressing his opinion and that this was recognized as his prerogative. And it is John who emphasizes this particularly, although he also speaks in detail of Peter's denial. (John 13:6ff.; 36ff.; 18:10ff.; 15ff.) This clearly shows a priority which becomes much more definite after the Ascension and which is recognized without the least trace of opposition. We may recall how Peter instigates the choice of a new apostle, how he explains the phenomenon of Pentecost and draws conclusions from it, and the like. Again this is emphasized by the fact that John stands beside him, yet the accent of authority does not fall upon the disciple who alone stood beneath the cross but upon Peter. (Acts 1:15ff.; 2:14ff.; 3:1ff.; 5:3 etc.)

The pre-eminence of Peter was not one of talent; we may say this with all respect. John was more highly gifted, and so was Paul. Nor was it a superiority of character; Peter is portrayed as rather unstable, and it was he who expressly denied his Master. (Matt. 26:69ff.) The pre-eminence of Peter was not the result of a particular love that Jesus had for him. It was John who could call himself "the disciple whom Jesus loved." (John 13:23) What, then, was the reason for Peter's priority? An account written not by Peter nor by one of his pupils, but by Matthew (16:13ff.) relates how Jesus in a solemn hour asked His disciples, "Who do men say the Son of Man is?" They replied, "Some say John the Baptist, others Elias, others Jeremias or one of the prophets." He said to them, "And who do you say that I am?" Then Simon Peter answered, "Thou art the Messias, the Son of the living God." And Jesus said to him "Blessed art thou, Simon, son of Jonas; not flesh and blood"—the biblical expression for unaided human nature—"have revealed this to thee but my Father in heaven. And I say to thee: thou art Peter [that is, the rock] and upon this rock I will build my church, and the gates [that is, the powers] of hell shall not prevail against it." This means that the pre-eminence of Peter is one of vocation. This may be connected with natural qualities and tendencies, but essentially it is a grace and cannot be logically explained or accounted for.

John recounts that after the resurrection of the Lord the apostles were once again in Galilee. Jesus appeared to them at the lake and gave to John and to Peter the presage of their future destiny; to John was given the mysterious prophecy of "remaining until the *parousia*," to Peter the charge and the power to feed the flock of the Lord, which meant essentially the same thing as Jesus' words at Caesarea Philippi. (Matt. 16:13ff.)

Around the small circle of the apostles a larger one gathered and these were called the "disciples." We meet them again and again, in a special way in the passage where Luke recounts (Luke 10) that "the Lord appointed also another seventy-two and sent them two and two before His face into every city and place whither He himself was to come." Then follow the important words about their mission. When they returned and narrated what they had done, Jesus, we are told, was mysteriously elated, and, "rejoicing in the Holy Spirit," spoke of His relation to the Father and the plenitude of His Messianic power, and then told them that an understanding of and participation in the kingdom of God rested upon a very different foundation than earthly greatness. (Luke 10:21 ff)

John speaks of "disciples" in another connection. In an authoritative pronouncement Jesus revealed the connection between redemption, sacrifice and Eucharist, and then they said "This is a hard saying and who can hear it," and "after this many of His disciples went back and walked no more with Him." (John 6:60, 66)

To the twelve Jesus entrusted His Message. They were called "apostles"; that is, those who are sent. They called themselves "the witnesses," and were so conscious of their importance that after the Ascension they assembled and made this statement:

> Judas, who was the leader of them that apprehended Jesus, was numbered with us and had obtained part of this ministry... let another take his bishopric. Wherefore of these men who have accompanied us all the time that the Lord Jesus came in and went out among us, beginning from the baptism of John until the day wherein He was taken up from us, one of these must be made a witness with us of His resurrection. (Acts 1:16–17, 20–22)

So they chose Matthias by lot to take the place that had been held by the traitor. Now the sacred number was complete again and they could carry out the mission to which the Lord had called them when He said after His resurrection:

> All power is given to me in heaven and on earth. Going therefore, teach ye all nations, baptizing them in the name of the Father and of the Son and of the Holy Spirit, teaching them to observe all things whatsoever I have commanded you; and behold I am with you all days even to the consummation of the world. (Matt. 28:18–20)

These words show that the apostolic mission was not confined to those who were first called, but constituted a true office which is related to the nature of the kingdom of God. Consequently, it extends beyond the circle of the first apostles. The choice of Matthias does not permit any doubt that the apostles were conscious of that fact, and accepted it as self-evident that they should plan for the continuance of the office.

The Pauline epistles show us that the establishment of new centers of activity in each case involved the appointment of a man who received the charge and the power of an apostle, the bishop:

> For a bishop must be without crime, as the steward of God; not proud, not subject to anger, not given to wine, no striker, not greedy of filthy lucre, but given to hospitality, gentle, sober, just, holy, continent, embracing that faithful word which is according to doctrine, that he may be able to exhort in sound doctrine, and to convince the gainsayers. (Tit. 1:7–9; also Tim. 3:1ff.)

And so it goes on through the ages, and will go on even to the end of history: that is the Church.

But what constitutes the core of this church? What are its contents? What gives to it its surety and validity? Jesus himself states it very clearly: "He that hears you, hears me, and he that despises you, despises me, and he that despises me, despises Him that sent me." (Luke 10:16) And at the end of Matthew's gospel we read: "Behold I am with you all days, even to the consummation of the world." (Matt. 28:20) When His messengers come, He comes; when they speak, it is He who speaks.

But there is more. In the account of the Last Supper we read:

> And when the hour was come He sat down and the twelve apostles with Him. And He said to them, "With desire I have desired to eat this pasch with you, before I suffer. For I say to you that from this time I will not eat it, till it be fulfilled in the kingdom of God." And having taken the chalice, He gave

thanks and said, "Take and divide it among you. For I say to you that I will not drink of the fruit of the vine till the kingdom of God come." And taking bread, He gave thanks, and broke and gave to them, saying, "This is my body, which is given for you. Do this for a commemoration of me." In like manner He took the chalice also, after He had supped, saying, "This is the chalice, the new testament in my blood, which shall be shed for you." (Luke 22:14–20)

The men to whom He was speaking were not modern psychologists and symbolists but men of antiquity who thought simply and in a corporeal way. When Jesus said to them, "This is my body" and "this is my blood," then it "is" that and does not merely "signify" it. So they knew that here He was giving them Himself, in the mystery of an inconceivable sacrifice. This too is contained in the new community which was here established. It is the central point, the holy of holies. Here again we are told what "the Church" is: the living Christ who imparts Himself to His own throughout the ages.

At the start matters were not yet shaped and organized in detail. We might say that the situation is similar to that which we find at the beginning of the book of Genesis, where we read: "In the beginning God created heaven and earth. And the earth was void and empty, and darkness was upon the face of the deep, and the Spirit of God moved over the waters." (Gen. 1:1–2) Then the Spirit takes hold, and when we read, "Let there be light.... Let there be a firmament made amidst the waters and let it divide the waters from the waters...." The stars shall be made, growth shall come, and the beasts...; then it is the Spirit that forms and arranges, for He is the source of all creation. Something similar takes place here.

Everything is there, in some fashion, but awaiting an event that shall shape and determine. Jesus has taught and has worked miracles. He has suffered, died, and risen. He lives in light eternal, Lord of all power in heaven and on earth, and He will "draw all things to himself." (John 12:32) His own are there, not yet comprehending, but ready and prepared for a great decisive event. He told them to wait. The Spirit would come, would teach them all things and give them all things. (John 16)

Through the Spirit of truth the Church is born and Christ's will is made manifest.

The Birth of the Church

Let us summarize once more: Jesus knew that His message is decisive for the salvation of men—men of all countries and of all the ages. Therefore He necessarily had a definite intention in regard to the manner in which this message would be carried "to all nations and even to the end of time," and would remain intact and unadulterated on this long journey. We today think immediately of writing and printing, but Jesus said not a word of these things. He knew of a book which contained the doctrine of salvation, but that book was the Old Testament. His own doctrine He entrusted not to a book but to men with whom He had lived and whom He had trained. He gave them the task of proclaiming the message, of bearing witness, of awakening life and of organizing. The way in which that was to be done He left to the future, to the circumstances and to the judgment of the apostles illumined by the Holy Spirit.

It was characteristic of the life of Jesus that the result—if we may be permitted to use the word in dealing with so sacred a subject—was not visible during His earthly life. He was to remain the sower, others were to reap the harvest. He himself had said, "In this is the saying true that it is one man that sows and it is another that reaps. I have sent you to reap that

425

in which you did not labour. Others have laboured and you have entered into their labours." (John 4:37–38) This was also true of Him. That which was to come forth from His prayer, His teaching, His actions and His suffering, lay beyond the tomb.

Everything was in the process of becoming—full of promise but without visible form. The future apostles were ready, but in terror of their foes. Their memory recalled the words and deeds and the fate of their Master, but they did not yet understand the true meaning and interrelation of these things. Their Master was everything to them, but they did not yet know who He really is, and their loyalty had not yet reached the point of triumphing over earthly things.

Therefore, after the death of Jesus, the disciples felt that they were in a state of expectancy. At the very last moment, in the deeply mysterious hour of His return to the Father, they asked: "Lord, wilt thou at this time restore again the kingdom of Israel?" (Acts 1:6)—the kingdom in which they—we may add this with reference to Matthew 18:1 and 20:20—would sit upon the "twelve thrones," of which Jesus had spoken in a very different sense. (Matt. 19:28) So they waited.

And now the book of Acts tells us:

> And when the days of the Pentecost were accomplished, they all were together in one place; and suddenly there came a sound from heaven, as of a mighty wind coming, and it filled the whole house where they were sitting. And there appeared to them parted tongues as it were of fire, and it sat upon every one of them. And they were all filled with the Holy Ghost, and they began to speak with diverse tongues, according as the Holy Ghost gave them to speak. (Acts 2:1–4)

The occurrence was observed; a crowd gathered in front of the house:

Now there were dwelling at Jerusalem Jews, devout men, out of every nation under heaven. And when this was noised abroad, the multitude came together and were confounded in mind, because every man heard them speak in his own tongue. And they were all amazed, and wondered, saying, "Behold, are not all these that speak Galileans? And how have we heard every man our own tongue wherein we were born?"...and they were all astonished and wondered, saying one to another, "What does this mean?" But others, mocking, said, "These men are full of new wine." (Acts 2:5–8, 12–13)

The time had come for the first testimony:

But Peter standing up with the eleven, lifted up his voice and spoke to them: "Ye men of Judea, and all you that dwell in Jerusalem, be this known to you, and with your ears receive my words. For these are not drunk, as you suppose, seeing it is but the third hour of the day; but this is that which was spoken of by the prophet Joel: And it shall come to pass in the last days (saith the Lord) I will pour out of my Spirit upon all flesh, and your sons and your daughters shall prophesy. (Acts 14–18)

And he continued:

Men of Israel, hear these words: Jesus of Nazareth, a man approved of God among you by miracles and wonders and signs, which God did by him. in the midst of you. as you also know; this same man being delivered up, by the determinate counsel and foreknowledge of God, you by the hands of wicked men

have crucified and slain.... Therefore let all the house of Israel
know most certainly, that God has made both Lord and Christ
this same Jesus, whom you have crucified. (Acts 22–23, 36)

This was the first proclamation of the message, and it contained a
sacred power:

> When they had heard these things they had compunction in
> their heart and said to Peter and to the rest of the apostles,
> "What shall we do, men and brethren?" But Peter said to
> them, "Do penance and be baptized every one of you in the
> name of Jesus Christ for the remission of your sins, and you
> shall receive the gift of the Holy Ghost." ... They therefore that
> received his word were baptized, and there were added in that
> day about three thousand souls. (Acts 37–38, 41)

This was the event for which they had been waiting. And what was it
that happened?

A mysterious power began its work. Its action is expressed by images
taken from the elemental forces of nature: a flaming fire and a rushing
wind. But the force itself is not a natural one, for we are told that the flames
took the form of human tongues, and the rushing wind produced words;
that is, it possessed mind and meaning.

In order to understand what was taking place we must turn to the Old
Testament and see how the Spirit works here. The word "spirit" as used
here does not mean reason, logic, calculation, but the religious spirit,
pneuma. In this concept many ideas are combined: first, that activity which
is invisible and yet so effective, the breath, the power and expression of
life; then the great breath of the world, the wind, which we do not
see—Jesus said to Nicodemus, "Thou knowest not whence it cometh or
whither it goeth" (John 3:8)—and yet it can fill the sails and shatter the

trees; then the soul, which no man grasps or measures, and yet we live and act by it. All this is involved and points to something greater and more mysterious which comes directly from God: the Holy Spirit.

He brings it about that there shall be a man somewhere, whatever his origin may be—Isaias, or Jeremias, or Jonas—who becomes a prophet, capable of understanding the meaning of God's action in time, here and now, and who has the courage to step forward and to proclaim, "Thus says the Lord!" The Spirit awakens the leader in the events of sacred history, for instance, that immeasurably great man, Moses. He calls the hero who fights not for his own glory, but for the accomplishment of God's will, as did Gideon or David. He enlightens the judge who administers the law among God's people; again we think first of Moses or Josue, or the figures of the book of Judges. He inspires the artist who works for the adornment of the holy place, as in the vocation of Bezaleel. (Exod. 35:30ff.) And all this is done not by way of natural talent, but so that the power of God is revealed thereby.

The Spirit penetrates the inmost recesses of life. As the breath draws the air into the interior reaches of the body, so the power of God is drawn by the Spirit into a human being and transforms it. Samuel said to Saul, "The Spirit of the Lord shall come upon thee ... and thou shalt be changed into another man." (1 Sam. 10:6) The Spirit brings it about that a man grasps a truth which of himself he could not understand; that an attitude awakens within him which would otherwise be beyond his capacity; that he experiences a presence of God which he himself could not attain. This is the Spirit who operated on the occasion we have described.

Let us disregard theory; let us look upon the phenomenon: What were these men who in the hour of Pentecost were seized and gave testimony, Peter and the eleven? What were they before this event? They were men whose conduct certainly does not give the impression of heroism. We are told explicitly that they sat behind closed doors, fearful that they might suffer the same fate as their Master. (John 20:19) But now they stepped forth and spoke.

We must also remember the particular time in which this took place: the weeks of the great pilgrimage, during which Jerusalem swarmed with men of all nations, excitable as such crowds always are, humanly, religiously, and politically. At any moment a spark could catch and fanatical rage could flare up against the followers of the man recently executed. It was a crowd such as this that the apostles confronted and to which they spoke: "Let all the house of Israel know most certainly that God has made both Lord and Christ this same Jesus whom you have crucified." (Acts 2:36) These were the same men who before this had hidden themselves in fear—and yet they were entirely different. This was the work of the Spirit.

Each spoke with compelling authority, not only as one who has had an experience might say to another: "It is so; I have experienced it." That would indeed be a kind of authority, but it would be the authority of one who had gained insight by natural means or who had endured suffering. This was different. This was an authority transcending the human, an authority that did not admit of argument, one that must be obeyed or rejected.

But what were they saying as they addressed the crowd so authoritatively? What was the subject of their speech? It was Christ. And how did they speak of Him? If we compare the relation of the Apostles to Christ before Pentecost with that which became manifest on this occasion we perceive a profound, an intrinsic difference. Of course He had been their Master before. They accompanied Him, listened to His words, observed what He did and how men behaved toward Him. They were witnesses of everything, so that they could say later that no one could be an apostle who had not been with them from the beginning and hence was capable of speaking from experience. (Acts 1:21ff.) But can we maintain that they understood Him? To some extent, naturally, they did understand Him. When He said that His disciples should avoid not only deeds but even words of hatred, should not merely pardon a limited number of times but should always be ready to forgive—and the other things that He taught them in regard to the proper attitude of children of God—then they understood the words in a general human sense. They also perceived the purity and selflessness of their Master, the power of helping and healing that proceeded from Him, the atmosphere of stillness which enveloped Him in spite of all the turmoil around Him. But always He remained, as it were, ahead of them, beyond them. They were always approaching Him from a distance—the distance of their Old Testament world and way of thinking.

But after the Spirit had come upon them a mysterious change of position took place. Now they spoke from His point of view. He was no longer "before" them. He was "in" them. As they spoke, He was speaking. Later St. Paul would write about this "in" from deep personal experience. He was in Christ and Christ in Him. "Now it is no longer I who live, but Christ lives in me." (Gal. 2:20) But there is more: When these twelve apostles speak, it is not as if a group of twelve men had had the same experience and then each one stepped forward (Acts 2:14) and stated: "I also vouch for this; I corroborate what our spokesman is saying." When we speak of "the twelve" this is not merely a number—twelve instead of twenty or a hundred—but a symbol, namely the twelve tribes of Israel, who must then be re-interpreted as the twelve tribes of the new holy nation, that is, the totality of the believers. These twelve, therefore, are not just a number but a figure.

How close and strong this unity is we may perceive by considering an event which followed soon after and had important consequences. Some time after the occurrences on the day of Pentecost, Paul went from Jerusalem to Damascus in order to carry on the persecution there. (Acts 9:2ff.) On the way the Lord met him and Paul collapsed on the road. This meeting was both a defeat and a vocation: Jesus turned the persecutor into His servant and apostle. Immediately Paul began to teach, and he did it with a power which still rings in his Epistles. If anyone had been capable of acting alone, merely as a result of his vocation by Jesus, then it was Paul. Humanly speaking, he must have been strongly tempted to do so, for the original apostles did not make things easy for him. When they chose Matthias they had made the rule that only one who had been with Jesus from the beginning could become an apostle. (Acts 1:21) But Paul had never seen Jesus in His earthly form. Therefore they felt that this additional apostle was somewhat irregular—quite apart from the fact that it was he who had so deeply disturbed the pleasant peace of the original community. How great was Paul's temptation to say, "I do not need you. I was called by the Lord himself." And at the beginning of the Epistle to the Galatians he does call himself most emphatically, "Paul, an apostle, not of men, neither by man, but by Jesus Christ, and God the Father, who raised him from the dead." (Gal. 1:1) The excitement of Paul's first experience had lengthy repercussions. We need only read in the second Epistle to the Corinthians how he speaks of the difficulties of his apostolic life, or note the tone in which the Epistle to the Galatians speaks of James and Peter and John "who are regarded as the pillars." (2:9) But he, who could say of himself "I have labored more abundantly than all [the others]" (I Cor. 15:10) went to Jerusalem and gave the apostles an account of what he had done and accepted their decision as to what he might maintain and what not. (Acts. 21:15-26; Gal. 2:1-10)

All this means that "the twelve" were not merely a group of men which might just as well have been larger or smaller, but they were—together with those who gathered around them—a figure, a whole, an organism, which stood in objective validity and authority. They were—the church!

If we consider all this, how shall we express what happened on the day of Pentecost? At first the obvious answer would seem to be: the Church was founded. But this would not correctly express the occurrence which the book of Acts relates. There was something which preceded. Jesus chose the twelve and entrusted His work to them; He spoke to Peter of the rock on which He intended to build His church. He made the Eucharist the core and the central mystery of the church that was to be, apart from the fact that He lived with them throughout this time, spoke to them, wove His sacred form into their minds and souls. But all this was not an accomplishment but a preparation, a foundation and a germ. And then, on the day of Pentecost, the Church was "born."

The Church is not an invented and constructed institution, however wise and powerful, but a living being which has come forth from an occurrence that is both divine and human, the event of Pentecost. She lives on through time, in the process of becoming, like every living thing. She changes as every thing in history changes with time and destiny and yet essentially she is always the same, and her inmost core is Christ.

This determines the way in which we must understand her. So long as we regard the Church as merely an organization which serves definite purposes, as a governing body which is opposed to the freedom of the individual, as a federation of those who have the same views and attitudes in religious matters, we do not have the right relation to her. She is a living being, and our relation to her must itself be a vital one.

But that is a subject which we must consider more carefully.

The living being of which we are speaking possesses a mighty power: According to the will of Christ it must leaven every period of history, penetrate into all corners of the earth and take hold of all nations. (Matt. 28:19ff.) It is of unshakeable solidity, a solidity which is the power of truth. Jesus himself compares it to a building which He will erect upon a rock-foundation. (Matt. 16:18) This motif of strength and solidity was marvellously developed by St. John in the Apocalypse. He unfolds in an impressive vision the image of the heavenly city. (21:9ff.) But at the same time the impression of rigidity that one associates with the image of a building, and the feeling of coldness that would be produced by the stones, is transformed into a thing of life as we read that the heavenly Jerusalem comes down from God, "dressed as a bride adorned for her husband."

But the concept of the Church as a living being was most emphatically stated and worked out by that apostle who would perhaps have been most tempted and most able to fashion Christian existence into an immediate and individual relation to Christ, St. Paul. We have already spoken of this, and of the fact that he used the ancient concept of the *corpus.* "The body, the Church," he says with forceful brevity. (1 Cor. 12:27; Col. 1:18) But he combines this concept with the idea of the spiritually transformed corporeality of the risen Christ. So he constructs the fruitful concept of the *corpus Christi mysticum* of which the believers are members. (1 Cor. 12:12ff.)

And then St. Paul's image expands into cosmic dimensions. The Epistle to the Ephesians (1:22ff.) and that to the Colossians (1:15ff.) announce with visionary power that the "body of Christ," transformed by the Spirit in the Resurrection, shall take hold of the whole world and draw it into the unity of one life whose fulness is ordered and guided by the ruling power of the sacred Head.

The vital powers of this Church are enormous. The individual persons are incorporated in it, yet each of these is also immediately related to Christ and has his own individuality. (1 Cor. 12ff.) Each one is a "member." We have already suggested a modern image: each one is a "cell" in this great living organism, carried, arranged and united by the molding force which proceeds from the sacred Head. The question arises how the individual life and personal dignity of each one is related to this mighty totality. The answer which follows immediately from the organic image would be that the individuality, the personal life and freedom of each one is not crushed by the vitalizing energy of the whole but on the contrary is emphasized and supported by it in order that what we call "life" may unfold. The passage of the Epistle to the Corinthians to which we have referred expresses it very clearly. The Church is a church of persons and personalities.

Here an important phenomenon becomes clear—that of authority. That Christ gave to the Church authority—that is, competence and power—is proved by words such as these:

If thy brother shall offend against thee, go and rebuke him between thee and him alone. If he shall hear thee, thou shalt gain thy brother. And if he will not hear thee, take with thee one or two more, that in the mouth of two or three witnesses every word may stand. And if he will not hear them, tell the Church. And if he will not hear the Church, let him be to thee as the heathen and publican.[1] Amen, I say to you, whatsoever you shall bind upon earth, shall be bound also in heaven, and whatsoever you shall loose upon earth, shall be loosed also in heaven. (Matt. 18:15–18)

At once the question arises: What is the nature of this authority—especially in view of the role which the Church has sometimes had to play in history? Here again it is Jesus himself who gives a very clear answer. It is a competence and power not of lordship but of service. When the mother of the sons of Zebedee requested for them positions of honor in the kingdom of God, Jesus said,

You know that the princes of the Gentiles lord it over them, and they that are the greater exercise power upon them. It shall not be so among you, but whosoever will be the greater among you let him be your minister, and he that will be first among you shall be your servant; even as the Son of Man is not come to be ministered unto, but to minister. (Matt. 20:25–28)

These words indicate the difference between the use which "Gentile" rulers make of their power and that which God demands of those who have authority in the Church.

And in order to connect in the minds of the apostles an image of the exercise of authority for service, that is, an authority based on love and selflessness, with the memory of their last gathering before His death, He had, before instituting the great mystery of the Church, the Eucharist, washed their dusty feet. He performed the service of a slave, and said,

> Know you what I have done to you? You call me Master and Lord, and you say well, for so I am. If then I, being your Lord and Master, have washed your feet, you also ought to wash one another's feet. For I have given you an example, that as I have done to you, so you do also. (John 13:12–15)

The Christian concept of existence can be summarized as follows: God is the Lord and the Omnipotent, and omnipotent is His sway. But His omnipotent rule is love and "love in seriousness"—in such seriousness that this love, as the life of Jesus reveals, becomes His destiny.[2]

This love—we must emphasize it again—indicates the ever incomprehensible decision of the Infinite that the finite should exist, should be itself, should flourish and reach perfection. God's love is His will that the person should exist in a state of dignity and freedom which may not be violated, which God himself respects and does not force even when it sets itself against His will.

This fundamental element of Christian existence shall again be realized in the Church—and shall be made possible by the personal working of the Holy Spirit. It begins with the renouncing of force and constraint, and with the confidence that the apparent powerlessness which ensues will yet lead to good. It also demands a silent reverence even if the person appealed to closes his mind or rebels, even if his freedom says no when it should say yes. The final criterion for the history of the Church is not the height of her cultural achievement, nor even of her religious culture, but the degree of clarity with which her members, both clergy and laity, recognize that the vital powers which Christ has given the Church become active only insofar as they take the form not of lordship but of love and service. This they must recognize, and must act accordingly.

The transformation of authority into service and of power into love is one with the charge to preach the gospel. For the gospel means the revelation of the mystery that God has eternally willed that His omnipotence should be love, love in all seriousness; and this will has been carried out in the creation, redemption and sanctification of men and of the world. But the history of the Church is the history of the understanding of this task attained by her members, of the sincerity of their will to fulfill it, and of the measure in which this attempt succeeds. But since the Church consists of human beings, this history is a concatenation of effort, advances and realizations. Between these lie periods of relapse when authority is understood as lordship and power as force.

We cannot apply the modern idea of progress to the history of the Church. This idea constitutes a fatal illusion. The noblest thing that lives in man is the will to become better and ever better; it is the yearning for perfection. But this will and this yearning are personal. They can be realized only in freedom—with the attendant danger of the possibility of *yes* and *no,* of success and failure. The idea of progress confuses all this with the concept of "evolution" which is derived from the determinism of nature. This deceives man about the character of his existence and paralyzes his noblest powers. The realization of the charge given to the church is of another kind. It takes place—or does not—in trial, decision, steadfastness or failure.

Hence the fundamental Christian concept of judgment refers also to the Church—more exactly to the embodiment of the Church in the individual cleric and layman. And much of the history of the Church, her persecutions, her powerlessness and failure—"much" not "all," for we must not forget that the Church also faces a resolute hostility—much of this is a judgment; that is, the consequence or rather the penalty for failing to carry out her great charge.

In our pluralistic age the repeated question, by what sign the Church can be recognized as the Church of the Lord, becomes particularly urgent.

In view of the thoughts we have suggested the answer must be, "It can be recognized by the fact that it turns authority into service, and power into love." This is implied in the statement of Christ which St. John records in the last discourse: "By this shall all men know that you are my disciples, if you have love one for another." (13:35)

Of course the questioner must also consider that this answer cannot be read off like the indicator of a barometer. There are certain prerequisites for receiving it, especially the will to understand and also to grant to the Church what we always claim for ourselves, the recognition of the insufficiency of all things human. And the Church is composed of human beings.

The answer to another question is also suggested by our reflections; namely, to what extent Church history is theology. This question becomes urgent when we see how Church history, under the pressure of the assumption that it must become "science" in the modern sense, is in danger of becoming a minor division of the history of scholarship. Church history becomes what it should be, namely theology, when it views the Church from the point of view of her mission. And this mission is to proclaim the message of God's love which operates in creation, redemption and sanctification. But this proclamation becomes effective only when the transformation of authority into love and of power into service takes place at the same time.

Of course the right viewpoint also demands that we recognize not only the faithful carrying out of the mission but also the failures. And this again is only possible when we permit ourselves to see clearly and to apply properly the criterion of reality and truth.

Finally we must indicate—though briefly—something which characterizes the living being which we call the Church: namely that it has a cosmic relation. This relation is essential to it even where its external measure is slight, for it is primarily and essentially of a qualitative rather than a quantitative nature, though it is quantitative also when regarded as a goal.

For, instructed by revelation, the Church sees the world not as the modern concept of nature sees it, which, even while recognizing the cosmos fundamentally as finite, yet acts as if nature were infinite, or more precisely, absolute, the one and all, without beginning or end, the simple existent, which is its own cause and can be understood through itself alone. Rather, the church regards the world as a creation, a work, determined and supported by the one and only absolute, the Creator. From this point of view she considers the world, in its smallest details, as a whole.

Whether the Church realizes this wholeness in her attitude, that means, gives to every creature the freedom of being and of development which is its due according to the will of the Creator, that is another question.

We must also add that this cosmic relation means something else than indefinite generality. The Catholicity which from her very origin is possible for the Church, and is the mission given to her, also implies unmistakable identity and clear recognizability.

Revelation and Mystery

We are speaking of the Church that was born through the Holy Spirit on the day of Pentecost. To her Christ entrusted Himself and His cause. She is not merely the sum total of those who acknowledge Christ, nor yet the community which grows from the faith of individuals sharing the same truth and their obedience to the same rule of life. She is rather a structure, a living whole. We may best express this by saying that she is a living being which was born at that time and has been growing throughout history, developing, struggling, suffering and fulfilling its destiny. But its content is Christ. He lives in the Church, works through her and gives Himself through her.

But we must consider more carefully the meaning of the statement that Christ is in the Church. It was St. Paul who spoke not only emphatically but prophetically of this Christian sense of "in." In all probability he did not meet Christ during His lifetime. But he says, "I give you to understand, brethren, that the gospel which was preached by me is not according to man. For neither did I receive it of man, nor did I learn it, but by the revelation of Jesus Christ." (Gal. 1:11–12) On the way to Damascus the risen Christ laid hold of him. Thereafter he said that Christ was "in" him.

In this same letter to the Galatians we read "And I live, now not I, but Christ lives in me." (2:20) What does this "in" mean? Evidently it does not mean that he is merely occupied interiorly with the person, the teaching, the work and the destiny of Christ; that he understands and loves Him and depends upon Him. St. Paul means more: that the Lord is really in him. But this certainly cannot mean that Christ is in him in a concrete way, as—if the reader will permit us to use the comparison for the sake of making our meaning clear—the embryonic child is present in the mother's womb.

If we understand him rightly, Paul's line of thought is as follows: When Christ died and rose again, something mysterious happened to Him. The Spirit—that same spirit by which the Son of God had become Man and by whose power He taught (Luke 1:35; Mark 1:10ff.)—penetrated and transformed Him. Then the Jesus, who lived an earthly life and was limited by all the bounds which confine us also, became the "Lord of Glory." This does not mean that He stripped Himself of His body; it is a significant fact that St. John recounts how Jesus appeared to His disciples after His Resurrection and showed to the doubting Thomas the marks of His wounds, as a kind of summation of His earthly existence. (20:27) Whatever Christ has done and suffered remains a living reality in Him for all eternity.

Nor does the statement mean that the Jesus of history was a mere man, though possessed of tremendous religious power, and that only after His death did He become the Christ of faith by the experience of the community. It is true that by his earthly birth He became man, but He remained what He was from "the beginning," the eternal Son of God. The Christ of glory is the same person as the Jesus of the humiliation, but now unhampered and exercising His power without any earthly impediment. Hence He can also dwell in the person who believes in Him. Modern man is a subjectivist and psychologist. He considers such a statement "physical" or "objective" or "mythical," or whatever word he may use to disguise his aversion to a clear designation of fact. But actually he has forgotten what is meant by, not intellect or logic, but the living spirit, *pneuma*, and spiritual reality.

This same Jesus also lives within that being which we call "the Church." In order to express this, St. Paul forms the concept of the *soma Christou*, the empirical yet spiritual, that is, the historical "body of Christ." In the Epistle to the Ephesians he says: "He has subjected all things under his feet and has made him head over all the Church, which is his body and the fullness of him who fills all in all." (Eph. 1:23) And again:

> Who is the image of the invisible God, the firstborn of every creature; for in him were all things created in heaven and on earth, visible and invisible, whether thrones or dominations, or principalities or powers. All things were created by him and in him. And he is before all, and by him all things endure. And he is the head of the body, the Church, he who is the beginning, the firstborn from the dead, that in all things he may hold the primacy. (Col. 1:15–18)

In the first Epistle to the Corinthians St. Paul also speaks of this mystery, in the passage where he tells of the variety of spiritual gifts which nevertheless form a living unity in the totality of the Church:

> For as the body is one and yet has many members, and all the members of the body whereas they are many, yet are one [single and unified] body, so also is Christ. For in one Spirit were we all baptized into one body, whether Jews or Gentiles, whether bond or free. (I Cor. 12:12–13)

Ancient sociology pictured the state, the commonwealth, as a body which comprises many members and functions within its unity. St. Paul gives this concept a new significance: Jesus Christ operates within the totality of the believer and by the power of His function as the head unites them into a living unity, the Church. We may also complete the image by saying that He is the soul of this body, permeating everything, the individual and the whole. Christ lives in the Church and she proclaims Him to the world. Through her word, her sacraments and regulations, her whole life and being—which is itself a miracle, for according to all the laws of history she should long since have disintegrated and vanished—she reveals the Lord.

As soon as we think about this, another thing obtrudes itself upon our thought, the possibility of being scandalized by the Church.

When the Son of God became one of us, this meant not merely that He touched interiorly a man named Jesus who lived in Nazareth, or became for him a prophetic experience, but that He entered into the unity of personal existence with him, so that thereafter what Jesus did was the deed of the Son of God and what Jesus experienced and suffered became the destiny of the Son of God. St. John says explicitly that he who sees Jesus sees the Logos: "We saw his glory, the glory as it were of the only-begotten of the Father, full of grace and truth." (John 1:14) He says the same thing at the beginning of his first epistle and it seems as if he wished to emphasize the tremendous message so forcibly that nothing might erase it:

> That which was from the beginning, which we have heard, which we have seen with our eyes, which we have looked upon, and our hands have handled, of the word of life: for the life was manifested, and we have seen and do bear witness and declare unto you the life eternal, which was with the Father and has appeared to us: that which we have seen and have heard we declare unto you. (I John 1:1–3)

Christ is the essential revelation. In Him, if we may say this, the eternal Son of God translated Himself into human terms. He who of Himself dwells "in light inaccessible," (I Tim. 6:16) who lives "in the bosom of the Father," (John 1:18) has come among us, has stood before us visibly in this man who was called Jesus of Nazareth; He spoke audibly in his words, could be touched in his body. Our own being offers a parallel for this. Our spiritual soul cannot be perceived by the senses but it is constantly translated by our body. The man is a soul become visible, audible, tangible in the body, spirit made manifest. This is a kind of indication of the way in which Jesus, the Son of God made manifest, is a living revelation.

But the situation may also have another effect. Someone might say: How can this be the Son of God when he appears in all respects to be a man? We recall the incident, when Jesus went into the synagogue in His native town. (Luke 4:14ff.) The temple-servant handed Him the scroll of the Prophet Isaias. He unrolled it and came upon the prophecy concerning the Messias who was to come and help all. (Isa. 61:1) Then Jesus said, "Today this scripture is fulfilled in your ears"—that is, in His person. And what happened? At first they praised the grace and power of His words. But then they wondered how He could have this power—He, a citizen of their town, whom they had known from childhood: "Is not this the son of Joseph?"—a man like all others, sharing our common humanity. Jesus called their attention to the danger inherent in this likeness, the danger of being caught in it, of not seeing the revelation: "Amen I say to you, that no prophet is accepted in his own country." Then their mood changed. Rage and deadly hatred broke out and they forced Him to the edge of the hill on which the city was built, to cast Him down. Is this not strange? For a moment they felt the divine power of His word, and then everything changed, and there was a prelude to that tragedy which was to be consummated on Calvary.

That which was to reveal the Son of God in Jesus, the fact that in Him the divinity can be translated into human terms and so beheld—this very

fact also conceals Him, so that there results a counterpoise which necessitates a decision—a yes or no. But it is more than that; we must say, a "yes"
that grows into love, and becomes faith—or a "no" that turns into hate,
and becomes scandal. The possibility that one or the other could be the
consequence of Christ's coming was inherent in the Incarnation. He himself was aware of it. When John the Baptist from his prison sent messengers to Jesus to ask: "Art thou he that is to come or look we for another?"
Jesus answered them with the words of Isaias about the Messianic miracles. These had been fulfilled, and the Messianic nature of Jesus could be
"seen and heard and handled." But He added immediately: "And blessed
is he that shall not be scandalized in me." (Matt. 11:2–6)

But what induces the proper decision? When does the one who encounters Christ see through the counterpoise of revelation and concealment? When he has good will. When, that is, grace enlightens him. The
Sermon on the Mount speaks more clearly, in saying: "Blessed are the clean
of heart, for they shall see God." (Matt. 5:8) This statement is primarily a
promise for eternity; but eternity begins even in time, at any given moment. And so the statement means also that those who are clean of heart,
that is, those who love rightly, love the right thing and in the right way,
shall be able to see aright. For in these matters it is the heart that guides
the eyes. The heart enlightens the eyes so that they may see and distinguish, or it blinds them so that things become confused.

For this too there is a parallel, in the relation of man to man, a dim
anticipatory sketch of the counterpoise attending our encounter with Him
who called Himself "the Son of Man." Man is the image of God, created
by the summons of His love for freedom and dignity. This is expressed
even in his erect stature, in his countenance and in all his expressions. He
who has clear vision sees this and responds with the reverence that is due
to such a being. But it can happen that someone says: "What is this creature that is born and dies, that is subject to so many needs, urged by instincts and tormented by fears? What is this two-legged animal?" This

results in the irreverence which does not see what a man is and which is active everywhere at present. For the nature of man is not plain and simple, cannot be immediately determined and grasped, but it reveals and conceals itself at the same time, so that one may recognize and respect man as a person, but also reduce him to a thing, use him and misuse him. So the eye must be able to see, in consequence of a heart that is "clean," ready to satisfy those demands which a person makes upon us and which make our relations to a person so much more difficult than our relations to a mere thing, but also much nobler and more rewarding. Man is always in danger of being "scandalized" by man—and isn't his being so almost a universal situation today?

And now, this necessity of deciding between faith and scandal, which is essential for our relation to Christ, where do we meet it, since the Lord is no longer immediately and historically present but has entered into His glory? Who exercises, if we may say so, the function of revealing and concealing at the same time with the resultant counterpoise? It is the Church which does this.

Christ entrusted Himself to her. In her He lives as "the way, the truth and the life" (John 14:6) eternally valid. But the Church does not stand in metaphysical remoteness, but in time. She is history. In historical concreteness she encounters the individual and "blessed is he that shall not be scandalized in her." The one she encounters may see the eternal in her. The very fact that she still exists after two thousand years is revealing. Man can perceive in her the radiance of the Christ who dwells within her. This is really what the person who comes to the Church is seeking, the mysterious interior life which is expressed in the Eucharist, in the Sacraments, in the Saints, in the transcendent truth of her dogmas. He can "see, hear, and handle" this if his heart is "clean," ready for true love. But he can also say, "What is this structure, one of many religious associations, which arose at a certain time and developed in various ways in the course of history? How can it put forth so great a claim?" He can point out deficiencies and faults in the Church, much slackness and indolence, externalization and lack of spirituality, and he may cry out in protest, "Does this thing claim to be the holy church of Christ?"

That this is so is part of her mystery. In her, Christ utters himself in time. His word may be perceived and faith ensues. But it can also be impeded by all that is evil, confused and disordered, and then scandal results. So there arises the counterpoise which necessitates decision. And this occurs not only once, but again and again, in every new situation.

Therefore when we say that Christ is in the Church we must not interpret this as meaning that He stands there visibly and tangibly, like a tree which can be recognized as a tree and nothing else, only as this particular beech or oak or fir-tree. But the statement means that He is in the Church after the manner of revelation, which always includes both manifestation and concealment. That there must first be an interior preparation, a clearness of vision which comes from a heart that is clean, loves rightly and seeks only the truth.

We must also not forget that to recognize the Church and make our decision in her favor is something living and organic. It cannot be done arbitrarily or at any time or in any situation or in any state of mind. Time is required for our ripening, and for daring to say "Yes," for deepening our understanding again and again. Aside from the fact that all is the work of grace and that God gives this when He wills and in the way which is proper in His sight.

Finally, we must remember and reflect with great seriousness on the fact that the Church consists of all those who profess faith in her. Each one of us reveals Christ and each one conceals Him. We can never speak as if the Church stood there and we—I in each instance—stood here and I could view and analyze and judge her, pointing out responsibilities and failures. I must always include myself in the image that I construct of her, must refer to myself the judgment I pass upon her. Then the image and the judgment will be different—as though I were speaking of the faults of a person whose life is closely bound up with mine. I tell what is good about him and reject what is faulty, but all in a spirit of love. Only then shall I penetrate more deeply into the nature of that mysterious reality which has been moving through history for two thousand years, loved as nothing earthly has been loved but also hated and persecuted with a bitterness never experienced by anything else.

The Church and Contemporaneity with Jesus Christ

The phenomenon considered in the preceding reflection is so significant, and so much depends upon our understanding it properly that we shall advert to it once more, and from a particular point of view.

When a young person begins to mature he naturally tests his attitude toward his faith. He experiences a crisis. He asks whether he can believe what he has been taught at home, in school and in sermons, indeed whether, according to the criterion of truth, he ought to or can be permitted to believe it. He asks whether and how it will give him support for his existence, and guidance for his life and his work. Perhaps he thinks at first that for the sake of honesty he should break with it. But then he finds the wish stirring within him to discover some religious foothold, and he makes a new effort to reach Christian truth.

And now I should like to speak of a personal experience which, however, I believe may be of significance for others also.

A statement in the New Testament had always touched me with that insistence which indicates direction and guidance. It is found in Matthew 10:39 and reads: "He that will find," that is, save, "his life shall lose it and he that shall lose his life for me, shall find it." This text refers primarily to martyrdom, but as usually happens when some such word falls into our interior life, it took on a very urgent significance for me, and as a result of the double meaning of the Greek word *psyche,* which means both 'life" and "soul," it seemed to say to me: "He who holds fast to his soul shall lose it and he who surrenders it will gain it." This statement deals with the fundamental mystery of the religious life, which is that a man attains to his real, divinely intended self only if he departs from his immediate "I," and gains himself in the true sense only if he gives himself up. Now the great question was: where does this departing and giving up take place? Who can call me in this way and demand my soul of me in such a way that the surrender really takes place, that I do not secretly remain with myself and hold fast to myself?

The first answer was: Only God can do that. But who is God? How must one conceive of Him in order to have the right idea?

The introduction to this book spoke of the phenomenon of structurized thought; that is, the fact that the process of cognition and the results of our efforts to know are partly determined by psychological tendencies. In connection with the problem of religion this brings up a disturbing thought. If someone speaks of God merely from his own experience and according to his own standards, then what he designates as "God" reveals a suspicious similarity to his own nature. One man sees in God the first cause of all events, another pure being, another the idea of good, others the foundation of the world or the secret of life or the spirit of the nation or the course of history—and so on, according as the particular tendencies of the person involved determine his choice and his relation to one or another side of the divine reality and cause him to lose sight of the living whole. Sometimes the similarity is so great that the "God" whom different persons acknowledge is really an ideal or wishful image of their own nature, and we can read in the image of the divine the character of the person whose thoughts construct it.

The way to truth, then, cannot be to "seek God" as we like to say, merely through our own experience and our own thought. For if the seeker pictures God in this way and establishes a relationship with Him, he really remains with himself and holds fast to himself—only in a more subtle and more closely binding manner than if he declared openly: "I do not want anything to do with God; I am sufficient for myself."

Then who is God in truth? How must we conceive of Him in order to have the right idea of Him, really to go to Him, to commit ourselves to Him and find freedom with Him? Evidently something is lacking. We lack a warrant which will guarantee that when we say "God" we do not actually mean "I." But where can we find this?

In answer there appears the figure of Christ. The more clearly our gaze is fixed upon Him the more plainly we see that His claim to be the revealer of the living God is justified. He stands in a close proximity to the true God which enables Him to know more of the mind of God than anyone else. He lives in a relation of unity with God which brings it about that what He speaks is spoken by God Himself.

So we understand the fundamental Christian truth of the Mediator and Redeemer. We see how for St. Paul and St. John "to speak of God" meant "to speak with Christ of God."

The meaning of Christ's statement in St. John's Gospel "I am...the truth" becomes clear. (John 14:6)

But in relation to that basic experience of which we spoke in the beginning, this means: The God who is able to demand our soul of us and to give it to us anew is only vouched for when we seek Him not through merely subjective experience and "autonomous" thinking, but when He approaches us in His reality and sovereignty in the words and the character of Christ. Jesus himself said, "No one knows...who the Father is, but the Son, and he to whom the Son will reveal him" (Luke 10:22), and very plainly and directly in St. John's Gospel "He who has seen me has seen the Father." (John 14:9)

Christ is not only the one who alone guarantees the knowledge of the true God, but He is the one through whom a living approach to God must be made if we are really to reach Him. as Jesus also says very pointedly in St. John's Gospel: "I am the way... No man comes to the Father but by me." (John 14:6)

All this means that the "freely accessible" God does not exist. For the one who claims to seek and experience and know God autonomously, He remains the Unknown "who dwells in light inaccessible." (1 Tim. 6:16) Man approaches Him only by following Christ. It is He who shows us the direction and teaches us the proper disposition.

But this is not really the end of the journey. The various studies and researches dealing with the life of Jesus, and the opinions about Him that circulate among men, show how varied and manifold is the image that men paint of Him. And that not only in the sense in which the image of Christ in the mosaics differs from that of the Gothic period or the romanesque or the baroque—differences stemming from the dispositions and interpretations of various periods of history, in which, nevertheless the essential element remained the same, namely the incarnate Son, consubstantial with the Father—but the differences touch His very nature. Again and again the essential point is lost, which St. Paul and St. John proclaimed so insistently: He is the eternal Son of God who became incarnate in time and remains man while "sitting at the right hand of the Father." Jesus is portrayed as a mere man or as a solar myth; as a sage like Socrates or a hellenistic mystic; as a friend of souls and a social reformer; a religious genius and a spiritual revolutionary; one of the line of prophets or the revealer of a Germanic way of life; a psychopath, schizophrenic or megalomaniac, and so forth and so forth. A more penetrating examination again reveals that disturbing similarity of the respective portraits to the persons who have painted them. Often it seems as if these figures of Christ were idealized self-portraits of those who imagined them.

In view of such portraits and their origin, how can we rely upon the word that "no man knows the Father but he," and "no man comes to the Father except through him?" In other words, where is the guarantee that Christ himself gives us?

Here we come to the Church.

Jesus knew that He and His message were absolutely decisive. So He wished this to be carried on "to all nations" and "even to the end of the world." (Matt. 28:19–20) But in His comments about this continuation of His message the concept of a book does not occur, as we saw in our first meditation. He does speak repeatedly of the written word of God, but always in reference to the Old Testament. But the means of propagating his own message would be the living proclamation by those whom He had chosen. (Acts 1:2) The methods by which they would carry out their mission were left to them: the spoken and the written word, commemorative action, deeds that gave testimony, and exemplary living, a combination upon which the fullness of the Spirit was bestowed through the events of the day of Pentecost and which thereafter continued to the end of time. This combination is the Church.

Christ guarantees the reality of the living Father; but the true image of Christ is guaranteed by the Church, or, more precisely, by the Holy Spirit who speaks in her. Of her Jesus says, "He that hears you hears me; and he that despises you despises me; and he that despises me, despises him that sent me." (Luke 10:16) In the words of the Church He is speaking; in His words the Father speaks.

But as regards the Scriptures, they are a living element of the Church. They have sprung from her, completed in the course of the first century and gathered into a valid canon by the Church herself around the turn of the century. It is the Church of Christ who again and again exhorts the individual to give up his own soul in order to receive it again renewed and restored to its true nature.

This exhortation is such that it cannot be pronounced by the autonomous will of the person addressed, but it springs from a reality which is independent of his pleasure. If he misunderstands the message, it corrects him. If he fabricates a Christ according to his own wishes, it defends the true image. If he eliminates from the figure of Christ the elements that scandalize him, it emphasizes these. In this constant encounter with the concrete, contemporary Church, the figure of Christ constantly rises up again intact and unimpaired in its sovereignty, bearing witness to the Father as He truly is.

All this means that the step which really led to the freedom of faith in the complete reality of Christ, and through him in the sovereignty of the living God, is the belief that Christ speaks in the Church, so that he who hears her hears Christ Himself. (Luke 10:16)

This statement may sound strange at a time when it has become for many a matter of course to hold that he who submits to the Church loses the freedom of the Gospel. In actual fact the Church educates us for Christian freedom. Of course this freedom means something else than the psychological possibility of choosing what suits our taste or the philosophical autonomy to judge right and wrong according to our own standards. It means that the one who is ready to believe is constantly freed from the constraint of psychological, sociological, historical and other presumptions and brought before the complete reality of the God who reveals himself in Christ.

The step into the Church is a true act of faith, and persevering in the Church is also a true matter of faith. Therefore they involve all the struggles and dangers that inhere in such a relation. But of this we must speak in greater detail.

In order to understand what the Church is, from the point of view adopted in our discussion, we may seek assistance from an author whose name one might not expect to hear in this connection, the great evangelical thinker Sören Kierkegaard. He wrote a remarkable book entitled

Philosophical Fragments and a commentary on it entitled, "A concluding unscholarly postscript to the philosophical fragments." This work poses a thesis which at first strikes us as odd. He says that in the fullest sense one can become a Christian only in "contemporaneity," using this word in its exact sense as historical, not psychological contemporaneity, with Jesus Christ. Only in that case can the decision to believe involve the risk that must be bound up with it if it is to be genuine. Only he can really become a Christian who lives in the same country and the same time as Christ and meets him in person.

According to Kierkegaard this meeting takes place as follows. A man comes along. For some reason or other a conversation begins and in the course of the conversation he declares that he is the Son of God and demands that the other believe this, for his salvation depends upon it. This claim not only sounds curious but it arouses indignation—or what is worse—laughter: You were born yesterday and will die tomorrow. You live in this country, wear a garment that was made in a certain place, eat bread that was baked in a certain house—and you claim to be the Son of God? (cf. John 8:57) But the strange thing is—Kierkegaard calls the situation and the assertion "the absolute paradox"—that the claim is right, for this man is really the Son of God. Only, the statement is made, so to speak, from the other side, from eternity. And how can the person addressed, who stands on this side, in time, and so in an uncertain situation—how can he attain certainty that the speaker really is what he claims to be—attain to that unique certainty upon which his eternal salvation depends—that is, faith? This is a tremendous decision. If he decides rightly, then he finds, through the man confronting him, a relation to the redeeming God. But if he is wrong? If the claimant is only a man like all others? Perhaps outstanding because of some talent? Or perhaps one who suffers from religious delusions? Then the person addressed is not merely mistaken but has committed himself to utter nonsense. He has, as Kierkegaard says, made himself ridiculous in a horrible way—ridiculous by eternal standards.

One could mention all kinds of reasons which would cause him to take the risk of faith. For example, the words of this man who is called Jesus and comes from Nazareth contain wondrous wisdom; he performs amazing miracles; his character gives the impression of holy purity; a mysterious influence can be felt in his presence, and so on. But do these constitute proofs which remove the danger of the step expressed by the words, "I believe that you are the Son of God and in you I believe in the Father?" Kierkegaard says no, for whatever amazing phenomenon I encounter, it is always human, enclosed in space and time and humanity, and therefore finite and debatable. Every reason for a "yes" could be countered by a reason for a "no." Everything that could possibly be a matter of experience is unrelated to the absolute magnitude of the matter in question. Therefore the step into faith always remains something tremendous, the risk of the "absolute paradox," the decision to expect the absolute and eternal from the finite and temporal; the confidence that this decision will lead to a conformity with the inscrutable intention of God and so to eternal salvation. Everything supports the probability that the person addressed will indignantly reject the proposal, that is, will be offended, scandalized. To penetrate this narrow defile, says Kierkegaard, is to have faith.

But what of the man who lives in a later age—years, centuries after the life of Jesus has ended? After countless persons have taken the step into faith and now can bear witness by their own lives that it leads to salvation? After wise, important, reliable men have meditated about Jesus of Nazareth, interpreted him and explained the greatness of his teaching? To assent to this, says Kierkegaard, is not really to believe, for the test of contemporaneity would be lacking. Is faith then impossible for men of later ages? No, says Kierkegaard; but they must lift themselves above the situation. They must put away what later times have thought and experienced and return to contemporaneity with Christ in their thought and life. This, he says, is difficult, and he does not hesitate to use for it an expression which is hard and destroys all enthusiasm and warmth of feeling, "a training for Christianity." This training the man of a later age must inflict upon himself; only so can he reach the essential situation which permits the decision of faith.

These thoughts express a deep Christian seriousness. But closer investigation reveals that such a "training for Christianity" is impossible, for we simply cannot escape the fact that we live in a later age, long after Jesus Christ. Kierkegaard's idea is, to use a word that he himself used, a "desperate" one. It grew out of his struggle against a rationalistic, moralistic Christianity which had become merely a matter of habit. And yet there is some truth in it. A serious faith can be attained only by contemporaneity with the messenger of the revelation. But where and how?

In the sense of his immediate historical reality Jesus of Nazareth can never become my contemporary—but his messengers can; and in them He Himself "comes" (Luke 10:16) and the sum total of His messengers is the Church. Every age is contemporary with her for she goes on through all the ages. The teacher who speaks of Christ and his message; the priest who explains the word and baptizes; the celebration of the Eucharist for which the congregation assembles around the altar; the bishop and the teachers of the faith, whom he ordains—all this is the Church. Through her I receive the message. The Church also includes the believing family in whose atmosphere I receive the spirit and the language of Christianity; the people of the congregation among whom I stand at the altar; the others everywhere in the world who know that they are one in the unity of faith. All these, living and teaching, are really and immediately my contemporaries. And their whole humanity, the good and also the questionable, joins in proclaiming the message and demands to be included and supported in the Christian "we."

In all of this Christ is present and speaks to me. He speaks to me not as an isolated figure, but as the Church.

But in what a strange relation she stands to him who speaks in her! Everything in the Church is so full of the human elements—commonplace, ordinary, even wicked human elements. How much has been perpetuated in theories, rules, regulations and prescriptions which did not belong to the original message! How many accretions have adhered to her in the long passage through history! What a great responsibility rests upon her for all that has been said and done, or left unsaid and neglected in her name!

So the question naturally arises: Is this the witness which I can and should believe? Is this the figure through which the Holy Spirit speaks—He who stepped into history on the day of Pentecost and shall "lead us into all truth," as Jesus promised? (John 16:13) The whole difficulty of what Kierkegaard called the "absolute paradox" rushes down upon us. But the way of faith leads through it, for hereby I find out about Christ. To think that one can have direct experience of Him is an illusion, for even the book of the New Testament which we might suppose would bring the reader immediately before Christ, really belongs to the Church. The enormity of the problems which arise at this point is attested to by all that we call New Testament scholarship and also by all those persons who say that they cannot find in these texts any morally binding word of God. And yet God is speaking here.

The step into the Church is certainly not what a commonplace polemic thinks it to be: an escape into indolence, a surrender of one's own responsibility to priest, bishop or Pope. This may be true in individual cases, of course, just as the will to make one's own decision may be subjectivistic self-assertion. But the truth is that we learn about Jesus only through the Church, and that it is in view of her that the decision of faith is made because she alone brings us into the condition of contemporaneity.

Indeed, this decision must be made again and again. Fundamentally and for the first time we make it when we enter the Church. But again and again we experience the effects of the all-too-human element in the Church. Again and again we hear—not only from others but from our own feelings—the objection: what I meet here cannot be the Church as

Christ meant her to be. And again and again we must decide: This is she; I believe!

But then we experience anew the reassuring, expanding and liberating effect that she produces. For the Church is that which the polemic against her not only does not see but turns into its opposite. She is the guarantee, intended by Christ Himself, that He can, out of the very freedom of His being, approach every man.

The Guardian and Dispenser of Truth

I n our last two reflections we considered the two-fold effect proceeding from the Church. She stands in history, and by the power of the Holy Spirit she proclaims the Savior through her existence, her words and her actions. She translates Him into the language of our human life, brings Him into relation with its forces and structures. But by the very fact that she does this—that she is human—all human qualities appear in her. Indeed, one is almost tempted to say that these human qualities develop most strongly in the religious atmosphere, or at any rate can be perceived here with particular intensity. Consequently a kind of veil is drawn over the message and makes it possible, indeed, rather natural, for men to reject the message as unworthy of credence. Therefore the Church is the everlasting sign, since the ascension of the Lord, before which men make the great decision for faith or scandal.

The content of the Church is Christ. In preserving Him she preserves herself, for without Him she is nothing. In understanding Him and His message she understands herself, for it is He who constitutes the meaning of her existence. In handing Him on to men she herself lives, for even though she exercises the most varied cultural influences in the course of history, her essential lifework consists in bringing the reality of Christ into our existence.

Let us try to see more exactly how this takes place, when the Church holds up the image of Christ in history and makes it plain to us, feature by feature.

Just as soon as the proclamation of the message began, after Jesus had ascended to the Father, the interpretation of His figure began also. Whoever speaks of Christ can do so only with the words and concepts that he draws from the materials of Jesus' personal existence and the historical situation. This implies the attempt to understand the sacred content, to explain it and bring it into relation with the thought of the time. But this immediately gives rise to the danger of misinterpretation.

The first New Testament documents that we possess are the early Epistles of St. Paul. Paul had never seen Jesus. He had heard of the Lord first from those whom he met in Jerusalem, and then in a very decisive way through his experience on the road to Damascus. So what he says of Christ is already an interpretation, and it becomes this more and more, the longer he thinks, prays and teaches and so penetrates more deeply into the sacred nature of Christ. If we look more closely we notice that Paul also meets with adversaries, who likewise interpret, but incorrectly. Among these are primarily the Judaists, who considered the ritual law of the Old Testament as binding even for the New and so questioned the sovereignty of Him who said of Himself: "The Son of man is Lord over the Sabbath." (Matt. 12:8) Through Paul the Church bore witness to the sovereignty of Him who was "obedient unto death," and proclaimed "Jesus Christ is the Lord." (Phil. 2:8, 11)

Another distortion of the real image of Christ is already referred to in St. Paul's Epistles (e.g., 1 Tim. 1:3) and then we find it recurring again and again throughout the whole of Christian history, constantly repelled by the Church and constantly reappearing. This distortion is gnosticism.

After St. Paul we find St. John waging a definite battle against it in his Gospel, his Epistles and the Apocalypse.

The gnostics begin with a concept of the world in which spirit and matter are opposed and hostile to each other. The spirit is good: it is God; matter is evil: it is the demon. From this point of view there can be no real Incarnation, for the Logos, who comes from the good God, cannot unite with the evil matter. Therefore, according to the gnostics, the Logos had only a phantom body on earth, lived a phantom life and died only in appearance. At the moment when the man Jesus died, the Logos departed from Him and returned to the Father. This sounds very spiritual, but actually it destroys everything, for the Christian message is not concerned with raising the soul to complete spirituality but with liberating man for a new and holy existence.

The message of Jesus does not concern the spirit alone but the whole man. He is to live his human life according to the will of God, to die the death which sin brought into the world (Rom. 5:12–14), but thereafter to rise again and as man have eternal life. But this presupposes that the Logos himself became man, really and entirely; that in the man Jesus the eternal Son of God died and rose again and eternally "sits at the right hand of the Father" in divine-human glory. To this the Church bears witness, and how energetically she does this we can see in the Prologue of St. John's Gospel, where we find the sentence: "The Word became flesh"; not only "man," but—with almost offensive harshness—"flesh."

After it has been made clear that there was a real Incarnation, the question arose as to how the divinity of Christ could be reconciled with the basic statement of biblical religion, that God is one; He alone is Lord of the world because He is Lord of Himself.

The world at that time was still largely polytheistic in its thinking. The religious impulse to express the manifold nature of the universe in many different divinities was still active.

Hence there was great danger that the unicity of God, or, out of regard for this unicity, the divinity of Christ would be questioned, and there began the long struggles with Arianism in all its variations and complications. These continued through the fourth and fifth centuries and were all the more serious because the theological discussions were closely associated with political affairs. Out of these struggles grew the doctrine of the inner life of God, which maintains that God is one and the only one, but also infinitely fruitful, since begetting and birth occur within Him. He is indeed the absolute Lord, dwelling in "inaccessible light," yet neither lonely nor speechless, but living a life which contains an "I" and a "Thou," a word and an answer.

Here emerges the doctrine of the triune life of God—so absolutely decisive for faith that one can show how its rejection is the first step toward atheism. For if God is the lone *monotheos*, then He requires the world in order to become living and fruitful. Thereby He ceases to be "God" who is "the Lord" and becomes an element—even though it be the prime element—of the world. The doctrine of the Trinity transcends all comprehension, for how could man understand the way in which God lives? And yet its elucidation is the result of great intellectual effort—the effort of an intellect which begins with Revelation and moves within the sphere of its premises so that it does not destroy the mystery but preserves and reveals it. It is the intellect of the Church or of the individual insofar as he is a part of the Church and thinks with her mind. This thinking is clear and imperturbable. Its result is the *lex credendi*, the dogma requiring obedience. But by this very fact the figure of Christ is preserved intact, and faith is freed from the bond of a naturalistic impulse of thought and led to unalloyed truth. Christ is of the same nature as the Father, for there is only one God. But he is related to the Father in the eternal communion of "I" and "thou," the eternal discourse of word and answer. This gives to the figure of Christ its real and proper depth.

The efforts to reveal the mystery—and this revelation also constitutes its preservation—continue. What is the relation of the divine to the human in the person of Jesus Christ?

In Alexandria there was a famous school of theology that was metaphysical and mystical in its thinking. This school directed its attention above all to the unity of the figure of Christ. It was also influenced by the ascetics of the Egyptian desert—men who firmly and fervently directed all their energy toward one thing, to find God and renounce everything for this purpose. When the question arose, in what relation the divine and the human elements in Jesus stood to each other, the school of Alexandria replied, "They blend into one nature." This idea was admirably simple, but it was detrimental to the truth of Christ. For how can man blend with God? What kind of a God would this be who would become fused with the human? What kind of humanity that would fuse with the divine? This concept would leave nothing intact, neither God nor man nor Christ himself.

Then the sober school of Antioch arose and emphasized the impossibility of fusion. For God alone is God and man is only man. So we see how the opposite of the Alexandrian interpretation was worked out as a result of the peculiar dialectic, by which an idea carried to the extreme brings out as a kind of repercussion the contrary idea. It was maintained that what took place in the incarnation of the Logos was a union not of being but only of will—a moral union; the will of the man Jesus being so completely surrendered to the eternal Son of God that it brought about a perfect unity. But this would again destroy the truth of Christ, for he would no longer be the mysterious one who could say "I thirst," and also "I and the Father are one," but would only be a man possessed of the highest religious endowments.

So the discussions continued, carried on with a passionate intensity unknown to us who have grown cool and dispassionate. The outcome, expressed in solemn decisions, was as follows: the unity of the living Christ is unique. It is an identity of the person in different natures. A "person" is not a thing, not an energy, not an event, but the way in which a spiritually determined being exists in itself, belongs to itself, is responsible for itself, in a word is itself, is an "I." This "I" in Christ was the "I" of the eternal Son of God. The human nature of Jesus was based upon this; the actions of the man Jesus determined by it. Thereby the divine nature of the Logos and the human nature of Jesus were wondrously united. Not mingled or confused; the union was chaste and holy. But it was so intimate that within it what belonged to one nature also belonged to the other. This expresses a manner of being, an existence which is unique and which is known to us only through revelation. Even in faith the understanding cannot fathom it, but for the one who contemplates it and ponders upon it it becomes a pure and shining light. A whole world of holy realization is opened to him when he inquires into what close proximity to the divine nature of the Logos the human nature of Jesus is brought by this union, and what takes place within it, and also what the incomprehensible humility of love implied in this union meant for the Logos himself. And then there is the mystery of union with God which all this made possible for redeemed man. We may think of St. Paul's doctrine that Christ is "in" the believer and the believer is in Christ.

This is a statement which "explains" nothing. On the contrary it deepens and intensifies the mystery. It surrounds it, so to speak, with protective concepts and in this way preserves the sacred reality of Christ pure, complete and unified. It is as if a spring bubbled up and then the well-builder came and enclosed it. Surrounded by the solid ring of the wall the spring flows continually providing life and refreshment. The reality of Christ surpasses the bounds of our understanding. Hence there is always the danger that reason will try to simplify it by taking away some of its elements. Then it will seem that Christ has been "explained." But He will no longer be "the Lord," whose sovereignty is high above all human standards. The dogma of the human and divine natures in Christ breaks the presumption of reason and prepares the throne for the incarnate Son of God. In obeying and believing, man enters into the freedom of divine truth.

In modern times a new question arose: Jesus Christ stands in history—but what does that mean? In history one thing always depends upon another and is conditioned by it: events arise from given causes and change when these causes are no longer operative, and so forth. How does Jesus Christ stand in this connection of psychological, social and cultural relations, this continual becoming, changing, and passing away?

The early Christian ages saw Him in a peculiar timelessness. We may think of the Christ of the mosaics enthroned in the apsides of the early basilicas. In His figure the eternal is so predominant that temporal conditions are quite unperceived. But in modern times these are the very things that impress our consciousness and determine our interpretation.

So, for example, the seeker may encounter the typical figures of great men and use these to interpret the nature and the influence of Jesus. He may note the image of the sage who guides us to an understanding of the meaning of life, and may consider Jesus a sage. Or he may meet the founders of the various religions and see in Jesus one of these. Or he may discover the phenomenon of a genius in whom religious feeling becomes creative and may use this to interpret the figure of Christ. Scholars who are interested in social problems see in him the great reformer who experienced the distress of men and wished to lead them by religious means to freedom and happiness. Historians of religion investigate the phenomenon of mythology and state that men's yearning for greatness and liberation usually attaches itself to a definite person and elevates him to an importance which he himself does not really have. This yearning may actually solidify into a figure in which there is not even a nucleus of reality. In this way there arises the theory of a "Christ of faith" for whom the "Jesus of history" is only the starting-point; or even the theory of a "Christ-myth," which has no connection at all with a historical person.

If we survey these attempts they appear as a kind of eddy whirling about the figure of the Lord. Each one of them contains an element of truth. Each theorist is striving, from his own particular viewpoint, to fit Christ into history. They are right in their striving—for the Son of God did really become man, and we may draw certain conclusions from this fact—but only as long as they are based upon a firm faith in the eternal divine sonship of the Lord. We may think of certain problems regarding the psychology of Jesus which have been scarcely inquired into; that is, the nature of the consciousness of the God-man, his will, his sense-perception, his prayer, the interior course of his life, and so forth. But all this may be handled only if we do not, to begin with, fit him into the forms of general human existence but work out the special categories which His divine-human reality demands. It must be a "theological psychology" which is as urgent as it is unexplored.[1] But as soon as these attempts break away from faith, they slip into relativism and the true Christ disappears.

What brings men to the Lord is a longing for redemption. The meaning of this term is found in the command given to Abraham: "Go forth out of thy country and from thy kindred and out of thy father's house, and come into the land which I shall show thee." (Gen. 12:1) This means that man must free himself from the self-will of his rebellious and confused nature and open himself to the revelation of God. But what do those different interpretations do? They draw Christ into the realm of the merely human—and in each case into that aspect of it which the speaker particularly values. If we have once become aware of this we need only open one of these "Lives of Jesus" to obtain a picture of the man who has written it. The image that he paints is always, positively or negatively, his own, merely magnified. It gives expression to a deep-seated danger from which the Redeemer shall deliver him, and the writer creates a Christ who confirms him in his state. He makes the Redeemer useless. From the point of view of the rebellious man who locks himself up within himself we might say he makes Him harmless.

All this the Church opposes, and declares: Christ is the Son of God, but He has entered into history. He became man in a certain country among a certain people and "in all things like unto us." But He is never absorbed by the merely human. He, the liberator, is Himself infinitely free in His actual divinity. For this basic reality of our redemption the Church carries on a struggle through all the ages. On this point she is steadfast and unflinching.

This attitude may on occasion lead to harshness. The Church herself is actualized in history, and that means in human beings. This makes it possible that the act of the preservation of the truth may be influenced by the human element in history, the determination to be in the right, to win and to dominate, the narrow view resulting from antagonism and strife, the equating of a love for eternal truth with mistrust of new questions and experiments. All this may happen. It is a form of that danger of scandal of which we have spoken and lays a heavy responsibility upon the persons who are to blame for it. But amid all these distortions what is taking place is the preservation of the one Christ, whole and entire.

Only from this point of view can we understand the existence of the Church and her history through the course of the ages: she preserves and unfolds the truth of revelation.

The Visibility of the Church

We have been trying, up to this point, to understand many things about the nature of the Church: how she was begotten by the will of Christ and born of the power of the Holy Spirit; how she contains the Lord himself, carrying Him on through history; how, again and again, she is the occasion of a division among souls, since she has inherited the characteristic of her founder, to be "set for... a sign which shall be contradicted" (Luke 2:34) so that he who encounters her either believes in her as the way to Christ or is scandalized by her.

Finally, we have glanced at the manner in which the Church raises the truth of Christ above those notions which endanger it and we have seen how, in consequence, this truth becomes ever clearer and deeper. If the reader has perhaps felt that the exposition was a matter of dry abstraction he might reflect that it is rather pure rationalism which inclines to turn into sentimentality, since it is unable to penetrate the thought with the glow of a real experience of truth, and so remains caught in barren abstraction.

The Church performs her service of the proclamation and preservation of the truth of Christ (John 16:14) in other ways as well: by the manner in which she preserves and carries out the central mystery of her life, the

473

Eucharist; by the arrangement of sacred times and places, symbols and actions, which we call the liturgy; by the charitable services which she renders to the poor and the suffering, and so on. The twofold effect would always be clear: that a reality is revealed which bears witness to God in the midst of this earthly life, and also that the human element emerges insistently and appears to justify the opinion that divine action is out of the question here. So we have considered how great and how revealing and yet how irritating the process is which has been continuing for nearly two thousand years. In the midst of questioning and thinking, of doubt and denial, a truth is upheld which does not come from the logic of the world but transcends all our concepts.

Now we wish to approach the problem of the church from a new point of view, the question of her visibility.

At times when the Church enjoyed unquestioned respect and esteem, her life developed with great splendor, but thereby often lapsed into a preoccupation with externals which was a direct contradiction of her interior mystery. So we can understand how in opposition to this tendency the spirituality and interiority of the Church were emphasized. But this reaction finally went so far that men said that the Church had nothing to do with exterior form and appearance, that the true Church was beyond all form and was invisible. So, when one asked where this Church might be found, the reply was that it was quite undiscernible. The Church would be where men believed. And if one asked wherein the doctrine of the Church consisted the answer was that there was no such doctrine; that the Church was the community of those who confessed faith in Christ. The external structure, the form subsisting in history, the complex of offices and duties, of sacraments and symbols, of ordinances and laws, which historically or empirically was called the Church, all this was regarded as something unessential, even as a falsification of the real and true purpose of Christ. What is the truth of the matter?

We see here a viewpoint which affects all things concerning faith. For example, in answer to the question who Jesus Christ is and what the New Testament concept of His divine sonship means, the reply is given: Jesus was a man of great religious power, such as has rarely appeared in history. His consciousness was wholly filled with the reality of the living God. He experienced what the Old Testament said about salvation through the fulfilling of the law, but went beyond this. In His experience God became so transcendently holy that the idea of attaining salvation through the fulfilling of the law appeared meaningless. So He was convinced that man could do nothing but surrender himself to the mercy of God. There was another experience: Christ felt in God a disposition toward himself which He called "love," and realized that God demanded of Him a corresponding disposition and manner of life, or, more exactly, gave Him the capacity for this. This experience deepened more and more and was finally expressed in the statement, "He is my father, and I am his son." There was a third point: Christ realized that He was called and was able to bring others also into this relationship to God. He interpreted the prophetic promise of the Messias in this way and felt Himself to be the one who was to bring salvation and establish the kingdom of the Father. But if we ask, "Is all this really true, is it honest-to-goodness reality?" then the ambiguous explanations begin: "Certainly, it is true, but interiorly, psychologically, as the content of experience, as a way of understanding our own existence in relation to God. To speak of a reality beyond this would be materialism, myth, or the like."

This way of thinking is characteristic of the present age—actually it is already outmoded. Certainly it is not in accord with revelation. If we take up the New Testament we see that it nowhere speaks of such a psychologistic, purely interior divine sonship. On the contrary, from the synoptic Gospels to St. Paul and St. John the tremendous fact emerges more and more clearly: The Son of God the Father lived in eternity. When the fullness of time had come, He entered into history. As St. John says, He "became flesh and dwelt among us." Those who were called saw Him with their eyes, heard Him with their ears and touched Him with their hands. (John 1:1–14; 1 John 1:1–3)

Similarly men speak of the Church, saying that she is not an objective reality, not something that exists definitely in space and time, having an unmistakable form in history, but that she is something purely interior, a relationship between those who believe in Christ. They maintain that Jesus never thought of a Church in the sense of an objectively historical realization and structure, of authority, office and regulation; that He desired a communion of the redeemed, but one that would continually grow through the breath of the Spirit, the opening of men's hearts, and the realization of the brotherhood of man and the universal fatherhood of God, and which would exist in reality insofar as this experience was realized.

This also is a modern way of thinking, modern subjectivism and individualism, which is already disintegrating and by a reaction becoming its direct opposite, the totalitarianism of political and economic powers. But the New Testament contains nothing of that sort. If we read what it says on the subject we see how forcefully it places the Church within the reality of history.

A most impressive proof of this can be found in the attitude of St. Paul, of which we have spoken once before. If anyone had been capable of dispensing with a visible Church, it would have been he. He emphasizes most strongly the fact that he had been taught interiorly and spiritually by Christ himself. (Gal. 1:12) How natural it would have been for him to draw the conclusions that we have spoken of and to say, "I need no visible institution. Christ knows me and I know him. That is sufficient." Then he might have gone on to conclude: this is sufficient for everyone who has the assurance of faith, and he might have taught his followers the same thing: "You know Christ and He knows you. This assurance is your salvation. It liberates you from all the old and new laws. You are no longer servants, but free children of God. And in this consciousness, which sets you free you also have communion with each other, a holy brotherhood under one Father." This is what Paul might have said, and this is how his teaching is often interpreted. But this is incorrect. Paul did not think in this way. He did not act in this manner or give such doctrine to his followers. But, as the Epistle to the Galatians records, (Gal. 2:1ff.) He went to Jerusalem and gave to the apostles, with Peter at their head, an account of His revelation, and He accepted what the original apostles proscribed for Him in regard to the question, so important at the time, about the relation of the Christian way of life to that of the Old Testament.

He did more than that. He was the first to attempt a rational interpretation, a theory of the Church. And for this, as we have already stated, he used a concept employed by ancient law to describe the state; that is, the concept of the *corpus,* the objective, organic unity, in which the individuals are the members, a unity that does not depend upon the will or the experience of the individual but subsists objectively in itself. With the help of this concept he constructed the idea of the *soma Christou,* the Church as the body of Christ. (I Cor. 12:12ff.) She is that great unity in which every individual is a member, and Christ is the head. This unity exists really and objectively in itself, founded and constituted, resting upon the apostles and their successors, expressing itself in valid doctrine, binding regulations and liturgical acts. The term for it is not "gathering" or "congregation," as modern individualism translates the Greek word *ekklesia,* but "Church." In every congregation the Church is present, but she herself and as such is more than the community of kindred souls meeting here and now, unless we give the word "congregation" a meaning which transcends the ordinary one and take it to signify the union of all the baptized believers, founded by Christ and constituted in the apostles. But this would be only a difference of terminology.

The central mystery of the Church is the Eucharist. The two realities are so closely connected that for Augustine, to mention one instance, the "mystical body of Christ," the Church, is almost fused with the concept of the Sacrament and that of the unity of faith. How does this view of Christianity interpret the Eucharist?

If we were to ask a person with this view, "What is the Eucharist?" he would reply: "It is the memorial of Jesus, (Luke 22:29; I Cor. 11:24) of His person, His love, His redeeming life, teaching and destiny. It is having a spiritual part in Him by memory and faith." But what is the meaning of the words "This is my body"? Then the person questioned would reply that these words must be taken symbolically, as "this signifies," that what takes place is a symbol of union, a condensation of what, originally, was the meaning of every meal, but in relation to Christ. As the Lord of the feast gave to His companions the bread and the wine, he evoked that union of divine sonship which He had created among them.

Again, the essential thing is taken to be purely interior, psychological, "spiritual." And again we must say, "This is a modern view." Sacred Scripture does not support it. Scripture says, this "is" my body, and so it must remain. If we combine the words of the synoptic Gospels with what St. Paul says in his first Epistle to the Corinthians (I Cor. 11:23ff.) and what we read in the sixth chapter of St. John's Gospel, we find that they proclaim something quite unprecedented: that Christ, in a manner transcending all natural thought and all that was revealed in the Old Testament, gives Himself, His living being, to mankind.

This is a doctrine whose complete range and implications become clear only when we consider that the Christian revelation concerns not merely a spiritual "soul" but the whole man, who shall attain his completion in the resurrection to eternal life.

Modern man is so conscious of the reality of the world, feels its material, political and technological reality so strongly that his religious life migrates from the realm of the visible and withdraws into complete interiority. Here we might remember the significance of St. John's statement, "This is the victory that overcomes the world: our faith." (I John 5:4) In view of this statement, faith means that we do not withdraw, but in daily endeavor strive to lift up the sacred, valid reality of God, of Christ, of His work and His organization against the powerful reality of the world.

Someone might readily object: "Do you not see that this view would confine the sovereign God? You must leave His freedom untouched—a perfect freedom unhampered by any human form. As soon as you say that this historical person 'is' the Son of God; this religious association 'is' His Church; this object of cult 'is' the body of Christ; you are impairing God's freedom."

This sounds very impressive, especially when we see how men sometimes treat the mysteries of faith. Then the demand that we must refrain from all such statements and leave the reality of God in its absolute freedom, a freedom defined by no assertion, limited by no form, appears to be the expression of the purest piety. But is it correct? It would be so if man on his own initiative sought to grasp God. But it is just the opposite. The demand is really the greatest presumption, for how can man think that it is his responsibility to preserve God's freedom when He, the Lord, is the very one who has bound Himself?

What could be more confining than the Incarnation? If the Son of God, as St. John says, was from all eternity "at the bosom of the Father" but in time "became flesh and dwelt among us," then He certainly confined Himself thereby. For if He was staying in Jerusalem He could not say that He was in Nazareth. If He did something on the third day of the week He could not say that it was done on the first day. If He was eating, truth forbade Him to assert that He was sleeping. These things constitute a confinement, an adaption to the differentiations and limits of earthly existence. When the soldiers of the chief council came and bound Him, who was it that was bound? Only the man Jesus, or the Son of God? Unless we want to be Docetists, who attributed to Christ only a phantom body, we must say, "It was the Son of God." And when Pilate pronounced his judgment, was it not the Lord, eternally free, who was bound and delivered over to death in the mystery of our redemption.

This is the very core of Christian thought, that the Son of God does not keep Himself isolated from human reality by some metaphysical barrier, but has entered into this reality and by this very fact has bound Himself. If we have once noticed this situation we see that it began much earlier, by the very fact that God created the world. Have we ever thought about that, not just "thought" but deeply reflected, with mind and heart, what it means that God created the world? He, the infinite one, created our finite world. However immeasurably it may extend into the realm of cosmic vastness or microscopic minuteness, however inexhaustible in its forms and unfathomable in its nature, in comparison with God it is still something "small." But since God has created it, it exists and nothing can alter that fact. Let us accept the thought: Since the creation of the world, God no longer exists without the world. Logically, that statement is non-sense, for the words "since" and "no longer" express the element of time and time only comes into being with the world. But we cannot speak in any other way. And the meaning of the statement is probably evident. It is something monstrous, something scandalous, unless we consider it with piety and obedience. But does this not indicate a "binding" of God, through His own sovereign will? And this bond shall never be severed, since Revelation tells us that this world of ours, after its destruction, shall arise as a "new heaven and a new earth." And is it not a "binding" that God created man, who shall never be annihilated? Hence there exists forever the sacred "I—thou" relation between God and man into which man has been called by God, and in which the one who has been called can say, "My Lord and my God."

The tremendous and incomprehensible thing of which revelation tells us and which, through faith, becomes the core of our existence, is just this sublime truth, that God has bound Himself for our sake. Therefore it is not proper for man to presume to concern himself about God's freedom, but he should accept with adoration and love what grace bestows upon him.

Not classical humanism, not oriental profundity of thought, not the modern concept of the superman has ever regarded man and the world as seriously as has the Christian faith. They have never been as highly valued as in the Christian revelation. If we ask how God is disposed toward man, into what relation with Himself God has admitted man, then we are told something which would be blasphemy if we asserted it on our own initiative. But, since God Himself says it, we may adore it and call it love—for this is the love of which St. John says that it originates not in man but in God. (I John 4:10) This is a mystery of magnanimity so great that it overwhelms us. Let us beware of trying to prescribe to God the Lord how He should be or what He should do. A god whom we conceive of according to our standards of what constitutes proper divinity would be a man-made image. The true God is as He reveals Himself. And He reveals Himself as the one who thinks and does those things which we have considered.

His sovereign freedom has also bound itself by the Church. And we must take care so that nothing false may creep into our thoughts about this Church. Let us not say "God must be free" and mean thereby, "I wish to be my own master." For the fact that God has bound Himself, which is basic for my Christian existence, means also that I myself am bound. If God wills that I should exist then He binds Himself in love to keep me always dependent upon Him. And so it would be blasphemy if I declared that I did not wish to exist. Rather, I should render Him the obedience of my existence and carry it out in the obedience of action. If God wills that the Church should exist, in the plain sense of an unambiguous historicity, then He binds Himself in love to realize His grace through her, and by that very fact I am bound to accept her as that which He wished her to be.

The Eschatological Character of the Church

T he following pages will deal with the Church from a point of view which has become important for Christian thought during the last decades, the *eschata,* the end of time and of all things. This point of view was predominant in Christianity during its early days and the time of persecution. When the Church was recognized and accepted by the world it receded. But today it has again become meaningful—perhaps as an omen of future tribulations and as an aid to perseverance in faith, but also as an indication that many of the ideas about the worldly glory of the Church and about the Christian life, which originated in the middle ages and the baroque period are now being recognized as what they are, namely, the responses to temporary emergencies which became disastrous illusions.

The word comes from the Greek, *to eschaton,* "the last," and it refers to the character of Christian existence insofar as it is redeemed, but also hampered by the times, by all times, by time as such; insofar as it is moving toward a final goal, the second coming of the Lord, the end of time, the resurrection, judgment, and eternity and insofar as this goal and purpose is already effective.

But we must at once make an essential distinction. Sometimes the concept of eschatology is treated in such a way that—to speak abstractly—the Christian principle involved is removed from all contemporary reality and transferred entirely to the expected future and the second coming of Christ. Here we have a new form of the old attempt to separate the content of the gospel of salvation from every earthly experiential reality and transfer it to the pure ideality of faith, thereby avoiding the decision and the scandal. A gospel so "eschatologized" is unreal and forms an intermediate stage on the way to complete disintegration. It gives rise to a concept of the Church according to which she is nothing more than a "value" of hope incomparably higher than any historical reality. This is a ruse of the conscience by which it evades the decision before the will of Christ.

As the expression is used in our reflections, it signifies a characteristic of the real Church. She is eschatologically oriented and also historically present, an object of hope and also of actual encounter here and now.

The meaning of the term "eschatological" we find first in St. Paul. Above all, Paul was under the influence of the event on the way to Damascus which determined his whole subsequent life, and in which he experienced the risen and glorified Lord as a power transcending all earthly measure—perhaps he was also under the influence of the words of Jesus recorded in John 21:22, "If I will have him to remain till I come, what is it to thee?" Accordingly the Apostle expected the return of the Lord and the end of all things in the very near future. So much so that it influenced his teaching about the attitude of the Christian to world problems. "The fashion of this world passes away," he says in the first Epistle to the Corinthians. (I Cor. 7:31) Therefore it was pointless to concern oneself about property or to found a family. (I Cor. 7:30–38) The whole existence of the Christian was based upon the expectation that Christ would soon return and establish His eternal kingdom. But this mood, which also influenced the life of the earliest Christian community—cf. the first chapters of the book of Acts 4:32ff., 5:1–11—changed after a while. In the later Pauline Epistles it is no longer influential.

St. John too, as we notice, expected Christ to return in a short time. The final sentences of the Apocalypse show this: "He that gives testimony of these things says, 'Surely I come quickly.' Amen. Come, Lord Jesus." Here we are at the end of the first century. Of course, it was a time of special tribulation, the beginning of the Roman persecutions, during which the thought that Christ's return was near became a comfort in view of the despotism, ostentation and arrogance of paganism.

But this mood also did not last very long. Faith fixed itself upon an indefinite time. The word "soon" became a relative term. It no longer denoted the measurable difference between a short space of time and a long one, but rather the insignificance of time as such in comparison with eternity. "Soon" took its meaning from the fact that no space of time, however long, can be compared with the timelessness of eternity.

What the concept of eschatology, understood in this way, means in relation to the Church, can be better understood if we begin with the corresponding nature of the existence of the individual believing Christian. And it is St. Paul who expounded the elements of such a theological doctrine both individual and social. In the second Epistle to the Corinthians he writes:

> For this reason we faint not, but though our outward man is
> destroyed, yet the inward man is renewed day by day. For our
> present momentary and light tribulation works for us exceed-
> ingly above measure an eternal weight of glory; while we look
> not at the things which are seen but at the things which are
> not seen. For the things which are seen are temporal but the
> things which are not seen are eternal. (II Cor. 4:16–18)

Here the apostle balances two elements of Christian existence against each other. First he calls them the "outward" and the "inward," then the "seen" and the "unseen." Later he speaks of "tribulation" and "glory," and then of the "temporal" and the "eternal." In another passage he mentions the living and immortal, and again the "old" and the "new." (II Cor. 5:4–17)

In the Epistle to the Romans we meet this contrast again. In chapters 3 to 8 it is developed at great length, especially by means of the two concepts of the "carnal" and the "spiritual" man. (esp. Rom. 8:3–11) This last pair of opposites is particularly impressive and at first glance seems to refer to the contrast between the life of the body and the life of the spirit; the body with its limbs, organs and impulses on one side, the spirit, with its powers and activities, its knowledge and its moral endeavors, on the other. From this we might conclude, as some have indeed concluded, that St. Paul is dualistic in his thinking, that for him only the spiritual is good and valuable, while the corporeal and material is worthless, indeed evil, and must be overcome. But if we look more closely we notice that in the term "carnal" the apostle also includes the spirit and its activities, that is, the whole man, and that, on the other hand the 8th chapter of the Epistle to the Romans speaks of the "redemption of the body"; indeed, that Christian hope is bound up with the hope of the whole creation waiting for the revelation of a redeemed and eternally perfected body. (Rom. 8:18–29)* And finally, in the first Epistle to the Corinthians, at the end of a veritable phenomenology of the corporeal, we read: "It is sown (that is, in burial) an earthly (natural) body; it shall rise a spiritual (that is, a transfigured) body. If there is an earthly body, there is also a spiritual body." (I Cor. 15:44)

So we see that St. Paul by the terms "carnal" and "spiritual" did not mean two parts or areas of the human entity but two religious conditions affecting the whole man. The "carnal" or "earthly" man is man unredeemed, natural, confused and blind; the "spiritual" man is the one in whom the message, the grace and the image of Christ are operative. This

---

* Cf. the interpretation, "The Yearning of Creation, Rom. 8:12–39" in *The Word of God*, Henry Regnery Co., 1963.

transformation begins with the first movement of faith, which is sealed by Baptism. At that moment the living Christ enters the believer. But what does that mean?

In the Epistle to the Philippians St. Paul speaks of Jesus who is in the form of a servant and of Christ the Lord who possesses "the body of glory." (Phil. 2:7; 3:20–21) He means one and the same Jesus Christ, first, as he was during his earthly life, bound by its laws and subject to its weaknesses, and then the risen Christ who had entered into glory after passing through death and resurrection, and who had appeared to Paul on the way to Damascus, transfigured and free of all limitations of finiteness—the "Lord" in the fullest sense of the word. This Christ, says the Apostle, enters into man by faith, and becomes, we might say, the soul of his life and being. As the spiritual soul is the interior form of a natural existence and turns matter into a living body, so the powerful figure of the risen Christ seizes the natural man who is willing to believe and produces in him the essential and ever-valid reality of the living Christian. In the Epistle to the Galatians we find a mysterious sentence, the key, as it were, of the life of faith. First the two words rising from the depths of a new self-consciousness, "I live"; and then the distinction, "Yet not I, but Christ lives in me." (Gal. 2:20) And we may continue the thought: by that very fact I really and truly live as the self that God intended me to be.

From this point a whole history begins, for the living Christ in man forms his nature, his body and soul, his thoughts, his love, his powers and qualities—all into a new man. The great antithesis, "the old" and "the new man," arises. The new man grows, whereas the old man decays, subject to the transitoriness of existence. The new man grows, through all that befalls him, in faith, obedience and effort to overcome. But he is concealed, as the passage from the second Epistle to the Corinthians tells us. He is invisible, because the old covers him. The old lies across the new, indeed, contradicts it. Who of us, if he examines the day or the year that has passed, must not confess that much, far too much, has gone wrong, was faulty, cowardly and petty? And so he might lose confidence and begin to wonder if the sacred message could really be true; and he must believe in his own Christianity and constantly renew his faith in the face of the contradictions of his daily experience.

The believer must be conscious of the fact that our whole present life is oriented toward a life to come, so that aging constitutes not a decrease but an increase. (I Cor. 4:16–18; 5:1–8) But that essential thing toward which the life of faith is moving, is not the children nor the race, not humanity, work or culture, but the perfection of one's own human nature. This too the believer must accept in faith: in eternity he shall be not merely a "soul," but a redeemed new man, fashioned after the image of Christ, and therein perfected as the true self intended by God.

So much for the eschatological element of Christian existence: man constantly experiences his own poverty and insufficiency and yet knows by faith that he is moving toward a new existence in which nothing of his humanity shall be lost. All that has been done rightly will be preserved therein. It is not without purpose that the risen Lord bears the marks of His wounds in His hands, for His earthly history, transformed, lives in His eternal form. Similarly the risen man shall retain all that he has lived and done for the kingdom of God, but all transformed into eternal glory. (II Cor. 3:17–18)

In the eighth chapter of the Epistle to the Romans we read: "For I reckon that the sufferings of this time are not worthy to be compared with the glory to come, that shall be revealed in us." (Rom. 8:18) For a moment we might think that what is here referred to is the glory of the liberated spirit, transcending all sense-experience. This is the teaching of dualism and idealism. But the epistle continues:

> For the expectation of the creature waits for the revelation of
> the sons of God. For the creature was made subject to vanity,
> not willingly, but by reason of him that made it subject in the
> hope that the creature also itself shall be delivered from the

servitude of corruption into the liberty of the children of God. For we know that every creature groans and travails in pain, even till now. And not only it, but ourselves also, who have the first fruits of the spirit, even we ourselves groan within ourselves waiting for the adoption of the sons of God, the redemption of our body. (Rom. 8:19–23)

So what is spoken of is not redemption from our corporeal nature, but the redemption of our earthly body for the eternal freedom of God, who is above all that we call "body" but also above all that we call spirit in a natural sense—God, inexpressible in His super-natural essentiality.**

But what is here proclaimed is the message of a future existence, which, however, already operates here and now and amid the mutability of things temporal, a vital power in the midst of daily suffering and dying and failure, a power that passes all comprehension. The confidence in this message we call "hope." (Rom. 6:24ff.) This hope is the most profound principle of the vital consciousness of the Christian, to whom, as St. Paul elsewhere says, the Holy Spirit imparts the certainty that in the midst of this transient existence he is maturing for a fullness of life that shall never wither or fade away.

What we have said gives us our starting-point in speaking of the eschatological element in the Church. Like the existence of the individual Christian, the Christian totality, the Church, can be understood only from the standpoint of the eschatological mystery.

But first we must clarify a few points. The Church is not a composite of the individual believers, nor is she the harmony of individual experiences in faith. She is independent of each individual, a reality confronting him, a figure which is self-based, a vital impulse transcending the individual. So she was willed by Christ and so she was born of the Holy Spirit

---

** Cf. "The Yearning of Creation," cited previously.

on the day of Pentecost. On the other hand, the individual believer cannot be considered a mere function of the Church. He is not only the material of which she is built, not only a differentiation of her common life in individual form. Rather, he is a person, established as such by the call of God and preserved by God's eternal appellation of "Thou." As a person he possesses dignity and freedom even in the Church; he has a responsibility and the right to fulfill it.

We cannot, in a totalistic fashion, derive the individual from the Church, nor in an individualistic way, derive the Church from the total number of individuals. And yet the Church cannot exist without the individual nor the individual without the Church. The Church, as well as the individual, is rooted in the saving and sanctifying will of Christ, in the creativity of His Spirit. But the individual becomes himself, a personal child of the Father, in the Church, and the Church is realized in the individuals as what she is, the living "body of Christ." The "isolated individual," who could dispense with the Church in his Christianity, does not exist, just as the Church does not exist as a purely objective figure or an independent sociological structure; but she lives in the individual, in each one according to his own unique way.

The relation between the Church and the individual then cannot be expressed by simple statements running along a single line, but only dialectically, so that in each case the one statement receives its meaning from the other and in reference to the other. Whenever a man, touched by the call of God, comes to the faith, he does so in the Church and through her, even though he is not conscious of her. And conversely the Church is realized, as the objective reality which she is, only in the individual believer, in each person in a unique manner, whenever an individual believes, and in all the circumstances of life under which he believes. Every vital act of the Church is—as dogma, mystery and sacrament, regulation and commandment—an act of the objective Church and confronts each individual as such, but it is carried out in view of the individual and his life which is his personal responsibility, and it is consummated in him. This gives the basic concept of the *Corpus Christi mysticum* its full meaning.

But we must add something here: the two "realities"—if we may call them so for the purpose of simplification—the Church and the individual, are not on a par, but the Church has a characteristic which has its source in the will of Christ and which, in its realization, depends upon her objective form: she has authority. She has been charged by the Lord to bring to the individual His truth, His instruction, in a word, Himself, in His spiritual reality and fullness of value, and to take care that the individual rightly understands the truth of Christ, accepts Christ's standard of values and carries these out in his own life.

This authority is not one of domination, so that the individual is subject to her, but the Church is the great servant of the individuals, and becomes by this service that which she really is. Her authority is the authority of service, and the acceptance of this authority, obedience, is the reception of the message of salvation and cannot be rendered superfluous by the maturity of the receiver. On the contrary, as the believer ripens to greater maturity he carries out more freely and consciously his obedience in reception and in action, so that the sacred relation of mission and proclamation on one side and of hearing and accepting on the other may be perfectly carried out. The Christian who truly understands himself knows that he is in harmony with the Church, so that the authority of the proclamation may be ever more purely and fully realized—an earthly image of that mystery in which the obedience of the Son is equal to the will of the Father.

This Church also contains the mystery involved in the concept of eschatology. The Church is historically real, real in earthly persons and earthly conditions. However she also bears within herself the life of the risen Christ and carries it out in preaching, liturgy and moral regulations. This interior life is not, if we may use this expression, enclosed in a vacuum by the earthly and historical reality, but it operates in every part, every phase, every movement of the historical, just as the whole life of the body operates in every limb, every organ, every cell, and thus strives to penetrate the earthly reality more and more. In daring phrases, which theology has not yet exhausted, St. Paul, in his Epistles to the Ephesians and the Colossians (Eph. 1:3–23, Col. 1:15–20) speaks of the manner in which this life reaches out even beyond the realm of man and the earth and grasps the whole universe, in order to transport this world into what the Apocalypse calls "the new heaven and the new earth." (21:21–22:5)

For the Church—or more exactly, for the individual who lives in her and perceives the fullness of spiritual meaning that she contains—the temptation may arise to identify her with her empirical reality and to forget that not only the individual believer but also the Church, "carries her treasure in earthen vessels," as St. Paul says (II Cor. 4:7); which means that she is influenced by all that comes under the heading of earthly limitation, historical conditions, and human imperfection.

Men may be tempted and, as history shows, have often succumbed to the temptation to identify the nobility of the Gospel message, and the new life which it awakens, with earthly magnificence, to equate the Church's authority to "bind," in carrying out her spiritual instruction and guidance, with empirical power. This leads, according to the historical situation, to pretensions to political, social or economic power or cultural brilliance. Thereby the true character of the Church is hidden, the fact that she is still a pilgrim, on the way toward a future existence. This is hidden and can be recognized only by faith. But the acquisition of this faith is not always easy.

Just as the individual, in view of what the Gospel proclaims about the mystery of divine sonship, must wonder whether it really applies to his own questionable existence—to such an extent that it is only through the assurance of the message that he can believe that he is that which it proclaims him to be—even so we can only believe about the Church that she is really the "one and holy," as the Creed calls her. Again and again the covering which conceals her seems to contradict her nature and her mission. Just as the individual must hope, transcending all possible empirical experience, that that which is ripening in him will some day, *en eschatois,* be revealed, so he must trust and hope, as a member of the Church, that she will, at the end of time, be revealed as the "new heaven and the new earth," the "heavenly city" and the eternal "bride of the Lamb," "coming down from God"; whereas her history can be understood only as a time of pilgrimage and concealment.

At the Council, when Pope Paul VI laid the tiara with its triple crown upon the altar so that it might be sold and its price might be used to feed the hungry, he intended this act both as a symbol and a multiple lesson.

The Church can be wholly understood only from an eschatological point of view. This fact, however, should in no way destroy the identity which exists between the Church for whose revelation we are waiting and the Church who at present repeatedly confesses her insufficiency.

If it makes sense to speak of something like a feeling of faith, then the experience in which the believer becomes conscious of the Church contains the confidence in a firm foundation laid by Christ, the surmise of a mysterious inner depth, and also the feeling of a powerful movement which passes onward through the transitoriness of time to a future which lies not beyond years or centuries but beyond time itself. But this is preceded, for the individual and also for the Church, by the judgment.

Epilogue

O ur reflections about the eschatological character of the Church should conclude this book. This is not to imply, of course, that the subject has been exhausted. In the course of our considerations the reader must have realized how copious it is. But what we have here set forth is not meant to be a systematic investigation of the problem of the Church, but matter for reflection. In connection with the Council a systematic treatise on the subject will probably be written some day, and we may wish that it will really cover the subject and not force it into one or another point of view, for this would do great and lasting harm.

It is not easy to write about the Church, and it becomes less easy the longer one thinks about her. When one does, however, it should be with love and with deep concern, for what we call "the Church" is as vulnerable as it is powerful. And every wound has long-lasting effects, although we can see again and again how great are the powers of renewal in that living entity which was born on the day of Pentecost.

Much might be said about the fact that the Church is a whole, great and inclusive, full of tensions and yet wondrously unifying. She is realized in the smallest congregation and yet extends over the whole world. Therefore, men will have to speak of her again and again, for she becomes conscious of herself in the thoughts of every age; she receives affirmation and contradiction and, consequently, a constantly renewed power to evolve and unfold.

This book, we must repeat again, is meant to provide reflections, thoughtful glimpses from one or another point of view. But the more one has learned of the Church the more one hesitates to make statements about her. So this book, of whose genesis we have spoken in the first chapter, was not written easily, but slowly and hesitatingly, and more than once the author asked himself whether he should not give up the work, especially when he realized how much would have to be said about the Church in connection with the Council and how much is already being said. He asked himself whether what he might produce was not already *passé* and would hardly fit in with the present age which is going about its business with such a strong consciousness of renewal. But the book has grown out of long years of experience, of reflection, and—I may repeat—of love and concern. So it may be of service.

Let us consider briefly the task which, in our estimation, must be performed by a book about the Church—one task of many, for in view of the many problems there must be many attempts to solve them. But one task, it seems to me, must be to express a particular characteristic, the comprehensive quality in the unity of the Church with her multiplicity of tensions yet her enduring identity—that which is meant by the word "catholic."

In considering this characteristic we may reflect upon the variety of images under which the New Testament—and the Old, by anticipation—beholds the Church.

There is one image which is today seemingly the predominant one in men's thoughts, the image of the people of God. It is marvellously vivid, full of movement, and expresses immediately something that is particularly important for the thought of our time, the historical element, the

Church's existing and working in time, her wandering and struggling. But we must not forget the other image which the Lord himself contributed to Christian thought when he spoke of the edifice that he would build upon the rock.

The Church, as St. Paul explains, developing the words of his Master, is that great whole which grows and matures as a living being and sends forth various particular forms—branches of the vine. This grows throughout the course of history and shall fill the whole earth, indeed, shall go beyond the earth and transform the whole creation. But the Church is also "where two or three are gathered together in the name of Jesus" and He is in their midst.

The Church will ultimately be that precious adamantine structure, built of noble gems glistening in the brightness of eternal light—as the final chapters of the Apocalypse describe her. But she will also reveal the tender beauty of the bride going to meet her spouse. She will be both, passing from one image to the other. This is of her very nature, and is in effect even in our day. There is in her a constant activity and also an abiding sameness.

The Church is so very much alive that she lives in every hour of history, determines it and receives from it material for growth. She is stirred to growth but also narrowed and hardened, questioned by each moment of history, and in answer unfolding what has lain hidden within her. But the Church is also the unflinching one, guarding the yea and nay of the truth, so that Scripture could make a very severe statement, that he who does not listen to her, knowing what he does, should be regarded "as a heathen and a public sinner."

But all these images, which express real powers, real responsibility and dignity, are again veiled by the mystery of the eschatological clement. They can be refuted at every point by the appearances of history. They must be believed and their fulfillment must be hoped for and awaited.

They express powers and qualities of majesty and dignity which are already operative in every place, however insignificant, but must not be interpreted in terms of earthly and historical glory. Their embodiment in transforming glory is reserved for the future—the absolute future which lies beyond the return of the Lord.

THE WISDOM OF THE PSALMS

Preface

I n the Psalms human and religious notes combine with basic motifs
of Revelation to form a powerful harmony. The fact that they belong
historically to an early age only makes the sound more penetrating.
It is not without reason that the Psalms became the basic material of liturgical texts. Therefore it may well be profitable to study some of them in
regard to these elements and in this way to bring them closer to the comprehension of our age.

It also seemed useful to clarify the differences between the Psalms
and the spirit of the New Testament in order to indicate more clearly the
essential quality of Christian piety. Our selection does not follow any particular viewpoint but simply presents passages which came to the special
attention of the author in the course of every day life.

Moreover, the meditations themselves have no systematic purpose.
They do not propose to present a whole, but some very essential elements
of this whole. Therefore, many thoughts which would in themselves be
important for the religious world of the Psalms are missing. Others again
recur more frequently as they are involved in the spiritual movement of
the meditation.

The text employed was the author's translation of the Psalms published under the title "German Psalter" (Munich 1950) by order of the German bishops.

In regard to the numbering of the Psalms our selection follows the Vulgate, that is, the Latin translation. Between this and the Hebrew Bible—and consequently the evangelical translation, which confirms to the Hebrew—there is a difference, which depends on textual viewpoints. For the purpose of facilitating orientation we have given each Psalm both the Latin and, in parenthesis, the Hebrew numeral.

The Spirit of the Psalms

The Psalms form a book of the Old Testament which is placed between the writings of the Prophets and the Wisdom Books and consists of a hundred and fifty religious poems: liturgical texts, personal prayers, meditations and didactic poems. They were collected over a long period of time. The earliest ones were composed by King David, that is, about the year one thousand before Christ; the latest ones date from the time of the Maccabean Wars, which took place in the second century before Christ.

Their length varies greatly. The long one-hundred-eighteenth Psalm contains almost one hundred and eighty verses. Shortly before this we find the shortest one, which is called the "little point in the Psalter," and which has only two verses.

The content of the Psalms also varies. There are some which thank for petitions fulfilled; others are filled with jubilation over the beauty of God's world. Some express the consciousness of great guilt. Many arise from immediate need and distress, persecution by enemies or some misfortune. Others have a meditative character and consider God's works in nature, the power with which He has guided the history of His people, or the wisdom of His law which orders the life of the faithful.

So there is great variety in the Psalms, but they are unified by certain features common to them all. There is, first of all, the simple fact of tradition which has always regarded them as a unity. Then there is the more important fact; that is, that these poems are prayers, words arising from believing hearts and carrying the events of life before God.

Therefore, the Psalms have played an important role in the history of Christian piety. They form the basic material for the prayer of the Church. The liturgy is interspersed with texts from the Psalms. Likewise, they are the sources of many hymns; words from the Psalms appear in the Christian Revelation as well as in everyday speech, etc.

And now we ask, what do the Psalms mean for us, for our life?

They have been called wonderful poems. The beauty of their language and the power of their images have been said to bring about that elevation of the spirit which is produced only by great art. This is true, but only to a certain degree. Certainly there are glorious poems among the Psalms. We may think, for example, of the great Psalm of Creation, the hundred-and-third, or the fiftieth which grew out of the consciousness of deepest guilt—the *Miserere*. But there are others, which, from the point of view of poetry, are only of average quality, and even some which are simply handicraft. We must be permitted to say this, and it is easier to do so because the essential meaning of the Psalms does not lie in their literary quality, just as the significance of the Pauline Epistles does not lie in the fact that they express so strong a personality, nor the significance of St. John's Gospel in the fact that it rises to metaphysical heights. The Psalms are the word of God, a word that He speaks as a man inspired by Him speaks his human word. Hence they are a revelation which leads to salvation.

But they are this in a special form, the form of a prayer. They do not proceed from the experience of a human soul, for instance, a prophet, who has recognized divine truth and now says, "Thus saith the Lord," although frequently this element is also involved. Examples of this occur in Psalms like the seventy-sixth, the hundred-and-fourth and the hundred-and-fifth, which interpret the history of the nation, or in those like the hundred-and-ninth, in which the figure of the coming Messias shines forth. As a rule, however, the Psalms spring from the emotion of a man, who in prayer, whether as an individual or in community, turns to God.

Therefore, the manner in which the Psalms should be handled is not to read them and think about them, but rather to let ourselves be caught up in their movement and lifted up to God. In doing this, however, we may have a singular experience. We may doubt whether the Christian can always appropriate these prayers. Do not earthly affairs play a role in the Psalms which is in contradiction to the Christian spirit? Do not passions break out in a manner which is incompatible with the spirit of Christ? Some of them, the so-called imprecatory psalms, for example the sixty-eighth or the hundred-and-eighth, actually use the language of open hatred. They call down all manner of evil, even the curse of God, upon their enemy. So it can happen that Christian feeling protests against this, and there are persons who demand that these Psalms be removed and that they all should be examined with an eye to such offensive material.

On the other hand, there is the fact that in the Psalms we are dealing with the word of God, and that man has no right to pass judgment upon this word or to change anything in it. If we take this fact as our starting point, and it is something which is a prerequisite of all proper meditation upon Revelation, then the very things which threaten to give scandal will be seen to point to something essential.

In order to remove the difficulties mentioned above, people have made many clever statements, and of course we must welcome anything that leads to a deeper understanding. But I believe that there is a point of view which leads us farther by the simple power of truth without any display of eloquence.

Who is speaking in the Psalms? A man who is no longer a pagan. The divinity he addresses is no longer that of the myths and mysteries. The latter was the mysterious depth of the all, the religious power of existence, misunderstood as the divinity of the world itself. When man moved in the realm of the pagan myths he accepted the world as the one-and-all, surrendered himself to it, and became subject to it. The man praying the Psalms has nothing to do with that kind of piety.

The one to whom the Psalms are addressed is the living God who is above the world. We cannot here discuss the difficult question what "gods" really are, so we shall speak, for the sake of simplicity, as if they really were something. In any case, they are dependent on the world. There wouldn't be any Zeus if the vault of the heavens and the order of the constellations did not exist; no Gaia, if there were not the dark and fruitful depths of the earth. The God of the Psalms is He who has no need of the world. He lives in Himself and through Himself. The name by which He revealed Himself in the decisive hour on Mt. Horeb, "Jahveh" (Ex. 3:13ff.) is rendered by "the Lord" in the Greek and Latin and hence also in the German translation. But He is "the Lord" not just because He rules the world, but because He is mighty in Himself.

This is the God whom the Psalms address. Faith in Him frees the man who is praying from the binding spell which lies on all pagan piety, however noble it may be in individual instances. Invocation of this God lifts man to a freedom which the world cannot give him—either in the most daring metaphysics or in the highest wisdom.

All this is true. But it is also true that the man of the Psalms is not yet a Christian. He has not yet heard the message of God's triune life and the freedom based upon it; nor has he received the message that this God loves the world, with a free, personal love, so much so that He takes upon Himself the responsibility for the guilt of His rebellious creature; that He Himself atones for this guilt and so creates a beginning from which a new existence proceeds. All this unknown to the man of the Old Testament. He is only on the way from paganism to Christianity. He is on the right way, but he has not yet arrived.

In the history of the Old Testament something has taken place that has been deeply impressed upon the memory of the people. It has actually become the fundamental principle for their concept of existence; that is, the long journey from Egypt—that country in which myth and mystery developed in such an impressive way—and through the loneliness of the desert, led by the personal presence of the living God into the Promised Land. This is the concept of existence of the man of the Old Testament: he is on the way.

This state of being on the way finds expression in the Psalms. In them we find all the powers and experiences which move man: the joys, the distresses, the fears, and the passions. Everything is brought before God, but not in a Dionysiac fashion; not in a general affirmation of existence, and not that the speaker says, "Live, the more powerfully and flamingly, the better! Hatred, revenge, reviling and cursing belong to life and are therefore good." Rather, the Psalmist says, "This is the nature of the man who speaks here. He is filled with earthly desires, with hunger for life, with passions of every kind, with hatred and vindictiveness, but he remains before God and shows himself to God as he is. The Holy One towers above all that is said and passes judgment on all things. If we take those songs which give the most offence—the imprecatory Psalms—and compare them with the forms of religious cursing which occur in pagan magic, then we can see the difference. The latter reveal the will to do violence to God and to force Him by enticements and incantations to carry out the work of destruction. We find nothing of this sort in the Psalms. God's liberty remains inviolate. At all times He is the Lord and the Judge. All passion, all hatred is put before Him, and, in consequence, there is a differentiation, for the truth comes out and there is a liberation.

Now someone might say, "But I am no longer on the way. I am a Christian. We must answer, "Are you really? Do you dare to say that your Christianity is complete"? What does it mean to be a Christian? Perhaps St. Paul gave the most complete answer when he said in the Epistle to the

Galatians, "I live, yet not I, but Christ lives in me." (2:20) And then he carries on the thought, "by that very fact I am my true self." Is this true of you? Can you say that you live in the consciousness of Christ's in-dwelling, that you have entered into his holy disposition and as a result become your true self? We need only ask this question to know the true situation.

That which lived in the man of the Old Testament still lives in us. Not in the same way as it lived in the men of that time when the work of Revelation and Redemption was not yet historically "consummated" (John 19:30), but in the sense of personal realization. We too are still on the way to being Christians. We have heard the message, have been baptized and believe—let us rather say we strive to believe—but we are still wandering and struggling. Here too St. Paul gave us the decisive expression when he said in the Epistle to the Romans that the new man in us, who is "conformed to the image of the Son of God" (Rom. 8:29) must make his way through the old, rebellious, confused man; that we must "put off" the old man, leave him behind us, and "put on" the new man; that we must pass from a servile and corrupt condition to the liberty and essential truth of the man reborn in Christ.

And if someone wished to insist on his rights and say, "But I have learned in the school of Christ; I do not harbor the hatred expressed in the Psalm"—then we could answer again, "Is that really so? Or is it only because you have not had the provocation? Are not the same potentialities in you, ready to awaken if the occasion came? Perhaps, they would be even worse.

An objection to the reality of the Redemption, which is frequently raised, is this: has the world become better since the death and resurrection of Christ?

Let us leave out of account all that has really become better and wholly different through Christ and his word; let us honestly admit the question: Has the world, in its historical totality, become better? Perhaps we must reply in the negative. Perhaps its immediate condition has in many respects become even worse.

The person of Christ has made clear the difference between good and evil. Good and evil have come "of age." The man who lives in the mythical state of consciousness does not really know what his existence is all about. Everything still flows together, like the forces of nature. The distinction between good and evil constantly passes over into that between beautiful and ugly, noble and ignoble or sound and unsound. Only in view of Christ do values and ways really diverge. Only He is the "Judgment."

If, after the coming of Christ, man desired the good it meant the morally holy, doing as Christ did, and it involved the seriousness of the Cross. Similarly, evil now meant opposition to the incarnate Son of the holy God, rebellion against Him who "came unto His own and His own received Him not." (John 1:11) No, they killed him.

So, evil has become more terrible than ever, open, conscious and voluntary. Never in pagan times did the things happen that have happened in the last forty years. And we, who belong to our time, have every reason to assume that the terrible things are in us also. It is only a question of how far God fulfills our petition, "Lead us not into temptation."

The Psalms can become very meaningful for us, because as we pray them we are revealed to ourselves. We take as our own the words which we find there. We learn to see our heart not as we wish it to be but as it really is; not only as we are familiar with it but also its hidden and dark depths. And we bring all this before God. We learn to understand that we are still involved in the fetters of existence; that we think constantly of earthly things. We hate; we wish evil to our enemies; we would like to destroy them if it were possible. But we come before you, Lord, with all that is within us. You are to see it; You are to judge it and we pray that You may heal us.

If we look at things in this way, then we see how important these texts are. We can actually say, the more their words offend us, the more reason we have to think that they reveal ourselves. We should accept this and in prayer voice our repentance and draw near to God.

Growth and Way

PSALM 1

We turn to the first of the Psalms. It forms the portal through which we enter the world of these poems and it reads:

Blessed is the man who hath not walked in the counsel of the ungodly, nor stood in the way of sinners, nor sat in the chair of pestilence.

But his will [delight] is in the law of the Lord, and on his law he shall meditate day and night.

And he shall be like a tree which is planted near the running waters, which shall bring forth its fruit in due season. And his leaf shall not fall off; and all whatsoever he shall do shall prosper.

Not so the wicked, not so; but like the dust [chaff] which the wind driveth from the face of the earth.

Therefore the wicked shall not rise again in judgment, nor sinners in the council of the just.

For the Lord knoweth the way of the just, and the way of the wicked shall perish.

The Psalm is very simple and unpretentious. We find in it neither lofty ascents to metaphysical heights nor violent emotion resulting from the tragic quality of existence.

It is constructed around three images which originate in the life of the people among whom the Psalm was composed but which also extend into the depths of all existence, basic images which every man can use to interpret his life.

The first image appears in the very first verse—the image of the way. A "way" is something that we take whenever we are going somewhere, and we are always going somewhere. A "way" means that we go on from a starting-point, proceed from one point to another and step by step. It would be a good thing if we could rid ourselves of the feeling that all this is a self-evident matter, not worth thinking about, but rather would realize the basic form that the image reveals. A "way" means that every step presupposes the preceding one and prepares for the next one; that the movement has a direction toward a goal which the one who moves finally reaches; that one may grow weary, but may also rest; may go in the right direction but also in the wrong one.

A "way" is a basic image which expresses everything that happens. When a plant grows there is first a seed; this becomes a shoot; then it develops further, step by step. Isn't this also a way—a way of growth and change of form? Here too what precedes prepares for what follows. The second stage depends upon the first and is a step toward what is to come. Nothing stands alone; everything is a link in the structure. There is also a direction; that is, toward the development of this particular plant and not another. There is danger and success, and so on.

In a work too there is a way. I begin, and then I proceed from one section to another. I cannot do first what comes second. Everything is prepared by what precedes and in turn brings about the realization of what follows. There is also a direction toward a goal, the completed work; there is weariness and resting, danger and conquest.

There is also a way in a personal encounter. I meet a person. Behind this there is already a long way, for I come out of my life and he comes out of his and each of us has had his destiny. Then there is a meeting; our mind receives an impression; interest awakens, confidence grows and in time there develops what is to come about: a friendship, an association, a love, together with all that it involves of crises and conquests, fulfilment and disappointment.

The way is a basic image, the manner in which the finite is realized in time and space. It appears everywhere, in wisdom and poetry, in myth and dream. This is the image which the Psalm uses as the expression of the actions of man.

At first it speaks of the wrong way. For if there is a right way there is also a wrong one. Motion involves the possibility of error. The man who speaks here knows this, for he lives in Palestine and is a neighbor of the desert. But what is the nature of the wrong way?

It consists of the actions of the man who follows "the counsel of the ungodly, stands in the way of sinners, sits in the chair of pestilence." If someone says to a person who is hesitating, "Don't be stupid; use your advantage; everybody does it and if you go about it cleverly no one will notice it"; if the person who is given this advice consents, he is going the wrong way. This is true also of the person who considers himself superior to holy wisdom; who thinks he knows better because some philosopher or writer holds this opinion; and who makes fun of old-fashioned prejudices because he knows life and is a realist.

To what extent is this a "way"? Let us suppose that someone consents to the possibility of dishonest gain. The first time it is difficult. He must silence his conscience and must overcome the opposition which has been built up by good training and proper business ethics. The next time it is easier because a connection has been made which lessens the resistence and facilitates the following of the impulse. A kind of incline has been formed which leads to dishonesty. This is a way.

An evil action is never the matter of a moment. Something always precedes and something follows. The worst lapse—into disorder and untruth, passion or hatred—is preceded by something, and this again by something else, and this by something earlier, and first of all there was a beginning. Then step followed step; each one helped to make a way, to make it broader, smoother, and more precipitous.

And then the Psalmist speaks of the good way, saying that the man who follows it takes delight in the law of the Lord. There is a way of looking at the good which makes it probable that one will not do it—the way of merely thinking "I ought to," of considering it merely as a duty. Of course, doing good is a duty that one "ought" to fulfil. But that is only one side of its nature; the other consists in the fact that the good is something great and that we are permitted to do it. Man has received from God the possibility of doing good, the wondrous privilege of being permitted to do it. To recognize this is what is meant by delight in the law of the Lord. He who looks upon the will of God merely as a yoke to be borne does not see how brightly the good shines.

Then the Psalm continues: the good way is the way of "the man who meditates day and night upon the law of God." Day and night let us—each one of us—honestly examine ourselves. How much of an effort do we make to learn to understand the good? How much time do we spend in trying to see what in our life is right and what is wrong? What small fragment of the attention which we pay day by day to the newspaper do we devote to this? Must we not answer, practically none? Then what is the state of our way?

And now appear the two other images, both beautiful and noble. The one says that he who takes the good way—and now we leave the image of the way and pass on to another—is "like a tree planted near the running waters." We think of the Orient where the sun blazes and destroys all vegetation. But beside a stream, itself a precious thing for the people of those countries, there is a tree whose roots reach down into the moist depths and absorb rich nourishment. The trunk grows up, like a pillar, strong and sturdy; the branches spread out, covered with verdure; they blossom and bear fruit.

This too is an ancient basic image. We may recall the tree of life which appears in myths and folk-tales and signifies an existence which is stable and shapely, whose roots reach the springs of water and which blossoms and bears fruit. It is like the man who is rooted in God's truth and whose life brings forth much fruit "in patience" as the Lord was to say, constant and never wearied.

This image is contrasted with another which represents the man who takes the wrong way: "Not so the wicked, not so, but like the dust [chaff] which the wind driveth from the face of the earth."

When the Palestinian farmer had harvested his grain he brought it to the threshing floor. This was elevated so that the wind could blow over it. The grain was threshed, the straw removed, and the rest remained, a mixture of grains and chaff. Then the farmer took the winnowing fan and threw the mixture across the wind. The heavy grains landed on the heap which grew higher and higher, the chaff was blown aside by the wind to be swept up and burned.

This is the image. What is its meaning? The man who takes the wrong way will not be like the heavy ripe grain, solid and filled with life, but like the chaff which is dry and empty, carried away by every wind and good for nothing but to be burned in a brief flame.

How rich is this simple Psalm! Only six verses compose it, but they are very compact and full of meaning. Of course we must explore it. We must ask questions, for only he who asks persistently receives an answer. Naturally, there are questions which remain unanswered, when the person questioned does not know; this often happens in the case of a man. But here, God is speaking. If the conscience in all seriousness desires an answer and the heart is ready to accept it, then it comes.

As soon as we read this Psalm we are also reminded of the New Testament. We may recall what John the Baptist says of the Messias: "He that shall come after me is mightier than I, whose shoes I am not worthy to bear; he shall baptize you in the Holy Ghost and fire." And then he continues: "Whose fan is in his hand, and he will thoroughly cleanse his floor and gather his wheat into the barn; but the chaff he will burn with unquenchable fire." (Matt. 3:11–12) It is the image of the Psalm! Christ is the one who separates and weighs the fruit; what is solid he carries into eternity, what is empty he gives to the wind.

The other image is also applied to Christ—indeed, he applies it to himself: "I am the way." That means first that he shows the way, by command and counsel. But beyond this it means that he himself is the way, is, in the matters of salvation, what the street and the path are in matters of communication. Therefore everyone who resists Christ loses the right direction, the way which leads to the Father. God, the living God, does not stand in the market place so that everyone can view and grasp him. He is not simply available, either for our religious needs or for our selfish and complacent thoughts. He is the hidden God, and Christ said explicitly, "No man comes to the Father but by me." (John 14:6) We come to the Father only through him whom the Father has sent to us; if we live in him, if he enters into us and we enter into him, he becomes our light and strength and food. He is the way. The man who does not wish to follow this way ends elsewhere than he had intended. When questioned about the true God, St. Paul replies that He is "The God and Father of Jesus Christ." (Rom. 15:6) Not a divinity attainable by free experience and imagination but He whom Jesus means when he says, "My Father"; this God and only He. Christ said, "He who sees me sees the Father." He is the epiphany of the Father and gives us eyes to see the Father. (John 14:9) Everything else leads us astray.

This is true, whether we like it or not. Everyone would consider it folly to travel north in order to reach a city situated in the south. The inexorable law which determines the way to the Father is even more powerful and absolute.

The Living God

PSALM 113 (114)

T he one hundred and thirteenth Psalm is dominated by an event
that was deeply imbedded in the memory of the chosen people:
the deliverance from their servitude in Egypt and the long journey through the desert into the promised land.

It begins with these words:

> When Israel went out of Egypt, the house of Jacob from
> a barbarous people
> Judea was made his sanctuary, Israel his dominion.

Before this Israel had been the property of masters and despots and
had to perform forced labor for them, to assist in building the cities and
fortresses of Egypt, the temples of Egypt's gods and the pyramids of its
rulers. Now Israel became the "sanctuary of God," the kingdom and abode
of Him who had called them. This deliverance and the journey through
the desert were indelibly impressed upon the consciousness of the people;
we constantly find traces of this in the Old Testament Scriptures. What
was the reason for this tremendous impression?

First of all, this period was the heroic age of Israel's history, the con-
solidation of the different tribes into a unified people who are surrounded
by dangers, battles and great deeds. But then there is something else, and
we must clearly understand its meaning, for otherwise we cannot understand the peculiarity of this people.

On Mt. Sinai, when "the Lord spoke face to face with Moses as a man
speaks with his friend," in deep consciousness of this favor the chosen
leader said to God:

> If thou thyself dost not go before, bring us not out of this place.
> For how shall we be able to know, I and thy people, that we
> have found grace in thy sight unless thou walk with us, that
> we may be glorified by all people that dwell upon the earth?

And God answered,

> This word also, which thou hast spoken, will I do; for thou
> has found grace before me, and thee have I known by name.
> (Ex. 33:11; 15–16; 17)

And so we find it repeated again and again that the Lord "went before
them," and there was a mysterious and mighty sign of this; the sacred
cloud.

In the book of Exodus we also read:

> The cloud covered the tabernacle of the testimony, and the
> glory of the Lord filled it. Neither could Moses go into the
> tabernacle of the covenant, the cloud covering all things and
> the majesty of the Lord shining, for the cloud had covered all.
> If at any time the cloud removed from the tabernacle, the
> children of Israel went forward by their troops; if it hung over,

they remained in the same place. For the cloud of the Lord hung over the tabernacle by day, and a fire by night, in the sight of all the children of Israel throughout all their mansions. (Ex. 40:32–36)

God dwelt among them. In a tabernacle—a tent—as they did. Of course, a strict commandment kept them from sacrilegious approach. But the "cloud" was a sign of His guiding power.

But what does it mean when it is said that God travelled with this people, that He dwelt among them, that He have them instructions and passed judgment through the mouth of Moses, that He fought their battles and took care of their needs?

If we had said to one who was among them at that time, "God is everywhere; how can He have dwelt among you and gone before you?," then he would probably have answered, "I know that He rules the world and what takes place anywhere takes place through Him. But He was with us as with no one else; He travelled with us and passed judgment among us, and when we were obliged to do battle it was He who conquered the enemy. This we experienced and it was as real as the course of the sun in the heavens, as true as it was that our feet trod the earth."

Here we have a mystery which extends through the whole history of Revelation. God, who simply is and therefore is at all times and places, can step into a special moment of history, and He has really done this. This does not only mean that His presence was experienced or His assistance became effective. Explanations of this sort would only blur the essential thing. The meaning is rather that which offends every rationalist, an express entrance of God into the finite, into time and place, which then "in the fulness of time" was completed by the incarnation of the Son of God, so that we could say—must say—that it happened in this place and nowhere else, in this year and not earlier or later; that He went a certain way and spoke to definite people.

It is a great mystery but it belongs to the core of Christian faith. It began when God drew near to His people in a definite coming, wondrous and terrible, and formed His covenant with them on Mt. Sinai. It was continued during the long journey through the desert. And, after this had terminated, it was realized in the temple in Jerusalem. Therein God dwelt, not merely experienced psychologically but in actuality, living and abiding there in person.

This presence of God was the reason why the journey through the desert and its events were so deeply impressed upon the memory of the people of Israel. Everything was colored by this immense fact and filled with eternal significance.

Now we understand the atmosphere of the following verses:

> The sea saw and fled; Jordan was turned back.
> The mountains skipped like rams and the hills like the
> lambs of the flock.
> What ailed thee, O thou sea, that thou didst flee; and thou,
> O Jordan, that thou wast turned back?
> Ye mountains, that ye skipped like rams, and ye hills, like
> lambs of the flock?
> At the presence of the Lord the earth was moved, at the
> presence of the God of Jacob,
> Who turned the rocks into pools of water, and the stony
> hill into fountains of waters.

What is recounted here is the passage of the Red Sea at the beginning of the journey and the crossing of the Jordan at its end. Then there is mention of earthquake-like events, perhaps the shaking of Mt. Sinai, at the appearance of God recounted in the nineteenth chapter of the book of Exodus. And finally there is a reference to the drought in the desert, when Moses at God's command brought water out of the rock. (Ex. 17:2ff.)

Everything is surrounded by the atmosphere of mystery: the sea "flees," the Jordan "was turned back," the mountains "skipped." These are not merely poetical images but an expression of the tremendous power that was working at the time.

And so praise breaks forth:

> Not to us, O Lord, not to us, but to thy name give glory.
> For thy mercy and for thy truth's sake; lest the Gentiles should say, "Where is their God?"
> But our God is in heaven: he hath done all things whatsoever he would.

What happened there shall be referred to its proper source. The composer of the Psalm is not writing a heroic lay. He is not concerned with national greatness or the glory of outstanding personalities from the history of Israel, a Moses or Saul or David, although of course this too enters into the picture, for he is a man and is recounting human history. But the essential thing that he announces is the glory of God, and what he voices is a prayer and a confession.

Israel plays a peculiar rôle in the history of nations. The destiny allotted to it—we shall speak of it again elsewhere in these meditations—was both great and difficult. It did not depend upon its own power, nor yet upon friendship and alliances with other nations. Between Israel and all other peoples, however akin they might be, there always arose the inexorable barrier of the call by Him who was not a *numen* of historical nations but the one who on Mt. Horeb rejected every name that might be bestowed by the world, and replied to Moses' question about His name, "I am the I-am." (Ex. 3:14)

Israel was His people. It was not to have any other determination. All other people were "gentiles" who created their divinities to affirm their natural historicity, Egyptian and Babylonian, Persian and Syrian, Greek,

Roman and Germanic. Their existence was bound up with the life of their believers. If the Egyptian nation was destroyed then its gods likewise perished; if the Assyrian nation perished then its temples and sacred places were empty and deserted. But the God of Israel was enthroned "in heaven," beyond earthly things, even though in guiding sacred history he journeys "in person" with the people whom He has called, or rather whom by His presence He has made into a nation. The gods of the gentiles "exist" and "will" as they must, because they are nothing more than the religious expression of cosmic powers. But He is the Lord, Lord of Himself and therefore Lord of all beings and He "does" whatever He will.

At the time of which the Psalm speaks something special happened to the chosen people. They migrated physically from political servitude—and also migrated spiritually from the world of paganism. When, summoned by the voice of God, they released themselves from an environment that had been familiar to them for centuries and moved into the desert, they also experienced who the mysterious and mighty one was whose voice guided them and whose presence encompassed them.

Israel had certainly had the opportunity to see what "gods" were, in Egypt with its ancient mythologies, its immense temples, its countless images, glorious works of human talent, but also a denial of the true Lord of the world. They had experienced the magical power of this world and now they were experiencing the powerful reality of the living God, the glowing sanctity of His presence. Now they knew the difference.

The existence of faith begins with the differentiation between the mighty powers of nature and of man's accomplishments on the one hand and the One "Who is" on the other hand. This differentiation is here made, so sharply, so keenly cutting through all ambiguity, that it is expressed in words of splendid naiveté:

> The idols of the gentiles are silver and gold, the works of
> the hands of men.

They have mouths and speak not; they have eyes and
see not.

They have ears and hear not; they have noses and smell
not.

They have hands and feel not; they have feet and walk not;
neither shall they cry out through their throat.

These figures, often gloriously beautiful from an artistic standpoint,
full of magical power for men's immediate feelings, become as it were
naked before the eyes of the speaker: "works of men's hands."

In the Prophets we find a word for the gods which practically annihilates them: they are "nothing," nothing expressed in images. Isaias says:
"Their land is full of idols; they have adored the work of their own
hands.... and idols shall be utterly destroyed." (Isa. 2:8, 18) And Jeremias,
"If a nation hath changed their gods, and indeed they are not gods. But
my people have changed their glory into an idol." (Isa. 2:11) Of course, they
are not a nonentity. In their images we find religious cosmic forces, and
often a deep experience of the world. But the insight given by an encounter
with the living God goes to the core. It penetrates all the religious, philosophic, aesthetic or other notions which man makes into an idol and sees
that they are nothing which has real existence in itself; they are destroyed
and vanish.

So grotesque is the contradiction between the presumptuous pretended majesty and the actual powerlessness, between the expenditure of
thought, art, and solemnity on one hand and the interior emptiness of the
images of the gods toward whom it is directed that, the Psalmist begins to
mock them: they have eyes and see not, have ears and hear not—they are
nothing! The educated man of our day is indignant at such words. He
considers them the expression of fanaticism and lack of culture. It is true
that it is not proper for everyone to speak in this way, but the man who
speaks in the Psalm has had the great experience of which the unbelieving

man of culture knows nothing, but which is decisive for everything. In view of this experience he is divinely right.

The whole history of the chosen people is dominated by this basic experience. It does not mean that now they were all pious and obedient. Some were, others—perhaps many—were not. There were very evil conditions among them, violence, dissension, immorality, impiety; indeed, the Prophets tremble with indignation at these things. But for the whole of their national consciousness God was a living reality while all about them images and myths of gods filled the world, often very artistically constructed, interpreted with deep wisdom, but in the last analysis—nothing.

Then we read:

> Let them that make them become like unto them, and all such
> as trust in them.

This verse shall be treated particularly at the end of our meditation, so we shall leave it for the present.

The Psalm continues:

> The house of Israel hath hoped in the Lord; he is their
> helper and their protector.
> The house of Aaron hath hoped in the Lord; he is their
> helper and their protector.
> They that fear the Lord have hoped in the Lord; he is their
> helper and their protector.

Over against the empty gods and idols arises the living one Who has revealed Himself to the chosen people on Mt. Sinai, "the Lord," Who has need of nothing, Who is not dependent on any people, but in the freedom of grace has called one that they may be His people and He may be their God and that in the course of sacred history. He may through them bring salvation to all nations. He is the hope of "the house of Israel," "the house of Aaron," two tribes of the people who here stand for all the others.

He is the hope of "all who fear the Lord." This does not mean to be afraid of Him, but to realize that He is the Holy One, the unapproachable One who has yet drawn near, the only real One who in grace turns His awesome power toward his people. Therefore they must turn away in fear from all that is opposed to Him, yet have unbounded confidence in Him beyond all finite powers.

From Him comes the "blessing." Only He Who has created can really bless. God's blessing is a kind of continuation in time of the act of creation. It gives duration and stability to that which has come into existence; it causes growing things to thrive, living creatures to become fruitful.

> The Lord hath been mindful of us and hath blessed us.
> He hath blessed the house of Israel; he hath blessed the house of Aaron.
> He hath blessed all that fear the Lord, both little and great.

This blessing comes out of sacred depths, out of the "interior" of God, if we may use this expression, out of His disposition toward His people of whom He is "mindful, whom He does not forget but keeps unchangingly in His presence.

And now a different turn of phrase succeeds that of meditation and prayer. It seems to be related to action. A person of authority, perhaps a priest, appropriates, as it were, the blessing of God and expresses it in liturgical words:

> May the Lord add blessings upon you, upon you and upon your children.
> Blessed be you of the Lord, who made heaven and earth.

And the chorus of those addressed answers:

> The heaven of heaven is the Lord's, but the earth he has given to the children of men.
> The dead shall not praise thee, O Lord, not any of them that go down to hell.
> But we that live bless the Lord, from this time now and forever.

Again we note the reference to God's unapproachable majesty. Heaven is the kingdom reserved to Him. But he has also given a kingdom to men—the earth.

A deep feeling reveals itself here at having a place and a right upon earth for life and work. Those who speak here are conscious of the roots of their existence. These are planted in the earth; God has planted them. This feeling is all the deeper because the person speaking has as yet no real consciousness of eternal life. Death does not extinguish life but it is a "descent into the depths" into the shadowy realm beneath the earth. So the whole feeling for existence, life, knowledge of the world and accomplishment of work is gathered up into the duration of life on earth. We need not particularly emphasize the fact that this has nothing to do with materialism. It has a special meaning in connection with the order of salvation of which we cannot speak at this point.

But let us return to the verse which we have set aside and which says of the idols and images of the pagans:

> Let them that make them become like unto them, and all such as trust in them.

This is a terrible sentence—especially in view of the aestheticism and frivolity with which men today speak of "gods." We may understand it against the background of the words which describe the origin of man. They are found in the first chapter of Genesis and read as follows: "God said, 'Let us make man to our image and likeness' . . ." (Gen. 1:26ff.) Then God who is Himself above all images, created a being in which His glory appears. He translated—if we may use this expression—His infinite inexpressible fulness of being into a finite image, man.

Man is the image of God. But wherein does this likeness consist? Scripture defines it by saying that God rules and that He has granted to man the power to do this also. We must understand correctly what this "also" means: God rules by his very nature because He is God; but man rules by grace because God gives him the power. He is under obedience to God; therefore, the world obeys him. By understanding, judging, acting, and shaping, he molds this world into his kingdom. Since he himself is in the service of the supreme Lord, it becomes the kingdom of God. This is the image and likeness.

If man had persevered in doing this, he would have become more and more "like" God. He would have taken over the world more and more perfectly and in purer and purer love would have returned it to God. But he rebelled. He wanted to rule by his own power and to possess the world for himself. The result was that he became the slave of the world. He betrayed the true Lord and so the world became his god. This is expressed by the gods, personifications of the power which the world gained over man when he fell away from God. And so man who was meant to be the image of God became like to the gods. What that means may become clearer if we look not only at Apollo and Athena, but also at the dark and dreadful and hideous forms to whom men have paid divine honors. Then our glance will become sufficiently sober to see even in the brightest Olympians the empty coldness, the anonymous "it."

This is a truth which we must recognize. What man is, is ultimately determined not by himself but by the divinity in which he believes. Rationalists are in the habit of saying that man conceives of divinity according to his character, his temperament and the needs of his life. Certainly there is something in this. But actually the situation is reversed: man himself becomes like the divinity in which he believes. And if he does not believe in any then it is this nothingness which determines his inmost being.

If, for example, a man is conscious of the fact that God has created him by calling him forth, so that he is one who is addressed by God; if he regards the various situations of his life as modes of this call, and his own action as the answers that he gives, then the core of his person becomes more and more solid, secure and free; his nature becomes ever richer and more receptive of eternity.

But if man conceives of divinity as pantheism conceives of it, as the world-spirit, the fundamental mystery or the basic nature of the universe, then there is no clear and binding "Thou," but only a hazy indefiniteness. Then this indefiniteness passes over into his inmost being and he loses the ability to answer the decisive questions of existence by a clear yes or no; this way and not otherwise.

And if he wishes to return to mythology, as in the twelve years of madness when the Germanic gods were to be revived; or as some philosophers and aesthetes do, who insist that for them the Greek gods are a valid reality, then man loses all seriousness, for the gods are "nothing," in whatever forms they may appear, political or philosophical or aesthetic.

But if divinity is absolutely denied and eradicated, and radical positivism or materialism dominates, then there is an evil emptiness in the depths of man's being. It may be covered by the coercion of power, the din of progress, the appearance of prosperity, but it is there, and it makes man interiorly defenseless and leaves him at the mercy of the state.

The God in whom we believe, the living and free, is our support and our defense; let us not forget that. In the measure in which He disappears from the consciousness of man, man's nature is corrupted. He no longer knows who he is. However exact his science, however advanced his technology, however refined his culture—actually he is disoriented and without support. He is at the mercy of every falsehood and despotism. It is exactly as the Psalmist says: man becomes like the God in whom he believes.

This is the tremendous experience of which the Psalm speaks. The people who had been in Egypt and there experienced what gods are, now learn who the living God is. This concerns us. The fundamental decision of our life consists in recognizing who He is, in view of the gods and the godlessness in politics, culture, poetry or wherever it may be. Only because God has established his being is man what he is. Only by receiving himself from God does he remain sure of himself. Only because he is addressed by God can he really say "I." For his whole existence is only the answer to the creative call: "Thou, be!"

Praise to the King

PSALM 95 (96)

A characteristic group of the Psalms consists of the "Royal Psalms" or, more exactly, the Psalms of "God, the King." In order to understand them we must consider what forms the core of the religious consciousness of the believers of the Old Testament: the fact that God made history with this people in a special, unparalleled way. How did this happen?

The Old Testament recounts in the twelfth chapter of the book of Genesis that God called a man named Abram—later called Abraham—out of his homeland and led him to Canaan. His descendants and relatives grew in number and prosperity. But then came a hard time of drought and famine and they travelled into the land which was a refuge at that time, Egypt. At first they were in favor, but then the attitude of the ruler and the people changed and they were enslaved. After a long time God again called a man, Moses, and through him led the people into freedom. On the peninsula of Sinai something occurred which happened at no other time in history: God made a covenant with this people.

This covenant is expressed in a thought which often recurs, for example in the book of Leviticus: "I will walk among you and will be your God and you shall be my people." (Lev. 26:12) This sentence must be understood in a special way. God would be a god to this nation not as every nation is a people of God, since He is the Creator and Lord of all, nor yet as the mythical consciousness spoke of the divinity of a people as the basis of their existence. Here we have something special: God calls this people and wishes to make history with them; moreover, a history whose content is the salvation of mankind, fulfilled in the kingdom of God.

It was a great thing that was granted to and also imposed upon the people of Israel: to be a nation among other nations, to possess a country, have a constitution, build a culture, wage war, like every other nation, but to do all these things not under the kind of leadership under which all other nations live—the wisdom of rulers, the intelligence of lawgivers, the efficiency of generals, etc.—that is, under the normal conditions which regularly produce history, but under the immediate guidance of God, revealed through those who were called by Him.

It is not easy to explain what that meant. This was not what cultural history means by a "theocracy." This indicates a form of government found in a primitive stage of development. In a theocracy a people or a tribe not yet acquainted with natural political values of the corresponding ways of life is led by priests in the name of a divinity and later goes on to oligarchical or monarchical forms of government. But in the case of Israel there is something different. The whole life of this people was to be a life of faith, a faith depending not upon truths which stood behind the veil of mystery either in the heights above or in the depths within, but upon realities of earth, of history. A faith and confidence, we may be tempted to say, of superhuman difficulty, constantly in danger of breaking under the tests to which it was put again and again.

This challenge necessarily brought about repeated conflicts. For instance, the general, Saul, would judge that it was high time to attack the army of the Philistines. But the prophet Samuel had announced the will of

God that Saul should wait until he himself should offer the sacrifice. But
Samuel delayed his coming and the army began to disperse (1 Sam. 13:4ff.)
Or the king Joakim decided that it was politically wise to ally himself with
the power of Egypt against the Babylonians under whose sovereignty the
Jewish state had passed. But God commanded through the prophet
Jeremias: "No; remain in alliance with the Babylonians although they have
inflicted bitter humiliations upon you." (Jer. 27) The harvest needed to be
brought in; every day was essential, but the commandment forbids working
on the Sabbath. There were commandments which seemed to mock all
reason, like that of the sabbatical year which returned after every six years
and in which the land should rest and no field should be tilled, nor vine
pruned. But God promised that what grew of itself would supply sufficient
food for all. (Lev. 25:1ff.)

If natural reason objected that this was folly, the answer would be:
God commands it and gives His word that all shall be well.

A final echo of this we may perceive in the promise attached to the
fourth commandment: "Honor thy father and thy mother that it may be
well with thee and thou mayest live long upon earth"—"be long-lived upon
the land which the Lord thy God will give thee" was the original reading.
(Ex. 20:12)

But that such an existence might be possible, this people must have
had a special religious experience, namely the immediate, living consciousness: God is with us. And this not in the sense in which it is taken
by everyone who believes in God and His providence, but in a special
sense. After the law had been given on Mt. Sinai and it was time to begin
the long journey through the desert, Moses spoke a strange word to God:
"If thou thyself dost not go before, bring us not out of this place." (Ex. 33:15)
He does not mean that God should be with them by His grace, but personally and expressly as a general is with his army. We shall not understand
the life of the Old Testament if we do not see in its core the consciousness

of an immediate powerful presence of God, moving, acting, making
history.

Especially on the long journey through the desert it must have happened again and again that the people were overwhelmed by the realization of this presence and broke forth into jubilant praise of their king,
praise of the God-King who gave testimony of Himself to His people. Such
experiences are the source of the royal Psalms.

One of them, the ninety-fifth in the book of Psalms, reads as
follows:

> Sing ye to the Lord a new canticle; sing to the Lord all the
> earth.
>
> Sing ye to the Lord and bless his name; shew forth his
> salvation from day to day.
>
> Declare his glory among the gentiles, his wonders among
> all people.
>
> For the Lord is great and exceedingly to be praised; he is
> to be feared above all gods
>
> For all the gods of the gentiles are devils [the work of men's
> hands], but the Lord made the heavens.
>
> Praise and beauty are before him, holiness and majesty in
> his sanctuary.
>
> Bring ye to the Lord, O ye kindreds of the gentiles; bring
> ye to the Lord glory and honour; bring to the Lord glory unto
> his name.
>
> Bring up sacrifices and come into his courts; adore ye the
> Lord in his holy court.
>
> Let all the earth be moved at his presence; say ye among
> the gentiles, the Lord hath reigned
>
> For he hath corrected the world, which shall not be
> moved; he will judge the people with justice.

Let the heavens rejoice and let the earth be glad; let the
sea be moved and the fullness thereof; the fields and all things
that are in them shall be joyful.

Then shall all the trees of the woods rejoice before the face
of the Lord, because he cometh, because he cometh to judge
the earth.

He shall judge the world with justice and the people with
his truth.

If we perceive behind these words the experience of which we have
spoken, the outburst of jubilant praise to the king—how the words come
alive!

"A new canticle" shall be sung. What is it that spoils the holiest prayer?
This happens when the words become old and trite. The Psalmist says that
the song shall be "new." Whether this means that the Psalm was actually
composed at that time, or whether the experience of the moment gave
rise to the strong feeling that nothing was ever felt or expressed in this
way, is a question that we may leave undecided.

"All the earth" shall sing to the Lord. The kingship of God among his
people shall radiate among all nations.

His name shall be praised. The name of God is God Himself. All
shall bear witness to the salvation which He bestows and which His
faithful ones experience. They shall tell of "His wonders among all people," of the deliverance from Egypt, the journey through the desert under
God's guidance, the victory in so many battles, the prosperity in the
promised land.

"The Lord is great and exceedingly to be praised; he is to be feared
above all gods."

We see that here "the gods" are not merely nonentities; their temples
and images, myths and cults fill the surrounding world: Egypt, Babylonia,
Assyria, and Persia. They are figures of religious power and beauty which

must have been overwhelming. The world was full of all this and in the midst of it this little nation lived and bore witness to God. All these gods are in themselves "nothing." They live by the blindness of men, but thereby they have great, sometimes overwhelming power. Only one is real, He, the Lord of the covenant of Sinai.

"For all the gods of the pagans are the work of men's hands"—personifications of the mystery of nature made by the imagination of men. "But the Lord made the heavens. He has no need of the world in order to be, nor of the human imagination in order to live. He lives of Himself and before all else.

"Praise and beauty are before him, holiness and majesty in his sanctuary." The attributes of the heavenly King become figures that surround Him.

In our passion for freedom and our cult of the individual personality we have forgotten what majesty is: holiness which lives and rules. Beauty and power and glory are the radiance of God, of which the prophets speak in such powerful and affecting words. (cf. Isa. 6)

This God shall be praised by "the kindreds of the gentiles." They shall offer sacrifices to Him in His holy courts, in holy adornment, in festive attire.

The praise of the God-King shall spread over the whole of creation. All things shall participate in the jubilant praise. The earth shall quake in ecstasy; the heavens shall glow with joy; the sea and the innumerable lives which it contains shall resound as with voices; the fields and beasts and trees shall glow. That which is always true but which lies dormant under the cover of everyday life, the fact that they are created by God, that He dwells in them and works in them, this shall reveal itself in an Epiphany of God in all that exists.

This is the jubilant praise of the King.

But what has become of the possibility that God should rule by a constant miracle and the people should obey Him in a faith surpassing all reason? Inexpressible things might have come of this, but it did not happen.

We must never forget that our life of faith rests upon a dark tragedy. At first there was the destruction of Paradise and its unimaginable possibilities; then the chosen people accepted the kingship of God at Mt. Sinai but constantly rebelled against it, "stiff-necked," so that the account of the journey through the desert is an account of the constant struggle of Moses against their opposition. At the end of the age of the "Judges" they demanded an earthly king "such as all other nations have." And when Samuel was indignant at their delusion, God said to him: "Hearken to the voice of the people in all that they say to thee. For they have not rejected thee, but me, that I should not reign over them. According to all their works they have done from the day that I brought them out of Egypt until this day; as they have forsaken me and served strange gods, so do they also unto thee." (1 Sam. 8:6–8) The history of the kings, who should have been God's stewards, is a continuous succession of faithfulness and apostasy, and those who fell away were more numerous than those who remained faithful. And finally when He stepped into history, Whom the prophets had foretold, the Messias, the Son of God, and wished to set up the kingdom of God in all the fulness of grace, then He was brought to trial because He presumed to claim royal dignity, and He was nailed to the cross. This is what happened.

We must think this over from time to time. We cannot let ourselves be satisfied by a few sentences from the Catechism. We are living in a vast historical whole, a series of events stretching from the beginnings of the human race to the present day, and going on toward an end of which the Lord said no one knows when it shall be reached, "not the day nor the hour."

We are living in the midst of these events. The great world powers have fallen away from the divine Lord and ever more definitely declared their independence. And now we are experiencing a new epoch: great nations, almost half of the earth, are saying not only, "without God!" but, "away with God!" They not only permit atheism and encourage it but they persecute the faith, destroy it methodically and completely in adults and in the mind and heart of children, so that in comparison the hostility of the Roman Empire seems almost harmless.

The sign under which everything stands is not only the announcement that "God is dead," which means that He no longer is operative as an experience or a historical motif, but it is the will to "kill" Him, to destroy the religious organization, to murder God.

So the troubled question arises: What can we do? Christ gives us the answer. The first statement that we hear from him is: "The time is accomplished and the kingdom of God is at hand; repent and believe the gospel." "Then"—this is the unexpressed continuation of the thought—"it will arrive." Not in the sense of the eschatological kingdom at the end of time, when Christ returns for judgment, but now, in the course of history, changing the conditions of the believer's existence. This did not happen, for those addressed by Jesus did not receive Him. (John 1:11) But His word was not destroyed. The kingdom of God is not "here," but always in the act of "coming"—in everyone of us if we "repent" and "believe," in every community, in every work, every stage of history, if men accept the call. Of course, the work of the kingdom of God is laborious, and it is attacked from within and without, hoping for the final, victorious coming of the Lord, when He shall summon the whole of history before His judgment and His victory shall be revealed.

It is wonderful to think that in me, in my great poverty, the kingdom of God can come. In what I am, how I live, in the way in which I carry out the duties of my state, in my family, in the way I carry my misfortunes, the kingdom of God can come. It can come in every thought, every action obedient to the call. This is the mystery of God's nobility; that is, that He does not force His kingdom upon us, but makes it dependent on us whether we accept it or not. He, the almighty one, entrusts His royal honor to our readiness; if we do not will it, it does not prevail in us. If we will it only in a lukewarm fashion, it comes only with difficulty and darkly. It is always we ourselves who open or close the door for Him, in all our thoughts and actions, in all we do or do not do.

The Creation of the World

PSALM 103 (104)

T he first sentence of Holy Scripture reads: "In the beginning God created heaven and earth"; that is, the world, everything. These words are easily said, but do we realize interiorly what they mean? Let us try to think in this way: Nothing finite *is*. But God is, absolutely. It is impossible that He should not be. To be is His name. This is how He revealed Himself when He said on Mt. Horeb "I am the I-am." (Ex. 3:14) In pure freedom, from the unfathomable depths of His decision, God wills that the world should be, and it comes into being. It does not exist absolutely, not by its nature, but by His will. Our minds cannot realize this step into being, but we must try to gain some sense of it and to surmise the mystery of God's omnipotent act.

The creation of the world was an event far surpassing all events. This was something whose accomplishment, humanly speaking, required not only wisdom and power, but also magnanimity, boldness and enthusiasm. What do these words mean when it is God to whom they refer? Here He is already at work who makes possible the primary beginnings of things, the one who is the mighty wind and glowing fire, the Holy Spirit. The next two sentences of Scripture read: "The earth was void and empty, and darkness was upon the face of the deep; and the Spirit of God moved over the waters," or, as another version has it: "A storm of the spirit fell upon the waters."

The "world" is the immeasurable totality of energies and forms, a tissue of relations extending into ever-increasing enormity and withdrawing into ever decreasing minuteness. All this was thought, willed and realized by God. Nothing was supplied for Him, neither models nor matter. And all these forms and arrangements, so full of truth, which science strives unceasingly to penetrate, only to see again and again that they continue to the vast unknown; this profusion of value and meaning, which ever and again impinges upon the human mind yet can never be fathomed—God has made them.

This cannot be the result of an arid, sober, though powerful activity, but here we have unfolding depths, creative thought, and flame and force.

Let us seek an image of this within the realm of human accomplishments. When a man of genius has an inspiration then he feels that this is not merely the result of his own small calculations and actions, but comes from another source, and yet it is he who produces the work. It is said that Beethoven, when he felt the stirrings of a new work, was terrified at the thought of what he would be compelled to endure. But how would it be with God?

What must creating mean for Him? Actually "creating," because man really should not use this word for his own activity. Man is unable to bring the least thing into being out of nothingness, he can only work at something which is already existing, use something already formed as the material of a new structure. But God creates. Nothing is, and He causes something to be. There are no beings, and He conceives the immeasurable profusion of forms which we call "the world." He does not do this in dull efficiency, not because He wishes to attain some end, but he creates in sovereign freedom, in prodigal profusion and in delicate precision. And—here we are speaking foolishly and in human fashion, for how else could we speak?—what a storm of ecstasy must have filled Him!

But when we have tried to find words that may hint at the marvellous thing that takes place there, our conscience calls us to order. What are we doing? Do we really expect to approach God through images of the colossal? And so we gather everything into that one thing which expresses true omnipotence: the complete effortlessness of the simple command, "Let there be."

This too, the effortless freedom which knows nothing of strain or of noise, this too is of the Holy Spirit, to whom the sequence of the Mass of Pentecost applies the beautiful term, lux beatissima, "most blessed light." He is the Creator Spiritus, the "creating Spirit." Everything has been created in Him. That is why it is "new." The work of man is always basically "old," even as it comes into being, because it gives form to something already existing. What God creates is new, original, and without precedent.

It is of this joy of God in creating that the Psalmist speaks. Not so much in definite words—although these too are not lacking; we shall notice them presently—but rather by the power of the images, the rhythm of the sentences, the interior movement that streams through all.

The Psalm opens with an invocation of the glory of God:

Bless the Lord, O my soul; O Lord my God, thou art exceedingly great.

Thou hast put on praise and beauty, and art clothed with light as with a garment.

Who stretchest out the heaven like a pavilion, who coverest the higher rooms thereof with water,

Who makest the clouds thy chariot, who walkest upon the wings of the wind.

Who makest thy angels spirits and thy ministers a burning fire.

What we find here is the early concept of the world. This considered the earth immovable, since the laws of the cosmic revolutions were still unknown. Above the earth rose that which we still call "the firmament," the lofty vault which spreads over all. Here, in the language of a nomadic people, it is called "a pavilion," a tent. Higher still towers the "room" of God, the unapproachable place where He is enthroned. This concept has long been outdated by science, but we must not forget that it is the picture which we see if we live by simple appearances.

In considering the Old Testament concept of the world we must remember two things. First, that we find in it nothing of pantheism. Pantheism is uncleanness of spirit; where the holy God speaks there is no place for it. God alone is God; the world is his creation. But thereby it is real, has a nature and a meaning. This is the first thing that we must bear clearly in mind, in order to have a proper understanding.

But God is in everything. He reveals himself in everything. The eye of the believer sees God's greatness in the vast expanse of space; he sees His mantle in the brightness of the firmament. And how luminous is He himself, light of all light, if the beams of the sun and the stars are His covering!

He is active in all events. If in a storm the heavy clouds race over the sky, it is He who rides in them, thundering in darkness. Again the storm is a great bird, bearing the Lord upon his wings. And again the winds are His messengers; the "burning fire" of the lightning is His servant.

For us the winds have become merely currents of air due to the variations of temperature and air-pressure; the lightning is an electrical discharge, differing only in degree from the spark in a radio. Science has determined events and made them transparent. This is right and proper. But is it the whole? If there were nothing more would not the world be meager and poor? Have men not always surmised that the mystery of God's work is revealed in all the phenomena of nature?

And now the Psalm speaks of creation:

Thou hast founded the earth upon its own bases; it shall not be moved for ever and ever.

The deep like a garment is its clothing; above the mountains shall the water stand.

At thy rebuke they shall flee; at the voice of thy thunder they shall fear.

The mountains ascend and the plains descend into the place which thou hast founded for them.

Thou hast set a bound which they shall not pass over; neither shall they return to cover the earth.

First God creates the foundation, the earth. The world of the Psalm is not the natural cosmos, but the existential world in which man lives, history takes place, and salvation is determined. Therefore the Creator first creates a solid place for these events, the earth.

At first there is chaos upon the earth, the primeval flood, the playground of primitive forces. But these too have a master. He "rebukes" their rage and they "fear" His command. He sets a boundary and an order for them and so there is a place for human life.

Again we find the image of the storm: the waters flee in terror before His thunder. There is an echo of things long forgotten, perhaps the great flood, perhaps something even earlier, primeval events. The image of the actual present which everyone can understand—a storm, an earthquake—is interwoven with the dark past and becomes awesome. The Psalms often speak in this way: the present is there, but beyond it, intermingled with it, there are events long past—or far in the future. This is prophecy, for which time becomes transparent.

Then the surface of the earth takes shape. Its forms are translated into movement: the mountains "ascend"; "the plains descend"; everything finds its place. Chaos retreats and now there is an order in which man can live.

> Thou sendest forth springs in the vales; between the midst
> of the hills the waters shall pass.
>
> All the beasts of the field shall drink; the wild asses shall
> quench their thirst.
>
> Over them the birds of the air shall dwell; from the midst
> of the rocks they shall give forth their voices.
>
> Thou waterest the hills from thy upper rooms; the earth
> shall be filled with the fruit of thy works.

In order to appreciate these verses fully, we must think of the people of the hot Mediterranean regions for whom flowing water was something inexpressibly precious. This water God sends forth from springs; He lets it flow in streams, and all living creatures draw their life from it. The trees grow; beasts of all kinds flourish; and the voices of the birds fill the trees with their harmony.

All that unfolds upon earth comes from God's creative power. We may remember what we mentioned before. For the early concept of the world there were no natural energies, no laws of nature. All events come immediately from God's initiative. When in ancient inscriptions the king speaks: "I built this or that city, constructed so many ships, waged this or that war," then the architect who planned, the slaves who moved the stones, the soldiers who fought, are disregarded, and only the ruler is named and the work that he commanded. In this way they thought of God's relation to the world. Whatever happens is his immediate work?

> Bringing forth grass for cattle and herb for the service of
> men,
>
> That thou mayst bring bread out of the earth and that wine
> may cheer the heart of man.
>
> That he may make his face cheerful with oil and that bread
> may strengthen man's heart.

The trees of the field shall be filled and the cedars of Libanus which he hath planted.

There the sparrows shall make their nests; the highest of them is the house of the heron.

The high hills are a refuge for the harts, the rock for the irchins.

But Scripture never thinks of nature alone, revolving upon itself. Nature is always related to man; natural history passes over into human history.

He hath made the moon for seasons; the sun knoweth his going down.

Thou hast appointed darkness, and it is night; in it shall all the beasts of the woods go about;

The young lions roaring after their prey and seeking their meat from God.

The sun ariseth and they are gathered together, and they shall lie down in their dens.

Man shall go forth to his work and to his labour until the evening.

Then the writer is overcome by emotion. Everything is so great, so full of life. There are so many creatures.

How great are thy works, O Lord! Thou hast made all things in wisdom; the earth is filled with thy riches.

So is this great sea, which stretcheth wide its arms. There are creeping things without number, creatures little and great.

There the ships shall go; this sea dragon which thou hast formed to play therein.

In the earlier Latin version the speaker, in imagination, is standing at the shore of the sea: *Ecce mare, spatiosum manibus*, he exclaims. "Behold the sea, so wide for our hands." We seem to see his gesture, his hands outspread to grasp the distance; but it is far too great for man to measure.

And in the sea there is a multitude of creatures, countless shapes. It is in the deep that animal life begins. In the account of creation we read:

> God said, "Let the waters bring forth the creeping creature having life, and the fowl that may fly over the earth under the firmament of heaven."

And God created the great whales and every living and moving creature which the waters brought forth according to their kinds, and every winged fowl according to its kind. And God saw that it was good. And he blessed them, saying, "Increase and multiply, and fill the waters of the sea, and let the birds be multiplied upon the earth." (Gen. 1:20–22)

The sea is also a place for man, a path for his ships, connecting lands and nations.

And in it, mysteriously mighty, "the dragon." Perhaps this refers to the largest of all living creatures, the whale; perhaps it is a mythical beast, the leviathan. It is difficult to decide. In any case, this too is no creature of pagan mythology, but it is created by Him who shows His sovereign freedom even in this monster. What a magnificent idea: The Lord enthroned on high has made this creature "to play in the sea." We are almost inclined to think that a gleam of humor is cast upon the giant image.

> All expect of thee that thou give them food in season.
> What thou givest to them they shall gather up; when thou openest thy hand they shall all be filled with good.

Whatever the animal may feed upon, plants or their proper prey, it is always the hand of God that supplies the food.

But if his bounty is withdrawn—perhaps a drought comes and the vegetation shrivels up, or a storm destroys everything or a pestilence breaks out—it always means that God in anger hides His face and life can no longer subsist. But then circumstances change for the better; a new growth appears and young animals come into existence, for God is kind.

> But if thou turnest away thy face, they shall be troubled.
> Thou shalt take away their breath, and they shall fail and
> shall return to their dust.
> Thou shalt send forth thy spirit, and they shall be created;
> and thou shalt renew the face of the earth.

Coming into being and passing away and being renewed are not a naturalistic process for the speaker. They are the constant action of God. His power awakens life and lets it flourish; His power determines its end and renews it again.

In this connection we see again what is the key to our understanding of the Psalm: the "spirit" of God, His creative breath.

At the beginning of our chapter we said that the whole Psalm really speaks of the Holy Spirit, the Creator, the Lord of all beings, that we can sense this in the movement that pulsates through the sentences, in the excitement of realization, the overpowering glory. The word "spirit" here brings this out openly.

The history of the word shows that many meanings are combined in it. First that of breath, that mysterious thing which we cannot see but which we feel, which continually moves in and out in our breast, makes speech possible and sustains life. Then the wind, the breath of the world which is also invisible and yet real, whether a breeze or a storm; of which we "know not whence he cometh and whither he goeth." (John 3:8) Then the soul, the interior being, intangible yet so intensive, which feels pain and joy and desire, which knows and wills and in dreams lives a mysterious life. Then the concept passes into that of spirit, especially that spirit which surmises and beholds the vision, and which awakens in the prophet as inspiration. All this comes together in the concept of the Spirit of God, or rather, it becomes the material by which the experience of his infinite creative power is expressed. It was overwhelmingly revealed on the day of Pentecost when the entrance of the Pneuma into history revealed itself by the elements of wind and fire, by prophetic speech and interior renewal.

It is this breath of God which is active in all things. It is He, the Spirit, who reveals himself in the interior movement of the Psalm:

> May the glory of the Lord endure forever. The Lord shall re-
> joice in his works.

These are wonderful verses, filled with reverence and the sense of God's nearness.

"The glory of the Lord" is His creation, the works of which He himself says that they are "good" and "very good," not merely in the sense of natural perfection but also in that God's glory radiates in them.

The believer of the Old Testament does not behold the world scientifically nor aesthetically, but prophetically, as a countenance through which God looks at him, God Who himself dwells in light inaccessible. And we should ask ourselves if there is not something here that we should recover. In the course of modern development our eyes have become dim. Not our natural eyes—although even these do not see clearly enough, otherwise we would not say about man the foolish things we say—but the eyes of faith, (cf. Rom. 1:18ff.) Have these not forgotten how to see the world as a "work" and so to see Him who made it? To see it as a form which conceals and yet reveals Him? And do we not have occasion to ask God to enlighten us?

And then the psalmist wishes that God shall "rejoice in His works." What profound intimacy with God enables a man to speak in this way! How close he comes to the mystery that God Who is eternally glorious in Himself willed that the world should concern Him so much that He could rejoice in it—and bear its guilt, indeed take it upon Himself and atone for it! Do we understand this mystery that transcends all reason, before which we can do only one of two things, be scandalized and renounce our faith, or recognize precisely in that which seems impossible the mysterious reality of God and believe it to be all the greater for that reason?

But again we are reminded that the world was created by the Spirit, not out of the dull necessity of nature. Its glory could not move a man so much if it were merely the result of dead causality. Certainly there are natural forces and natural laws, but they are more than what science and general culture behold in them. Every form of nature is a mysterious document, plain to him whose eyes are open. In every event of nature the man of the Bible is addressed by Him who works all things.

> He looketh upon the earth and maketh it tremble; he toucheth
> the mountains and they smoke.

This is an earthquake or the eruption of a volcano, but, fundamentally, it is also a revelation of God's activity.

> I will sing to the Lord as long as I live; I will sing praise to
> my God while I have my being.
> Let my speech be acceptable to him; but I will take delight
> in the Lord.
> Let sinners be consumed out of the earth, and the unjust,
> so that they be no more.
> O my soul, bless thou the Lord.

But there is a dreadful discord in this world which God made: the existence of "sinners" and the "unjust."

The "sinners" are those who think they can do anything they please—lie, rob, destroy. But someone who had experienced it, Hagar in the desert, said of God "He who sees me" and some day the judgment will come. The "unjust" are those who say, "There is no God." (Ps. 13:1) Then, as now, they declared that the world is autonomous, a structure of natural forces and natural laws. And they think this explains everything. In reality they make the world barren and dark. It would be vain for man with his little mind to try to bring a little light into such an existence. Then, after a few thousand or million years the earth would be glaciated and all would be silent and dead. How could anyone paint this picture and think that it was the final answer, the answer of science?

We have used the word "science." I hope that the reader will not suspect me of despising scientific work. True scientific research is something noble; it is a striving to reach by natural intelligence what it can attain: the laws of nature, the course of history, the structure of language, the system of law. But all this, in spite of its importance and the abundance of its material, is not the end. Beyond it there is mystery, and it is of this that faith speaks.

But it becomes disastrous if science claims to be able to explain matters of faith. Then it is doing something for which it cannot be responsible. Similarly, it would be disastrous if one who is speaking about revelation and faith would claim by means of these to be able to judge the things that belong to science. That would not be fitting. Everything must be kept in order. Then everything serves God.

The World Praising God

A mong the Psalms there is a group which has a particularly joyous character, the so-called Psalms of praise. Their composer feels the glory of the works of God and through them the greatness of Him who created them. The emotion he feels at this is expressed in solemn words.

The Psalms of praise are found throughout the whole book. In the hundred-and-forty-eighth, that is, at the conclusion of the book, the whole of creation, man and things, unites as it were in a great finale and sends its praise up to God. The Psalm reads:

> Praise ye the Lord from the heavens; praise ye him in the high places.
> Praise ye him, all his angels; praise ye him, all his hosts.
> Praise ye him, O sun and moon; praise him, all ye stars and light.
> Praise him, ye heavens of heavens, and let all the waters that are above the heavens praise the name of the Lord,
> For he spoke and they were made; he commanded, and they were created.

He hath established them forever and for ages of ages; he
hath made a decree, and it shall not pass away.

Praise the Lord from the earth, ye dragons and all ye
deeps,

Fire, hail, snow, ice [mist], stormy winds, which fulfill his
word;

Mountains and all hills, fruitful trees and all cedars;

Beasts and all cattle, serpents and feathered fowls;

Kings of the earth and all people, princes and all judges of
the earth;

. Young men and maidens; let the old with the younger
praise the name of the Lord, for his name alone is exalted.

The praise of him is above heaven and earth, and he hath
exalted the horn of his people.

A hymn to all his saints, to the children of Israel, a people
approaching to him. Alleluia.

How would we have to go about it if we wished to gather up all existence so that its fulness and also its unity became clear and we could carry
everything before God in one song of praise?

Perhaps by seeking the outermost point of our living world from
which we could see and perceive the whole in all its relations. Here the
idea of the poles of the world might help us—not the astronomical
physical poles but those of the world of living beings. These poles are
not situated above and below, but above and within, in the sublime and
the interior. They are the "places" in which our mind finds God: His
loftiness and His nearness.

So we might—taking the second way first—plunge into the depths,
the depths of the soul, as St. Augustine does when in the account of his
first decisive religious experience he says: "And admonished from above"
(as St. Paul also says) "to return to myself I entered into my inmost being

under Your guidance and I could do so because You were my helper" (Conf. 7:10); into the inmost depths, where, if we may use this expression, our being touches nothingness, where the hand of God holds us. This would be the point of which we could say "We cannot go farther."

From there we might move outward, layer by layer, into feelings, imagination, thoughts, and then into the word, which comes from within, then farther into our relations with men, those nearest to us and those farther removed, one group after another, even to the whole of mankind on the earth. Then we could extend our thoughts beyond the world into the universe with its cosmic laws, and so we might gain a glimmer of the immense whole which extends from the interior center into the outer vastness.

That would be a good way. But we could take another, soaring up to the highest attainable point and then descending from there to the world of man, to ourselves and our daily life. This is what the Psalm does.

The very first verse soars upward: "Praise ye the Lord from the heavens; praise ye him in the high places." These must not remain mere words. If we wish to understand them we must feel something of what height really is. There must be something of that urge which drives man from the valleys to the mountains, higher and higher, until he stands on the summit and looks down and around. Every earthly summit is a symbol of absolute height which can never be attained but is hinted at in every mountain.

Those who stand in the high places shall praise God. These are the "hosts of God," the angels, the world of spirits whom God created before material things, and who serve His will. But in the word "hosts" another meaning is implied. The angels are meant, but also the stars. The speaker lives in the south where the radiant constellations are so much brighter and more perceptible than in our more northerly lands and hence impinge so much more upon men's feelings. And we must not forget that for the ancients the stars were not merely astronomical bodies as they are for us, but were thought of as powers having a mysterious majesty, moving and guiding. The concept of the stars was fused with that of the angels, and something of this still lingers in modern thought. These sparkling powers are addressed: angels and stars shall praise God.

"Praise him, ye heavens of heavens." For the man who is speaking the earth is a large flat disc, the solid foundation of his world. Above it rises the heavenly height. It gives to him who looks up the feeling of inaccessibility and infinity.

This heaven is itself divided. In the center is the solid vault. We can still see the reflection of this concept in the word "firmament." Beneath the vault is the moving mass of air; above it the upper ocean from which the rain descends. Higher still is the throne-room of God. These most lofty regions are exhorted to praise God.

"For He spoke and they were made." It is the decisive word. What the Psalm means by "praise" is possible only if the world is the work of God. If it is "nature," in the modern sense, then there is no praise. Then nothing ascends from the world to an eternal, holy source. Then nature does not proclaim truth and breathe forth joyousness, does not in gratitude lift up its being to its creator. What philosophers and poets of this kind say is the shreds of vanishing faith or empty rhetoric. In reality everything simply exists—dull and mute.

Praise proceeds only from the knowledge of the inexpressible fact that "in the beginning"—not of time, for time came into being when God created the world, but in the beginning absolutely—there was nothing; that then God commands and finally the world is made, and now in the mind and heart of him who knows by faith, gratitude springs up because the magnanimity of the creator permits him to exist.

If there is only nature, then an honest mind cannot "praise," anymore than it can "ask" or "thank." These terms simply become words unjustly appropriated and lacking half their meaning. Nature does not expect or perceive praise.

"He hath established them forever and for ages of ages." God created the world with its abundance of creatures and the structure of its laws. In consequence of this it is meaningful; we can see it and know it, live and work in it. This is good. We may think of the words in Genesis, "God saw all the things that he had made and they were very good"; that is, they were valuable in themselves, worthy of being.

This was the first movement of the sacred symphony which is developed in the Psalm: the praise of God from the heavens.

Then it descends: "Praise the Lord from the earth, ye dragons and all ye deeps."

After the first great impression which the inhabitant of Palestine would receive, that of the countless multitude of stars, the next would be that of the mysterious depths of the sea. To persons familiar with the sea it always appeared to be the primeval source of life. When the book of Genesis recounts the creation of an animal life it mentions the fish first and that is a truth which is confirmed by science. The primeval source of life in the depths of the sea, and the height of heaven where stars and angels dwell—two unfathomable mysteries which call to each other and respond—both of these shall praise the Lord.

After height and depth have been called upon the path of praise moves into the atmosphere: "Fire"—the lightning—"and hail, mist and snow, the stormy winds which fulfil his word"—all these shall praise Him.

Then the mountains and hills are called upon, the topographical features of man's abode in which the earth strives upward, movements toward the "height." And did not the revelation of the name of God take place on Mt. Horeb? The covenant was made and the law was given on this same mountain, which is also called Sinai. And Jesus again and again went "up into a mountain alone" for sacred converse with the Father.

"Fruitful trees and all cedars": these mysterious beings, so silent yet so alive, which grow from the depths of the earth into space, bud and blossom and bear fruit. Some of them man plants and tends and he eats their fruit; but there are also those which grow of themselves. The cedars are mentioned particularly, glorious creatures which appear in Scripture as symbols of strength and beauty. All these shall praise Him who made them.

Also the beasts of the earth, the free wild creature as well as the tame and domesticated ones, the "cattle." All that flies and creeps shall praise Him who is the creator of all.

At last, the Psalm moves on to mankind; first to the great units called people or nations who are represented by their kings; the judges who hold court; and then to the "young men and maidens, the old men and the children." All these, mankind in the diversity of characters, classes and functions, accomplishments and destinies, shall praise the name of God and refer their existence to their Creator.

We are told that God has a name. He himself revealed it on Mt. Horeb: "The I-am." (Ex. 3:14) There is a chassidic story which recounts that a student finished his studies and left his master to live his own life. One day he came to visit the master and knocked at the closed shutters. The master asked, "Who is there?" and the student replied, "I am here." There was a long silence and finally the master said with great seriousness, "Who may dare to say 'I am' except one alone, God?"

No one, knowing what he is doing, can dare to say simply "I am," or "I am so-and-so"; only God. To be is His nature, and His name is He himself in the form of a word. All men shall praise Him, for they exist only because He willed that they should be.

"The praise of him is above heaven and earth, and he hath exalted the horn of his people." He is "above" all, because He is mightier, wiser, and more enduring than all; He is the creator and Lord of all. Among the many nations there is one that is "his people." He has chosen them, called them and by a covenant has made them His own. He has granted them hymns of praise, given them the grace of praising Him as their special privilege.

What does it mean, to praise? Let us turn to the simplest reality. If we praise a person, what do we say? "You did that well"—that refers to his work; or perhaps, "You are wise"—that concerns himself. Praise means that whatever is well done, good or beautiful is recognized and valued as such, and that the person who has accomplished it or to whom it belongs is told this. Then it brings joy to him who hears this and also to him who unselfishly expresses it.

But can this be done in relation to God. Evidently it can. He himself did it. In the story of creation (Gen. 1) we read that whenever a day was ended and the work stood in its perfection, "God saw it and it was good." And at the conclusion, "God saw all the things that he had made, and they were very good." God approves of everything that was brought into being by His creative power and gives it the right to exist. He declares that it is good that it should be and that it is an honor to God that He created it. His honor is the glory of being who He is and of having created what He created. "I will not give my glory to another" (Isa. 42:8) He said. No one shall ever say that someone else created the world or that it is uncreated and exists in its own right. No one shall ever say that the world is meaningless or wrong insofar as He created it. And God will demand a reckoning of everyone who by sin or negligence spoils His work.

When man praises he freely accepts this glory of God. He recognizes the wonder of God's work and expresses this in words. Actually, the world should praise God, but it is unable to do so. Trees, beasts, sea and stars are voiceless. The soul and heart of man must know and feel His glory and his mouth must convey the praise to God.

Is it easy for man today to think in this way? Do we find it "right and just, proper and availing for salvation" to praise God for heaven and earth and sea, for beast and tree? Hardly; but why?

Something gets in the way, something that determines the thought of modern man within the last few centuries—the concept of nature. This is for him the simply existent, the self-evident, self-valid, and self-based; that for which one cannot conceive a beginning or an end, and whose cause cannot reasonably be sought for. The man whose mind is ruled by this view can only say, "How mighty is the world!" He can feel its fulness and say, "How good that the world exists!" He may be lifted to enthusiasm by its beauty. But all this is not what the Psalm means by the praise of God, for the world, so conceived of, claims to exist by its own power.

But the world is not "nature" but "creation." This concept of course includes all that philosophy, poetry and science can say about nature, but it takes on a different meaning. The concept of creation restores the world to God's hand. Anyone who tries to realize this recognizes also how difficult it is. But it must be done, otherwise we fall into unbelief, living with the idea of a universe which knows nothing of God, and only adding a few Christian accents. Only insofar as we think of the world as God's creation can we pray the Psalm properly.

Once Again: The World Praising God

We have considered Psalm 148, but we have not exhausted its meaning—how could we!—so we shall meditate upon it once more. As we do this many of the ideas of the preceding meditation shall recur, but in a new interpretation they shall take on a new meaning.

Let us consider the text again:

> Praise ye the Lord from the heavens; praise ye him in the high places.
>
> Praise ye him, all his angels; praise ye him, all his hosts.
>
> Praise ye him, O sun and moon; praise him, all ye stars and light.
>
> Praise him, ye heavens of heavens, and let all the waters that are above the heavens praise the name of the Lord.
>
> For he spoke and they were made; he commanded, and they were created.
>
> He hath established them for ever and for ages of ages; he hath made a decree and it shall not pass away.

Praise the Lord from the earth, ye dragons, and all ye
deeps;

Fire, hail, snow, ice, stormy winds, which fulfill his word;

Mountains and all hills, fruitful trees and all cedars,

Beasts and all cattle, serpents and feathered fowls;

Kings of the earth and all people, princes and all judges of
the earth;

Young men and maidens; let the old with the younger
praise the name of the Lord, for his name alone is exalted.

The praise of him is above heaven and earth, and he hath
exalted the horn of his people.

A hymn to all his saints, to the children of Israel, a people
approaching to him. Alleluia.

This Psalm develops a basic act of religious life, the praise of God. But
what is praise?

As long as we ask this in a general way the meaning soon becomes
clear: it is something conscious, lofty, festive. It arises at the sight of things
and is addressed to Him who made them. But we want to ask more definitely: the author of this Psalm, who speaks in the atmosphere of the Old
Testament, what does he mean when he speaks of praise?

First we would think that his emotions have been stirred by the beauty
and greatness of the world. Perhaps we ourselves have had a similar experience, for instance after a period of illness when we lived in isolation in a
sick-room. Our senses had become keener, our feelings more vivid; and
when we stepped out of doors for the first time the beauty of a leaf, a
flower, a tree almost overwhelmed us and demanded expression in words.

There is something else in the Psalm: the feeling that a free agent is
behind this wonderful world. Something that happens of necessity, that
goes on according to law, does not awaken this feeling. But the marvellous
work, at which the Psalmist wonders, is not of necessity, God "spoke and

they were made." What was operative here was magnificent generosity, the generosity of God, His sovereign liberality.

What the Psalmist sees and experiences here is not "natural" nature, not something that can be grasped by the senses or the reason alone, but in it God is speaking. It bears witness to Him. The man who wrote these words felt the spirit of God in the world. In these great phenomena—the sea, the sun, the stars, the living and growing things—he sensed the presence of God. Everything was permeated by the divine mystery. This is what he realized. It filled him with wonder and gratitude, and he gathers it all up in this word: Praised be He who has made it.

If we look more carefully we notice something else. The text does not say: "God, I praise thee, because thou hast made all this," but "Thou sun, thou moon, ye heavens and seas, praise the Lord!" The creatures are exhorted to give praise.

The one competent to praise the Creator is always the man himself, the person speaking. I should praise. Suppose for a moment that I have just been created, that I am aware that through God's omnipotence I have come into existence—or, more correctly, I am permitted to exist; I have been set free to be, to live, to think and feel and speak. I am able and am permitted to do all this. If I could be aware of this, this blessed novelty of being permitted to be, then praise would spontaneously break forth: "Lord, praise be to Thee for this"—and these words would express the very depths of my being.

But here heaven and earth and stars are called upon—it is they who should praise. But they cannot do this; they have neither consciousness nor freedom, nor speech. In them praise is fettered; it sleeps. So man comes, takes all this into his heart and gives speech to that which has been voiceless. He says, "O sun, you should praise the Lord. But you are unable to do so; therefore I take your place; at this moment I am 'sun' for you, and with my words I carry the praise of your being to God."

This is man's function, to translate into words of praise the essential praise that lies in all things. Of course, one cannot do this at all times. It was certainly a moment of great exaltation for the Psalmist when he was able to do so, and his words have been given to our humdrum existence so that we may enter into his feelings and make his words our own.

The very first verse introduces the theme powerfully: "Praise ye the Lord from the heavens, praise ye him in the high places." The angels are addressed; they should praise God. After the thought has soared at once to the greatest height it descends slowly step by step.

Sun and moon shall praise Him, the sparkling stars, the highest heavens. The Old Testament thought of heaven as composed of different levels. There was the firmament, a crystal vault, to which the stars were attached. Above it lay the upper ocean; beneath it the realm of clouds and weather. Above all was the abode of God, where He was enthroned, surrounded by His angels. All these mighty creatures shall praise the name of the Lord. "For he spoke and they were made." This is the revelation upon which all is based: nothing is eternal, nothing self-evident; everything is created, is the work of God.

The work of creation—we think of it according to the teachings of science—is so ordered that it can be misunderstood as autonomous nature. The fact that something has been made obtrudes itself the more strongly the more imperfect it is. The more perfect it is, the more it is, so to speak, released from its dependence upon the maker and appears to be self-sufficient. The world has this mysterious quality and that is what we misunderstand when we speak of "nature."

"He hath established them forever." It is not like the work of man, which is made today and disintegrates tomorrow. It remains. This does not refer to the variations which also belong to that which we call "nature": the rhythms of light, the movements of the constellations, the seasons, the birth and death of individual beings. All this is part of an order which abides. But the reference is to the structure of the whole, the impression of solidity, reality, dependability which every element of creation produces. And in a deeper sense the fact that no mythical, demonic power of destruction prevails over the existence of the world.

The firmament and the stars are beneath the realm of the angels who immediately surround the throne of God; now the thought descends to the regions of our life.

There is the earth. There is the sea with its depths, the old mysterious realm where all life originates. There is the fiery lightning and the hail, mist and snow, storm-wind, mountains and hills. There are fruitful trees and cedars, the mighty giants of Lebanon, wild beasts and domestic herds, creeping things and the birds.

The Psalm finally reaches mankind. The nations of the earth are called upon, and the rulers who represent them; princes and judges who rule them, young men and maidens, old men and children—all shall praise the name of the Lord. The name of the Lord is He himself, God in the form of the word. The majesty of God is what provokes praise, the fact that power and glory are in Him personified and so can receive and appreciate the praise. This majesty is greater than earth and heaven. It is not created, but it is revealed in creation, revealed as that which surpasses all that is created.

At last comes the final class by whom God is praised, the people of God which "approaches" Him, bound to Him by the covenant, by His dwelling among them in history.

It is a mighty descent; on each step new praise breaks forth.

Did the praise cease after the composition of the Psalms?

Certainly not. In Old Testament times the Psalms were sung in the temple services and they were prayed by individuals in their devotions. Indeed they gave the form to personal prayer. Jesus prayed them. They resound in his words upon the cross (Matt. 27:46) and the "Magnificat" (Luke 1:46ff.) echoes them. Even today they form the chief constituent, we might even say the basis, of the prayer of the Church, the Liturgy.

This form of divine praise, which makes itself the voice of voiceless creation and turns its "essential" praise into speech, awoke again in later times. We find it frequently in Christian poetry, most perfectly perhaps in the *Canticle of the Sun* of St. Francis. This begins:

Most High, Omnipotent, Good Lord.
Thine be the praise, the glory, the honour and all benedic-
tion; and it continues
Be thou praised, my Lord, with all Thy creatures, above
all by Brother Sun
Who gives the day and lightens us therewith;
and he is beautiful and radiant
with great splendour.

Again the gaze of the poet ranges over the various regions of creation.
The earth also is invoked:

Be Thou praised, my Lord, of our sister,
Mother Earth

We hear the ancient note from mythology but reborn of faith.
Then comes a note of which the Old Testament knew nothing,

Be thou praised, my Lord, of those
who pardon for thy love
and endure sickness and tribulation

Here speaks the fervor which can even make that which is difficult
into a subject of praise.
Blessed are they who will endure it in peace—as if he were overwhelmed by the thought, how wonderful is the man who does this!
Finally the song of praise takes a very bold step:

Be thou praised, my Lord of our sister, bodily Death.

In itself—in spite of all idealistic and materialistic rhetoric—death is for a living man the ultimate terror. But here the union with God is so boundless that it can change the picture and call death "sister."

The man who voices this praise is close to all things. Not in pantheistic fashion; for him too the word is valid, "He commanded and they were created." There is no mingling of God and the world, but the closeness which he feels is that of creature to creature. In their createdness all things are brothers and sisters. In this intimacy he can set free the word that is bound in them and lift it up. God receives, as it were, the glory of the work that He expended on creation, receives it back from the mouth of the man who believes in Him and loves Him.

The word of praise has largely disappeared from our lips, just as today the joy in beauty seems to be disappearing and poets vie with each other in words of strife and anguish. Only very seldom do we find one like the Spaniard Jorge Guillèn, who speaks of light and joy.

But we must re-acquire the ability to praise; not in an artificial way, certainly, but we can, for instance, when we are out-of-doors, accustom ourselves to think: "God has created this." Present-day man is of the opinion that a religious act must be wholly spontaneous; otherwise it is not honest. He who says this does not know what prayer means. There is a kind of prayer that arises spontaneously, and blessed are they to whom it is granted. But there is also the prayer of service, of practice, and this is the rule. The thought: The world is created the heavens, the light of the sun, the mountain, the trees, all are created, and praised be He who has created them—all this is prayer and we must strive to acquire it again.

God's Understanding

The great one hundred-and-thirty-eighth Psalm is the song of God's knowledge. But before reading it we shall, as we often do in our meditations, work up to it by considering our own experience. We shall do this by asking what is the relation of the world to knowledge and to truth for man today.

Nature contains an innumerable multitude of forms, objects, and events in infinite variety, ranging from unattainable immensity to indistinguishable minuteness. They are in the most varied relations and orders, and are determined by laws and filled with meaning. Is all this known? This question perhaps seems strange to modern man. For him the world exists but has no knowledge of itself and is not comprehended in any consciousness. Essentially and originally, it has nothing to do with truth, only with reality. We can speak of truth only after man knows the world. It is he who brings truth into it.

But how long has man existed? Science says, he has been on earth for perhaps a million years. And how long shall he continue to exist? Again, science can attempt to calculate: until the cooling of the earth has caused it to be glaciated. Or, as we must say in view of recent history, until political despotism, the inquisitiveness of scientific research and the drive of technology have destroyed the necessary conditions of life.

During this time—how short in comparison with the duration of the universe—the light of knowledge in search of truth is shining and it extends as far as the existence of man extends. But what is that compared with the mental darkness which preceded it and which shall follow it?

And where do we find men? We find them on this tiny sphere of the earth, lost in space, and then only in the habitable and inhabited portions of its surface. What of the other heavenly bodies, and the immense and empty interstellar spaces?

And how weak is knowledge even where it claims to have attained to truth! If one has honestly labored in the service of truth and become capable of forming a judgment, and then looks and listens to find out how much that is really worth while is contained in conversations, in newspaper articles, in speeches and lectures and the opinions of experts, what does he find? Is he not finally discouraged, offended and even disgusted by the thoughtless way in which people claim to see truth where there is no truth?

What does man know of that which should above all be known to him, man himself? At first he seems to know a great deal. Anthropology, taking the word in its broadest sense, is constantly advancing and the amount of data is incalculable. But is it clear to anthropology what man is? Sometimes we would be inclined to think that true comprehension of man is in inverse ratio to the amount of anthropological science.

What do we know, each one of us, about others? Just so much that we can associate with them, on the street, in our occupation and in society. We have approximate surface knowledge, and often not even that, or things would be different. Beyond this, do we know anything about those who pass us on the street, with whom we associate in shops, offices or professions? Do we know anything of their inner life? Of their destiny?

We do observe a little of the surface, a few traits of character, a few habits, but beyond this there is darkness.

He who is more closely connected with another sees more, of course: a father, mother, lover or friend. But can he really fathom the interior, the sentiments of the heart, the depths of character, the hidden need? And is it not true that sometimes love, of its very nature, does not see truly, because it is selfish and wishes the loved one to be what it would have him, because it is hypersensitive, lazy, cowardly and does not wish to see? And the ultimate depths, where man is a person and where he is bound up with his destiny, there no glance can penetrate.

If all this is so, then "knowledge" in our world is a tiny island of mental brightness surrounded by impenetrable darkness.

Is this the opinion of Revelation; that is, that the world is a boundless darkness, a vast unknown, in which a little light breaks, faint and flickering, where man is found, but quickly extinguished, leaving all once more in darkness and silence?

No, Revelation tells us that the world is known, every individual thing, every relation and also the whole. Its essence and its value, its existence and its meaning, its coming into being and its enduring—all are known. That world of which unbelief speaks and which lies in the darkness of mere being does not exist. This concept is the result of rebellion. Revelation says that the world is known from its very beginning, from its very foundation, because it is created. It is known by its Creator. His knowledge is not consequent upon its being, so that there would first be a world and then God's eye would be fixed upon it, but it was known before it existed. Even more: when it was made, the act of omnipotence which created it was at the same time the act of omniscience which held it in the light. Only as a result of God's creative knowledge does the world exist at all.

In the first chapter of St. John's Gospel we read: "In the beginning was the word." Not "the deed" as the rebellious Faust said. Not the blind urge of which idealism speaks, but the truth breaking out into the word. But the "word," the *logos*, is only another name for God's eternal Son. He is essential truth, for in him the Father is revealed to himself. "And the word was with God"; the eternal Son is turned to the Father, born as truth and responding as truth. "And the word was God," eternally existent. "All things were made by the word, and without him was made nothing that was made." These are powerful statements, unfathomable, inexhaustible, but every spark that we receive from them enlightens the mind and instructs the heart. They tell us that in the beginning, from the first reality of the world, there is no darkness, because everything stands in the light of God's knowledge. And it is in man's power to receive this light into his consciousness or to shut it out. This he can do, so completely that he turns the work of the *logos* into the dark impenetrability of modern "nature."

We too are in the light, for we too are created by the power of God which is one with His truth. We too are penetrated by the knowledge of God as a result of our being created, whether we know it or have forgotten it, whether we wish it or rebel against it.

What a tremendous thought! Everything that is, is known. Everything moves in the region of God's light. Everything by its being and enduring expresses the image of truth which the thought of God implanted in it in creating it.

Our own knowledge is no autocratic illumination but it must strive to retrace the lines of meaning which the knowledge of God has traced in thinking and creating. Similarly our self-knowledge is the endeavor to think that which God knows about us. Our truth is in His knowledge, and we know only so much about ourselves as we know through Him.

This is a thought that can give us peace—peace and breadth of vision. How wonderful it is that everything abides in truth and that untruth is only a shadow between us and all that is. Actually and essentially everything abides in truth, all creatures and we ourselves. Our soul and body, our powers and qualities, our work and our destiny—all are in the light of God.

But then our feelings may change. Is it not terrifying to realize that all that we are and do and think, our whole being, is known?

Out of this conflict of feelings emerges the one hundred-thirty-eighth Psalm, with which we shall deal. It is long and therefore we cannot consider it entirely and in detail. But let us look at the first part:

> Lord, thou has proved me and known me; thou hast known my sitting down and my rising up.
>
> Thou hast understood my thoughts afar off; my path and my line thou hast searched out.
>
> And thou hast foreseen all my ways, for there is no speech in my tongue.
>
> Behold, O Lord, thou hast known all things, the last and those of old; thou hast formed me and hast laid thy hand upon me.
>
> Thy knowledge is become wonderful to me: it is high, and I cannot reach it.
>
> Whither shall I go from thy spirit? Or whither shall I flee from thy face?
>
> If I ascend into heaven, thou art there; if I descend into hell, thou art present.
>
> If I take my wings early in the morning [take the wings of the morning-light] and dwell in the uttermost parts of the sea.
>
> Even there also shall thy hand lead me, and thy right hand shall hold me.
>
> And I said, "Perhaps darkness shall cover me, and night shall be my light in my pleasures."

But darkness shall not be dark to thee, and night shall be light as the day; the darkness thereof and the light thereof are alike to thee.

For thou hast possessed my reins; thou has protected me from my mother's womb.

I will praise thee, for thou art fearfully magnified [that I am wondrously made]; wonderful are thy works and my soul knoweth right well.

My bone is not hidden from thee, which thou hast made in secret, and my substance in the lower parts of the earth.

Thy eyes did see my imperfect being and in thy book all shall be written. Days shall be formed, and no one in them.

If we have noted these words carefully, then we have felt a great power, a power of light which penetrated all.

We can understand the piety of the Old Testament only if we remember that there everything is penetrated by the experience of God's reality. For the Jews of that time he was not merely an idea, an indefinite power or a personal experience—He was for them more real than the ground upon which they stood, real not only in a general sense but in this particular place, in this particular moment, because their whole history was to be a history of God's activity and presence. And this presence meant that they were known by Him.

In the book of Genesis there is a wonderful passage which tells that Hagar, Sara's maidservant, fled from her mistress into the desert. There she sat down beside a wall, at a loss what to do. Then God appeared to her and told her that she should return to her place, and then we read:

And she called the name of the Lord that spoke unto her, "Thou the God who hast seen me." For she said, "Verily here have I seen—him that seeth me." Therefore she called that well

"the well of him that liveth and seeth me." The same is between
Cades and Barad. (Gen. 16:13–14)

We feel the power in the words, "He has seen me." It is the power of
truth which nothing can stop. It is this of which the Psalm speaks.

In the silence of a quiet hour we shall consider its words and identify
ourselves with the speaker. Then it may perhaps be granted to us to be
faintly aware of the glance of the great quiet eyes.

The Psalmist has become conscious of the fact that God knows him,
and this thought is developed more and more powerfully. Would it be
possible to shut out this knowledge? No, for it penetrates everything.
Could one escape it? Perhaps by fleeing to the height of heaven? But there
God dwells from all eternity. Or to the depths of the lower world?—"Thou
art there." Or by taking "the wings of the morning light"? When the sun
rises in the clear atmosphere of the Orient the light flashes over the earth
in a moment. If he could flee as swiftly as the light rushes over the earth,
far away "to the uttermost parts of the sea"—not the sea which bounds
Palestine, but the shoreless ocean—even there would God's "hand lead
him." He could not take one step if it did not hold him. He would fall into
space otherwise, because going becomes possible only when God provides
the way and guides the steps.

Then the Psalmist attempts to measure how deep God's knowledge
extends, and he must say to himself that God sees not only the body but
also the soul, and within the soul the course of the thoughts, and these
from afar; that is, he sees these thoughts when they are still on the way
from the depths of the soul into the light of consciousness and still far
removed from it, even then they are known by God.

He speaks even more boldly: when he was not yet born nor formed
in the womb—the image of the man's mother and that of the mother of
all living creatures, the earth, are blended—even then God's eyes beheld
what the person being formed would do later in the course of his life.

No distance in space, no remoteness of soul, no veil of potential futurity is able to withdraw anything from the glance of God.

According to our relation to God the fact of his knowledge becomes our comfort or our terror, for this knowledge is in itself the judgment. If God knows all, then he knows my actions, both good and evil. He knows not only what I do but also why I do it, knows my motives and my purposes both open and secret. And He not only knows all this, but He judges it. He measures it according to His measure, and His measure is valid, without error or uncertainty. Hence I stand not merely in the light of His glance but under the verdict of His judgment. This clearly states my condition, however men may be disposed toward me, whatever I may think of myself. Herein lies the ultimate seriousness of existence—and this may weigh very heavily upon us.

But there is not only the bitter sense of helplessness before the incorruptible judge, but the feeling of confidence before the one who is all-gracious. This causes a man to say, "Lord, I know that I am not justified before you. Wherever you look you find evil in me. I myself see this, how much more You for whom men's hearts are open. And yet, I consent that You see me. I wish to stand in the light of Your glance. All that I am I surrender to Your truth."

There is a knowing which is merely knowledge, the ascertainment of facts and structures of meaning. This is unmerciful. Let us think of the way in which a research-scholar or scientist turns his instruments upon the object which he is examining, or the way in which an unsympathetic judge ferrets out the actions of a person accused. God's knowledge is not like that. It is one with His love. He himself has created the object of His judgment and He continually preserves it. God's truth is thought but also heart; it is light, but also warmth.

And the man who is united with God believes, and believing means surrendering to Him. Believing, he says to God: "You shall know everything, my being, my actions, my thoughts, my joys and my sorrows, my successes and my failures, what I possess and what I have lost; the good and noble as well as the evil, ugly, base and disgraceful. All shall come into your light. There it will all be safe, even what is worst.

His light is love and salvation. It will guide all aright.

God's Shepherding Care

PSALM 22 (23)

Many of the Psalms grew out of the history of the chosen people, others out of the personal life of the individual. Among these the twenty-second is particularly impressive. Before turning to it we want to try to understand the manner of life from which it proceeds, the life of the shepherd. This type of life has become strange to us. We no longer know anything of the world in which a man lives with his flocks whom he knows and loves, from whom he derives his food and clothing, and who dwells largely in lonely places with their dangers and mystery. From him to his flock flows a constant stream of ever watchful knowing and caring. He leads them to pasture and to the water, takes care of them if they are sick, protects them against robbers and wild beasts. Comparing the relation between God and man to that between the shepherd and his sheep implied nothing at that time which might offend man's dignity.

It is to those times that our Psalm belongs. According to tradition it was composed by David himself, who came as a young shepherd from the flocks of his father to the army of King Saul, a sling-shot in his pocket and his staff in his hand.

The chosen people were a pastoral people. The book of Genesis tells how God's command came to Abraham, their ancestor, in Mesopotamia, and how he, obeying the call, travelled with his family and his flocks into the promised land. His descendants became numerous. At the time of a severe famine they took refuge in Egypt and there were reduced to slavery from which they were delivered by Moses. Led by him, the Israelites fought their way through the desert with their flocks, and finally, under Josue, took possession of the promised land.

The shepherd with his flock was a familiar sight for these people and the relation of shepherd and flock became quite naturally an image of the conditions of human life.

The Psalm reads:

> The Lord is my shepherd and I shall want nothing.
> He hath set me in a place of pasture.
> He hath brought me up on the water of refreshment [living water].
> He hath converted my soul.
> He hath led me on the paths of justice [the right way] for his own name's sake.
> For though I should walk in the midst of the shadow of death
> I will fear no evil, for thou art with me.
> Thy rod and thy staff they have comforted me.
> Thou hast prepared a table before me against them that afflict me.
> Thou hast anointed my head with oil and my chalice which inebriateth me how goodly is it! [My cup runneth over]
> And thy mercy will follow me all the days of my life
> And I shall dwell in the house of the Lord unto length of days.

A great depth of feeling pervades this poem. The man who is speaking feels that he is a member of God's flock and he has firm confidence in his shepherd. His shepherd is the Lord, so he shall "want nothing."

How often something was wanting in a land which consisted largely of stony plains. These had only a sparse vegetation, and often the flock had to search a long time before finding grass. If they really found a green pasture, how precious it was! He who has God as his shepherd is always granted this abundance, the image of all good gifts.

"He hath brought me up on living water." In the land of the Bible water is scarce and so it became an image of life and of value. This is true especially of "living water" in contrast to a cistern in which only rainwater gathered, which soon became brackish; a spring which constantly flows and delightfully quenches thirst. In order to describe the wonders of Paradise the book of Genesis tells of its rivers; four of them, in streams of cool abundance, which made the land fruitful.

He who commits himself to God's care is brought to an abundance whose inexhaustible supply does not merely quench thirst from time to time but provides satisfaction and security, copious draughts, a super-abundance of life. There his soul—and the word means his whole being—finds refreshment.

"He hath led me on the right way." Let us recall again the holy land, which was, in large part, a desert with few roads. How easily a shepherd could lose his way and wander into arid land where the flock might die of thirst, or into dangerous places where robbers might attack them. God leads his flock "on the right way."

But He does this "for his own name's-sake." The name is the revelation in which God made known who He is: the mighty One, but also the One who is kind and provident; the One who has bound himself to this people by his covenant. Not because He, like the pagan *numina*, was the mythical personification of the nation but because He by his free grace chose this people and made it the bearer of the history of salvation.

"Though I should walk in the midst of the shadow of death," or " in a dark ravine," "I will fear no evil, for thou art with me." In mountainous regions it can happen that the sun sets swiftly, suddenly as it does in southern countries, and the shepherd with his flock must pass through a narrow gorge. This can be very eerie. Wild beasts may attack or robbers may rush out. The flock huddles together and follows the shepherd. But they are unafraid, for his "rod and staff" give them confidence.

The "staff" means the shepherd's crook, the symbol of the watchfulness, the experience and the calm confidence of the man who is closely bound up with his flock and knows the landmarks. The flock depends upon this. Perhaps we can also suppose that the shepherd as he walks strikes the ground with his long staff so that the sheep hear the sound and even in the darkness are certain of the shepherd's guiding presence. The "rod" means the club which the shepherd carries for protection and with which he defends his flock.

So the Psalmist says to God, "With You I am safe."

The image of the shepherd is succeeded by another, also taken from the real life of that time, the image of host and guest.

"Thou hast prepared a table before me." The traveller has come a long way; now he arrives at the home of his friend and is well taken care of, for a guest is sacred, and the host is responsible for him, with all that he has.

He prepares a table before him against them that afflict him. The traveller has enemies; perhaps they have pursued him. Now, however, he is safe, and the host, sure of his power, proudly defies all enemies. They can see how the guest takes his ease and they feel powerless to harm him.

"Thou hast anointed my head with oil." It was an old custom, which is also referred to in the Gospels, for example, in the passage telling how Jesus is invited to the house of a Pharisee and then rebukes him for his lack of courtesy: "I entered into thy house—my head with oil thou didst not anoint but she" —Mary Magdalene—"with ointment hath anointed my feet." (Luke 7:44–46)

The oil smoothed the long hair. It was mixed with perfume and diffused a pleasant fragrance. It was a part of hospitality to give this pleasure to a guest.

"My cup runneth over"—not sparingly measured, not half-full, but running over. The host who does this says "You are welcome to everything."

"Thy mercy will follow me all the days of my life." Usually the situation is reversed; it is the man who follows after happiness and seeks to grasp it, but it flees and he stretches out empty hands. Here it is blessedly otherwise; God's mercy itself follows the man loved by God, practically pursues him and reveals inexhaustible kindness.

"I shall dwell in the house of the Lord." This probably does not refer to the temple, but to the whole country which belongs to God and is His house, in which the man who trusts in Him is His guest. Wherever the believer may dwell, in the house of the Lord, he is hospitably received, protected and showered with gifts.

Here there is an intimate closeness, an unconditional confidence which entrusts itself to the holy and mighty One. In order to understand this we must go back to the basic religious experience of the chosen people, the fact that God had bound them to himself in a special way.

This does not mean the providence which God exercises over all His creation, but it refers to the event which the first chapters of the book of Exodus recount: God came to this people and in a mysterious way drew them to himself. God, who has no need of the world—nor of this people, for He constantly passes judgment upon it—has spoken and freely brought to pass what He has promised, faithfully confirming it: "I will walk among you and will be your God, and you shall be my people." (Lev. 26:12) Out of this covenant comes the consciousness which is expressed in the image of the shepherd and his flock. This is the reason for that confidence which knows no doubts.

The books of the Old Testament are filled with accounts of events which show how the history of this people grew out of the covenant. Not out of the political wisdom of its kings, not out of the valor of its soldiers, not out of the industry of its workers—important as these may be—but out of the constant merciful action of God.

We shall quote just one example from the book of Judges.

There we are told how Gedeon marched against the Midianites, the pillaging tribes of Arabs who repeatedly invaded the land of Israel from the desert:

> Then Jerobaal, who is the same as Gedeon, rising up early and all the people with him, came to the fountain that is called Harad...and the Lord said to Gedeon, "The people that are with thee are many, and Madian shall not be delivered into their hands, lest Israel should glory against me and say 'I was delivered by my own strength.' Speak to the people and proclaim in the hearing of all, 'Whosoever is fearful and timorous, let him return.'" So two and twenty thousand men went away ... and only ten thousand remained. And the Lord said to Gedeon, "The people are still too many. Bring them to the waters and there I will try them."...and when the people were come down to the waters the Lord said to Gedeon: "They that shall lap the water with their tongues, as dogs are wont to lap, thou shalt set apart by themselves; but they that shall drink bowing down their knees shall be on the other side." And the number of them that had lapped water...was three hundred men, and all the rest of the multitude had drunk kneeling. And the Lord said to Gedeon, "By the three hundred men, that lapped water, I will I save you and deliver Madian into thy hand." (Judges 7:1–7)

It is not the people themselves who are making their history. It is God. He acts, and by acting reveals himself.

We find the image of the Psalm beautifully echoed in the New Testament. There Jesus appears as the true shepherd, in passages like the following:

> And Jesus went about all the cities and towns, teaching in their synagogues and preaching the gospel of the kingdom and healing every disease and every infirmity. And seeing the multitude he had compassion on them, because they were distressed and lying like sheep that have no shepherd. (Matt. 9:35–6)

Or the parable of the sheep that had strayed from the flock and that he follows into the desert until he finds it, and then he carries the weary sheep on his shoulders and restores it to the flock. (Luke 15:4–6) And there are other passages.

Especially impressive is the tenth chapter of St. John. There Jesus says, "The thief"—one who might have been lurking in the dark ravine—"cometh not but to steal and to kill and to destroy. I am come that they may have life and may have it more abundantly. I am the good shepherd." And again,

> The good shepherd giveth his life for his sheep. But the hireling, he that is not the shepherd, whose own the sheep are not, seeth the wolf coming and leaveth the sheep and flieth...because he is a hireling and he hath no care for the sheep. I am the good shepherd and I know mine, and mine know me, as the Father knoweth me and I know the Father. And I lay down my life for my sheep. (John 10:10–15)

What depth of meaning this adds to the image! Christ came in the freedom of his love to lead them to life, to the fulness of life, abundant as flowing water. He knows those who believe in him and they know him. It is the intimate knowledge of the Redeemer and the redeemed, an intimacy like that between Creator and creature, or perhaps even closer because of the love with which Christ "loved them unto the end." (John 13:1) He cares for them, because they are his, bought at the price of his atonement.

And now we read an unprecedented sentence. Christ knows his sheep as the eternal Father knows the Son and as the Son knows the Father. Do we see how here the relation between the shepherd and his flock is drawn into the abyss of the divinity? It is inconceivable what here shines forth from the intimate life of God into the life of the man who is united to Him by faith.

He says even more: "I lay down my life for my sheep." The intimacy of Jesus with his own extends even through the end, through death. It is a covenant unto death, just as the gift of himself in the Eucharist is a sacrament proceeding from the death of Jesus. It was established the evening before his passion, as his "body which was given for us . . . his blood which was shed for us." (Matt. 26:26ff.) And St. Paul says, "As often as you shall eat this bread and drink the chalice you shall shew the death of the Lord." (1 Cor. 11:26) The union here is as profound as that between one who dies for another and the one for whom he dies, when he who does this is the almighty God.

But the relation, like all true relations, also applies in reverse; and now the image of the dark ravine receives its final meaning, for the shadow is our own death. There no one will be with us, neither father nor mother, neither brother nor sister, neither lover nor friend. There science does not help us, nor art nor culture. We go alone through the dark ravine. But Christ is there; he alone, because he died for us, after living for us, and then rising from the grave, conquered death. In this way he accomplished a mysterious identification with us. He entered into our destiny so divinely and powerfully that he lives the life of each believer, as St. Paul says, "I live, yet no longer I, but Christ lives in me." (Gal. 2:20) Whenever a believer says, "I," Christ says, "I," in him. Whenever a believer endures his destiny, it is Christ who endures it in him.

And in turn the Father grants what St. Paul asks for his Christians, "That Christ may dwell by faith in your hearts; that being rooted and founded in charity you may be able to comprehend, with all the saints, what is the breadth and length and height and depth, to know also the charity of Christ which surpasseth all knowledge, that you may be filled unto all the fulness of God." (Eph. 3:17–19)

Perhaps we have at some time had a presentiment of our own death, have envisioned the hour of absolute loneliness, when everything will fall away; everything will abandon us. And the more ambitious the words that were spoken, the more completely shall everything which they promised disappear including wealth, progress, and culture.

Only our confidence in Christ will not be deceived. He remains. He accompanies us. He dies with everyone who believes; and he will "raise him up again, in the last day." (John 6:39)

The Voice of the Lord

PSALM 28 (29)

I n the Psalms we encounter human life with its joys and sorrows, but also the world of nature. However we must make a distinction here. It is not nature in the way in which it is treated by our lyric poets. Nature for its own sake has no place in the Old Testament; it is always regarded from a religious point of view, or, more exactly, it is always related to the personal God and to the destiny of the man who is addressed by God, and only so does it attain its full meaning.

Nature is the work of God's creative power, a revelation of His glory, the instrument of His might. His word is active in all things. There is as yet no conception of what we call the laws of nature. The Old Testament knows nothing of these. Knowledge of natural laws comes only at the beginning of the modern age. In the Old Testament everything that takes place is the immediate work of God. We might almost say that here the word of God, His will, that rules, bestows and punishes, takes the place of the laws of nature. When it rains, it is God who sends the rain; when the sea is moved, it is He who stirs up the water; when the trees grow, it is God's power that causes their growth; when the grain ripens it is He who gives bread to man. Of course, ultimately, it is really God who causes these things, but He does it by intermediary causes: the energies of nature, the power of growth in the seed, the organs of life. But these intermediary causes play no part in the conceptions of the Old Testament, and God does everything immediately even to the last detail. Hence the religious intensity of the language, but also many difficulties; for example, the question: What is the cause of evil? Does God bring this about also? The Old Testament never quite solved this problem.

But, in a different sense than in mythology, everything is filled with God. Yet He is never Nature itself, neither its order, nor its soul. God is very close to nature but there is never a fusion. Always He is the Lord, Lord of nature because He is Lord of himself. His hand fashions all that exists; His word is active in every occurrence; but He does not need nature nor does He intermingle with it. Nature never succeeds in being God or becoming a part of Him. He always rises above it, is far beyond it, sufficient unto himself, unapproachable in His majesty.

The manner in which God is related to nature in the Psalms corresponds to the relation of man to nature. Man has need of nature and his emotions are touched by it. He admires it or feels its menace, but he is never submerged by it or absorbed in it. Even the strongest emotion has nothing of the Dionysiac element.

Man is, or at least is intended to be, the lord of nature by means of grace; God is the Lord by His very essence. Man experiences his own lordship by being in a personal relation to God; this raises him above any interrelation with nature. Even in the moments when he is most moved by it, it is never nature that man addresses. When he speaks he is always thinking of the Creator and Lord of nature.

This is the secret of the nature Psalms. By the manner in which they speak of the shining heavens and the stormy winds, of the mountains and the fields, of fertility and drought, they always speak of the God of revelation who said on Mt. Horeb, "I am the I-am." (Ex. 3:14)

One of these Psalms which we shall now consider is the twenty-eighth.

Bring to the Lord, O ye children of God, bring to the Lord the offspring of rams.

Bring to the Lord glory and honour; bring to the Lord glory to his name; adore ye the Lord in his holy court. [in holy adornment]

The voice of the Lord is upon the waters; the God of majesty hath thundered; the Lord is upon many waters.

The voice of the Lord is in power; the voice of the Lord in magnificence.

The voice of the Lord breaketh the cedars; yea, the Lord shall break the cedars of Libanus,

And shall reduce them to pieces, as a calf of Libanus and as the beloved son of unicorns.

The voice of the Lord divideth [strikes out] the flame of fire.

The voice of the Lord shaketh the desert; and the Lord shall shake the desert of Cades.

The voice of the Lord prepareth the stags [twists the oaks from their roots], and he will discover the thick woods; and in his temple all shall speak his glory.

The Lord maketh the flood to dwell [is enthroned above the flood], and the Lord shall sit king for ever.

The Lord will give strength to his people; the Lord will bless his people with peace.

Let us examine the thoughts of this Psalm. It begins with the invocation: "Bring to the Lord, O ye children of God, bring to the Lord glory and honour." The children of God are the lofty beings of heaven, the angels. They behold God's glory and they see and understand what He does in the world.

Here we have the mighty course of a storm. The angels see it and behold God's power revealed in it. They are overwhelmed and their emotion is transformed into an act of adoration. We are tempted to speak of a cosmic liturgy here. In the heavens, around the throne of God, are the angels. They experience what takes place "below," on earth, and they cast themselves down before God and praise Him. They do this "in holy adornment," in solemn vestments, as heavenly liturgists. This is an image that is developed in the last book of the New Testament, in the Apocalypse.

Now the experience begins. The Psalmist is perhaps out in the open country. Some may think of David, watching his flocks. And then the storm breaks, "the voice of the Lord"—this phrase runs like a *leitmotif* through the whole Psalm.

It refers first of all to the thunder with its mighty crash which resounds through the world; then also to all the powerful forces unleashed: the storm-wind, the lightning. "The voice of the Lord" is the power of God, insofar as it does not create and construct, but menaces and lets us feel that He can break and destroy, and that all endures only by His grace.

"The voice of the Lord is upon the waters." At first reading, it appears that this might refer to the falling waters, the rain. But then it is repeated, "The God of majesty hath thundered; the Lord is upon many waters." Here something more powerful is brought into the picture, the rain of which the book of Genesis says, "The fountains of the great deep were broken up and the flood gates of heaven were opened; and the rain fell upon the earth forty days and forty nights." (Gen. 7:11–12) This refers to the waters which once flooded the earth when the sins of men became so great that God wanted to destroy all life from the face of the earth. (Gen. 6:5–7) It is the great flood, an historical event. But there seems to be another thought behind it. The world does not need to exist. It is not a natural necessity; it depends on the free will of God. Man is the final expression of the world. His conduct determines the meaning of its existence. If he is guilty, the possibility arises that God may recall the decree of creation. "It repented him that he had made man on the earth and he was touched inwardly with sorrow of heart." (Gen. 6:6) And so the same power that created could annihilate the work which had so disappointed its Creator. All this is indicated apocalyptically by the image of the storm.

"The voice of the Lord breaketh the cedars," those mighty trees of Libanus which are sometimes as much as twelve feet in diameter and which have been almost exterminated by the greed of men. That the voice of the Lord breaks them is a supreme proof of His power.

The voice of the Lord makes Libanus leap like a calf; the roll of the thunder shakes the mountains, their towering solidity turns into the image of a young and gamboling beast. "The voice of the Lord strikes out the flame of fire." The thunder, in which God speaks and threatens, strikes out the lightning, just as a man, striking a flint, brings out the spark.

"The voice of the Lord twists the oaks from their roots." It is like a powerful hand that grasps the trees and twists them as we might twist a willow twig. "He will discover the thick woods." The lightning strikes the trees and peels off the bark so that the interior becomes visible.

"And in his temple all shall speak his glory." This refers not to the people upon the earth, but to the angelic liturgists above, in the temple of heaven. "The Lord is enthroned above the flood"—probably the great flood of Genesis—"The Lord shall sit king forever." But then the thought returns to earth: "The Lord will give strength to his people; the Lord will bless his people with peace."

It is marvellous how the areas are interwoven. The whole spectacle is viewed from heaven, where the angels are. It takes place upon earth, but is drawn into the activity of the angels, knowing and glorifying God.

The activity portrayed in this Psalm—that the creatures of God, the angels, but also man who prays and sings, behold what happens upon earth and bring it into their adoration—are we today capable of this? It is a question that may disturb us.

It was not difficult for medieval man. He viewed the world as antiquity had viewed it; that is, as a cosmos. If we, for example, look at Dante's "Divine Comedy" we find its most complete image. The world appears as an enormous sphere, entirely filled and penetrated by the powers of God. It was the work of God and, with a few changes, could easily have been turned into a prayer like our Psalm. We need only think of the Canticle of St. Francis.

But then the exact sciences began to prevail and they created the modern concept of "nature." Medieval man could never have understood what this means. For him everything had a symbolic meaning; everything revealed God. The medieval cathedrals express this divine symbolism which underlies every object and every relation. But science asks for the natural *how* and *why*. Everywhere it finds the fact which is as it is, immovable and unchangeable, proved by experiment and expressed by a law which states what must happen, and how and why. At the same time, man begins to conceive of the world as not only great but infinite. Where then is God? Man no longer seems to have a proper place for Him. So he tries to draw Him into the world and a modern pantheism arises which conceives of God as the World-Soul. In our day the intoxication with infinity is passing away. The world is again viewed as finite. But science gives it more and more the character of a cold exactness, an enormous composite of energies and laws, while technology finds in it the material for more and more colossal operations.

This is the present situation, and this concept also affects the Christian believer. So it becomes difficult for him to draw the world into the act which is directed to God; that is, into his prayer. But it is man's task to do this. How can it be done?

We have probably been conscious of this problem. If we read, for instance, the nature poems of Goethe, which are filled with a pantheistic religion, we may have noticed that we cannot make them our own. We have become too sober—sober in a great sense, but also in an evil sense.

We cannot accept this way. Perhaps we must find our way by means of the thought that God is "He who is," absolutely; the One who exists of himself.

And now I would like to say something which is, in itself, unreasonable. But perhaps it will help us to bring before the eyes of our mind and into our feelings something that cannot be reached by "reasonable" statements.

St. Theresa of Avila once said, "God alone suffices." Thereby she meant that God alone could satisfy wholly the deepest longings of man. That is true. But I would like to give the words another meaning and say, "If God is, that is 'sufficient.'" Let us suppose—and this is the "unreasonable" supposition—that it were absolutely demanded that all potential being and meaning, life and value, work and happiness must be realized, or else there would be a crying void. This demand would be fulfilled by the fact that God is. That would be enough. Nothing else would be necessary.

This God has created the world and man—each one of us. He did this not because he was compelled to by some necessity but in complete freedom. He willed it because He willed it. And he did this, we say, out of love. The meaning of this—when God who has infinite love and fruitfulness in himself, has love for the finite, for man—surpasses all reason. It is not God who constitutes the problem, that is, whether He is, and who He is and how He is, but the finite, that is, how it can be and why, and for what reason. God is not the question, but man—man and the world.

Therefore, in a conversion, a *metanoia*, of thought, which we must accomplish in sheer reliance on revelation, the question which we have asked is reversed, and so is the answer. Atheism, which constantly spreads and grows ever more decidedly, states just the opposite: man, nature, and the work of man which uses the stuff of nature, are the only realities and suffice for everything. "God" is a creation of man, necessary and meaningful as long as man is still immature. Now man has become mature and takes the final step of maturity. Now he no longer needs "God." Man and his world constitute the whole. This satisfies in many persons the self-love of present-day man. Actually, it is a revolt against absolute truth.

To believe means to make a decision in favor of the truth. The believer sees the greatness of the world, overcomes the claim of its apparent independence, and, in faith and prayer, restores it to the hand of God.

The Longing for God

PSALM 62 (63)

There is a religious feeling, which seems to be very rare, although it really should arise very strongly from the depths of man's being; that is, the longing for God. It really should dominate our whole interior life; for the fact that man is created is not something that had significance only "once upon a time," at the beginning of things, but it is the basic character that determines all human affairs. Whatever man is, he is as a created being; whatever he does, he does on the basis of his created nature. Therefore, the longing for God ought to be the elementary expression of this fact. That is not so reveals to a thoughtful person much of our profoundest history.

It is true that upon creating him God set man free. He placed him in true reality and responsibility, although it is a mystery how something finite and conditional can be possible, how it can occupy space and have the power of being "beside" the infinite and absolute. We accept it as self-evident that the finite should exist; everyone of us accepts it as entirely self-evident that he himself, who considers himself the center of all that is, should be. This is so much the case that present-day man has begun to create an image and concept of existence in which there is nothing but man and the world. This is metaphysically grotesque since the opposite is really the case, that God is the self-evident one, the absolutely sufficient and that it is sheer grace, indeed a miracle of God's creative will that the world and man, that I and the world, exist. This is so, and the nature of God's absoluteness is revealed by the fact that He is not despotic, but magnanimous, nor crushing, but creative. The fact that we have been created is a bond between God and us, more real than that between the child and the mother. This bond should be felt, and not only in times of need but again and again, the more strongly and more intensively existence is felt. But God creates in such a perfect and magnanimous way that man can forget the fact and can think he is self-based, or else that he proceeds from the totality of the world, from "nature."

But in many of the Psalms the longing for God breaks forth very powerfully, most powerfully perhaps in the sixty-second. This is a very ancient Psalm; many still attribute it to King David. It expresses a powerful feeling which touches our heart. It reads as follows:

> O God, my God, to thee do I watch at break of day. [in longing]
> For thee my soul hath thirsted; for thee my flesh, O how many ways!
> In a desert land, and where there is no way and no water.
> So in the sanctuary have I come before thee, to see thy power and thy glory.
> For thy mercy is better than life; thee my lips shall praise.
> Thus will I bless thee all my life long, and in thy name I will lift up my hands.
> Let my soul be filled as with marrow and fatness, and my mouth shall praise thee with joyful lips.
> If I have remembered thee upon my bed, I will meditate on thee in the morning,

Because thou hast been my helper, and I will rejoice under the covert of thy wings.

My soul hath stuck close to thee; thy right hand hath received me.

But they have sought my soul in vain, they shall go into the lower parts of the earth.

They shall be delivered into the hands of the sword; they shall be the portions of foxes.

But the king shall rejoice in God; all they shall be praised that swear by him, because the mouth is stopped of them that speak wicked things.

He who reads attentively perceives the power of these words. They speak of a very ancient time; more than two and a half millennia have passed since the Psalm was composed. It begins: "O God, my God." Not a God who is generally prescribed, but his own, the one whom he has experienced, who is the meaning of his life, his own in a way in which He is no one else's.

"To thee do I watch in longing." He does not speak in a merely external fashion, according to custom, in such a way that he could do otherwise or refrain from doing it, but from a deep impulse. He has need of his God. But does he have to seek Him? God is there, everywhere, within us. True, but things are there; there is a wall between God and ourselves. They do not impede by their own nature, for God has created them. But the fact that our attention and desire are bound to them makes them a barrier. Man himself is also a wall between the God within him and his own life, because in self-will he shuts himself up within himself. Therefore man must seek, and must strive to penetrate all that divides him from God.

And then comes the wonderful verse: "For thee my soul hath thirsted." Let us not misunderstand these words. "Soul" does not mean abstract mentality, but what is most alive in us, that which grows and breathes and feels. The next words make this very plain. "For thee my flesh, O how many ways!" How beautifully concrete are these sentences! Like "a desert land where there is no water"—this is how the Psalmist feels. He knows how it is when the wells are dry and the earth lies parched by the sun. "So am I," he says, "my body, my soul, my whole being thirsts for thee, O God." Blessed is the man, we think, who needs God as the earth needs the rain!

"So in the sanctuary have I come before thee," he continues, "to see thy power and thy glory." The Psalmist stays in the temple and waits until he receives that for which the temple exists. For the temple is God's house, filled with Him, and he who crosses the sacred threshold can feel how the glory of God impresses itself upon him.

In order to understand what is involved here we shall read the verses of Isaias which speak of the great theophany:

> In the year that king Ozias died, I saw the Lord sitting upon a throne high and elevated, and his train filled the temple. Upon it stood the seraphims.... And they cried one to another, "Holy, holy, holy, the Lord God of hosts, all the earth is full of his glory." And the lintels of the doors were moved at the voice of him that cried, and the house was filled with smoke. (Isa. 6:1–4)

This is the vision which was to strengthen the prophet for his difficult task. But even simple faith could experience something of the sort, the epiphany, God's glory becoming visible, flashing in the temple, turning to man and reviving him more than a drought revives a thirsting man, refreshing body and soul. Without such an experience, the religious life of the Old Testament could not be understood.

"Let my soul be filled as with marrow and fatness" when I approach thee. Again, let us observe the marvellous realism. It is not colorless thoughts that seek God, not only weak feelings, but an elementary longing, for which the living holy One is as real as bodily food when man is sitting at the table during the sacrificial banquet, satisfying his hunger.

The touch of God is very real to the Psalmist even when he turns to Him outside of the temple. "If I have remembered thee upon my bed, I will meditate on thee in the morning." He cannot sleep at night; he begins to think. As if drawn by an interior force his mind turns to God. Then something comes over him and stills his longing. "Thou hast been my helper, and I will rejoice under the covert of thy wings." It is the ancient image of the eagle who covers his young with his mighty wings.

Then comes another verse full of realistic imagery. "My soul hath stuck close to thee; thy right hand hath received me." The Psalmist reaches out to God, and God grasps him with His mighty hands, so that nothing can separate them.

"But they have sought my soul in vain; they shall go into the lower parts of the earth." It is the spirit of the Old Testament that finds expression here, not that of the New Testament. The Old Testament did not abolish hatred; it strove only to separate it from merely personal feeling and to connect it with the destiny of the nation. He who belonged to the chosen people and fought for its cause felt that his own was thereby sanctified. Whoever attacked him, attacked the people of God. This may help us to understand the violence of the emotion in this Psalm: the enemies "shall be delivered into the hands of the sword; they shall be the portions of foxes." It is the converse of the strong feeling that was first directed toward God.

The longing for God seeks not only to know Him, or to fulfill His commandments. It wishes to have a part in God Himself.

Is this pantheism? What does this term really designate? A confusion of feelings and thoughts. The feeling expands and no longer distinguishes between spirit and matter, between "I" and "Thou," between God and the creature. Everything is confused in a vague unity which is neither genuine nor permissible because it mingles things that cannot be combined. But our Psalm recognizes the majesty of God, who alone can say, "I am the I-am," who does not need the world, but has called it into being, because He wished to do so. The Psalmist wishes to have communion with Him, not to sink into the primordial foundation of the world or to be dissolved in the streams of existence, but to have communion in the dignity of a free person. The "I" remains before the eternal "Thou," but it feels a mighty urge toward Him, in order to have a part in Him.

Perhaps the reader will ask, "Why do you speak of such feelings and dispositions, if they are no longer ours, if they float before us as something great and high, but we cannot realize them?" But let us look more closely. The basic feeling of a man who breaks forth from his created nature is the longing to have a part in God. St. Augustine, in the first chapter of his *Confessions*, said "Thou hast made us for thyself, O Lord, and our hearts are restless until they rest in Thee." Let us attend to these words. God has made us for himself; He has not set us down as a fragment of abandoned reality, but has created us in such a way that our created nature is an urge toward Him. He created us for a purpose—the movement toward God.

If this is so, then this urge of longing exists in each one of us, though often intimidated by criticism, choked by life's commonplaces. We are a part of the world, it reaches out for us, draws our attention, our feelings and desires toward itself. This covers the depths, drowns out the basic voice. Therefore we must say to ourselves in faith: "He is; He exists for me and I must strive toward Him, must make myself free so that the inmost depths may be revealed. I must create silence around myself, so that I may hear the still, small voice."

Natural life teaches us that an organ which is not used atrophies. We have within us the possibility to be near to God, to have a part in Him. St. Augustine defined the human soul by saying that it is "capax Dei" that is, that it is capable of grasping God. Let us not permit this capability to perish.

Why are there churches, these lofty edifices in which silence prevails if it is not so that one may enter, sit down and recollect oneself; and, after a while, we no longer sit but kneel, for the presence of God has become perceptible.

Or else at home, as the Psalm relates, at night when we cannot sleep. If we do not reach for a book, or a sleeping tablet, but entrust ourselves to the silence, recollect ourselves and become attentive, then it may happen that the consciousness awakes that He is here. I am before Him. I long for Him—and then the longing is stilled. It is stilled and yet it grows. For this is the wondrous thing, that the longing for God grows stronger the more deeply it is stilled.

Of course, we must not forget something which constitutes the most difficult point in the religious life of present-day man: the fact that the religious feeling, the religious perception which immediately responds to existence, is constantly growing weaker. This is one of the reasons which induce men to look upon the divine as a false value and faith as unnecessary.

This decrease of religious sensitivity is a historical phenomenon over which the individual has no power. So he will not attempt to feel a longing for God of which he is not honestly capable, but he will carry out his will to have a part in God according to the grace given to him, namely in spiritual acts of attention, of moral obedience, of trust and faithfulness, and of self-conquest for God's sake.

The Fear of the Lord

I will praise thee, O Lord, with my whole heart, in the council of the just and in the congregation.

Great are the works of the Lord, sought out according to all his wills.

His work is praise and magnificence, and his justice continueth for ever and ever.

He hath made a remembrance of his wonderful works, being a merciful and gracious Lord.

He hath given food to them that fear him. He will be mindful for ever of his covenant,

He will shew forth to his people the power of his works,

That he may give them the inheritance of the Gentiles. The works of his hands are truth and judgment.

All his commandments are faithful, confirmed for ever and ever, made in truth and equity.

He hath sent redemption to his people; he hath commanded his covenant for ever. Holy and terrible is his name.

The fear of the Lord is the beginning of wisdom, a good understanding to all that do it; his praise continueth for ever and ever.

In order that we may better understand this Psalm we shall first call attention to something: when the believer of the Old Testament tries to comprehend the truth of the Revelation, the divine message given to him, then he looks back upon the history of his people. In the Old Testament to believe does not mean to accept some reasonable doctrine or way of life as true but to be included in a history carried on by God.

The central point of this history is mentioned in the Psalm, the covenant of Sinai. There God promised this people that He would be their God and they should be His people. He carries on a history with this people. To believe means to be a part of this history, to be conscious of the deeds that God has performed in it and to rely upon what He will do in the future. Even the creation of the world belongs to it. This is the beginning of the history, the earliest of God's works, followed by all the others which took place within the world.

From this point of view we must learn to understand the Psalm. For example, when it speaks of justice, this does not mean a general way of acting, which we may describe by saying that God gives to each man what is right according to moral laws, but justice is what results from the covenant of Sinai, from God's commandments and promises. The works and deeds of God which are referred to are not only the works of the creation and preservation of the world, which concern all men, but also, and above all, what God has done for this people from the calling of Abraham down through the centuries to the time in which the speaker is living. And finally, the term "the just man," which occurs in the Psalms again and again, does not mean the man who lives according to the moral law which is relevant for all, and who comes before God on the basis of a religious experience possible for everyone, but it means the man who lives in obedience to the law of the holy covenant.

The Christian can no longer think in this way. His existence as a believer no longer rests upon the basis of a particular people, which, guided by God, makes its way through history. When the Christian speaks of man he means the inhabitants of the earth, and when, after the coming of the Redeemer, he speaks of the people of God he means all those who believe in Christ. For us the content of faith tends to take on the nature of a system of statements generally valid, of which we are convinced, something like a system of philosophy, only more lofty, more all embracing, distinguished by holiness and salvation. We easily forget that faith still means remaining in knowledge and confidence within the providence of a personally acting God, only that His works and deeds are now carried on within the confines of humanity as a whole. For even the Creed, the confession of faith, properly considered, is less an arrangement of valid verities than an account of the "great works" of God.

To believe means, for us also, to be sure that God is acting, throughout all time, from the creation of the world until its end. It means doing at any one time that which is demanded of us, and following God in His actions toward their goal; that is, the return of Christ and the victory of the Kingdom of God. So it is good if we again and again break through the appearance of a mere doctrinal system and say, "God is acting here and now, doing something with me also. I place myself in his activity, go with Him, act and strive." In this connection the meaning of "hope" becomes clear: it is the confidence that in spite of all opposition of disbelief and disobedience, in spite of seeming impossibility, the promises of the Gospel are being fulfilled and the birth into a new life will be realized for us and for the whole creation.

The whole Psalm is a representation of past events, of the "great deeds of God" which are past in regard to external time but still present in the memory of the believer. We find narrative, thanksgiving and praise, admonition and instruction, signs of God's disposition and a pledge for the future.

But perhaps, in a groping fashion, we can say more: God performed these deeds in other days, whenever, according to His counsel, the proper time had come. But God Who here works in time, is also beyond all time and place. So the deeds which He performs in sacred history do not pass with time, but transcend it and remain in a living eternity. Therefore we may say that what has happened operates in every moment of time, as soon as the believer thinks about it. For the man of the Old Testament sacred history has a kind of sacramental character; through prayerful thought, it comes to life and operates in the thinker; it blesses the moment, enlightens and strengthens and becomes effective for the future in the process of the history of salvation. The manner in which faith—the faith of the congregation in liturgical celebrations, of the family in their devotions and of the individual in private prayer—recalls past deeds of God—points forward, we may say, to that commemoration which our Savior will institute when he says, "As often as ye shall do this, do it in commemoration of me." (Matt. 26:26–28; 1 Cor. 11:23–25)

So the Psalm recalls the works of the Lord, His "wonders," particularly the deeds on Mt. Sinai and during the long journey through the desert, when He made His covenant with the people, indeed, made them into a nation by His covenant, gave them self-consciousness, law and order. He led them by the pillar of fire, taught them by the words of Moses, and later of the prophets, strengthened them in battle and gave them the promised land.

This commemoration is found in the Psalms again and again, and by it the events of the past are brought into the actual moment and connected with the history of salvation.

But we shall deal particularly with one verse of our Psalm, the tenth, which reads: "The fear of the Lord is the beginning of wisdom."

What is meant by "the fear of the Lord? We probably must begin by recalling that this concept has become strange to us. Who speaks of it today? And if anyone does, the modern ethics of autonomy has made it a thing of slight value for people today. Also, after Nietzsche proclaimed the message of the kingdom of man, after the governments of almost half the earth seek to do away with God and to set up the state as a divinity, just what is the fear of the Lord?

First of all, we must remind ourselves what it is not. It is not "being afraid" of God. There is such a thing. It exists in a morbid form when God becomes a dark "other," and the thought of Him becomes an oppressive feeling of constraint or a fetter for a timid conscience.

Besides this there is another fear before God which occurs when men have created an image of human existence into which God does not seem to fit, because His reality would shatter it, and consequently He is banished from it. Let us recall that Nietzsche, of whom we have just spoken, declared that if man wishes to realize himself and carry out his work, God cannot exist. And how many repeat this; Let us think of the political atheism of our time, whose concept of state and culture excludes God. All this makes of God a strange despotic power which forces itself upon man, and against which man must defend himself in order to gain freedom for himself.

And finally, is there not, even in the believer—the man touched by the sacred message—a fear growing out of the thought of what would happen if he really surrendered to God, His will and His love?

All this—and more—is fear before God, and it is basically foolish. For I can be afraid only of "another" who is opposed to me and wills what is harmful to me. But God is not at all "the other," the rival in existence, which that sort of philosophy considers Him to be. Everything exists through Him, for He has created it. I *am* only because He called me into being and keeps me. I exist and say "I" because He says "thou" to me and maintains me as such. If I can think, plan, freely decide, act and create, it is only because He permits me to be the image of His sovereign lordship in His world.

Here we have the ancient rebelliousness which is not willing to say, "I through God," but insists, "Either He or I." Therefore, since man wishes to be, God cannot be permitted to be. This is the deepest fear before God.

But "the fear of the Lord" means something very different. It means, above all, the clear consciousness that God really *is*. This is not a mere idea or a mere feeling, but a reality. More than this: if we ask what really *is*, then the proper answer is "He." Only thereafter, through Him and before Him, I. He alone could say, "I am the I-am!" (Ex. 3:14) Man should know and confess, "I am His creature." To accept this fact interiorly, and to be shaken by the greatness of this God, that is the fear of the Lord.

Furthermore, God is not only the One Who is real of Himself, He is also the Holy One, the One Who is essentially pure and good, the One in Whom there is no falsehood, no violence, no envy. There is in Him nothing that is wrong. Whatever we call good, whatever we strive for—if we strive morally—is a reflection of Him, and it is all supported, penetrated, and fixed by that inexpressible something, peculiar to Him, and attested to by its own being, which we call "holiness" and before which we kneel. To believe, to feel, to live in consciousness of the fact that He is the only basically Holy One, and that we live in His sight, subject to His judgment and cannot stand before it—that is the fear of the Lord.

Our verse says, "The fear of the Lord is the beginning of wisdom." What does that mean?

Scripture often speaks of the "foolishness" of man. Wherein does it consist? Whence does it come—all that is evil, confused, destructive in the life of the individual and in history?

Basically, these things are present because man permits himself to slip into an attitude which would only be possible if he were God. For, to decide autonomously about good and evil, to establish his aims according to his own will and without consideration for God's commandment—to do this he would have to be God himself. But this is not the case, and therefore his action is foolish, senseless and spacious and ends in emptiness. But he who knows that God alone is holy and eternal, and that man is created and subject to God's judgment, has a standard. He learns how to distinguish true from false, good from evil.

We have had a terrible lesson, for twelve years, showing what can happen when there is no fear of the Lord. No one of these who were then in power bowed before God, whatever they may have said to the people about "providence" and "positive Christianity" in order to subject the nation to their will. So they said that whatever is useful for the nation is right, but the "nation" was simply a cover for their own greed for power and otherwise a delusion. Crime was lord of the land, and it all ended in horror.

He who has the fear of the Lord in his heart distinguishes between what has value and what is worthless, what endures and what passes, what is valid and what does not matter. As soon as he thinks of the great distinction, between the eternal God and ephemeral man, the fog lifts. Many a philosophy, many a political theory, many a concept of culture or of education proves to be false, deceptive, a "dizziness of mind" as someone has said. The consciousness of the living God operates as a touchstone to separate reality from unreality.

Wisdom is something different from knowledge. A man may possess the knowledge of all the libraries and yet be a fool. Wisdom means the ability to distinguish between what leads to life and what leads, however distantly, to death.

The way in which a man lives depends fundamentally upon whether he knows who God is and "fears" Him. But where do we now hear the admonition of the Psalm? Do we read it in a book of philosophy? Does it live in the poetry of our time? Does the public atmosphere allow it to be heard? Is it not true that present-day man feels insulted if something like the fear of God is attributed to him? Fear—he replies—how so? Man is real; God is a word used by priests to subject man to their will. God is a hypothesis which has become superfluous; He is a mist that will soon disappear from the earth.

We should accept the thought of the fear of God. It is our guarantee that we shall not gain knowledge and power while forgetting the truth of existence.

The consciousness of sacred history awakened again and again in the believer of the Old Testament the fear of the Lord. When he considered how God created all things, how He did not leave man to his fate after the rebellion in Paradise but received him again in grace; how He delivered Israel from the Egyptian slavery and made them His people by the covenant of Sinai, led them through the desert and gave them the promised land; how He remained divinely faithful to them in spite of their continued unfaithfulness, and again and again called them to repentance by His messengers and instructed them in His holy will—then the reality of God was deeply impressed upon him. In the seventy-sixth Psalm we read,

> I remembered the works of the Lord, for I will be mindful
> of thy wonders from the beginning.
> And I will meditate on all thy works, and will be employed
> in thy inventions.

The believer recognized that he was God's creature and from the experience of God's greatness he gained the clearness of sight to discern the emptiness of pagan gods though surrounded by gigantic pagan powers, and he received strength to remain obedient to the one Lord.

We also will do well if we again and again renew our consciousness of the history of our existence. It makes a great difference how man regards his origin: if he thinks he comes from the dull necessity of a purely natural evolution or is aware that he has been thought by God's wisdom, called by His majesty and preserved in a sacred "thou." This certainly does not mean that we should overlook the genuine results obtained by true science. But these must be taken up into the great truth which makes man human, that God created him and made him in His image. The Christian believer also has the right to see in the history of the Old Testament the history of his salvation; only he sees it as continuing in the coming of the Redeemer whom the prophets foretold, in the life of Christ, his teaching, his death and resurrection and in the founding of the Church by the Holy Spirit.

From this he gains the consciousness that he is only man, but made in the image of God. He learns to live in the sight of God and to know that he is going through the passage of time toward the return of Christ, the judgment and the new creation. For him also this means that God is magnified, and he himself, man, is only a creature, but truly a creature, son or daughter of the Father, brother or sister of Christ, led by the Holy Spirit. And the fear of God, which is basically only truth carried out in life, will preserve him from falling a prey to the subtle as well as violent deception of self and of nature.

Transitoriness

PSALM 89 (90)

T he thought of transitoriness runs through the ancient world like a dark stream: life is short; everything passes. Even the greatest possessions and the most joyful experiences do not change this. This feeling also runs through the Old Testament. In order to understand better how strong it is, we must remember that the thought of eternal life long played no role in the Old Testament. It entered into consciousness only late, in the last centuries before Christ.

This had a special effect. The Old Testament seeks to place the earth immediately in the hand of God, to make it His kingdom; therefore man's glance should be directed only to this world. It is a curious attitude. We should misunderstand it if we called it worldliness. The believer turns to the earth in order to make it God's possession, that He may be its king. Therefore the thought of an eternal life after death should not be permitted to turn men's glance aside.

This will help us to understand better the melancholy seriousness of this Psalm:

Lord, thou hast been our refuge from generation to generation.

Before the mountains were made, or the earth and the world were formed; from eternity and to eternity thou art God.

Turn not man away to be brought low, and thou hast said: Be converted, O ye sons of men.

[Thou turnest man to dust and sayst: return anew, ye sons of men.]

For a thousand years in thy sight are as yesterday which is past, and as a watch in the night.

Things that are counted nothing shall their years be.

In the morning man shall grow up like grass; in the morning he shall flourish and pass away; in the evening he shall fall, grow dry and wither.

For in thy wrath we have fainted away, and are troubled in thy indignation.

Thou hast set our iniquities before thy eyes, our life [secret sins] in the light of thy countenance.

For all our days are spent, and in thy wrath we have fainted away.

Our years shall be considered as a spider [a sigh]

The days of our years in them are threescore and ten years,

But if in the strong they be fourscore years what is more of them is labour and sorrow.

For mildness is come upon us and we shall be corrected

[For they pass swiftly and we fly away]

Who knoweth the power of thy anger, and for thy fear can number thy wrath?

So make thy right hand known, and men learned in heart, in wisdom.

[Teach us to number our days that we may attain to wisdom of heart.]

Return, O Lord, how long? And be entreated in favour of thy servants.

We are filled in the morning with thy mercy, and we have rejoiced and are delighted all our days.

We have rejoiced for the days in which thou hast humbled us, for the years in which we have seen evils.

Look upon thy servants and upon their works, and direct their children.

And let the brightness of the Lord our God be upon us; and direct thou the works of our hands over us, yea, the work of our hands do thou direct.

This song is one of the most beautiful in the book of Psalms. It is entirely filled with the experience that everything passes, especially human life. But we must note at once how this transitoriness is regarded. The Psalmist does not say: "Everything passes; we must die and then what becomes of us?" But the Psalm begins by looking at God. To Him the Psalmist says: You were always there. You were there for every generation. You were always there as a refuge. Our existence was always in your sight and directed toward you. You were there before the mightiest and most solid objects, the mountains, before the whole earth, even before the universe. "From eternity"—that is the immeasurable past, in which God always was—"to eternity"—the immeasurable future in which He will always be there. And now "O God, thou art."

This "thou art" suddenly lifts the concept of God above all that we call "time." God simply "is." As He said to Moses on Mt. Horeb, "The I-am is my name." (Ex. 3:14) This word distinguishes Him from all the gods of mythology, removes Him from all connection with mountain and sea, earth and the universe. He is and He lives in His own special way, different from all that is created.

This eternity makes the transitoriness of man inexorably plain; but not in the way in which mythology consigns man and the world and the gods to destruction. The fact that perishable man looks toward the eternal God brings, in some mysterious way, a glimmer of the eternal even to human life.

This God is personal, the eternal "I." So the transitoriness of mythology, to which everything is subject, disappears—the hopelessness, the deadly melancholy. In the Psalm transitoriness is regarded from the point of view of the living God. It is willed by Him, but by that very fact assured of a divine meaning and touched by a hope which cannot as yet be expressed but is surmised. In a relation to this God by faith there is something of eternity even in man's passing away.

The Eternal One has decreed that men must die. But He wills also that others shall be born, hence this passing away and coming to be is not a result of the laws of nature or a mythological inevitability of death, but it is known, and willed by God and He is responsible for it.

This continues throughout the ages. The longest periods of time are nothing before the eternal, even as yesterday, which has passed away. Before the eternal power of God they are like something which a wave passes over and washes away; like a dream when one awakens and it is gone in a moment; like grass which is green and blossoms in the morning and in the evening is cut down and withers.

Then there is a new note: "In thy wrath we have fainted away." Behind the experience of transitoriness is the consciousness of guilt. Perhaps memory recalls a historical event, a disobedience to divine guidance which was followed by a catastrophe, a sacrilege which aroused the wrath of God. Our deepest consciousness is aware that death and sin are connected, that man would not die if he had not sinned. We think of the primordial commandment in Paradise:

The Lord God commanded man, saying, "Of every tree of
Paradise thou shalt eat, but of the tree of knowledge of good
and evil thou shalt not eat. For in what day soever thou shalt
eat of it, thou shalt die." (Gen. 2:16–17)

But other sins were added to this first one: "Thou hast set our iniquities before thy eyes, our secret sins in the light of thy countenance." The
wrath of God has caused the days to be so empty and fleeting. "We have
spent our years like a sigh." They have been not like a breath of wind but
like a sigh from a burdened heart.

"The days of our years are three score and ten." It is a statement of the
life-span of man, which we find in all languages. "But if in the strong they
be fourscore years what is more of them is labour and sorrow." This is how
it appears to one who looks back upon a long life. "For they pass swiftly
and we fly away" like startled birds and all is gone in a moment.

"Who knoweth the power of thy anger?" Who really considers all
this? Most men do not think; rather, they just live from day to day, and
this makes everything even more shadow-like.

Then comes a wonderful verse, which we shall consider more closely
later on: "Teach us to number our days"—to weigh, to feel how it is with
them—"that we may attain to wisdom of heart." The feeling of transitoriness, which brings only melancholy to the man without faith, shall give
rise to wisdom, wisdom "of heart."

The following verses entreat God with a childlike insistence that He
may graciously give joy for all the difficulties that have been experienced,
that He may grant as many good days as there have been bad ones, so that
the scales of life may be balanced.

At the end there is the beautiful conclusion which rises like a vault
above the whole song: "Let the brightness of the Lord our God be upon
us; and direct thou the works of our hands over us; yea, the work of our
hands do thou direct."

It is a wonderful Psalm. One could say much about it. But we will confine ourselves to the twelfth verse. "Teach us to number our days." We are to do this, not anxiously to count how much time still remains, nor pessimistically to despair of the meaning of life, but in order that the numbering, the considering and comparing may bring us wisdom.

How does one attain to wisdom "of heart?" By comparing our human life with the life of God, God, of whom Revelation tells us that He simply is. Not for a short time or a long one, nor even an endless time, but simply and absolutely. Essential being, that is God. To be and to be Himself, that is His name. With this immeasurable one, of whom we cannot say that He lives a thousand years, or all the years of astronomy, but that He *is* absolutely, the believer compares the short life of man.

This will bring wisdom; the gift of distinguishing, the gift of weighing; the ability to understand what is meaningful and what is not.

Wisdom is knowledge. But there are various kinds of knowledge. First, there is that of the mind. This determines a situation, examines it, and looks for the circumstances, for causes and effects, until one can say, "This is how it is; this is what happened." Perhaps even when dealing with matters which involve natural laws, "This is what must happen." In other words, it is science. A very important thing. But is it wisdom? Certainly not. One may know all the scientific formulas in the world, may be a great scholar—and yet a great fool. Wisdom is something else.

There is also the knowledge of prudence which a man acquires if he lives with his eyes open and tries to understand why things go as they do. Prudence means the knowledge of the ways in which we must act toward others if we wish to associate with them without clash or damage; of what we must do if we wish to attain certain goals when dealing with people of different types. We cannot approach a hypersensitive or conceited person with a simple moral request. We must appeal to his personal feelings. A person who seeks intellectual knowledge cannot be approached through his feelings. He desires reasons; and so on. This is prudence. But not yet wisdom. A man can be an experienced politician with unfailing skill, and yet be a fool before God.

What then is wisdom? It is concerned that life should have meaning, have a part in what endures. Wisdom takes care that in the end a man should not stand empty-handed. It is based upon the gift of distinguishing what is valuable and what is cheap, what endures and what passes, what is genuine and what is specious. So the Psalm says that the distinction on which all distinctions are based is this: God alone is "God," eternal, living and holy; man is merely man, created and transitory, but capable of knowing truth and experiencing value. He is in duty bound to do the good and responsible to God for the use he makes of his life.

He who attacks God's truth condemns man to folly. Hence the dreadfulness of the experiment which is being tried today: to form men without God, nations without God. This is being undertaken for the first time. What will come of it no one knows. But one thing is certain: it will destroy the power of distinguishing; it will destroy wisdom. And, the inmost core of man, his personal integrity, will suffer irreparable harm.

When we read the verses of our Psalm we feel the transitoriness of all things and the question arises, "What can I do about it? How can I stop this sinister stream, or at least check its flow?"

One may say, "I must fill it with thrilling events, with interesting, exciting things. I must experience, see, enjoy, grasp." And wisdom answers, "You fool! This will only make the stream flow faster. The more you pack into your life, the more you fill it with excitement, the more fluid it becomes!"

Another answers, "I must bring weighty matters into my life, must found industries, take part in politics, accept offices, take on responsibilities." He works, organizes, speaks, struggles. And what is the result? Do not the terms follow each other the more swiftly? Do not the heavily laden days grow ever shorter? And at the end he stands holding his head and wondering what has become of all his labors.

But if we ask, "What then shall I do? Wisdom, counsel me!" then wisdom replies, "You must learn to distinguish. You must bring into your life things that are of divine character, things that do not merely pile up or excite, but that have value."

And what has value? Wisdom replies, "the good!" When we have performed a duty, even though it was unpleasant, the situation changes, the action is past, but something remains: the good that has been done. This has a divine character.

Or if I act kindly toward a person, whom perhaps I do not like, try to understand him, help him—in this fulfillment of the divine command something takes place which remains. Many things around it fall apart; the encounter passes, the excitement dies down, the person—I as well as the other—will die; but the fact that at this moment charity was practiced, that remains, for it has a divine character.

Or I may have a friend, who like every man, possesses good characteristics and bad ones. Some things about him please me, others repel. I might be inclined to think: I will accept what pleases me and not the rest. Wisdom says, you cannot do that! You cannot pick out things belonging to a person, for everything in him belongs together. His best qualities are interwoven with his greatest weaknesses. If you do not accept the person entirely you lose him. This acceptance is patience. It is a divine characteristic; God has patience with you and with everyone. You must do the same, and then your friendship will endure. You may try to influence your friend, to emphasize his good qualities and soften the others, but first you must accept the whole.

The most beautiful thing in the world comes to pass when a person loves another. This does not mean passion, although even this has its good points; rather, it means the wonderful thing that a man, who by nature thinks first of all of himself, now opens his heart and embraces another. Then the other becomes as important to him as he is to himself, perhaps more important, and so the two feel secure in each other.

But wisdom says: it is foolish to attempt to force this love, to demand that it shall spring up, to require that it shall last, to urge when the other hesitates, to seek to purchase love by complaisance and favors. All this would be foolish because love can live only in freedom. It must be given and always given anew. And if it has been given for ten years, this is no guarantee that it will be given in the eleventh year. Indeed, this is the goal, for the nature of love involves eternity, but this is an eternity which does not proceed from security but ever and again from the freedom of the heart. This is why love dies if it is not honored by freedom; if the feeling arises that love is regarded as a matter-of-fact thing about which no effort needs to be made. One cannot force love, but one can serve for it, surround it with consideration and courtesy—then it flourishes. To understand this is wisdom.

So we might speak of many other things—also of this—and it would not be unimportant—that it is a part of wisdom to be careful of one's own wisdom. It is a virtue which is easily spoiled. If one is too conscious of it, or emphasizes it, then wisdom itself becomes folly, and a greater folly than that which it sought to overcome.

The Dark Side of the Human Heart

Psalm 136 (137)

A mong the one hundred and fifty psalms there are several which
cause difficulties for the Christian reader and may even seem to
provoke a protest. To these belong particularly those which we
call the Psalms of vengeance and imprecatory Psalms. One of these, the
hundred and thirty-sixth, we wish to consider, and we shall not evade the
difficulties which it poses for Christian feeling. Nevertheless, we shall see
that the Psalm is important for us also.

> Upon the rivers of Babylon, there we sat and wept, when
> we remembered Zion
>
> On the willows in the midst thereof we hung up our
> instruments.
>
> For there they that led us into captivity required of us the
> words of songs.
>
> And they that carried us away said: Sing ye to us a hymn
> of the songs of Zion.
>
> How shall we sing the song of the Lord in a strange land?
>
> If I forget thee, O Jerusalem, let my right hand be
> forgotten.

Let my tongue cleave to my jaws if I do not remember thee,

If I make not Jerusalem the beginning of my joy.

Remember, O Lord, the children of Edom, in the day of Jerusalem,

Who say, raze it, raze it even to the foundation thereof.

O Daughter of Babylon, miserable; blessed shall he be who shall repay thee thy payment which thou hast paid us.

Blessed be he that shall take and dash thy little ones against the rock.

Let us first visualize the situation of which the Psalm speaks.

From 597 to 587 B.C. the southern kingdom with its capital, Jerusalem, was ruled by king Zedekias. As a result of previous wars he was a vassal of Babylon, but he was caught up in the intrigues of the great powers and—against the warnings of the prophet Jeremias—he let himself be persuaded by Egypt to revolt against Babylon. A large Babylonian army invaded the country, devastated it and besieged Jerusalem for two years. In 587 the city was captured and destroyed. The people were dragged to Babylon, and only after seventy years, when the Persians had conquered the kingdom of Babylon, were they permitted to return to their home.

The experience which is expressed in the Psalm comes from the time of this exile. The Psalmist had himself witnessed the destruction of Jerusalem or had heard of it from eye-witnesses. He had then lived in Babylon, but at the time of the composition of the Psalm he was no longer there.

Now he recalls an experience of his exile, how at one time captive Israelites—perhaps temple-musicians, persons who performed at the temple-festivals and accompanied their festive songs with the music of harps—were in mockery challenged by Babylonians, "You singers, sing us the songs that you sang in the temple!" At this the Psalmist was overcome by a feeling so powerful that the song breaks off with a terrible discord.

"Upon the rivers of Babylon, there we sat," he begins. Perhaps the captives had a camp near a river. There, where they could perform their ritual ablutions, they may have held a kind of religious service. Now they were sitting on the shore; their thoughts turn to Zion and they weep in bitter sorrow. Babylonians pass by, see the conquered people and mock them: "Sing for us! You are great musicians! Sing us the songs that you sang in the temple." But they take their harps and hang them on the trees. That is their refusal.

"How shall we sing the song of the Lord in a strange land?" The faith of Israel, the service of the God who had revealed himself to them, is very closely bound up with the land into which Moses and Josue had led them. God, Jerusalem, Temple, Palestine, faith, and salvation formed a whole. Now it was torn apart. They did not understand how this could happen, and bitter sorrow came over them.

> If I forget thee, O Jerusalem, let my right hand be forgotten.
> Let my tongue cleave to my jaws if I do not remember thee,
> If I make not Jerusalem the beginning of my joy.

If only we had a spark of this fervor! If only God and His kingdom were one-tenth as important to us as the holy city was to these men!

Then memories arise; the terrible pictures of destruction with which the conquest had ended. There the triumph of victory, the intoxication of slaughter had raged. For the ancient peoples a city was more than just a human habitation, security and wealth. It was a divine foundation and order, an image of the existence of a nation and their gods. Probably the besiegers had heard something of the claim of Israel, who regarded the

Lord not as a national divinity, as other people did, but as the one, sole God, so that the enmity of the pagans against the God of Revelation was mingled with their destructive fury. All this came to mind, and longing and sorrow bred hatred.

This hatred is directed above all against their old neighbors, the Edomites

Remember, O Lord, the children of Edom, in the day of Jerusalem. The Edomites were Semites, but between them and the Israelites a deep dislike prevailed as often happens among related nations, as well as related persons who hate each other more profoundly than strangers. For the Edomites the destruction of Jerusalem was a great triumph. They considered the Babylonians the executors of their own impotent enmity.

"Remember them"—that was a curse—as they cried "Raze it, raze it."

The Babylonians raged in the holy city, slaughtered, plundered, and destroyed. Their greatest fury was directed against the Temple, the embodiment of all that the conquered people stood for. There is a Psalm which is totally devoted to this terrible mystery, Psalm seventy-three. There we read:

> Lift up thy hands against their pride unto the end; see what things the enemy hath done wickedly in the sanctuary.
>
> And they that hate thee have made their boasts in the midst of thy solemnity.
>
> They have set up their ensigns for signs,
>
> And they knew not both in the going out and on the highest top, as with axes in a wood of trees.
>
> [They were as those who swing their axes in a thick wood.]
>
> They have cut down at once the gates thereof, with axe and hatchet they have brought it down.
>
> They have set fire to thy sanctuary; they have defiled the dwelling-place of thy name on the earth.

They said in their heart, the whole kindred of them together.

. Let us abolish all the festival days of God from the land.

And beside all this horror stand the Edomites and urge them on: "More, more, raze everything to the very foundations."

This image rises in all its horror before those who remember, and now their hatred turns to those who perpetrated the outrage: "Babylon, destroyer!" and the desire for vengeance leaps up: "Blessed is he who can requite the evil that you have done to us!"

Babylon appears as a woman, the mother of the nation. The thirst for vengeance turns toward the most vital thing, her children and finds delight in their destruction: Blessed is he that shall take and dash thy little ones against the rock."

If we read these verses, not aesthetically but seriously, and even, as happens in the case of every Psalm, feel called upon to pray them, then we ask ourselves, "What is this? How can the word of God ask us to make these words our own in prayer?"

People have puzzled a great deal about how this is to be understood. Some have maintained that Edomites and Babylonians and in general those against whom the words of the imprecatory Psalms are turned should be taken symbolically, as the enemies of God, or, more exactly, the disposition of the enemies of God, and that it is this which is hated. But it is perhaps simpler and more in accord with the text if we take the Psalm as it stands. Scripture does not say, "What this man says is good," but "Man is such that he says these things." And if the reader protests, then Scripture replies, "Yes, you are like this too! In you also there exists what in the Psalmist is mingled with zeal for God, even if it varies according to the period of history and the nature of experience. In your case also it only awaits the opportunity to break forth."

But one may protest further and say, "The Psalmist was one who believed, who waited for the Messias. Such a man could not harbor feelings of that sort." This is a serious objection, and we must answer it.

What happens when a man is touched by grace and believes? He is not magically transformed. No magic power of good comes upon him; he does not suddenly become a different person. To hear the call of God and to stand within the covenant—or let us speak of ourselves: to hear the word of Christ and decide to follow him, does not mean to be at once a changed man. The new thing comes into man as a germ and he is as he is. A word, a truth, a scene from the life of the Lord falls into the soul and begins to grow. But with this there still exists what was there before.

St. Paul spoke of this from his own experience. To be redeemed, to adhere to Christ, means that within the "old" man there has sprung up the beginning of a "new" man. But the old man is still there with all his urges and inclinations, good as well as bad. Two centers are now active, two men are contending with each other. Ofter the new man is overcome by the old, or at least covered and contradicted so we can hardly notice that he is there. Only slowly does the new life make its way and grow stronger, and by means of self-denial the new man comes to his growth.

Strictly speaking, no one could say, "I am a Christian," but only "I want to be one." It would be in harmony with the Apostle's thought if we said that the new man is so concealed that we cannot know of his existence but must believe in him because of the word of the promise.

The great figures of Scripture make this clear to us. Let us think, for example of one of the patriarchs, the man who was so dear to Cardinal Newman, Jacob, the grandson of Abraham. He must have been a man of powerful religious experience, quite enviable in this respect. We may recall his vision at Bethel or his struggle with the angel of the Lord at the river Jabbok (Gen. 28:10ff. and 32:22ff.) Yet this same man by trickery deprived his brother of his birthright and deceived his dying father. (Gen. 25:29ff. and 27:1ff.) Who dares to judge and to say that a man who does this cannot be a patriarch, that is, a bearer of the promises of God? Jacob was both, a man seized by God and also a man who labored sorely under the weight of his humanity.

Or we may think of that other great figure in the Old Testament, King David, of whom God himself bears witness, calling him "my servant David." But then we read, what merciless wars he waged and how much blood stained his hands, so that God forbade him to build the temple (2 Sam. 7:1ff.); and how he broke up the marriage of his subordinate officer, Urias, and treacherously sent him to his death (2 Sam. 11). And yet he is David, and the Messias calls Himself his son. This does not mean that what he did was right, or that he who professes faith in God can permit himself to do evil on the side. But it means that we should not have a rigid, moralistic way of regarding the man of faith, but should view him as what he is, a living man, and should remember that we "are" not Christians but are "becoming" Christians.

We may say, "I trust that God will give me grace to become a Christian, and this may give us a feeling of deep joy. But we may not say, "I am a Christian and it is proper for me to pass judgment on the Christianity of others." We are always on the way.

So we must also not despair of ourselves. Sometimes we are tempted to lose courage when we notice again and again the same faults: anger, uncharitableness, sloth, untruthfulness. Shall we ever escape them? There is only one answer to this: you must go on, day by day, hour by hour, for you are not yet a Christian, but by honest effort you will become one.

Security in God

PSALM 90 (91)

T he ninetieth psalm is one of the most beautiful, if it is proper to
speak of greater or less beauty in regard to words in which God
is speaking. The reader who projects himself into the Psalm will
find that a place opens for him and therein he will feel a silent presence
which is wholly power and wholly goodness. He will be taken by the hand
and taught how to come to an understanding with this gracious power,
and, if he follows, he will be secure. Before quoting the text, it appears that
two brief suggestions will help us to understand it better.

Three persons appear in the Psalm, if we may count in this way. We
shall soon see why the reservation is made. There is, first of all, the person
who is speaking the Psalm. He has had a deep experience and because of
this speaks with authority about life, its difficulties and dangers; also about
what happens if man unites himself to God in a living confidence.

Then there is a second person, who does not speak but listens. But we
know how the words spoken by one person are completed by the heart
and mind of the hearer. So there must be a good and profound listener to
complete the words of the speaker of the Psalm. And, if we read it properly,
each of us can say, "I am the hearer," and therefore strive, to let the words
that he hears sink deeply into his soul. Finally, in the last three verses, a

third person speaks, the one who really counts, He who by His nature has the right to speak—God. He confirms and ratifies what the first person has said.

We must notice something else. The Psalm consists wholly of images; one follows the other, but all say the same thing. All speak of the dangers and distresses of life, of the confidence of the man who really believes, and of the constant kindness of almighty God.

We do not understand images by turning them into concepts. They must be taken as what they really are, namely images. We must call them up in our imagination, enter into them, feel their impact; then we receive their message. But this is not possible if the reader or speaker hurries through them. So he must proceed slowly, pausing again and again. He must put his own troubles into the images and accept the comforting words as directed to him here and now.

And now the text:

He that dwelleth in the aid [under the protection] of the most high shall abide under the protection [shadow] of the God of Jacob.

He shall say to the Lord, Thou art my protector [refuge] and my refuge [fortress], my God, in him will I trust.

For he hath delivered me from the snare of the hunters and from the sharp word [from the destroying pestilence].

He will overshadow thee with his shoulders and under his wings thou shalt trust.

His truth shall compass thee with a shield; thou shalt not be afraid of the terror of the night,

Of the arrow that flieth in the day, of the business [pestilence] that walketh about in the dark, of invasion or of the noonday devil [the evil that strikes at noonday].

A thousand shall fall at thy side, and ten thousand at thy right hand, but it shall not come nigh thee.

But thou shalt consider with thy eyes and shalt see the reward of the wicked.

Because thou, O Lord, art my hope [Because the Lord is thy protector]; thou hast made the most high thy refuge [fortress]

There shall no evil come to thee, nor shall the scourge come near thy dwelling [tent].

For he hath given his angels charge over thee, to keep thee in all thy ways.

In their hands they shall bear thee up lest thou dash thy foot against a stone.

Thou shalt walk upon the asp and the basilisk, and thou shalt trample under foot the lion and the dragon.

Because he hoped in me [was faithful to me] I will deliver him; I will protect him because he hath known my name.

He shall cry to me, and I will hear him; I am with him in tribulation; I will deliver him and I will glorify him [honor him].

I will fill him with length of days, and I will shew him my salvation.

We have seen how one image follows another, again and again. Each brings the same message. Each one receives it from the preceding one, strengthens and deepens it and passes it on to the next one.

God is as wise as He is knowing, as kind as He is powerful; He is faithful as no man can be. Therefore, he who entrusts himself to Him is truly secure.

The Psalm begins at once with an image: "He that dwelleth under the protection of the most high shall abide under the shadow of the God of

Jacob." A traveller walks in Palestine, a country largely desert under the burning sun, and its paths beset with dangers. We recall how Jesus in his parable about true neighborliness speaks of the road which leads from Jerusalem to Jericho, where robbers carry on their nefarious business. (Luke 10:30ff.) The man travelling in this country endured many hardships and fears. Now he comes to the house of a friend and finds relief. The shadow of his roof shelters him and the protection of the walls permits him to sleep safely. He who recognizes that God is kindly disposed toward him and is able to do what He wills, experiences His protection not only now and again, but he "abides" therein, as if in his own home and speaks with firm conviction "my refuge and my fortress!" A second image appears within the first, called up by a single word. In a country which is haunted by wild nomads there are fortified places on the heights, surrounded by walls and closed by strong gates, into which one can flee. "You are my fortress!" God Himself is the fortress. He who trusts in Him abides in Him.

"He hath delivered me from the snare of the hunters." The hunter sets snares and baits them in order to catch birds and small game. Similarly there are snares laid for men: lurking temptations, possibilities of going astray, occasions of error and folly, excess and hatred, which occur in the various situations of life.

Another danger is mentioned immediately, which was especially terrifying for people in tropical countries, "the destroying pestilence"—the terrible plague against which ancient times had only slight remedies.

"Under his wings thou shalt trust." The image of the bird who protects his young with his strong wings is very familiar to the Scriptures. We may think of the eagle who hovers over his nest (Deut. 32:11); or of the image which Jesus employed when he stood on the height and saw the city of Jerusalem before him: "Jerusalem, Jerusalem,...how often would I have gathered together thy children as the hen doth gather her chickens under her wings!" (Matt. 23:37) In the Psalm the image is used of God Himself:

"He will overshadow thee with his shoulders and under his wings thou shalt trust."

Another image is interwoven with this: There is a battle; someone is in danger of being overcome; perhaps he is wounded. Then a friend comes and holds his shield over him. This is what God does: "His truth shall compass thee with a shield."

"Thou shalt not be afraid of the terror of the night, of the arrow that flieth in the day." The terror of the night can be anything that threatens in the darkness. It can also mean the sinister quality of darkness itself which paralyzes man's heart.

But in order to interpret the Psalms more exactly we must note their poetic technique. Each verse consists of two lines, both of which say the same thing but with a different turn, a different emphasis, a different image, the so-called parallelism, a similarity of meaning. This results in the quiet soaring quality of the language of the Psalms, and also its impressive, persuasive nature. Because of the similarity of meaning one can at times, when the significance of one line is not clear, infer its meaning from the other line. So we read: "Thou shalt not be afraid—of the arrow that flieth in the day," that is, the hostile attack which comes during the day, nor of "the terror of the night," the attack which comes in darkness and hence is much more dangerous. "Nor of the pestilence that walketh about in the dark." Again we have a reference to the terrible foe that always threatens in the Old Testament and has already wrought such havoc among the people, and with which God through Moses and the prophets threatens those who are unfaithful to Him.

"Nor the evil that strikes at noonday." Perhaps this again refers to the pestilence which grows more dangerous with increasing heat, or perhaps to the rays of the sun which can be fatal to man in the noon-day heat.

"A thousand shall fall at thy side and ten thousand at thy right hand." In both phrases the right hand is referred to because it was unprotected in battle. The warriors carried his shield on his left arm; there he was protected; his right hand wielded the weapon, and there he was in danger of being wounded. The Psalm speaks of a danger so great that on this unprotected side tens of thousands, a countless number, fell, but the evil did "not come nigh" this one man because God stood there.

"But thou shalt consider with thy eyes and shalt see the reward of the wicked," those who depend on their own strength, who rebel against God and even deny Him. Their fate shall reveal more clearly how different is the lot of the man who is bound to God by perfect confidence.

Of the greatest trial to which faith may be subjected this Psalm does not speak; that is, the fact that the wicked and the unbelieving flourish, that they seem to be in harmony with the powers of existence, so that they succeed in everything. Other Psalms do speak of this, for example the seventy-second. These make it clear how hard the trial is, and we cannot say that the difficulty is overcome by a higher knowledge. It is opposed by a more decided emphasis on confidence which shall be rewarded at last, even though late. The real answer to the question would have to proceed from an insight into the ripening and transforming power of suffering. But this insight can only be obtained in the school of the crucified one. The Old Testament never solved the problem of suffering and of evil.

"Because the Lord is thy protector; thou hast made the most high thy fortress. Again we have the image of the fortified citadel on the height, into which the people round about flee when the enemy approaches, and where the traveller who is far from home may also seek refuge.

"There shall no evil come to thee, nor shall the scourge come near thy tent," as when you sleep during your journey at night in a tent whose weak walls give no protection.

And now comes the beautiful image which has become so much a part of our speech and thought that we are no longer aware of its origin: "He hath given his angels charge over thee, to keep thee in all thy ways."

The holy messengers and warriors, who joyfully and exactly fulfil the will of God, protect the man who trusts in the Lord.

Indeed, they do more, wonderfully more: "In their hands they shall bear thee up, lest thou dash thy foot against a stone." On the bad roads there were sharp edges, and it could happen that a man who walked barefoot or in sandals might be injured. To prevent this the angels put their hands under the feet of the traveller.

The wayfarer also passes over many dangers, serpents and adders, lions and dragons, without being aware of the evil that threatened, for he is protected.

Now God speaks: "Because he was faithful to me I will deliver him." Faithfulness to God is faithfulness to Him who is himself wholly faithful. So it is truth, and truth does not enslave but frees.

"I will protect him because he hath known my name." This word leads us into even greater depths. We shall return to it again at the end of this meditation.

"He shall cry to me and I will hear him." A cry to God is not lost in emptiness. He, the omnipotent, the beginning, before whom there was nothing; the Lord, as no one else can be Lord—He is kindly disposed to the one who cries in faith and He "hears" him, "inclines his ear and hears," as the prophet says. We feel the mystery of God's turning to us. He, who knows everything, knows in various ways: as creator from the origin of all being; as judge in the incorruptibility of His judgment. He also knows as divine Providence, loving and gracious. His turning is help in itself. This is continued in the "nearness" of God to the one who cries. Again we have a mystery, that the omnipresent God is not only present through His all-encompassing reality; not only pervades and keeps in existence all that is; but as person is present where His creature lives; more correctly, assigns a place to him that he with his finite existence may be "before" and "with" Him who *is* absolutely and of Himself.

God "delivers him and honors him." What a thought! How marvellous, and yet how necessary that God should honor man! What would become of us if He stood before us only in His power? But He is noble, as noble in His attitude as He is great in His power. He does not wish to have slaves. He has given a meaning to all things and He rejoices in their being as they are. He has given life to the animals and all their movements are His gift. He has called—not placed—man into existence and He keeps him in this state. So the attitude of honor is basic to man's creation and then appears everywhere in God's providence until it is consummated in the mystery which is spoken of in the New Testament as the divine adoption by which we are children of God.

"I will fill him with length of days." In the Old Testament the idea of eternal life does not play a particular role. For a long time it does not even appear, and even later it has no decisive influence. What matters is life here on earth, with God and for His cause. So the promise is that he shall have a long life, and shall die satisfied with life.

And then "I will shew him my salvation." The salvation is the nearness of God, the fact that God *is* and turns to His creature in grace. The eyes of the man who is devoted to God in faith behold this truth.

The Psalm is deep and beautiful. Perhaps we have sometimes wished that we had some good prayers for use in our personal devotions. Sometimes we want to pray and do not know how. And constantly to pray an "Our Father" may not be very meaningful; on the contrary, it may endanger the sacred prayer and dull our appreciation of its mystery. So it might be well if we chose several Psalms, made them our own and had them ready for use in our prayer. The ninetieth Psalm, which we are here considering, could well be one of these.

We want to return again to the words of the verse which reads, "I will protect him because he hath known my name." This means first of all that the man here spoken of can distinguish the living God and His worship from the gods of pagan myths and cults. Palestine was surrounded by gigantic pagan religions: Egypt, Babylon, Persia, Syria—gods upon gods; some of them mighty figures, some glorious, some terrible or even disgusting. They surround the man of our Psalm. Of him God says that, among all the fictitious figures which made so great an impression on the human mind, he knows only the true and living God.

The sentence may have a second meaning. The name of God is God Himself. So God says of the sanctuary at Silo "where my name dwelt from the beginning." (Jer. 7:12) And he says to David that his son "shall build a house [i.e. the temple] to my name." (2 Sam. 7:13) So he who knows the holy name knows God, and is familiar with Him.

And a final thought. Have we ever really thought about the name of God? When we ask anyone this question he is usually surprised. Does God have a name? Yes, He has. He Himself spoke it—we have mentioned this before—at the time in which Old Testament history really begins, on Mt. Horeb. There he told Moses to go to Egypt and set his people free. Moses replied, "I shall go to the children of Israel and say to them, 'The God of your fathers hath sent me to you.' If they should say to me, 'What is his name?' what shall I say to them?" God said to Moses "I am who am." He said "Thus shalt thou say to the children of Israel, 'He who is hath sent me to you.'" (Ex. 3:13–14) So God's name is "I am the I-am." Herein speaks the majesty that takes no name which comes from without. And it means that God is the one who alone is real of Himself and possesses all power. We, as men, "are" not in the true sense. Of course we exist, but only "before" Him and "toward" Him. But God is He whose essential nature means that He is. An abyss of a name. An abyss for the mind that ponders upon it. A vaster abyss for the heart which experiences it. When this takes place there opens within the man himself, the finite man, a corresponding unfathomable depth, of which he otherwise is unconscious.

When we kneel down and pray as we should pray, after having become recollected and interiorly silent—for otherwise there is no prayer, only a succession of words—when we are in watchful silence and say to ourselves, "God is here," then we might be tempted to continue, "And I too am here." But if we do this, our heart objects, "That is not right. You cannot say, 'God is here, and I also.' But if He 'is here' then you are not 'also' here, you are only 'before Him.' The unapproachableness of God's majesty stands between." Then it may happen that we receive the grace to experience the name of God.

But this God, who is absolute reality of Himself and in Himself, is the one with whom the Psalm brings us into intimacy, and this results in profound confidence.

NOTES

The World and the Person

Nature and Creation

(Nature, Subject and Culture)

1. See Guardini, *Hölderlin, Weltbild und Frömmigkeit* (1955), p. 361.

(The Created-ness of the World)

2. It seems that the concept of God's Lordship is the Biblical expression for His freedom. As "Lordship," God's freedom is different from that of man, which in its ultimate nature implies obedience. Only in man's obedience to God is his dominion over the world justified and, in the last analysis, even possible.

3. There is an idea—and it is actually not merely an idea, but an attempt to overcome this state of things—namely, Nietzsche's demand for the *amor fati*, the absolute acceptance of existence as it is. From this point of view, it is a matter of accustoming our inmost feeling to the thought that nothing exists but the world and that it is finite. Man must gradually learn to exist from the world alone. The doctrine of the continual return of the same thing strengthens this pronouncement and demand to the utmost—even to horror: e.g., the howling of the dog in *Zarathustra*. It is an attempt to completely change man's inmost feeling about existence, to train the merely world-related man who desires nothing but finiteness and hence no longer protests against it.

4. Of course, even seriousness can degenerate. There is a way of "taking the world seriously" which is not Christian and is only possible if one evades that which is really important. The way in which modern man takes nature, himself and culture seriously is slightly grotesque to the eye that is sobered by faith because all that appears so much a matter of life and death, does not really exist. And the fact that a nonentity is embraced with such seriousness is a mockery of Satan. In this way, the Christian takes neither the world, nor himself nor nature seriously. In the face of all this, he has the sense of humor of the redeemed. And only within the confines of this God-given lack of over-seriousness does the world flourish. Only in the holy liberty of its createdness does it thrive. The world does not wish to become an idol. It desires that charming lightness of touch which finds its final expression in the "freedom of the children of God." "Autonomy" is a kind of tetanus in which the world suffocates.

(God and "The Other")

5. See my interpretation of the Psalms in *Gläubiges Dasein*, Würzburg (1955), p. 65ff.

6. In this connection, see my book, *Religious Figures in Dostoievski's Work* (Leipzig, 1939), especially the chapter "Godlessness," p. 213ff.

7. Hence the belief in creation sets a task for religious practice—namely learning the right attitude toward God. It is necessary to learn that He exists sovereign, independent of the world, its Creator and Lord. Yet not the "other," but He whose existence enables me to be, who is of such a nature that, the more strongly He influences and dominates my life the more truly I become myself.

   The whole modern view of the autonomy of the world and of man, the whole battle against heteronomy in its different forms, the concepts of nature, the subject and culture in the sense in which we have discussed them, seem to rest ultimately on the notion which made of God the "other." Thereby He was forced from the true nature of His being into the concept of a being beside or above man, a concept quite alien to Him. That this happened was the result primarily of man's rebellion. But we do not grasp the situation entirely or justly if we see it only in this way. The man who rebelled had suffered much. It is very painful to think of God as the "other," and pain is pain even if it is one's own fault. Moreover, there are offenses which cannot be straightway set right and difficulties which do not simply disappear when man turns toward what is right. In order to see truly that the suffering involved in thinking of God as "the other" is the result of guilt one needs help, spiritual training and a proper regulation of life, but these were often lacking. Figures like Nietzsche do not spring up by chance or merely from ill-will. They are the reply to serious sins of omission. If the faith in God the Creator and Redeemer is to be a living one, then men must see Him in His nature and His mystery and understand themselves in their true relation to Him and realize that they possess their freedom and dignity from Him. But this does not come about through mere assertion. How closely these deep matters are connected with very practical ones is revealed in the manner in which authority and obedience are conceived of and carried out. The relation of religious authority to the individual is basically understood in the same way as the relation of God to the world. In the matter of authority, opposition is naturally very clearly defined. Not what the individual wishes but what the authority commands is right. And yet it involves an ultimate decision whether we think of and carry out this relation in such a way that we are merely conscious of the opposing "other," or whether in him we somehow perceive the true relation of God to the world. If that is not the case, if we see only the command, the law, the officials, then something basic is destroyed. The relation loses its deepest meaning and psychological necessity leads to rebellion. This is particularly true in the matter of conscience. In our Christian education of the conscience, in dealing with the concept of sin, in the matter of training and development of the conscience, in our whole attitude toward a command, we have good reason to examine ourselves and see how we have failed or been remiss in this respect.

The Poles of the Sphere of Existence

(Above and Within)

1. But the phenomenon can also be reversed. Then the lower order, the depth, is considered of primary value. This is the case in the chthonic cosmologies, in particular forms of experience which are still encountered and for which the center of gravity lies in the womb, since this signifies fruitfulness, security, unconsciousness, unity, innocence, etc. From this point of view the "above" would be considered of lesser value. This attitude manifests itself in an antipathy to the intellect, the concept, the form, justice, and the spirit. But this second possibility must be disregarded here, because otherwise the whole matter would become too complicated.

(Christian Inwardness)

2. This section appeared as a separate essay in the publication *Unterscheidung des Christlichen* (Mainz, 1935), p. 305ff. Because of the continuity of the argument it had to be repeated here, but it has been entirely re-worked for the purpose.

3. "Depth" is here used not as the opposite of "height" but as direction inward.

4. The distinction is a rough one. Of course, a spiritual element is also present in instinctive action, quite apart from the fact that it reflects earlier actions which were spiritually determined and which influenced the fundamental attitude. To a considerable extent,

education means creating, through spiritual influence, a situation in which we may assume that what is right and proper will be done instinctively.

5. Cf. also Guardini, *Religious Figures in Dostoievski's Work* (1939), p. 256ff.

6. Cf. Guardini, *The Conversion of St. Augustine* (1935), p. 132ff.

7. This is a quality of truth which, in western philosophy, probably first emerges in a decisive way in the writings of Plato. It occurs in Heraclitus, but rather as a manifestation of harsh pride. In Plato, it comes out clearly and becomes a universal element. His concept of existence is constructed essentially in the direction of height. Since his time we have the notion of the ideal. The "idea" is absolutely "above." The way to it is an upward one. And one rises upward not only through intellectual keenness and effort but through love—*Eros*. It is this which raises the thought aloft and gives it boldness and consciousness of direction. The *Symposium* is the canticle of this height. The notion of the ascent was later very fully developed and opposed to that of descent, in that design of the origin of the world and the task of man which Neoplatonism worked out. The former is the descent into heaviness and depth, the latter the ascent to that *One*, which is also the *Beginning*.

8. Cf. Nikolai Hartmann, *Ethik* (1926), p. 247ff.

9. This is by no means immediately evident to our natural feelings, which instinctively rate a noble steed or a beautiful wild beast higher than a wretched man. So it signifies a decisive step in our personal development if we overcome this dependence on a merely vital excellence.

(The Summary)

10. This statement does not indicate a naive anthropocentrism. It expresses as much responsibility as self-assurance and it leads to discouragement as well as to presumption.

11. I hope to be able at a later date to submit more definite material on the Christian concept of death.

12. For the metaphysics and theology of this very noble concept see Guardini: "The picture of the angel in Dante's *Divine Comedy*" (Leipzig, 1937), p. 101ff.

The World—Its Enclosure and Openness

(The World as the Whole of Existence)

1. Another question is: how far I am really gathered to a point, that is, unified; how far is my person realized and not living in distraction?

(The World as "the Whole," "a Whole" and the Mighty)

2. This insight, or rather view, has consequences also for the problem of the existence of God, more exactly, the problem of His place. Religious imagination and feeling is more conservative than the profane; it still conceives of God dwelling in the empyrean and of His working through gaps in the world-structure. But as soon as a change of view such as we have indicated takes place, it brings it about that for the immediate imagination and feeling God no longer has a place, and this may lead to a formal "either-or" between experience of the world and faith in God.

From this result practical problems of religious education: the behavior of faith, such as prayer, the presence of God, coming before God, seeking His face, must be adapted to the new picture of the world. But there are also theoretical problems, for the question, "where" God is, has a theological content. What symbol must be substituted for the existence of God in itself and in the world if the space beyond the world and the gaps within it can no longer be used?

Cf. for this the little essay on "The Distance of the Andromeda-Nebula" in my book, *Spiegel und Gleichnis (Mirror and Parable)* [Mainz, 1932], p. 271ff.

3. It is true that there also appear to be experiences of another sort. Nietzsche, for example, tried to understand it in such a way that the correct representation of it would be not a system but a battle-field—more exactly, the possibility of countless battle-fields which need have nothing to do with each other, the possibility of innumerable, uncombinable Heracleitan happenings and battles. But it is an argument against this theory that we can determine its source, for it indicates an opposition to the prevailing opinion of the time.

4. Only one real break seems to go through the world: that between degree of value and actual power, meaning and force, virtue and happiness, justice and success. Actually, the two should always coincide. The good man should be happy, the pure beautiful, the just successful; in general, that which has value should have reality. But this is not the case. It is the fairytale which takes this situation for granted. Fairytales constantly tell of this unity because it does not exist in reality. At this point, revelation discloses the fact of sin. Someday, after death, this unity shall come into being. The process through which it is realized is called Resurrection. Its content is "the new creation," "the heavenly city Jerusalem," "the bride" (Apoc. 21). The confidence that it shall come we call "hope."

5. Shakespeare is the poet whose work reveals the mightiness of the world in an overpowering manner. No one else portrays it as so great, so sweet and so terrible.

6. This too reacts upon the relation of God and the world. Before this might of the world God seems to become unreal and pale. There appears the menacing phenomenon that religion is regarded as hostile to values, unpleasant, insipid, insignificant and boring. The

question arises, how, in the face of this world-power, God's reality and value can be experienced in a new way. To establish a "life-value of faith" does not seem to suffice for this.

7. The manner in which the world is experienced is also varied: it may be as a constant production of mythical forces, or else as deprived of its enchantment, rationally fathomed, possessed by calculation, mastered by technology; as strange and terrible, or as friendly and providing security, etc.

(The Boundary and Nothingness)

8. Cf. Guardini, *Die Bekehrung des Heiligen Aurelius Augustinus (The Conversion of St. Augustine)* [1935], p. 246ff.

(The World's Enclosure within Itself)

9. It would be an important task to investigate the psychological, ethical, ideational and other mechanisms and mental operations which are involved in this.

10. Cf. Guardini, *Hölderlin, Weltbild und Frömmigkeit* (1939), p. 144ff.

11. Cf. Guardini, *Hölderlin* (1939), p. 161f. and "The Image of the Angel in Dante's *Divine Comedy*" (1937), p. 43ff.

12. Just as in Hölderlin, Christian ideas operate in Rilke. Of course, they have taken on a purely secular form and serve the development of the "naked world." So we also find in Rilke a "Purgatory" in which the dead "learn to be dead," and must "make up for life," until they have achieved their complete existence and now stand entirely in the beyond, more exactly expressed, in the whole.

13. This is secularized Christian charity, completely absorbed into the world.

14. As a minor parallel phenomenon, significant however as a symptom, one might mention occultism. Of this much is probably mere trickery, the greater part is self-deception or an uncritical effort of

religious sentiment to establish itself somewhere, specifically at the place of death. The phenomenon is likewise not genuine when it is made to serve apologetic purposes, for instance, to support faith in eternal life or in the reality of God. But it also has a genuine sense, one which entirely contradicts revelation. For it attempts by means of experimental investigation to prove that there is a realm beyond death in which the dead continue to live. But this existence does not lie "in the hand of God." It is not removed, but belongs to the world. Characteristic of this is the attitude of the occult experience and research, which is quite without faith in the Christian sense of the word, and at times completely irreligious, and also the curiously earthly, often all too earthly character of the "manifestations." One might suppose that positivism, of which we said that it knows no hereafter, is here at work, in order to appropriate this hereafter in the most irreligious form possible.

(The Situation of the World and the Redemption)

15. For the whole of this see Guardini, *Das Wesen des Christentums* (*The Nature of Christianity*) [1938].

16. See Guardini, *Das Christusbild der paulinischen und johanneischen Schriften*, Würzburg (1961), and *Drei Schriftauslegungen* (1958), esp. p. 69ff.

17. The parable of the bad and the good shepherd expresses this by saying that he is the "door" through which the flock "go in and out and find pasture" (John 10:1–8).

18. How great and how real the struggle is becomes clear only when we truly understand the forces which are there wrestling with each other. "Flesh" and "spirit" do not mean body and spirit in the philosophical sense, but the old and the new man in the theological sense. The spirit also, as a part of man's being, is "flesh," as long as it is unredeemed; correspondingly, the body also becomes "spirit" when man is renewed

by God. Cf. the exposition given in the first Epistle to the Corinthians of the "spiritual" body of the resurrection (1 Cor. 15:25–58).

The Structure of the Personal Existence

(Person and Personality)

1. The same thing could be said of the pure action whose intention is not to attain some purpose but to do what should be done for its own sake: to satisfy a sense of honor and to fulfil justice. But we shall confine ourselves to an analysis of creative activity.

2. Nature itself can also be understood as a work of creation, not as its own but as God's.

3. Every break-through of a higher form and activity first of all brings it about that the perfection of the preceding condition is shaken, so that in contrast to it the new appears barbaric. As soon as the mind begins to act, the charming perfection of the animal vanishes. In contrast to the perfect animal, the existence ruled by the mind appears brutal. And yet it is essentially higher, and it is proper that the other should be sacrificed to it. So the existence of European man, driven by the restlessness of the mind has a higher meaning than the existence of primitive man with its certainty and beauty bounded and yet perfected by nature.

4. This will depend on whether the objective power that has been attained is counterbalanced by a corresponding degree of reverence, wisdom, goodness of heart and strength of character and in this way the possibilities are submitted to the proper standards. If we look back over the period since the beginning of technological production we find much reason to be troubled. Man's domination of nature increases with incredible speed, but man does not appear to increase in maturity, certainty of direction and strength of character. It seems

as if there arose from the accomplishments of men a power which transcends man and goes its own way.

(The Person in the True Sense)

5. It is another question what happens to the concrete man under such circumstances, what influences these exercise upon his personal attitude, how far this is suppressed or falsified, what changes the condition of ownership actually undergoes through the personality which can never be extinguished, to what extent a man can create for himself a sphere of personal existence even in this state of degradation to the level of a thing, etc.

6. On the meaning of the personal quality in regard to sociology see my essay "On Social Science and Order among Persons" in the volume *Unterscheidung des Christlichen* (1935), p. 23ff.

7. This idea is based upon Augustine's definition of spirit which proceeds from the content of its act. According to this the spirit is that being which should have the truth, the good, and ultimately God as the content of its act. Then there is the other statement—also taken from Augustine—that reality means not the mere fact of existence, which is the same everywhere, no matter what its content, but that there are endless grades of reality depending upon the rank of the value realized. But whereas the attribution of value in all other areas depends on the created nature and the quality itself, the value of the spirit depends upon itself, as the content of its act which springs from its freedom. Hence the degree of value of the spirit is determined by its own freedom, so also its degree of reality, the security or insecurity of its reality, its health and disease. And yet the spirit has not produced its own existence but has received it. Therefore the decrease of reality, which results from the act that negates value, cannot take away its being as such. The spirit, in becoming evil, cannot annihilate

itself, but only precipitate itself toward nothingness, without ever being able to reach it. That measure of value with which the act of the Creator has originally invested the spirit and which guarantees its existence, is withdrawn from the power of its will. It cannot annihilate itself by an evil will. But it can, by means of the act which negates value, render its being so questionable that it becomes merely the bearer of frustration; that is, of perdition and despair. For this whole matter, see Guardini, *The Conversion of St. Augustine* (1933), p. 86ff.

8. Perhaps we find here the deepest meaning of the charge which God laid upon man after everything had been created, and by His own witness—"and God saw all that He had made and behold it was very good" (Gen. 1:31)—had been declared meaningful and worthy of being: "and God created man to His own image, to the image of God He created him; male and female He created them. And God blessed them, saying, 'Increase and multiply, and fill the earth and subdue it, and rule over the fishes of the sea and the fowls of the air, and all living creatures that move upon the earth.' Then God continued, 'Behold I have given you every herb bearing seed upon the earth, and all trees that have in themselves seed of their own kind, to be your meat. And to all beasts of the earth and to every fowl of the air, and to all that move upon the earth, and wherein there is life, that they may have to feed upon.' And it was so done" (Gen. 1:27–30). Everything has been "given" to man, not as an object to do with as he pleases, but as a work of God having a being of its own which man is to handle with understanding and reverence. To see and acknowledge *that* is justice, the primary moral attitude basic for all others.

9. This expresses most emphatically the uniqueness of each person. The one who says "I" exists only once. This fact is so radical that the question arises whether the person as such can really be classified, or what the

classifications must be in order that man may be placed in them as a person. Can we—to take an elementary form of classification—count persons? We can count figures, individuals, personalities—but can we, while doing justice to the concept of "person," say "two persons" and have the statement mean anything? We can say "a friendship," "a marriage"; then we mean a personal duality which exists in an overlapping form conceived of originally in a personal way—but "two persons"? Here the reason balks. In this direction lie the tasks which are imposed by human dignity. They demand such great mental effort, moral depth and existential seriousness that man evades them. He makes things easy for himself, disregards the person and acts as if he had to deal only with individuals, often as if he dealt only with material entities. The same thing holds true in regard to actions.

10. Certain forms of human moral breakdown and of illness consist in the separation of these "layers." If a man becomes a mechanism this is a defection from dignity and duty but it can also be a paralysis in the spirit and hence an illness. The same thing is true of the appearance of the animal type in man. Here belongs also the problem of animal figures in religion, of the animal divinities, idols, etc. See on this matter Guardini, *Religious Figures in the Work of Dostoievski* (1939), p. 270ff. and *The Lord* (1938), p. 683ff.

11. What the realm of impersonal nature means for man is another problem; to what extent he may submerge himself in it; to what extent his "health" requires this and wherein at the same time the danger of this contact consists.

The Personal Relation

(The Relation of "I" and "Thou")

1. Cf. Guardini, *Hölderlin, Weltbild und Frömmigkeit* (1955), p. 28f, 471ff.

(The Person and the Other Person; Language)

2.   *Hölderlin and the Nature of Poetry* (1937), p. 7.

3.   There is an anecdote recounted in the Chronicle of Salimbene, telling that Frederick II of Hohenstaufen tried to find out the original language of mankind. According to the tale he had several orphaned infants brought to a house and ordered that they should be given every care but he strictly forbade anyone to speak to them. In this way he expected to learn what language they would spontaneously utter. But the children did not begin to speak Hebrew or Greek or Latin—which according to the opinion of the time were the possible original languages. Nor did they begin to speak in the tongue of their parents. They died. This story is full of deep meaning and indicates that speech is not a product but a presupposition of human life.

4.   But in order to exist personally, man must also be silent. Not mute; muteness is a lack of words and suffocates the person. Silence on the other hand presupposes the person. Only the person can live in that recollected stillness which we call silence, and only the person can turn to another and enter into this stillness with him. Indeed, silence belongs to the word. In muteness the person suffocates; in chatter, it withers. The word and silence are incomplete phenomena, only when combined do they represent the true whole, for which there is no name—somewhat as light and darkness together form the complete unity of the phenomenon. Light alone and darkness alone, glare and gloom, destroy. But living brightness and living darkness are mutually related. They form the unity of the biological rhythm, for instance as the connection of day and night, or that spiritual unity which lies in the relation of transparency and mystery—not enlightenment and superstition.

It is another problem whether and under what circumstances there can be a pre-verbal or extra-verbal understanding which cannot be communicated. It seems to occur in some instances of high mental tension which under certain circumstances approach illness. It also occurs in definite, very pure religious experiences, especially in the true mystical contact. Both phenomena give us the impression that in them man is approaching a boundary which it is dangerous to cross. And indeed it is of the nature of man that this danger should exist. But it is the zone of the word and of the silence bound up with it that has been allotted to man and constitutes his proper and natural habitation.

The Person and God

(The Human and the Divine Person)

1. I have been told that these ideas are related to those which Ferdinand Ebner developed in his book *Das Wort und die Geistigen Realitäten* (*The Word and the Spiritual Realities*) [Innsbruck, 1921]; *Wort und Liebe* (*The Word and Love*) [Regensburg, 1935]. I have read only bits of Ebner's works. So I am glad of the agreement, but I can permit my comments to stand without reference to him. I am really indebted to Theodor Haecker for turning my thought in this direction but I could not specify any particular work or statement of his.

2. Cf. Guardini, *Das Wesen des Christentums* (*The Nature of Christianity*) [1938].

3. In the Synoptic Gospels we also find significant statements about the Christian person, especially the doctrine of the divine sonship and of Providence. But it is easy to turn this into an apparently natural and merely humanly-ethical morality. That is why St. Paul is so important. If men say that he introduces psychological and theological complications into the simplicity of the first Gospels, they completely misunderstand him. As a matter of fact, he only makes

explicit the true meaning of the synoptic accounts. Cf. Guardini, *Das Bild von Jesus dem Christus im Neuen Testament (The Portrait of Jesus the Christ in the New Testament)* [1938], pp. 99ff.

4. Cf. Guardini, *Das Christusbild der paulinischen und johanneischen Schriften*, Würzburg (1961), p. 32ff.

5. Cf. Guardini, *Der Herr* (1961; 1982), p. 485ff.

6. Cf. 1 Cor. 15:42–49. The concept of the Spirit also has a history, that of the Old Testament prophecy. And this also ties up with an event that took place shortly before, which completed prophecy and had its effect everywhere in the churches: namely, the irruption of the Holy Spirit on the day of Pentecost (Acts 2:1–41).

7. How completely it pervades even the first three Gospels I hope to be able to show more clearly in the near future.

8. In all this we are dealing not merely with theory but with the interior direction of man's entire life; with the relation of goal and way; with the perspectives of Christian existence. On their preservation and proper execution depend the truth and the health of Christian life. One might say many things about this; for example, in connection with the question of the structure of Christian prayer and of the liturgy in particular, the place of Christ in it, the manner of addressing God, and so forth.

Christian Personality and Love

(The Nature of Christian Love)

1. To what extent they were successful, and whether here too the person did not evanesce into something alien, must be left unsettled.

2. We are purposely avoiding the expression "child of God." As this is usually understood, it has taken on a definite connotation, the quality of gentleness, intimacy, "childlikeness"—but since we are dealing here

with something absolutely mature, this would somehow suggest the infantile. What Christ means by the child of God takes certain traits from biological childhood in order to distinguish the Christian from the individual who is "grown up" in the wrong sense, the calculating, hard, sceptical man, and to express the pure receptivity and humility of which Christ is speaking. Otherwise, the new birth indicates something which implies full personal maturity and responsibility.

3. I hope in the future to present a more detailed treatment of the fact that the reality of Christ shatters all psychological categories.

4. So the charm of an animal, the natural sureness and wisdom of its instincts, appear more genuine than the movements and the natural actions of a man motivated by the mind but also troubled. Beside a deer or a panther, a man, especially a city-dweller, seems a barbarian. We have already spoken of this. But unless we are romanticists, and here that means traitors to our own dignity, we will not for a moment doubt that the existence of man in comparison with that of the animal is not only of greater relative value, but absolutely in the right.

Providence

(Inadequate Interpretations)

1. This is the meaning of Nietzsche's "Will to Power."

2. In this connection, phenomena such as luck, chance, success, etc. take on a special meaning.

(Providence and Environment)

3. This is probably the point indicated by the ancient oracle when it attempted to change destiny by its pronouncements. It revealed to the questioner the way in which he could change the structure of his attitude and so influence the course of events around him. If a man

becomes more truthful, more magnanimous, more unselfish, more free and loving in the depths of his being then his destiny can actually change.

4. We probably do not need to emphasize that we have not in this study considered all the problems involved in the doctrine of Providence. We have dealt with a definite aspect of it which is particularly meaningful for the Christian view of the world and of man.

The Church of the Lord

Between Two Books

1. *Op. cit.*, 4th ed., 1955, p. 19.
2. This chapter of theology seems to have come to an end after being called "theology" as such for centuries.

The Will of Jesus

1. We do not intend to give a theological definition of the Church, but trust that its image will unfold from one meditation to another.

The Birth of the Church

1. That is, an enemy of the community.
2. Cf. Guardini, *Johanneische Botschaft*, Würzburg 1962, p. 102ff.

The Guardian and Dispenser of Truth

1. For this see my book, *The Human Reality of the Lord: Contributions to a Psychology of Jesus*. Würzburg, 1965.

The Virtues: On Forms of Moral Life
Copyright © 1963 by Catholic Academy in Bavaria
Translation copyright © 1967 by Regnery Publishing
Originally published as *Tugenden: Meditationen uber Gestalten*
Published with permission of Sophia Institute Press, through arrangement with Matthias Grünewald, Mainz and Ferdinand Schöningh, Paderborn

Alle Autorenrechte liegen bei der Katholischen Akademie in Bayern
Romano Guardini, Tugenden: Meditationen über Gestalten sittlichen Lebens,
6. Auflage 2004
Verlagsgemeinschaft Matthias Grünewald, Mainz/Ferdinand Schöningh,
Paderborn

Nihil Obstat: Rev. Thomas F. Sullivan
Censor Librorum
Imprimatur: Rev. Msgr. Francis W. Byrne
Vicar General, Archdiocese of Chicago
Date: July 11, 1967

The Scripture quotations found in the book have been given in the Douay-Challoner translation, except where an exact rendering of the German Scripture translation was made necessary by the specific use to which it was put by the author.